# Global Gender Issues
# in the New Millennium

# Dilemmas in World Politics
## Series Editor: Jennifer Sterling-Folker, University of Connecticut

Why is it difficult to achieve the universal protection of human rights? How can democratization be achieved so that it is equitable and lasting? Why does agreement on global environmental protection seem so elusive? How does the concept of gender play a role in the shocking inequalities of women throughout the globe? Why do horrific events such genocide or ethnic conflicts recur or persist? These are the sorts of questions that confront policy-makers and students of contemporary international politics alike. They are dilemmas because they are enduring problems in world affairs that are difficult to resolve.

These are the types of dilemmas at the heart of the Dilemmas in World Politics series. Each book in the Dilemmas in World Politics series addresses a challenge or problem in world politics that is topical, recurrent, and not easily solved. Each is structured to cover the historical and theoretical aspects of the dilemma, as well as the policy alternatives for and future direction of the problem. The books are designed as supplements to introductory and intermediate courses in international relations. The books in the Dilemmas in World Politics series encourage students to engage in informed discussion of current policy issues.

## BOOKS IN THIS SERIES

***Global Environmental Politics*, Sixth Edition**
Pamela S. Chasek, David L. Downie, and Janet Welsh Brown

***International Human Rights*, Fourth Edition**
Jack Donnelly

***The United Nations in the 21st Century*, Fourth Edition**
Karen A. Mingst and Margaret P. Karns

***Global Gender Issues in the New Millennium*, Fourth Edition**
Anne Sisson Runyan and V. Spike Peterson

***United States Foreign Policy in the 21st Century: Gulliver's Travails***
J. Martin Rochester

***Democracy and Democratization in a Changing World*, Third Edition**
Georg Sørensen

***Southern Africa in World Politics***
Janice Love

***Ethnic Conflict in World Politics*, Second Edition**
Barbara Harff and Ted Robert Gurr

***Dilemmas of International Trade*, Second Edition**
Bruce E. Moon

***Humanitarian Challenges and Intervention*, Second Edition**
Thomas G. Weiss and Cindy Collins

***The European Union: Dilemmas of Regional Integration***
James A. Caporaso

***International Futures*, Third Edition**
Barry B. Hughes

***Revolution and Transition in East-Central Europe*, Second Edition**
David S. Mason

***One Land, Two Peoples*, Second Edition**
Deborah Gerner

***The Global Spread of Arms***
Frederic S. Pearson

FOURTH EDITION

# Global Gender Issues in the New Millennium

························◄O►························

## ANNE SISSON RUNYAN

*University of Cincinnati*

## V. SPIKE PETERSON

*University of Arizona*

WESTVIEW
PRESS

A Member of the Perseus Books Group

WESTVIEW PRESS was founded in 1975 in Boulder, Colorado, by notable publisher and intellectual Fred Praeger. Westview Press continues to publish scholarly titles and high-quality undergraduate- and graduate-level textbooks in core social science disciplines. With books developed, written, and edited with the needs of serious nonfiction readers, professors, and students in mind, Westview Press honors its long history of publishing books that matter.

*Design by the Perseus Books Group*
*Composition by Cynthia Young*

Library of Congress Cataloging-in-Publication Data
Runyan, Anne Sisson.
    Global gender issues in the new millennium / Anne Sisson Runyan, University of
    Cincinnati, V. Spike Peterson, University of Arizona.—Fourth Edition.
        pages cm.—(Dilemmas in world politics)
    Includes bibliographical references and index.
    ISBN 978-0-8133-4916-9 (pbk.)—ISBN 978-0-8133-4917-6 (e-book)    1. Women—
Political activity.    2. World politics—21st century.    I. Peterson, V. Spike.    II. Title.
HQ1236.P45 2013
320.082—dc23

                                                                                2013027993

10  9  8  7  6  5  4  3  2  1

*To our sisters,*
*for all that we share*

# Contents

*Acknowledgments to the Fourth Edition*  xi

*Acknowledgments to the Third Edition*  xv

*Acknowledgments to the Second Edition*  xix

*Acknowledgments to the First Edition*  xxiii

*Acronyms*  xxv

**1  Introduction: Gender and Global Issues**  1

The Intersectional Study of Gender  2

Gender as a Lens on World Politics  5

Gender and Global Issues  8

Gender and Global Crises  11

Gender Gains: Repositionings of Women and
   Men in World Politics  17

Global Crises: Remasculinizations of World Politics  25

Mapping the Book  30

**2  Gendered Lenses on World Politics**  39

How Lenses Work and Why They Matter  40

The Power of Gender  54

The Power of Gender as a Meta-Lens in World Politics  64

Feminist World Politics Lenses  73

Global Gendered Divisions of Power, Violence,
   Labor, and Resources  82

**3  Gender and Global Governance**  99

Feminist Approaches to Politics  102

Women Actors in Global Governance  104

Barriers to Women's Participation in Global Governance  111

Institutionalizing Global Gender Equality    121
Neoliberal Governmentality and the New Global Politics of
    Gender Equality    131
Women in Politics versus Feminist Politics    133

4    **Gender and Global Security**                                139
Feminist Approaches to Security    142
Gendered Security    144
Women, Militaries, and Political Violence    148
Men, Militaries, and Gender Violence    158
Gendered Peacemaking, Peacekeeping,
    and Peace-Building    169
(De)Militarizing Feminism    173
Disarming Security    177

5    **Gender and Global Political Economy**                       181
Feminist Approaches to Global Political Economy    185
Women, Gender, and Development    188
Anatomies of Neoliberal Globalization    193
Women, Gender, and Neoliberal Globalization    200
Gendered Financialization    215
Gendered Resources    221
Gendered Divisions of Resources    223
Toward Resisting Neoliberalism    232

6    **Gendered Resistances**                                      237
Feminist Resistance Politics    238
Toward Degendering World Politics    255

*Suggested Activities for Research and Discussion*    273
*Web and Video Resources*    281
*References*    289
*About the Authors*    309
*Index*    311

# Acknowledgments to the Fourth Edition

For the first time in two decades, I, alone, am writing these acknowledgments. Spike elected to pass on continuing this project to engage in other life activities. Its history and our longtime collaboration on it remain close to her heart, and she remains a coauthor of this fourth edition in honor of her guiding force, which launched the project, and in recognition of her wisdom and words, which still grace the work in this latest permutation. I am so grateful to her for all that we have shared along the way and for our continuing friendship.

I also appreciate how supportive she was of my reimagining and reworking of the third edition, which we both agreed had to capture contemporary feminist international relations and transnational feminist thought and scholarship that foreground intersectional and anti-imperialist analysis. Developments in gender and world politics inquiry to which we were contributing in other projects had complicated germinal, "first-generation" feminist international relations (IR) thinking, which gave primacy to "the woman question" and which our first edition helped formulate and disseminate and our second edition largely updated. We also saw processes of governmental and corporate co-optation of feminism as political, economic, and environmental crises were accelerating, which demanded an analysis of the paradox of increased attention to gender in the international arena at the same time that neoliberalism and militarism were deepening. This observation constituted the central theme of our third edition and led us to focus on complicating and repoliticizing feminist approaches to world politics. The concerns we raised have been affirmed by other feminist scholars who noticed similar patterns at the same time as and since our last edition. Our critical approach to the neoliberalization (and militarization) of feminism also has been reaffirmed by the ways in which the issue of women's global "empowerment" has been taken up problematically in popular culture of late.

In this edition, I continue our focus on how the increased visibility of women as world political actors (in governance, militaries, macroeconomic institutions, and peace-building) and yet as the most victimized in the world (by poverty, disease, disasters, and domestic and international violence) has made gender equality a new (at least, rhetorical) priority in official and now popular imaginations. I continue to find in the now more popularized forms this increased visibility have taken, such as celebrity-studded philanthropic campaigns, often sponsored by corporations, that encourage "rescue missions" of poor women in the global South by Western consumers, can reinforce the very structural processes that are productive of gender and other interrelated inequities and the human and planetary crises such inequities reflect *and* induce. Such campaigns, in prescribing individualist and market-based solutions to gender inequality consistent with official responses I also continue to document and update, shift attention and energy away from political analysis and activism and do little to stem direct and structural violence. At the same time, there have also been some very visible and popular political uprisings through-out the world (Arab Spring, Occupy movements) since the last edition to which I attend in this one that tell us that collective political resistance and change are still possible, and that there are other ways of living, doing, sharing, and being that are more consistent with contemporary feminist perspectives on and commitments to social justice. The common thread throughout all our editions of this book has been identifying the gender and gender-related barriers to the furtherance of more just, less violent, and environmentally sustainable political, economic, and social thought and arrangements—a theme consistent with the Dilemmas series, which assumes, as we do, that this is the central challenge of world *politics*.

Although I have not altered central arguments made in the third edition, this edition reflects some of the latest thinking on gender from feminist, masculinity studies, queer, and transgendered perspectives on it and some of the most recent research on gender in world politics in the areas covered. New also in this edition are some further evolving critiques and reformulations of feminism, particularly from postcolonial perspectives and in an age of both official and popular neoliberal co-optations of it and new poststructurally informed movements oppositional to neoliberalism (and neocolonialism) that are reworking its meanings in different ways. In recognition as well of how much more challenging it is to teach this much more complicated and complicating treatment of gender*ed* world politics, which still addresses "women" (and "men") but much more intersectionally and in other ways more disruptive of these categories and the multiple hierarchical dichotomies or binaries they promote, I have re-organized and reworked several chapters and added more visual aids in the form of textual tables and figures for each chapter that draw out key terms and ideas in the text. I have also interspersed more references to popular culture and given more attention to social media as spaces of both depoliticization and politicization. As a result, I have also added more websites and a list of videos to the resource list that can be used in conjunction with the text. Finally, I have added a section that provides suggestions for further research and discussion activities beyond the questions posed at the beginning of each chapter to promote critical engagement with the subject matter.

As always, I am grateful to the burgeoning community of feminist IR and transnational feminist scholars, happily so large that I no longer know most of them but benefit from their work and especially all the new work that is continually represented in the pages of the *International Feminist Journal of Politics*, for which I am an associate editor. My many friends and supports in that community (too many to name, but you know who you are!) keep me going. As always, I am also indebted to my students and student supports. Anna Laymon, who recently graduated with her MA in Women's, Gender, and Sexuality Studies from the University of Cincinnati after completing her powerful culminating MA project on military sexual assault, helped me with the research to update parts of the book. Sean Keating, my fantastic graduate assistant while I directed the Charles Phelps Taft Research Center at the University of Cincinnati in 2012–2013, helped with graphics and the end stages of the manuscript production. And as always, I am most thankful for the love and support of my partner, Al Kanters, who continues to nurture me along with our delightful twin-sister cats and to help me heal from the loss of family members, especially my mother, whom I miss every day.

I finally thank Westview Press for continuing to see value in this project, the editorial staff I worked with at Westview for their careful and kind assistance, and the many faithful and new users of this book who engage in and engage students in the kind of intellectual activism that can indeed make better worlds.

*Anne Sisson Runyan*

# Acknowledgments to the Third Edition

Far from being merely a third edition, this book is a significantly new treatment of global gender issues for the new millennium. The events on the ground and the massive shifts in feminist inquiry and theory to analyze and respond to them since our second edition have necessitated an almost total rereading and rewriting of the relationship between gender and world politics in the new millennium. Our task has been eased by, and our text is highly reflective of, the contemporary feminist international relations (IR) scholarship that is now regularly represented in the pages of the *International Feminist Journal of Politics,* which arose out of the Feminist Theory and Gender Studies (FTGS) Section of the International Studies Association (ISA). The advances in such scholarship that this journal has fostered enabled our own rethinking and re-representation of both gender and world politics. The major advances in transnational feminist inquiry in general, which have been influenced by, intersected with, and contributed to feminist international relations (or feminist world politics) scholarship, have also lighted our way. These two connected, expanding, and varied bodies of knowledge have enabled us to document, analyze, and respond to the full-fledged crises of the incendiary violence unleashed by the global "war on terror" and economic and planetary meltdowns resulting from unbridled global capitalism. As contributors to these bodies of knowledge, we hope we have done justice to the theories and research of our many feminist colleagues around the world.

Many of these colleagues are also our friends who have supported our work since the late 1980s when we began working together to produce early feminist interventions in IR. We have returned to our collaboration once more to produce what we hope is one of the latest words (but far from the last or most exhaustive word) on the state of world politics from feminist perspectives.

To faithful readers and users of our previous editions, please note that gone are almost all the illustrations, graphs, and tables, as well as the glossary and questions for discussion, that were useful in early stages of teaching feminist IR and prior to the world of images now available on the Internet. We have concentrated instead on text that attempts to illuminate the complexities of injustice in and resistance to world-politics-as-usual, in language friendly to a range of levels but representing some of the most sophisticated analyses in feminist postcolonial and poststructural thought. We hope it will be as useful and used as previous editions. We thank Westview for its continued commitment to this endeavor and its staff who ably assisted us this time around.

We are indebted to so many colleagues and friends that we cannot possibly list them all here. However, we would first like to thank two students who served as research and manuscript production assistants and without whose help this would have been a much harder undertaking. Marjon Kamrani, doctoral candidate in Political Science and Women's Studies graduate certificate student at the University of Cincinnati (UC), provided the front-end research assistance for this endeavor. Marjon has become a part of our FTGS community as she produces her own feminist IR dissertation. Holly McEntyre, who has almost completed her joint MA/JD in Women's Studies and Law at UC, has provided the lion's share of the back-end work, carefully and professionally tracking the back-and-forth production of the text and helping us pull together the final manuscript. Holly has been Anne's right hand throughout her studies, serving as Anne's graduate assistant through most of the years Anne headed and served as graduate director of what is now the Department of Women's, Gender, and Sexuality Studies at UC. She cannot be thanked enough for all this support. As we noted in the acknowledgments to the previous editions of this text (which we retain in this edition to sustain the memories and threads of our running collaborations on this project), we do this, first and foremost, for the students—ours and yours—in the hope that commitments to social justice are reproduced and extended in the process.

Anne also thanks her department members and staff for their support, and especially Deb Meem, Amy Lind, and Michelle Gibson for taking on leadership roles in her department so that Anne could take the long-awaited sabbatical needed to work on this third edition. Feminist community is so important in our "neoliberalized" work environments, and Anne is fortunate to have so much of it.

For their friendship as well as their exceptional scholarship, Spike thanks the community of academic activists centered around the Department of Women's Studies and Institute for LGBT Studies at the

University of Arizona, and the Gender Studies Institute at the London School of Economics where she greatly enjoyed being a Visiting Scholar in 2007 and 2008. Among many, Spike appreciates two recent graduate students—Amber Ussery and Kara Ellerby—for their teaching skills and critical scholarship. As ever, Spike is indebted to friends and family—near and far—whose love, laughter, partying, and passionate activism "keep her keepin' on." Her heartfelt thanks to these and all who dare to imagine—and create—a world with less pain and much more dancing.

Many of the members of our wider feminist community are reflected in this book, but we especially acknowledge those who have been among our longest-term mentors, collaborators, friends, and sister-partiers (!): Cynthia, Ann, Jindy, Marianne, Jane, Marysia, Cindy, Sandy, Lily, Anna, Simona, Carol, Francine, Deborah, Gillian, Berenice, Val, Shirin, Kathy, Judy, and Laila. There are so many more who have inspired us, changed us, and supported us. Thanks to you all.

We also pay tribute to our families for nurturing our feminist sensibilities as they nurtured us. Anne especially dedicates this edition to her sister, Margery, who is among the many sisters to whom it is broadly dedicated. Our partners, Al and CJ, sustained us through this project (as well as much else over time), providing the care and emotional support that are always so desperately needed by anyone writing a book (as they have repeatedly learned and have so lovingly accepted time and time again).

Finally, we take this opportunity to "hug" each other. Although separated by space and somewhat differing trajectories over time, we have maintained our intellectual and affective connections and lovingly supported each other through thick and thin. The depth of our friendship defies description, but it has made possible so much and has given us so much.

*V. Spike Peterson*
*Anne Sisson Runyan*

# Acknowledgments to the Second Edition

Contrary to common assumptions and our expectations, a second edition can be more difficult than the first. In this case, we faced the challenge of both documenting how the world has radically changed and reflecting how the field of gender and international relations has substantially grown since the early 1990s. When our first edition appeared, the Cold War had barely subsided and the process of globalization or global restructuring was only beginning to be analyzed. There were also few book-length treatments of gender and world politics available. Unfortunately, the few hopeful signs that the world was changing for the better in the early 1990s dissipated quickly. Encouragingly, however, the reassertions of oppressive world-politics-as-usual have been met by the broadening and deepening of local, national, and transnational women's and other gender-aware social movements committed to political, economic, social, cultural, and ecological justice. Feminist challenges to the study of international-relations-as-usual have also proliferated, within as well as outside of the discipline. We take particular pleasure in noting the extensive book and journal literature produced by members of the now ten-year-old Feminist Theory and Gender Studies section of the International Studies Association.

It is these women and men, struggling in progressive social movements and doing critical work in academe, whom we especially thank for continuing to build supportive, caring, and joyous communities that enlarge the space for feminist transformations of the international relations field and world politics more generally. We cannot do justice to the breadth and complexity of their work, but we do acknowledge how crucial these communities of activists, scholars, teachers, and friends are to our well-being and that of the planet.

Thanks also go to the many teachers around the world who have used the first edition of our book to introduce the study of gender and international relations to students in their undergraduate and graduate courses. It is for them and for their (and our) many students—who are the future of feminist international relations thought and feminist world politics practice—that we prepared this second edition. We can only hope it will continue to serve this important purpose and its readers well.

In addition, we wish to thank the many people who suggested changes to and provided new materials for this second edition. They include Marianne Marchand, Sandra Whitworth (and her students), Margaret Leahy, Laura Parisi, Cynthia Enloe, and several anonymous reviewers. We could not address all of their insightful comments without producing an entirely new book, but we have accommodated many of their suggestions and are grateful for the time and energy they invested. Many thanks, too, go to the numerous artists, cartoonists, and photographers whose images of gender injustice and women's struggles enliven the pages of this book.

We also acknowledge Westview Press for seeing the need for and encouraging us to produce a second edition. Thanks in particular go to the series editor, George Lopez; the Westview editorial staff in New York, including Leo Wiegman, Adina Popescu, and Kwon Chong; and Jane Raese and Kristin Milavec as well as other Westview production staff members in Boulder. Special thanks go to Christine Arden for competent and insightful copyediting. We all weathered the storms of ownership and staffing changes at Westview and look forward to its continued commitment to publishing progressive texts on world politics.

More personally, Anne is indebted to her support staff at Wright State University, including Joanne Ballmann for her extraordinary manuscript production skills and many kindnesses; Women's Studies secretary Pamela Mondini and Women's Studies student assistant Jacqueline Ingram for their help with correspondence, research, and photocopying; and graphic artist Bruce Stiver for the production of charts and graphs. Anne is also grateful for the faculty development grant and other travel and research funds that were provided by Wright State University's College of Liberal Arts to subsidize the preparation of the manuscript.

Anne further thanks family, friends, and colleagues nearby and far away for nurturing and nourishing her feminist ideals and work. Although her sister Malinda did not live to see the first edition and her father passed away during the preparation of the second, they live on in her commitments to social justice, which they shared. Her mother, whom she now can take care of, continues to teach her and her remaining sisters to remember. To her husband, Albert Adrian Kanters, she owes her deepest gratitude for his loving support of her work and her life for so long. And to Spike go love and sisterhood always.

Spike is indebted to a number of overlapping communities. Closest to her heart, because they provide affirmation, sustenance, and partnership-in-partying, are close friends: especially rosie, eva, paula, and jane. A wider circle of feminists in Tucson, family in Illinois, and friends around the world constitute a community of support and inspiration for which Spike expresses deep gratitude and affection. Students make a different difference. Their questions, insights, challenges, contributions, and, often, friendship make academe a place worth being. Friends among the Feminist Theory and Gender Studies section constitute another special community. Their personal support, solidarity of spirit, and professional interventions in the field of international relations make it, too, a place worth being. Less concrete but equally crucial, the scholarship and activism of feminists around the world are sources of inspiration to Spike. Being critical of domination takes courage; doing it with love in your heart and in your strategies takes much more. Spike honors and thanks the loving radicals who combine these traits, and especially the many who face dire consequences for doing so.

Finally, Spike is still learning to decipher Anne's handwriting—and still learning from her how to love better. But the best part is how they laugh together.

*V. Spike Peterson*
*Anne Sisson Runyan*

# Acknowledgments to the First Edition

Venturing into new terrain requires vision as well as commitment. Our thanks go first to George Lopez, the series editor, for recognizing the importance of gender as a dilemma in world politics. Jennifer Knerr's professional guidance and personal warmth were invaluable for keeping not only our efforts but also our enthusiasm on track. Of the many other people at Westview who eased our task, and editorial board members who supported our project, we thank especially Marian Safran, Libby Barstow, Deborah Gerner, and Karen Mingst. From start to finish, the farsightedness and expertise of Lev Gonick and Mary Ann Tetreault have enhanced this project and its product.

Exploring new terrain requires bold spirits and reliable support systems. Among the bold spirits, we thank our foremothers, who took great risks to clear new paths, and our feminist colleagues, who also take risks in order to pursue and expand those paths. Our support system is the global community of feminists who refuse to separate theory and practice. Of the countless women and men who make up this community, we thank especially our friends in the Feminist Theory and Gender Studies section of the International Studies Association, who have given us invaluable support, encouragement—and permission to party. In particular, because the integrity of their energy makes such an important difference, we acknowledge our appreciation of Simona Sharoni, Theresa Scionti, and Judy Logan.

More personally, Anne thanks her secretary, Jackie Brisson, and her student assistants, Michele Sylvestri and Mary Burns, for their tremendous assistance with research, photocopying, mailings, and tracking down addresses and phone numbers (mostly of illustration copyright holders, many of whom were very gracious and helpful). It was, indeed, an all-women struggle at SUNY-Potsdam that brought Anne's part of the book to fruition. She also thanks her husband, Al Kanters, who, as always, lovingly cared for her basic needs throughout this project. It is the reproductive work of men like him that makes the productive work of women possible. She is also grateful to family members, friends, and colleagues, close by and far away, who have so strongly supported her feminist ideals and her feminist work. Finally, she offers her heartfelt appreciation to Spike, who has been not only an intellectual partner but a dear friend and true "sister."

Spike leaned heavily on the research assistance and emotional support so effectively rendered by graduate students Stacey Mayhall, Jacqui True, and Anwara Begum. Words only begin to convey how the community generated during the states seminar has enhanced Spike's quality of life. She is indebted to this group especially—and students more generally—because they not only make the hard work worthwhile but also keep her mentally and physically dancing. "It doesn't get any better than this." Her deepest thanks, as ever, go to family and friends whose love, affirmation, and inspiration keep her going—and growing; to those whose ways of being, loving, and knowing offer a lighted path: thanks especially to beryl, eva, rosie, and ozone. Finally, she wants to let Anne know that the best part of this project, like their friendship, was/is learning to love better, for which Anne gets the credit.

*V. Spike Peterson*
*Anne Sisson Runyan*

# Acronyms

| | |
|---|---|
| 1325 | United Nations Security Council Resolution 1325 (2000) |
| 9/11 | attacks on the United States on September 11, 2001 |
| AI | Amnesty International |
| AIDS | acquired immunodeficiency syndrome (*see* HIV/AIDS) |
| APSA | American Political Science Association |
| AWID | Association for Women's Rights in Development |
| AWSA | Arab Women's Solidarity Association |
| BPA | Beijing Platform for Action |
| CEDAW | United Nations Convention on the Elimination of All Forms of Discrimination Against Women |
| CIA | Central Intelligence Agency (US) |
| CWGL | Center for Women's Global Leadership |
| DAWN | Development Alternatives with Women for a New Era |
| DDR | disarmament, demobilization, and reintegration |
| DOD | Department of Defense (US) |
| DRC | Democratic Republic of Congo |
| ECOSOC | United Nations Economic and Social Council |
| EPZs | export-processing zones |
| EU | European Union |
| FAO | Food and Agriculture Organization (UN) |
| FMF | Feminist Majority Foundation |
| FTGS | Feminist Theory and Gender Studies (Section of the International Studies Association) |
| GAD | gender and development |
| GATT | General Agreement on Tariffs and Trade |
| GDI | Gender-Related Development Index |

| | |
|---|---|
| GDP | gross domestic product |
| GEM | Gender Empowerment Measure |
| GI | military, noncivilian serviceperson (*formerly* government issue) |
| GII | Gender Inequality Index |
| GPE | global political economy |
| HBO | Home Box Office |
| HIV/AIDS | human immunodeficiency virus/acquired immunodeficiency syndrome |
| ICC | International Criminal Court |
| ICERD | International Convention on the Elimination of All Forms of Racial Discrimination |
| ICJ | International Court of Justice |
| ICRW | International Center for Research on Women |
| ICTR | International Criminal Tribunal for Rwanda |
| ICTs | information and communications technologies |
| ICTY | International Criminal Tribunal for the Former Yugoslavia |
| ICW | International Community of Women Living with HIV/AIDS |
| IDPs | internally displaced persons |
| IFIs | international financial institutions |
| IFJP | *International Feminist Journal of Politics* |
| IGLHRC | International Gay and Lesbian Human Rights Commission |
| IGOs | intergovernmental organizations |
| ILGA | International Lesbian, Gay, Bisexual, Trans, and Intersex Association |
| ILO | International Labour Organization |
| IMF | International Monetary Fund |
| IOM | International Organization for Migration |
| IPU | Inter-Parliamentary Union |
| IR | international relations |
| IRA | Irish Republican Army |

| | |
|---|---|
| ISPM | Instituto Social y Político de la Mujer (Women's Social and Political Institute) |
| IWPR | Institute for Women's Policy Research |
| IWRAW | International Women's Rights Action Watch |
| IWTC | International Women's Tribune Center |
| LGBTQ | lesbian, gay, bisexual, trans, queer, questioning |
| MDGs | Millennium Development Goals (UN) |
| MST | military sexual trauma |
| NCRW | National Council for Research on Women |
| NGOs | nongovernmental organizations |
| OECD | Organization for Economic Cooperation and Development |
| OSAGI | Office of the Special Adviser to the Secretary-General on Gender Issues and Advancement of Women (UN) |
| PBS | Public Broadcasting System (US) |
| PPSEAWA | Pan Pacific and Southeast Asia Women's Association |
| PR | proportional representation |
| PTSD | post-traumatic stress disorder |
| R&R | rest and recreation |
| RAWA | Revolutionary Association of the Women of Afghanistan |
| SAPs | structural adjustment programs |
| SERNAM | Servicio Nacional de la Mujer (National Office for Women's Affairs) |
| SIPRI | Stockholm International Peace Research Institute |
| SOFAs | Status of Forces Agreements |
| TFNs | transnational feminist networks |
| TNCs | transnational corporations |
| TRIPs | Trade-Related Aspects of International Property Rights |
| UK | United Kingdom |
| UN | United Nations |
| UNAIDS | Joint United Nations Programme on HIV/AIDS |
| UNDAW | United Nations Division for the Advancement of Women |
| UNDP | United Nations Development Programme |

| | |
|---|---|
| UNEP | United Nations Environment Program |
| UNESCO | United Nations Educational, Scientific, and Cultural Organization |
| UNFCCC | United Nations Framework Convention on Climate Change |
| UNFPA | United Nations Fund for Population Activities |
| UNHCR | United Nations High Commissioner for Refugees |
| UNICEF | United Nations Children's Fund |
| UNIFEM | United Nations Development Fund for Women |
| UN-INSTRAW | United Nations International Research and Training Institute for the Advancement of Women |
| UNITAR | United Nations Institute for Training and Research |
| UN-SWAP | United Nation System-Wide Action Plan |
| UN Women | United Nations Entity for Gender Equality and the Empowerment of Women |
| US | United States (of America) |
| WCAR | World Conference Against Racism (UN) |
| WCC | World Council of Churches |
| WEDO | Women's Environment and Development Organization |
| WEF | World Economic Forum |
| WHO | World Health Organization |
| WID | women in development |
| WIIS | Women in International Security |
| WILPF | Women's International League for Peace and Freedom |
| WLUML | Women Living Under Muslim Laws |
| WREI | Women's Research and Education Institute |
| WSIS | World Summit on the Information Society |
| WTO | World Trade Organization |

# 1

# Introduction:
# Gender and Global Issues

Why does gender matter in world politics? What difference does it make to view world politics through a gender(ed) lens? What becomes visible when we see "international relations" as interconnected relations of inequality—among genders, races, classes, sexualities, and nationalities—as opposed to simply interactions between and among self-interested states? What are the costs of being inattentive to gendered dynamics in world politics for addressing a myriad of world problems that ultimately affect us all?

In this introductory chapter, we present an overview of the contemporary relationship between gender and world politics. We begin with a conceptual discussion of gender and why adopting a gender(ed) lens is important for understanding the changing nature of global governance, global security, and global political economy in which gender issues have become more salient in national and international policymaking. As a result of several factors we discuss, a host of international development, financial, and security institutions have now made the link between raising the status of women worldwide and developing democracy, reducing poverty, and lessening armed conflict.

With these foundations, we then move to the central conundrum or dilemma focused on in this text: despite some elevation of gender issues on national and international policymaking agendas that have led to some gains by some women, there have also been significant setbacks to achieving greater social equity and justice for most women and many men. These setbacks have arisen from contemporary global crises resulting, at least in part, from the gendered nature of world politics. Thus, throughout this text we attend to this contradiction between increased international attention to gender issues that *repositions some women and men* in world politics but leaves unabated global crises rooted in *the power of gender.* We emphasize that the power of gender acts as a *meta-lens* that fosters dichotomization, stratification, and depoliticization in thought and action, thereby sustaining global power structures and crises that prevent or militate against meaningful advances in social equality and justice. We employ the matrices of the *gendered divisions of power, violence,* and *labor and resources* not only to track the positioning and repositionings of diverse women and men in relation to global governance institutions, global security apparatuses, and global political economy formations, but also to show how the power of gender operates in these contexts to maintain interlocking inequalities based on gender, race, class, sexuality, and nationality (including inequalities among nations and with respect to national origin). We argue that inattention to the interlocking nature of these inequalities—an insight derived from *intersectional analysis*—has resulted in problematic gender equality policymaking. Such policymaking tends to target only women and fails to take into account inequalities among women. It further deflects attention from such interlocking forces as neoliberal governmentality, militarization, and globalization, which undercut equality and social justice efforts. These forces are responsible for what we refer to as the *crises of representation, insecurity,* and *sustainability* that diverse women and men are resisting at local, national, and transnational levels.

## THE INTERSECTIONAL STUDY OF GENDER

Gender "is not a synonym for women" (Carver 1996). Rather, it generally refers to the socially learned behaviors, repeated performances, and idealized expectations that are associated with and distinguish between the proscribed gender roles of masculinity and femininity. As such, it is not the same as and may be wholly unrelated to sex, which is typically defined as the biological and anatomical characteristics that distinguish between women's and men's bodies. Contemporary gender studies find that sex, too, is socially constructed because it is only through the meanings given to and the marshaling of particular biological and anatomical characteristics that sex difference, as an unequivocal binary, is naturalized and enforced, including surgically when children born with ambiguous sexual organs are made into either "girls" or "boys" to sustain the idea that there are only two sexes (Fausto-Sterling 1992, 2000). As a result, gender analysts challenge not only the biologically determinist idea that dualistic gender identities and roles arise from natural sex difference, but also the notion that sex difference itself is natural and dualistic, calling into question even our assumptions about a world made up of only "females" and "males," "girls" and "boys," "men" and "women." Thus, the study of gender is as much about the socially constructed categories of "men" and masculinity as it is about the socially constructed categories of "women" and femininity. Contemporary gender studies that partake of intersectional analysis, which holds that gender cannot be understood in isolation from other identity categories and relations of inequality, also recognize that there are multiple genders, as well as sexes, because race/ethnicity, class, sexuality, and other cultural variations shape gender identities and performances.

Because the particular characteristics associated with femininity and masculinity vary significantly across cultures, races, classes, and age groups, there are no generic women and men (or other sexes or genders). Our gender identities, loyalties, interests, and opportunities are intersected and crosscut by countless dimensions of "difference," especially those associated with ethnicity/race, class, national, and sexual identities. "Acting like a man" (or a "woman") means different things to different groups of people (e.g., transgendered people, heterosexual Catholics, Native Americans, British colonials, agriculturists versus corporate managers, athletes versus orchestra conductors, combat soldiers versus military strategists) and to the same group of people at different points in time (e.g., nineteenth- versus twentieth-century Europeans, colonized versus postcolonial Africans, prepuberty versus elderly age sets, women during war versus women after war). Men may be characterized as feminine (e.g., Mahatma Gandhi, "flamboyant" gay men) and women as "masculine" (e.g., Margaret Thatcher, "butch" lesbians). Gender is shaped by race (models of masculinity and femininity vary among Africans, Indians, Asians, Europeans), and race is gendered (gender stereotypes shape racial stereotypes of Africans, Indians, Asians, whites). Moreover, because masculinities and femininities vary (by class, race/ethnicity, sexuality, age), some expressions of gender (Hispanic in the United States [US], Muslim in India, Turkana in Kenya) are subordinated to *dominant* constructions of gender (Anglo, Hindu, Kikuyu). There are thus multiple masculinities that not only vary across cultures but also confer different levels of power. What is referred to as "hegemonic masculinity" (Connell 1987, 1995) is the ideal form of masculinity performed by men with the most power attributes, who not incidentally populate most global power positions. These are typically white, Western, upper-class, straight men who have conferred on them the complete range of gender, race, class, national, and sexuality privileges. "Subordinated masculinities" (Connell 1987, 1995) are embodied by those who lack one, some, or all these privileges and thus are rendered "feminized" on these scores. Although all femininities are subordinated to all masculinities, it is also the case that some femininities are subordinated more than or differently from others. The idealized image of Western femininity remains associated with Victorian notions of womanhood that celebrated the gentility, passivity, decorativeness, and asexuality imposed on white, middle- to upper-class women, who were the only ones who could enact such standards. Working-class women, women of color, and/or lesbians or trans-women are either denied the (dubious) status of feminine because they cannot meet these standards or are feminized (that is, devalorized) in other ways through processes of *racialization* and/or *sexualization*. For example, since the times of slavery and colonization, women of color have been labeled as naturally oversexual, thereby not only being unworthy of (white) male protection but also particularly open to (white) male sexual exploitation.

Finally, the specific meanings and values conferred on masculinity and femininity have also changed over time as well as across cultures. For example, Western ideals of "manliness" have undergone historical shifts: from the early Greeks through the feudal period, the emphasis of idealized masculinity was on military heroism and political prowess through male bonding and risk-taking, whereas more modern meanings of masculinity stress "competitive individualism, reason, self-control or self-denial, combining respectability as breadwinner and head of household with calculative rationality in public life" (Hooper 1998: 33). Moreover, not all cultures have associated either of these conceptions of masculinity with leadership qualities: "queen mothers" in Ghana and "clan mothers" in many Native American societies have been accorded power and leadership roles in these matrilineal contexts on the basis of the feminine quality of regeneration of the people and the land (Okojo 1994: 286; Guerrero 1997: 215). Furthermore, there is some play in gender roles even within patrilineal or patriarchal cultures, given that men are not exclusively leaders and warriors and women are not exclusively in charge of maintaining the home and caring for children. Cultures also vary in the play allowed to the display of nonconforming gender behavior, such as that not associated with a person's assigned sex; sometimes even "third genders" are even revered. Polities also vary in terms of acceptance of and resources available to people who choose to change their assigned sex. Due to the variation in meanings attached to femininity and masculinity, we know that expressions of gender are not "fixed" or predetermined; the particulars of gender are always shaped by context.

Because models of appropriate gender behavior are diverse, we know that femininity and masculinity are not timeless or separable from the contexts in which they are embodied, acted out, and observed. This illustrates how gender rests not on biological sex differences but on *interpretations* or constructions of behavior that are culturally specific, that shift as contexts change, and that typically have little to do with biological differences, which themselves are not fixed as some bodies are born neither "male" nor "female" and gender and sex assignments can be altered. In short, there are multiple genders and gender orderings, but gender is always raced, classed, sexualized, and nationalized, just as race, class, sexuality, and nationality are always gendered. Hence, gender analysis must avoid stereotyping (or reducing people to unfounded caricatures), essentializing (or assuming "natural" and unchanging characteristics), and singling out any one identity as descriptive of a whole person. Instead, gender analysis must adopt intersectional analyses to make sense of our multiple, crosscutting, and differentially valorized identities. However, as we argue in the next section, these variations still rest on concepts of gender differences and do not necessarily disrupt gender as an oppositional dichotomy and as a relation of inequality.

## GENDER AS A LENS ON WORLD POLITICS

Studies of gender arose not because other axes of difference and bases of inequality (e.g., race/ethnicity, class, religion, age) are less important than—or even extricable from—gender. Rather, gender became a significant lens through which to view world politics as researchers and social movement activists informed by feminist perspectives (which we address in the next chapter) that focus most centrally on the problem of gender inequality increasingly documented the institutionalization of gender *differences* as a major underpinning of structural inequalities in much of the world. Through a complex interaction of identification processes, symbol systems, and social institutions (explored in subsequent chapters), gender differences are produced—typically in the form of a *dichotomy* that not only opposes masculinity to femininity but also translates these opposi-tional differences into *gender hierarchy,* the privileging of traits and activi-ties defined as masculine over those defined as feminine. Thus, although it is important to recognize the cultural variation in how gender differences are formed and expressed, a *gender-sensitive lens* also reveals the political nature of gender as a system of difference construction and hierarchical dichotomy production that constitutes virtually all contemporary societ-ies. Gender is about power, and power is gendered. How power operates in this way starts to become visible in an examination of the relationship between masculinity and femininity.

Although the specific traits that mark gender-appropriate behavior vary cross-culturally, they constitute systems of politically significant struc-tural power in the following interacting ways. First, males are expected to conform to models of masculinity (that are privileged) and females to models of femininity (which are subordinated). There are multiple models of masculinity within cultures, but one typically has hegemonic status as the most valued and esteemed model, and it is associated with elite (class, race, and culturally privileged) males. Within particular cultures, these expectations are taken very seriously because they are considered funda-mental to who we are, how we are perceived by others, and what actions are appropriate. In this sense, gender ordering is inextricable from social ordering of power, authority, work, leisure, and pleasure.

Second, because masculine activities are more highly valued or privi-leged than are feminine activities in most of the world most of the time, the identities and activities associated with men and women are typically unequal. Thus, the social construction of gender is actually a system of power that not only divides the world into "men" and "women" and mas-culine and feminine, but also typically places some men and masculinity above most women and femininity. Consider, for example, how consis-tently institutions and practices that are male-dominated and/or repre-sentative of hegemonically masculine traits and style (politics, making money) are valued more highly and considered more important than in-stitutions and practices associated with femininity (families, caring labor). This elevation of what are perceived as masculine traits and activities over those perceived as feminine is a central feature of the ideology or system of belief of *masculinism.*

Third, because the dichotomy of masculine and feminine constructs them as polarized and mutually exclusive, when we favor or privilege what is associated with masculinity, we do so at the expense of what is associated with femininity. Politics, as conventionally defined, is about differential access to power—about who gets what and how. Therefore, the privileging of masculinity is political insofar as relations of inequality, manifested in this case as gender inequality, represent men's and women's unequal access to power, authority, and resources.

Like other social hierarchies, gender inequality is maintained by various means, ranging from psychological mechanisms (engaging in sexist humor, blaming the victim, internalizing oppressive stereotypes), sociocultural practices (objectifying women, creating "chilly climates" for women's advancement, harassing women sexually, trivializing women's concerns), structural discrimination (denial of equal rights, job segregation, marginalization of reproductive health issues), to direct violence (domestic battering, rape, femicide, or the systematic murder of women). Also, like many social hierarchies, gender inequality is "justified" by focusing on physical differences and exaggerating their significance as determinants of what are in fact socially constructed, learned behaviors. Thus, Arthur Brittan has argued that by denying the social construction of gender, masculinism serves to justify and "naturalize" (depoliticize) male domination because "it takes for granted that there is a fundamental difference between men and women, it assumes that heterosexuality is normal, it accepts without question the sexual division of labor, and it sanctions the political and dominant role of men in the public and private spheres" (1989: 4).

Like the abstract concepts of family, race, and nation, gender "in the real" sense is always inflected by such dimensions as race/ethnicity and class, which vary depending on culture and context. What does not appear to vary is what we call the *power of gender* to conceptually and structurally organize not only identities and sexual practices, but also virtually all aspects of social life in all cultures. Indeed, a gender-sensitive lens reveals that masculine and feminine "natures" are not simply inscribed on what are assumed to be distinct male and female bodies, but also are applied to other objects, including things, nonhuman beings, groups, institutions, and even nations and states. Consider references to a ship or car as "she," invocations of "mother nature," characterizations of opposing sports teams as "wimpy" while one's own is "mighty," notions of "motherlands" and "fatherlands," and categorizations of "strong" and "weak" states. Everyday parlance is rife with gender appellations and metaphors. This constant gendering of natural, artificial, and social worlds through language and, thus, thought, is no trivial matter. It directs us to how the power of gender operates to set up and reinforce dualistic, dichotomous, or either-or thinking *and* to foster hierarchical thinking in which those people and objects assigned masculine qualities are valued or given power over those assigned feminine qualities.

Thus, our approach foregrounds not only how a gender-sensitive lens reveals the nature and extent of gender and other related inequalities that structure and are structured by world politics, but also and most insidiously how the power of gender operates as a meta-lens (explored more fully in the next chapter) that orders and constrains thinking and thus social reality and action, thereby serving as a major impediment to addressing inequalities and the global crises we begin to explore below that stem from, sustain, and even worsen inequalities. On one level, the power of gender upholds masculinist ideology, which refers to individuals, perspectives, practices, and institutions that embody, naturalize, and privilege the traits of masculinity at the expense of feminized and other alternatives and are thus engaged in producing and sustaining relations of gender inequality. On another level, the power of gender works to pervade our everyday naming, speaking, clothing, working, entertainment, and sports as well as, we further argue, dominant approaches to knowledge production, governance, militarization, and economic relations. At its deepest level, the power of gender as a meta-lens continually normalizes—and hence depoliticizes—essentialized stereotypes, dichotomized categories, and hierarchical arrangements. In these multiple and overlapping ways, the power of gender is political: it operates pervasively to produce and sustain unequal power relations. Thus, lenses that ignore or obscure how gender operates systemically and structurally are conceptually inadequate for understanding how power works in world politics and politically inadequate for challenging interrelated social injustices and global crises.

## GENDER AND GLOBAL ISSUES

We observed as our starting point for the last edition of this text that it was not long ago that gender had no place in the study of world politics, but gender analysis now constitutes an accepted and burgeoning part of international relations inquiry and a significant national and international policy tool. Since then, this observation has found its way into popular literature and the popular imagination. Soon after our last edition came out, *New York Times* columnist Nicholas D. Kristof and coauthor Sheryl WuDunn published what became a national best seller, *Half the Sky: Turning Oppression into Opportunity for Women Worldwide* (2009), which has also been adapted into a traveling exhibition for museums and other showplaces as well as a two-part documentary aired initially through the US Public Broadcasting System (PBS). This journalistic and popular treatment of how central raising the status of women has become to national and international policymaking does not credit the decades of feminist IR scholarship and the centuries of international feminist thought and activism most catalyzed during and since the United Nations (UN) Decade for Women (1975–1985), which we had argued were most responsible for putting gender on the map of world politics. However, it does detail just how salient gender, when it is reduced to being synonymous with women, now is in the highest echelons of international development, financial, and security institutions.

In terms of intergovernmental organizations (IGOs), no less than the World Bank, the United Nations Development Programme (UNDP), and a host of other UN agencies, and in terms of nongovernmental organizations (NGOs), no less than the leaders of such groups as CARE, Doctors Without Borders, the Center for Global Development, and the Hunger Project as well as corporate foundation heads and economists with Goldman Sachs, Nike, and the like have all concluded the same thing: "'Progress is achieved through women'" (Kristof and WuDunn 2009: xx). Even international security experts have begun paying attention to gender on the basis of a perceived relationship between the marginalization of women in politics and society and the growth of "terrorism," particularly in Islamic countries. "As the Pentagon gained a deeper understanding of counterterrorism, it became increasingly interested in grassroots projects such as girls' education. Empowering girls, some in the military argued, would disempower terrorists. When the Joint Chiefs of Staff hold discussion of girls' education in Pakistan and Afghanistan, you know that gender is a serious topic on the international affairs agenda" (Kristof and WuDunn 2009: xxi).

Even though this newfound interest at the highest levels of world political institutions in gender, but more accurately in women, can be read as a feminist success story, as *Half the Sky* seems to suggest, we as longtime feminist IR scholars are troubled by the instrumentalist way that gender has become so salient. On the one hand, high-level attention to gender can be traced to tracking the positionings of women in world affairs that became possible when governments around the world—since the first UN conference on women, held in 1975—committed to provide data regularly to the UN that disaggregated the roles men and women play in state governance, militaries, diplomatic machineries, and economies. By the end of the last millennium, the data regarding how men and women are situated differently around the world revealed, starkly, the extent of gender inequality. The UNDP unequivocally concluded that "no society treats its women as well as its men" (1997: 39). Such a conclusion was based on reports to the UN Committee on the Status of Women that, although women composed one-half of the world's population, they performed the majority of the world's work hours when unpaid labor was counted, yet in aggregate were poorer in resources and poorly represented in elite positions of decision-making power (Tickner 1993: 75). Feminist activists and scholars who advocated for and performed such tracking did so for the purposes of uprooting gender and other social injustice.

On the other hand, as the story goes in *Half the Sky,* it was only when women became "engines of economic growth," as they were brought into the formal labor force in huge numbers out of their own economic necessity and for the purpose of fueling the world's factories as the preferred source of "cheap" and "obedient" labor, that women suddenly were noticed by economic elites as a previously "untapped resource" that could be better harnessed to serve national and transnational corporations and capitalism. "The basic formula was to ease repression, educate girls as well as boys, give girls the freedom to move to cities and take factory jobs, and then benefit from the demographic dividend as they delayed marriage and reduced childbearing" (Kristof and WuDunn 2009: xix). A further dividend of breaking down patriarchal authority in homes and communities and the violence against women and girls that is justified by patriarchal authority would be a reduction in women's and their children's poverty as women and children make up the vast majority of the world's poor. Similarly, as indicated above, women became visible to security elites only when it appeared that raising the status of women could constitute a counterterrorism tool. Thus, the empowerment of women has become only a means to an end, not an end in itself—just the latest mechanism to manage global problems as opposed to representing an actual commitment to gender equality and social justice. That inequalities might be leavened some is secondary to shoring up world-politics-as-usual priorities of capitalist economic growth and state and interstate security, which we argue below are productive of the very global crises that "empowering women" is now supposed to solve.

Beyond how problematic these instrumentalist reasons are for why gender is being embraced by national and international officialdom, *Half the Sky* also gives the impression that gender injustice, and the complex of social injustice of which it is a constitutive part, is not a deep structural phenomenon upon which the international order rests. While the book and its multimedia companions are peppered with stories of individual women's agency to change their circumstances in the global South and foregrounds the work of NGOs that assist them to do so, it suggests that these individualist activities and humanitarian charity to such NGOs by more economically privileged people, primarily in the global North, are all it will really take to turn things around for the most oppressed women and thereby "unlock" their "power as economic catalysts" (Kristof and WuDunn 2009: xxii). Highlighting even the poorest women's agency and tapping into desires to bring about social change are laudable, but such an approach obscures how women's poverty in the global South is directly related to past and ongoing wealth accumulation in the global North. It also lets off the hook governments, IGOs, and transnational corporations (TNCs) whose actions have heavily contributed to and sustained women's subordination over centuries. And it paints a very narrow and capitalist-centered vision of women's empowerment, reduced to turning "bubbly teenage girls from brothel slaves into successful businesswomen" (Kristof and WuDunn 2009: xxii).

In the next section, we offer a very different approach to thinking about gender and its relationship to global issues. Rather than seeing and casting "women" as instruments for solving global crises in ways that do not disrupt world-politics-as-usual priorities and do not require political action (only market levers), we argue that contemporary global crises are outcomes of world-politics-as-usual priorities that themselves are products of gender(ed) dynamics, which are not being fundamentally disturbed despite some gains by some women.

## GENDER AND GLOBAL CRISES

As we document throughout this text, despite the attention now given to gender in policymaking circles, relatively little has changed in the material conditions for most women. Even with such policies as gender quotas (to get more women into elective office) and gender mainstreaming (designed to avoid building gender discrimination into any government policy) that have been heavily promoted and used by the UN and other IGOs, causing their adoption across many parts of the world, there has been only a modicum of effect on the repositionings of women.

While some women have gained from the recent legitimation of gender inquiry and policy at the international level, global crises have deepened at the same time. Even though previous "hot" and "cold" wars since the times of the first colonial conquests have wreaked considerable havoc and violence that continue to this day, the rise in international violence in the new millennium is often pegged as a "post-9/11" phenomenon following the September 11, 2001, terrorist attacks on the United States. The George W. Bush administration chose to respond to this through wars in Iraq and Afghanistan, as well as a legitimation of torture and rendition in the name of national security and the global "war on terror," thereby justifying any violence across the globe done in its name.[1] The onset of the global economic crisis in 2008 is tied to the deregulation and manipulation of financial markets in the North with reverberations in the South, but these have earlier roots in neoliberal restructuring at least since the 1970s. At the same time, past colonizations and imperialisms continue to exert effects materially and ideologically, whether in the forms of gross economic inequalities, civil wars, ethnic cleansing, or the rise of a range of fundamentalisms. The planetary crisis of global warming has its roots in the industrial revolution, although the poisoning of the atmosphere has certainly accelerated as global capitalist-led industrial production has permeated the globe in more recent years.

Such crises are undermining modest gender gains as they worsen economic, political, and social inequalities, ratchet up violence, and threaten the very foundations of human and other life on the planet. We refer to these interacting global crises throughout the text as the *crises of representation, insecurity,* and *sustainability.* The crisis of *representation* entails inequalities not only in political representation in formal power structures but also in NGOs and social movements, which can hamper more complex and fuller analyses of "global" problems that can take different forms in "local" contexts. Without a range of perspectives from varying social locations, proposed solutions by the few (and most privileged) can do more harm than good. Moreover, the crisis of representation refers to how groups are "framed" in problem analysis and solutions. For example, if "Third World women" are constructed "under Western eyes" as only "victims" or potential "entrepreneurs" then they are denied agency and the ability to exercise their own approaches to local and global problem-solving (Mohanty 1991). The crisis of *insecurity* relates not only to the direct violence of international and intranational conflict, but also to the structural violence of political, economic, and social priorities and inequalities that leave wide swaths of people subject to unemployment, underemployment, poverty, disease, malnutrition, crime, and domestic and sexual violence. The crisis of *sustainability* refers to a crisis both of social reproduction and of resource depletion. The former is shorthand for the systematic disabling of households and human communities to cope and care for each other and future generations, whereas the latter is short-hand for the systematic disabling of the environment to sustain human communities. Both are the result of narrow constructions and obsessions with "growth," the pursuit of which enslaves all and militates against repri-oritizations that are not market-based. We relate these crises to the gen-dered divisions of power, violence, and labor and resources (described at the end of Chapter 2) from which they arise and that sorely limit the repo-sitionings of women and other subjugated people(s) to have a say in world politics and to resist global power structures and the crises they induce.

The seeming contradiction between rising international attention to empowering women to ameliorate gender inequality—which is now seen by many UN agencies and many member states as a significant source of global political, economic, and social problems—and the deepening of global crises that are undermining this acknowledgment and its im-plementation constitutes our central theme. This contradiction relates to some current conundrums in feminist IR inquiry. First, despite some gender policy gains at international and national levels, attention to the relationship between gender inequality and global problems is still insuffi-cient. Second, policymaking bodies have interpreted gender equality nar-rowly to mean only raising the status of women relative to men, without regard to inequalities among both women and men that arise from class, ethnicity/race, sexuality, and national divisions. Just as problematically, such bodies have used stereotypes of women and men to promote raising the status of women so that women are cast—whether as peacemakers, responsible debt payers, or innocent victims—as the solutions to global problems, while certain men—usually lower-class men and men of color or of the global South—are cast as backward, violence-prone rogues who stand in the way of gender equality and constitute the main sources of global problems. Some feminist scholars and activists have sometimes con-tributed to this kind of stereotyping or "framing," for example, when argu-ing for women's empowerment on the world stage. But this stereotyping is more pernicious when taken up by policymaking power structures to deflect attention away from larger causes and results of gender and other inequalities, which include militarization and global capitalism.

To complicate the category of "women" and the notion of "gender," we engage in intersectional analysis in order to minimize reproducing stereotypes of women and men that can be deployed by policymakers to avoid the more complex challenges of changing world-politics-as-usual. The concept of intersectional analysis emerged within these studies as a result of the work of black US feminist theorists in the 1980s and beyond (Collins 1991) who recognized that the lives and experiences of women of color were underrepresented in dominant Western feminist theories about women's subordination that were based on the experiences of largely white, Western, middle-class, and/or working-class women. Intersectional analysis holds that gender is always raced, classed, sexualized, and nationalized, just as race, class, nationality, and sexuality are always gendered.[2]

Here we expand upon what we mean by intersectional analysis. First, as we have already argued, women, men, and other genders have multiple identities simultaneously, describing themselves or being described not only by gender but also by race, class, sexual, and national markers, such as a black, American, working class, gay male. Second, these identity markers, however, are not just additive, merely descriptive, or politically or socially neutral. Some parts of our identities carry privilege, and others do not. For example, male privilege, which an individual may be able to exercise in the home over women and children, is offset in other, more public arenas if the individual is a racial minority in the larger demographic and thus subject to racism; a sexual minority within the person's own race or a wider demographic and thus subject to homophobia; and/or not a member of the owning or managerial class and thus subject to classism. Being an American may confer some privileges, such as citizenship rights, including voting rights, that are denied to nonnaturalized immigrants (of color or not), but we also know that racism (and classism) can trump those formal citizenship rights, as in the case of black Americans who were routinely kept from voting through Jim Crow laws, poll taxes, and literacy tests long after they won the formal right to vote.

Third, different parts of our identities become politically salient at different times. This casts us into pigeonholes that deny the complexity of our identities, and when some aspects of our identities are given rights but others are not, it can create a kind of schizophrenia within the individual and divisive mentalities within and between seemingly cohesive social groups. Consider the case of suffrage for African American women. The common notion is that African Americans were given the vote before women in the United States, but in fact only African American men were enfranchised first; African American women had to await the enfranchisement of women generally. Thus, their gender separated them from the category of "African American," which was coded as meaning only black men. At the same time, although many white women suffragists had been abolitionists, their anger over the enfranchisement first of only black men prompted racist arguments as to why white women were better entrusted with the vote to uphold white civilizational values. This effectively discounted black women, who had to organize separately. Thus, because of their race, African American women were also separated from the category of "women," which was coded as meaning only white women (Giddings 1984). A more contemporary example is the idea that a black man cannot also be gay because dominant constructions of black men's sexuality, foisted by whites and internalized by blacks from slavery on, are so tied to images of aggressive heterosexuality.

This brings us to the fourth meaning of intersectional analysis—namely, the kind of masculinity or femininity one is assumed to have rests on the meanings given to one's race, class, sexuality, and nationality. To amplify on an example we provided earlier, Africans brought as slaves to the Americas were defined by their captors as subhuman with largely animal instincts, which included the assumption that animals mate indiscriminately. The idea that slaves, whether men or women, were "oversexed" was a convenient mythology for male slaveholders who could thereby justify their sexual assaults on female slaves while upholding slavery and later lynchings in the name of protecting white women from "naturally" sexually predatory black men. The contemporary terms for this kind of thinking are the gendered racialization and sexualization of groups to render them as "other" or different and less than the groups doing the labeling. As raised earlier, hegemonic masculinity—currently identified with and exercised by those individuals, groups, cultures, organizations, and states coded with the full privileges of Western-ness, whiteness, wealth, and maleness born out of long histories of conquest and colonization—carries the highest representational (or labeling) power to render others "other." If we focus only on a narrow definition of gender or singular notions of masculinity and femininity, we miss the complexity of unjust social orders and fail to see how they are upheld often by pitting subordinated groups against each other, especially when such groups are coded as homogeneous without both crosscutting and conflicting interests within them that hold potential for coalitions and more comprehensive resistance to unjust social (and world political) orders.

Contemporary feminist scholars engage in intersectional analysis to avoid the practice of "essentialism," or the assumption that, for example, all women or all men or all those within a given race or class share the same experiences and interests. Only by recognizing how, for example, some women have benefited by the racial, class, sexual, and national origin oppression of other women, whereas many men subordinated by these very characteristics still exercise gender oppression, can we advance a more comprehensive notion of gender equality that sees it as indivisible from racial, class, and sexual equality and equality among nations. Unfortunately, the new focus on gender equality observable at the international level has largely separated gender equality from these other forms of equality. As a result, international efforts to increase gender equality can fail to address other sources of inequality (such as race and class discrimination) that disadvantage certain groups of women. At the same time, when such efforts blame only men, and mostly nonelite men, for gender inequality and fail to address forms of discrimination that subordinated men experience (based on class, race, and/or sexuality), then subordinated men may withhold support for gender equality. A narrow focus on gender equality also maintains the power of gender even as the socioeconomic positionings of women and men may be somewhat altered.

Another reason to avoid essentialism is also to avoid "universalism," or universal prescriptions for how to achieve comprehensive gender equality. Not only do women not share the same experiences or interests as a result of their multiple identities derived from their differing social locations in the world, but also the sociopolitical, cultural, and historical contexts in which women live vary significantly, requiring varying strategies for social change. These complex realities have made many feminists skeptical of resorting to "global" solutions just as they have recognized that "global" problems take many and differing "local" forms to which agents of social change must be attentive to create context-specific and context-sensitive solutions that do not backfire (Grewal and Kaplan 1994). This skepticism also extends to global actors, whether IGOs or NGOs, because they tend to be among the elite whose interests and analyses may reproduce inequalities on the local level even as they purport to be ameliorating them (Spivak 1998). Thus, global norms and global actors are double-edged swords that can both reduce and reproduce inequalities. On the other hand, local efforts to reduce inequalities at the local level that are not attentive to how those inequalities may be, at least partially, the result of more global processes that produce similar inequalities across locales risk failing to see these interconnections, thereby leaving inequalities largely intact or simply shifting them to "other" places.

Such insights that arise from intersectional analysis help us to make sense of the paradox between increased global attention to gender equality and deepening global crises associated with reassertions of masculinism and other subordinating ideologies. This form of analysis guides our examination of the power of gender as an ordering system that valorizes or privileges what is deemed masculine and devalorizes or subordinates what is deemed feminine in order to naturalize inequalities and power relations not only between and among women and men, but also between and among states, cultures, institutions, organizations, policies, practices, and even ideas and perspectives in the global system. As can be seen in Table 1.1, the processes of *masculinization as valorization* and *feminization as devalorization* powerfully organize our thinking as to what is valued and thus prioritized and what is not valued and thus denigrated in world politics. We address these processes more fully in the next chapter and clarify some of the terms used in the table later in this chapter, but suffice it to say here that the power of gender operates to naturalize a host of dualistic hierarchies and informs and intersects with other powerful ordering systems (based on race, class, sexuality, and so on) that blind us to developing less crisis-ridden and more just forms of world politics.

## GENDER GAINS: REPOSITIONINGS OF WOMEN AND MEN IN WORLD POLITICS

### *Gender and International Relations Inquiry*

Gender analysis in IR inquiry has become a subfield of the discipline, and feminist perspectives on world politics that generated gender analysis in IR now appear alongside or in combination with other, longer-legitimated ones, such as (neo)realism, idealism or (neo)liberalism, and (neo-)Marxism, and more recent ones, such as constructivist, poststructuralist, and postcolonial perspectives. We explore feminist lenses on world politics in Chapter 2 in significant detail, but here we briefly introduce the development of gender inquiry in IR and its impact on giving gender substantive consideration in world politics thinking.

TABLE 1.1

**Masculinization as Valorization and Feminization as Devalorization**

| Masculinized | Feminized |
|---|---|
| Men | Women |
| Sexual majorities /normative genders | Sexual minorities /nonnormative genders |
| White(nd) | Racialized |
| (Neo)colonizing | (Neo)colonized |
| Western | NonWestern |
| Global North | Global South |
| War | Peace |
| International | Domestic |
| States | Families/communities /social movements |
| Market economy | Care economy |

Feminist IR scholars generally do not subscribe to the conventional definition of international relations as being the power struggles between sovereign states in an anarchic world in which there is no supranational government to control state behaviors through the rule of law. Rather, these scholars favor an alternative definition of IR: "the identification and explanation of social stratifications and of inequality as structured at the level of global relations" (S. Brown 1988: 461). In this sense, feminist perspectives on IR understand power in broader and more complex terms than more traditional IR scholars do and have sought to put the relations of people, as agents and within social structures, back into international relations. To do so, these IR scholars have relied on feminist sociopolitical theorizing in other disciplines, including the now-well-developed (inter)discipline of women's and gender studies.

In general, gender analysts in IR operate from feminist perspectives, which, although varied, share minimally a concern with the problem of gender inequality as a motivation for research. They have found in their examinations that individuals, institutions, and practices associated with masculinity (men, states, war-making, wealth production) remain highly valued (or valorized) in political and world political thought, whereas those individuals, institutions, and practices associated with femininity (women, local or international political formations, peacemaking, poverty reduction) have been more typically devalued (or devalorized) and even dismissed in such thinking until very recently. Again, this is key to what we mean by the power of gender—the pervasiveness of gender as a filtering category, or meta-lens. That is, gender-sensitive research does more than document the pattern of excluding or trivializing women and their experiences while inflating men's experiences and power. It documents how gender—characterizations of masculinity and femininity—can influence the very categories and frameworks within which scholars work.

Gender inquiry in IR began with the question "Where are the women?" in international affairs, as they appeared absent in typical accounts of the rise of great powers, their leaders, their weaponries, and their wars, as well as in dominant theories about the nature of and interactions among states and their economies. At first glance, activities associated with masculinity (e.g., competitive sports, politics, militaries) appear simply as those in which men are present and women are absent and only the men engaging in these activities need be attended to. Gender analysis, however, reveals how women are in fact important to the picture (enabling men's activities, such as providing reasons for men to fight), even though women and the roles they are expected to play are obscured when we focus only on men. Through a gender-sensitive lens, we see how constructions of masculinity (agency, control, aggression) are not independent of, but rely upon, contrasting constructions of femininity (dependence, vulnerability, passivity). In an important sense, the dominant presence of men and the overvaluing of masculinity depend on the absence of women and the devaluing of femininity. Because of this interdependence, using gender analysis in IR does not merely reveal heretofore-unseen conditions and roles of women in world politics, but "transforms" what we know about men and the activities they undertake in international affairs. Hence, the study of gender alters our understandings of the conventional foci of IR—power politics, war, and economic control—by exposing what more deeply underpins them and why they are given such prominence over other ways of thinking about and acting in the world.

Thus, the seemingly simplistic question "Where are the women?" has yielded many insights. First, it has revealed that women are not absent in world affairs, even though they are rarely present in the top echelons of states, corporations, and IGOs. Instead, they tend to play roles that

1. grease the wheels of world politics, such as military or diplomatic wives who enable men to make war or peace by taking
   care of men's needs through freeing them for combat or creating
   social environments for men to negotiate, or sex workers who
   provide R&R (rest and recreation) to combat troops in service to
   sustaining militaries;
2. produce the wheels of world politics by sustaining everyday life
   in households and serving primarily as low-paid workers in defense plants, assembly work, agribusiness, and domestic, sexual,
   social, and clerical service industries—thereby undergirding
   the world's production of weapons, goods, and services—while
   also being situated as the predominant consumers of goods for
   households; and/or
3. derail the wheels of world politics through social movements
   and NGOs that protest world-politics-as-usual, whether in resistance to dictators, global capitalism, nuclear weapons, or natural
   resource depletion and destruction (Enloe 1989).

Such observations have led to an understanding that women are, in fact,
central to the operations we associate with world politics, but their centrality in relation to greasing and producing the wheels of world-politics-
as-usual rests upon their invisibility and conformity to "acting like
'women'"—that is, subservient to men. Second, the positioning of women
in world affairs has also illuminated the positionings of men. Prior to
gender inquiry in IR, the fact that men dominated positions of power in
world politics remained unremarked upon. It was just assumed that men
would hold such positions of power, and there was no interest in why or
with what effects. Asking the "man question" in international relations
(Zalewski and Parpart 1998; Parpart and Zalewski 2008) draws attention
to what "acting like 'men'" means for the conduct and outcomes of international politics.

As we have already discussed, evidence from feminist and nonfeminist
sources has been accumulating to substantiate the claim that gender equity is strongly related to the quality of life for everyone in every country
(Eisler, Loye, and Norgaard 1995; Eisler 2007). The conclusion reached
from this research by powerful international bodies is that "empowering
women and improving their status are essential to realizing the full potential of economic, political and social development" (UN 1995: xvii). IGO

and state policymakers—facing new challenges in post–Cold War and post-9/11 contexts that feature widening violent conflicts, economic inequalities, social and cultural divisions, and environmental breakdowns—have become increasingly open to accepting that the improvement of women's positions can bring improvements in world conditions. From this acknowledgment has flowed an unprecedented array of national and international gender policies, referred to by one feminist IR specialist as "the new politics of gender equality" (Squires 2007). This shift in policymaking, which constitutes in a sense the repositioning of gender on the world politics agenda from relative absence to increasing presence, relates to the repositionings of women (and men) that constitute a running theme in this text.

### Gender in International Policymaking

Angela Merkel of Germany, Michelle Bachelet of Chile, Ellen Johnson Sirleaf of Liberia, Benazir Bhutto of Pakistan (assassinated in 2007), Hillary Rodham Clinton of the United States, Julia Eileen Gillard of Australia, Dilma Rousseff of Brazil, Iveta Radičová of Slovakia, and Park Geun-hye of South Korea—these are only a few of the women who have become or sought to become heads of state and/or government over the past decade. Although 2008 was the first time that a woman was taken seriously as a candidate for US president, as of 2012 seventeen women were serving as elected heads of state and/or government and about ninety women have served as presidents or prime ministers of 34 percent of the world's countries since 1953 (Hawkesworth 2012: 27). Their numbers are still comparatively very low, but arguably women as world leaders have become less anomalous. Nevertheless, severe barriers to women's achievement of high office remain (discussed in Chapter 3).

Among the recent developments that could significantly increase the numbers of women heads of state and governments is the adoption of some form of gender quota in at least ninety countries (Dahlerup 2006b: 3). Drude Dahlerup identifies this as "a global trend" stretching back to 1990 when the UN Economic and Social Council (ECOSOC) supported the goal lobbied for by women's movements to have 30 percent of world decision-making positions held by women by 1995 (2006b: 6). As of 2012, only 19.5 percent of the world's parliamentarians were women; however, by then, thirty countries had reached or exceeded the 30 percent target,[3] with postgenocide Rwanda still topping the list at 56 percent (and in 2008 becoming the first country with more female than male legislators), followed by the Nordic countries, and a mix of Latin American and other western European and African states in 2011 (Hawkesworth 2012: 31). Almost all these have legal or party gender quota systems in combination with proportional representation systems (defined and discussed in Chapter 3). Although quota systems vary in form and efficacy, they were specifically promoted in the Platform for Action arising from the UN Fourth World Conference on Women, held in Beijing in 1995, which was unanimously supported by the world's governments, as the "fast-track" way to increase women's political representation.[4] Following that conference, in Latin America alone eleven out of nineteen governments had adopted either constitutional or legal gender quotas by 2000 (Araújo and García 2006: 83), and by 2011 in the fifty-nine national elections held that year, women gained more than 10 percent more seats in the seventeen countries with legislated quotas than in those without them.[5] There are many reasons for this recent "contagion" of gender quotas, but among them is a growing international consensus or norm, advocated by women's movements worldwide and supported by feminist scholarship, that gender equality in the form of women's greater political representation, ideally to the point of parity with men, is necessary for polities claiming or aspiring to be modern and democratic.

Gender mainstreaming also gained momentum and increasing acceptance during the same period that gender quotas were advancing. Although definitions vary somewhat, gender mainstreaming refers generally to integrating the principle of gender equality into any (inter)governmental policy (not just those associated with so-called women's issues, such as family and violence against women) to ensure that in practice it does not, wittingly or unwittingly, increase or sustain inequalities between women and men (Squires 2007: 39–40). Gender mainstreaming was first advocated in the context of economic development policies once feminist research revealed that approaches taken by funding bodies like the World Bank, such as the promotion of capital-intensive agriculture for export, tended to privilege men, who had or were given more access to capital, agricultural inputs and machinery, and land ownership. Women, although heavily involved in subsistence agriculture, which was the main source of family food consumption, were not seen as farmers or landowners and thus did not benefit from this kind of funding. This disparity not only increased men's power over women in agricultural work and families, but also contributed to producing more hunger and malnutrition when women's work of subsistence farming was increasingly so devalued and unsupported. The World Bank and a number of other supranational institutions, ranging from the UN and the Organization for Economic Cooperation and Development (OECD) to the European Union (EU), as well as many development agencies within states in the North, have been convinced by such findings to adopt gender mainstreaming, also called for in the Beijing Platform for Action (BPA), to try to avoid such outcomes (Squires 2007: 42). There have been numerous downsides to this approach (which we address in Chapter 3), but its institutionalization represents a sea change in its recognition that gender is infused in all (world) political issues and legitimizes the need for "gender experts" in world politics.

No less than the UN Security Council, arguably the most male-dominated and masculinist body in the world (that is, steeped in the most hegemonic masculine values associated with power politics), has also acquiesced to giving some attention to gender. For example, Security Council Resolution 1325, passed in 2000, calls for women to be present at peace negotiating tables, a goal long advocated by women's peace movements that have claimed women have greater interests and different stakes in ending war. As we explore in Chapter 4, it is not that women are inherently more peaceful, but rather that their predominantly civilian status means that they often bear the high structural costs of wars over time. In those wars, some past and some recent, where there has been little separation between the battlefront and the home front and civilians are purposely targeted, civilians constitute the highest proportion of those left homeless, diseased, and hungry; turned into refugees; and made victims of sexual and domestic assault (by enemy and "friendly" combatants) as indirect consequences of warfare. Although on average for the past few centuries combatants have died from the direct violence of war fighting in about the same numbers as civilians caught up in armed conflicts, civilian deaths in "total wars," such as the world wars, and in wars in which they are targeted for direct violence, such as massacres, have been higher and civilian suffering and death from indirect warfare violence are staggering (Goldstein 2011: 258–260). The majority of combatants are men, and the majority of civilians are women and children (both female and male), despite some increases in women in state and nonstate militaries and in child soldiers (both male and female) pressed into combat. Women, as can be seen in the case of postgenocide Rwanda, also are critical to the mending of postconflict societies as they tend to be the backbone of civil society, most centrally re-creating households and communities.

Predating this Security Council resolution was a significant codification and prosecution of rape as a war crime following the highly visible use of systematic rape in the early 1990s in the wars in the former Yugoslavia and in Rwanda. Systematic wartime rape not only neutralizes women as threats, but also seeks to weaken men's resolve to fight by "soiling their women" while also trying to wipe out an enemy culture or ethnicity by impregnating women with "alien" seed or keeping them from reproducing altogether. The assumption that rape was merely a natural "spoil of war" (for men) had kept it from being fully recognized as an international war crime until feminist activists and events in Bosnia and Rwanda made it clear that rape was a direct violation of women's human rights, rising to the level of torture as an instrument of warfare.

The ideas that women have human rights and that women's human rights expand traditional definitions of human rights were significantly advanced by the UN Convention on the Elimination of All Forms of Discrimination Against Women (CEDAW),[6] initially adopted in 1979 following the UN Decade for Women and going into force in 1981. By 2000, only 25 countries (including, most glaringly, the United States, as well as a smattering of Muslim and least-developed countries) had failed to ratify CEDAW, making it the second most widely ratified human rights convention (UN 2000: 151). As of 2013, 187 out of 194 countries had ratified CEDAW, with only the United States, Iran, South Sudan, Sudan, Somalia, Palau, and Tonga as outliers. Through CEDAW and subsequent UN conferences on human rights, particularly throughout the 1990s, women's movements and NGOs made the case that "women's rights are human rights," achieving international recognition that reproductive and, to some degree, sexual rights are just as important as and connected to political and economic rights. As long as women are denied choices about if, when, and under what conditions they bear children or terminate pregnancies, are subject to sexual and domestic abuse, and are limited in their sexual expressions and orientations, they will not be able to exercise their political and economic rights. Although women's and other human rights continue to be violated on a massive scale, the widespread ratification of CEDAW has given women's movements throughout much of the world a major tool through which to hold their governments accountable for continued abuses.

## GLOBAL CRISES:
## REMASCULINIZATIONS OF WORLD POLITICS

Just as women were gaining voice and ground in international forums and policymaking arenas, particularly in the first decade of the post–Cold War period, a series of political, economic, cultural, and environmental shocks heightened both direct and structural violence in world politics. While so-called hot wars raged in the global South (often as a result of East-West conflict) throughout the Cold War period and into the post–Cold War time (including conflicts in the global North arising out of the unraveling of the former Soviet Union as well as the first US-waged war against Iraq), decisions made in the aftermath of 9/11 produced not only wars in Afghanistan and Iraq waged largely by the United States, but also the so-called global "war on terror." Far from reaping the substantial peace dividend hoped for by this point in the post–Cold War era, world military spending, after a dip in the 1990s largely due to reductions by former Warsaw Pact nations, skyrocketed again to peak Cold War levels, with US military spending accounting for about half of the total (Goldstein 2011: 19). Although the Stockholm International Peace Research Institute (SIPRI) announced recently that 2012 saw the first slight reduction—0.5 percent—in world military expenditures in the new millennium, this was driven largely by the United States ending or diminishing its wars in Iraq and Afghanistan and by austerity measures, affecting military but even more social spending, instituted in the United States and the West as a whole since the 2008 financial crisis. However, these were also offset by increased expenditures across other regions of the world, although the United States remains the largest military spender by far.[7] As the Women's International League for Peace and Freedom (WILPF) documented in 2010,[8] one year of world military spending at 2008 levels would pay for the UN operating budget for 700 years and for 2,928 years of funding UN Women, the umbrella agency for gender equality at the UN, at its present funding level. Vastly improving a range of indices crucial to achieving gender equality, such as gender parity in secondary education, reduced maternal mortality, and full reproductive and sexual health services, would cost only 20 percent of what is spent on militaries each year and less than the UN-recommended minimum of .07 percent of gross national income annually that almost no developed country presently donates in nonmilitary international aid. The choice to privilege military spending at the expense of making populations more vulnerable to social, economic, health, and environmental harms is referred to as *structural violence*. Most "developed" and "developing" countries have consistently made the choice to engage in structural violence against their own people and the world's people.

Another major source of structural violence is neoliberal globalization, or the expansion (and imposition) of global capital interconnecting the world's economies, which, in its contemporary form, began in the 1970s and accelerated in the 1990s onward (Peterson 2003; Marchand and Runyan 2000, 2011). Much of the world is still struggling with the aftermath of the 2008 financial and ensuing economic crisis, precipitated as they were by poor and poorly regulated lending practices by US-based transnational banks and investment firms, which, for a time, artificially propped up the global capitalist economy in which almost all countries and many of their peoples were expected to become deeply enmeshed. Critics of globalization have long argued that extremely unregulated capital flows render the global capitalist system unstable. Advocates of deregulation have argued that an unfettered market would raise all boats, but it has, in fact, only enriched the few at the top; created unprecedented income and wealth gaps between the rich and the rest; shifted sites of industrial production to places with minimal or no labor and environmental standards and enforcement; and based wealth production not on the production of goods and services but on risky, faulty, and even fraudulent financial-sector mechanisms. Another net result of unbridled global industrial capitalism is global warming, around which there is finally close to world consensus that it is "man-made" and is threatening polities, economies, and life as we know it on the planet as a result of climate change and the "natural" disasters it accelerates.

Undergirding globalization is the economic philosophy or ideology of neoliberalism, which was developed by economists in the global North and imposed there and on the global South. Critics refer to this as a form of economic or market "fundamentalism" (Klein 2007), as it represents a total faith in the market, unfettered by state regulation and protections for citizens, and a total belief in the dismantling of the welfare state through the privatization for profit of public services, leaving no accountability or universal access to satisfaction of basic needs. The ensuing economic insecurities have also unleashed a variety of other fundamentalisms, including political, religious, ethnic, and cultural ones. Neoconservativism combines a neoliberal faith in the market with a view that the only role for the state is a coercive one: first, to control other states through strong national defense and offense (which is part and parcel of a militarist ideology), and second, to control populations through the imposition of laws that limit civil liberties and human rights, insisting that people conform to a particular set of behaviors deemed "moral." The rise of neoconservativism is closely related to the rise of patriarchal religious fundamentalisms—whether Christian, Judaic, or Islamic—especially when they are espoused by state elites and determine the "moral" codes upon which they seek to order and control society. Ethnic and other cultural fundamentalisms, whether they are based on conceptions of the "traditional" or the "modern," when espoused by elites produce similar intolerances for those who are "different" or dissent from the imposed social order. All these fundamentalisms result in structural and/or direct violence, ranging from political, economic, and social discriminations to ethnic cleansing and religion-based wars.

What is less acknowledged as a fundamentalism—and is an ideology that feeds and cuts across all other fundamentalisms—is masculinism, which justifies and "naturalizes" gender hierarchy (that is, makes it seem natural rather than socially and politically constructed and thus subject to change). As a number of feminist scholars (Faludi 2007; Joseph and Sharma 2003; Hawthorne and Winter 2002) observed in the aftermath of 9/11, women virtually disappeared as expert commentators on world affairs, particularly in the US media, where talking heads became almost exclusively military men who controlled the public discourse and espoused aggression—a decidedly masculine value—as the only acceptable course of action. Feminists and other critics from the academy and social movements of the ensuing wars were feminized—that is, portrayed as weak, naive, and dangerous—and many received death threats to further silence them. A similar pattern emerged in the United States in the post–Vietnam War period, during which we saw what Susan Jeffords (1989) calls the "remasculinization of America" as neoconservatives took power under Ronald Reagan in the 1980s. Seeking to put behind them the defeat in Vietnam that led to a more chastened view about the value of military conflict to solve problems and secure geopolitical objectives, neoconservatives—through public discourse and policy and even popular culture—rehabilitated the Rambo-esque masculinist and militarist values of might makes right, unfettered by "feminine" considerations about the costs and usefulness of war. The post-9/11 remasculinization of America under yet another neoconservative government was justified with resort to the necessity of war arising from some inevitable "clash of civilizations" in which one ethnic and religious fundamentalism must combat another (the West/Christianity against the East/Islam), but also with resort, at least for a short time, to the claim that the war in Afghanistan was about civilized men (in the West) saving women from barbaric men (the Taliban).

As Susan Faludi (2007) observes, this latter justification has a long pedigree in US history, naturalizing, for example, the European colonists' genocide of Native Americans. Moreover, as others have observed, the voices of Afghan women went unheeded, although they warned that the invasion and new government installed would simply put another set of violent patriarchs (or male rulers who believe in the subordination of women) in charge (Russo 2006; Farrell and McDermott 2005). Thus, they and other outside observers concluded that women's human rights were neither a reason for the war, despite the early rhetoric about this from the George W. Bush administration, nor could they be achieved by war, which most often vastly increases insecurity for women. A more comprehensive examination of gender and global security appears in Chapter 4, but suffice it to say here that masculinism is deeply implicated in increasing militarization and the silencing of alternatives to armed conflict and of nonviolent conflict resolution.

Masculinism has also shaped and propelled globalization. Charlotte Hooper's (2001) study of the discourse, or language, used by Anglo-American neoliberal economists and leaders to promote globalization in the 1990s reveals a new kind of hegemonic masculinity emerging: it combined older forms of "hard" masculinity that celebrated war heroism and risk-taking frontiersmanship with newer forms of relatively "softer" masculinity that applauded rational calculus, technological prowess, and global networking. This new model served to elevate global capitalist development to the most manly pursuit, even over war, to which all men and manly countries should aspire. Those (whether women or men, movements, organizations, institutions, or states) who were concerned with what globalization was doing—the loss of industrial jobs and the shift to low-wage service economies in the global North, the exploitation of labor and the environment in the global South, the decline of the welfare state and the privatization of social services, and the lack of interest in human development and environmental protection in favor of capital accumulation that went to only the very few—were seen as anachronistic (feminine) and thus should be brushed aside as being unready for the brave new world of the "new economy." Infusing martial values into the global capitalist cause, already replete with competitiveness values, encouraged the hubris that enabled the risky ventures that recently brought the world economy to its knees.

Long preceding the 2008 economic crisis, however, evidence had been piling up that most women were bearing the brunt of the new economy (Marchand and Runyan 2000). For example, as reproductive workers in the voluntaristic economy, or household members given by gender ideology the most responsibility for the creation and care of family and community members on an unpaid basis, women—who are also the largest consumers and providers of social services because of their reproductive roles—have lost the most with the reduction or privatization of social services. The retreat of the welfare state, particularly being accelerated now in the West under masculinist austerity measures post-2008, has meant that women have had to take on additional roles in the private or domestic sphere that used to be public services, for which women also used to be paid or paid better. As productive workers in the cash economy, women, who have been rendered as "cheap" labor by gender ideology, became the preferred labor force in low-wage service and light-industrial assembly work created by offshore production. Some women have benefited to a degree from this newfound employment, but their working conditions—including low wages, lack of union protections, poor health and safety regulations, sexual harassment, and polluted and dangerous workplaces and living spaces—have kept them in subordinate and precarious positions. Subordinate men, such as those in the working classes, have suffered as well, having their skills, wages, and jobs "feminized" (devalued or eliminated). But this effect, too, boomerangs on women in such forms as enduring higher incidences of domestic violence, taking full responsibility for both wage and reproductive work, and/or being left behind to sustain the household alone when men migrate for jobs elsewhere or having to migrate themselves to find work, thus leaving their families behind. Chapter 5 more fully addresses the impact of gender on the global political economy, and the impact of the global political economy on gender, and this analysis promotes our thinking alternatively about how to make more sustainable and just economies.

So how do we make sense of the contradiction of the rise of the new global politics of gender equality (or the repositionings of women and men) at the same time that remasculinizations of states and economies have been in ascendance? Our short answer is the power of gender, the principle concept informing this book and its other running theme. As a filtering and organizing mechanism that produces both worldviews and world structures, the power of gender is particularly resilient and adaptive, accommodating some changes in the positionings (or repositionings) of women and men, while sustaining, through shifting formations of what constitutes ideal forms of masculinity and femininity, masculinist values in world politics that devalue other ways of identifying, seeing, structuring, and acting in the world. Our somewhat longer explanation lies in the interactions of gender with the other identity markers and power relations of race, class, nation, and sexuality that intersectional analysis reveals. These provide more complicated pictures of social orders, enabling us to see how even the concept of gender equality is manipulated to privilege some women over other women and some men over other men—with the result being a general continuation of unjust social orders and political and economic relations. These also bring our attention to how divisions and inequalities created among women and among men have disabling effects on resistances and alternatives to world-politics-as-usual unless all inequalities are confronted in those resistances and alternatives. Figure 1.1 graphically depicts the ways in which interlocking ideologies of classism, racism, sexism, and heterosexism are at the heart of a range of also interconnected global systems (defined more in the concluding section of this chapter) that require resistance and alternatives.

As laid out in the following map of the book that concludes this chapter, our examination shows the power of gender at work in the lenses we use to analyze world politics in the contexts of global governance, global security, and global political economy. In the process, we explore what it would take to degender world politics.

## MAPPING THE BOOK

*Why "Global Gender Issues"?*

We share skepticism about invocations of "global" problems and solutions for several reasons: they can erase differences in social locations, experiences, and interests that must be recognized to unravel the depth, breadth, and multiplicity of power relations in world politics; they may privilege global actors as the only meaningful ones in world politics; and they often misrepresent world political inequalities and the crises that arise from them as being produced and experienced in the same ways across the globe, when in fact some actors are more responsible than others for such

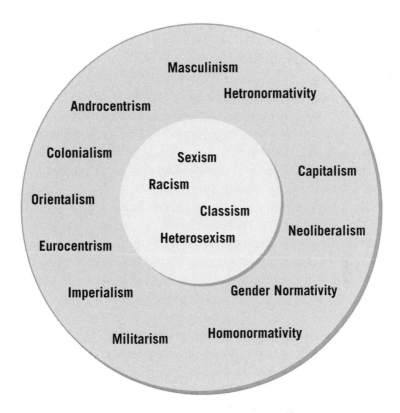

FIGURE 1.1  Intertwining and Mutually Constitutive Ideologies in Intersectional Gender Analysis

problems. The manifestations of such problems differ in kind and degree in varying local contexts, and the experience of such problems depends on one's social location so that some people are more insulated from and some are more exposed to them. We continue to retain the term *global,* however, to foreground not only the interrelationships between the conventional constructs and practices of global governance, global security, and global political economy inequalities they both engender and rest upon, but also the interconnections among differing "local" (including national) manifestations of inequalities as a result of these "global" constructs and practices.

We also share skepticism about a narrow, overarching, and unitary conception of gender and reject essentialist approaches to and universalist claims about it. We retain the term *gender,* however, to signify gender as a power relation that is inextricable from other power relations and sig-nificantly affected by and affecting them. Early feminist IR scholars have been taken to task for not attending enough to the intersections of gen-der, race, class, sexuality, and nation (Chowdhry and Nair 2002), but we use gender—specifically in our concept of the power of gender—to refer to a hegemonic (or dominant) worldview or meta-lens that produces and reproduces these intersecting oppressions. The latter, in turn, enables the production and reproduction of hegemonies in world politics, that is, the extraction of consent (or tacit acceptance) by dominated groups to unjust social orders maintained by dominant groups.

Our continued use of the term *issues* (in combination with "global" and "gender") is not intended to mean that there is a homogeneous set of inter-ests and issues that all women share globally. Nor is it meant to reduce the global politics of inequality to "women's issues." Rather, it is suggestive of a different and wider conception of not only what issues from global pro-cesses, namely, savage and interconnected inequalities and injustices, but also why these are world political issues, that is, subject to political debate and change, not the result of some inexorable, natural, or necessary pro-cesses that cannot be questioned. We organize our investigation of global gender issues according to major lines of inquiry in IR—global governance, global security, and global political economy—not to suggest that these are the only ways to think about world politics or to categorize knowl-edge about world politics, but rather to show how gender, in an intersec-tional sense, is deeply implicated in these "global issues" and the crises they induce.

## The Repositionings of Women, Men, and Gender

As we have begun to argue, gender is salient both as a substantive (empir-ical, concrete) topic in world politics and as a dimension of how we study (analyze, think about) world politics. The former we characterize as the ef-fects of world politics on gender. In subsequent chapters, we provide data on women's positions (or roles) relative to men's in the contexts of global political, security, and economic structures and organizations. But we em-phasize *repositionings of women and men* (including repositionings among groups of women and among groups of men) where these have occurred, as the result either of recent global attention to gender policymaking or shifts in the nature of war-making and the global economy. These data flesh out what we refer to as the gendered (understood intersectionally) divisions of power, violence, and labor and resources, which are addressed respectively in the chapters on global governance (power), global security (violence), and global political economy (labor and resources). Although overall patterns continue to show that men in aggregate hold more privileged positions in global power structures, whereas women in aggregate are subordinated in and by those structures, there is evidence that some women in some national and sectoral contexts are advancing (e.g., moving "up") and more men are becoming more vulnerable to the vicissitudes of violent conflict and economic change. These (still overall limited) shifts show that gender roles are far from static, but they also reveal that other power relations, such as race, class, sexuality, and nationality, play significant roles in determining which women "move up" and which men stay down or "move down."

Another common feature of our "issues" chapters (3, 4, and 5) is attention to the repositioning of gender in global policymaking. Not long ago, gender was absent as an explicit focus of policymaking by IGOs. Today, gender—either referring to women or to gender equality between women and men—is on the agenda of many IGOs in relation to a range of political, security, economic, and social issues. We address recent key gender policies but also critique them in terms of, on the one hand, their appropriations and depoliticizations of gender analysis and demands and, on the other, their insufficiencies in repositioning women and men, attending to inequalities not only between but also among women and men, and alleviating the global crises to which they acknowledge gender is related.

## The Power of Gender

As our other recurring theme, we deal with gender as a dimension of the way world politics is studied, thought about, and thus conducted by referring to the effects of gender on world politics, or *the power of gender* as a meta-lens, or mental ordering and filtering system, that produces and reproduces global inequalities, injustices, and crises. Chapter 2 elaborates the power of gender as a meta-lens; other chapters reveal how it operates to perpetuate inequalities between and among women and men, insufficiencies in the repositionings of diverse women and men, and appropriations of equality, nonviolence, social justice, and environmental sustainability demands. Thus, the repositionings of women and men and the power of gender are two *interacting* themes—two sides of the same coin—that frame and cut across the material presented in this text.

These interacting phenomena provide a gender-sensitive lens on global processes that foregrounds the relationship between gendered thinking and actors and gendered actions and consequences. Those consequences have most severely culminated in what we refer to throughout the text as the interlocking global crises of representation, insecurity, and sustainability, but we also deal with them one at a time and in more depth in the issues chapters. Such a lens alters both "what" world politics is and "how" we view it. We see the extent and structure of gendered inequalities, the role of gender in combination with other inequalities in structuring the experience of women *and* men (and other genders) worldwide, the significance of gender in relation to other power relations in shaping how we think about world politics, and the process by which gendered thought shapes world politics itself. In shifting our vision, a gender-sensitive lens, which is most concerned with uprooting the power of gender from which inequalities and injustices flow, also shifts our attention from questions of order, control, and growth at any cost (which are ostensibly best left in the hands of experts at the top) to questions of representational equity, nonviolent security, and human and ecological sustainability that actually require multiple voices from multiple social locations to address.

*Feminist Lenses in World Politics Inquiry*

Although a gender-sensitive lens on world politics alerts us to the power of gender as a hegemonic worldview or meta-lens, there are multiple gender lenses, or feminist perspectives, in world politics inquiry. These are addressed in Chapter 2, but here it is important to point out that we are applying a range of these lenses in our engendered examinations of traditional categories of world politics inquiry: global governance (Chapter 3), global security (Chapter 4), and global political economy (Chapter 5). The employment of multiple feminist perspectives foregrounds the substantial body of work that now exists in feminist IR,[9] affords more complex and sometimes conflicting analyses of these world political constructs, and ensures no single or hegemonic analysis that produces fixed or static approaches that foreclose debate within gender inquiry. At the same time, we point to weaknesses in and appropriations of gender inquiry and policy when they fail to address the power relations among women and among men that forestall more comprehensive critiques and resistances to processes that widen and deepen global and local inequalities. Our final chapter (6) examines some resistances, both activist and conceptual, that seek to change the inequalities between and among women and men and/or transform perspectives on world politics. Although varied, incomplete, and sometimes conflictual, resistance strategies attempt to confront the crises of representation, insecurity, and sustainability through enabling more participatory and nonhegemonic governance, nonviolent forms of security, and more just and environmentally sustainable economies.

## Clarifications of Terms

Recognizing that readers of this text will come from differing disciplines and educational levels, we offer some clarification of terms we use that may be less familiar. This is less of a glossary, which assumes agreed upon and fixed meanings, and more of a clarification of how we use terms whose meanings are multiple and sometimes contested. Where appropriate, less familiar terms not addressed here are defined where they first appear in the text.

For additional clarity, we note that when we use "gender" as a noun or adjective, we are most often foregrounding the masculine-feminine dynamic conventionally emphasized in feminist and gender-sensitive accounts. When we use "gender*ed*" as an adjective, we intend something more complex and intersectional, referring not only to masculinity-femininity, but also to how gender is always crosscut by other axes of difference. We sometimes list these dimensions—race, ethnicity, class, religion, sexuality, nationality, age, ability, and so on—but at other times prefer "gendered" as a less cumbersome shorthand signaling intersectionality without listing specific differences.

Similarly, although we largely refer only to "women" and "men" or "males" and "females" or use notions such as "both genders," we understand, as indicated in the beginning of this chapter, that there are multiple sexes and genders and that "women" and "men" are themselves socially constructed and nonhomogeneous categories (Fausto-Sterling 2000). Implied or explicit references to "elites" in the text signify those privileged in the particular context by (especially but not exclusively) gender, class, ethnicity/race, sexuality, and nation.

We often refer to the ideologies of "heteronormativity" and "heterosexism," which assume an essentialized (natural, universal) binary of sex difference (male and female only), privilege exclusively heterosexual desire (for the "opposite" sex), and maintain that the only natural and hence appropriate or respectable expressions of desire, intimacy, sexual identity, marriage, and family formation are heterosexual. The rigid gender dichotomy presumed in both ideologies promotes masculinism, devalues what is feminized, and fosters the demonization and even criminalization of nonheterosexual relations. We most often use "sexual minorities" to signify individuals and groups who contest or do not conform to hetero-normativity and normative gender identifications. Although "LGBTQ" can capture an array of sexual and nonnormative gender identifications (lesbian, gay, bisexual, and trans identities—which can include transgen-der, transvestite, transsexual—as well as queer and questioning identities), we note here that engaging in particular sexual practices need not consti-tute assuming a particular sexual identity, that these Western-originating terms are less widely circulated elsewhere, and that those who engage in same-sex or other minority sexual practices or nonnormative gender ex-pression do not necessarily identify as LGBTQ (particularly outside the global North) or fit into these categories (such as intersex people who are born with ambiguous sex organs). "Homonormativity" refers to the assumption that all sexual minorities do or should conform to Western conceptions of lesbian, gay, and bisexual identity and to Western forms of LGBTQ politics, which when imposed on other cultures and political con-texts is often referred to as "global gay" politics. Gender "queer" can refer to a range of sexual minority identities, but "queering" more typically re-fers to analytical processes and social practices that defy heteronormative and homonormative readings of social reality and performances of nor-mative sexual practices and gender identity. Heteronormative "patriarchy" refers not only to male-dominated or masculinist rule but also to rule that enforces heterosexual norms to achieve that end.

Although we have addressed "sexualization" and "racialization" defini-tionally to some degree, we want to stress that they carry two meanings that are often in tension. They refer in one sense to processes of identifying an individual or group as one or another sexuality (straight, gay, queer) or race (white, black, Asian) by attributing to them particular and often ste-reotypical ideas and practices associated with that label. In a second sense, the attributing process often emerges from a position of normative privi-lege and presumed superiority, which effectively stigmatizes (or "others") the objects of attribution, especially by constructing them unidimension-ally—as "only" their race, class, or sexuality. It is in this sense that privilege permits whites to be less aware of "having a race" themselves and more often to "racialize" others, even as the social construction of "race" permits some who are excluded from "whiteness" through economic or religious discrimination at one juncture to be "whitened up" by altered alignments at another (southern Europeans, Jews, Irish). References to "white," then, also can refer to those who gain the status of "whiteness," regardless of ac-tual skin color, as a result of class and other privileges.

Racialization is also historically inextricable from the expansionary and colonizing practices of European elites who deployed Enlightenment ideas ("reason," "science") and new technologies (gunpowder, steam engine) to enhance their power over foreign populations, thus enabling the extraction of resources and labor to fuel European "modernization" and geopolitical dominance. "Eurocentrism" is an ideology of European superiority that arose from this conquest and is often used interchangeably with "Western-centrism" in more recent times. "Orientalism" (Said 1979) is one effect of Eurocentrism (or "Occidentalism"), consigning the "non-West" to the status of cultural, political, economic, and technological backwardness. Such backwardness is assumed, in Eurocentric and Orientalist thinking, to need stimulation from the West to "develop" or "modernize" or "progress." It is for this reason that we try to resist such labels as "developed" versus "developing" countries or the oft-used terms "First" and "Third" Worlds, as they maintain notions of upward continuums and hierarchies. Moreover, like "industrialized" and "nonindustrialized," they are not accurate because there are postindustrial, industrial, and nonindustrial formations in most countries. We instead use, where possible, the terms "global South" and "global North" to denote social locations of subjugation and privilege, respectively. At times we invoke the global North or North or the global South or South to refer to the geographic locations associated with the First and Third Worlds, but at other times we mean to include nonprivileged groups in both the geographical South and North when we refer to the global South. We also remind readers that there are elites in the South who share the privileges of the global North.

Although after World War II resistance to direct colonial rule was largely successful, the global North continues to exploit the global South through less direct and differently manipulated forms of "neocolonial" or "neoimperial" rule (sometimes referred to as "recolonization"). Most recently, "neoliberal governmentality," or the marketization of all life, has been put forward as the current form of neoimperialism. "Neoliberalism" refers to what we earlier called market fundamentalism, and "governmentality" is a form of governance that posits a right or normative order and entails a range of often noncoercive disciplinary mechanisms that enable conformism of human subjectivities to it (Foucault 1991). Neoliberal governmentality is sometimes used interchangeably with a contemporary notion of Empire. "Empire" today refers not to sovereign actors pursuing economic and military power beyond their territories but to a deterritorialized, decentered apparatus of rule operating across all dimensions of the social order and constituting the paradigmatic form of "biopower" in which subjectivities inculcate "self-discipline" to conform to market and other dominant logics (Hardt and Negri 2000: xii–xv). The United States leads but does not (or cannot) control this new form of rule. The Bush administration, however, forcefully promulgated a cultural logic and normative order presupposing global capitalism and the "war on terror" as inseparable components of the only "right" conceptualization of democracy and world order—an orientation that has somewhat changed under the Barack Obama administration but has not significantly or sufficiently disturbed the dynamics of Empire. This contextualizes what we mean by "the imperial(ist) impulse": the practice of thinking and acting from a position of presumptive power and moral superiority in ways that reproduce essentialized and oppositional categories that silence, condemn, or preclude alternative ways of thinking and acting, and do so in the name of knowing unequivocally the one "best" answer, policy, or global project. It is a key argument of this text that the power of gender constitutes just such an imperial(ist) impulse by underpinning, naturalizing, and reproducing it.

## Notes

1. The Obama administration came in taking a strong stand against the lax definitions of torture enabled under the Bush administration, planning to close the military prison for terrorist suspects at Guantánamo Bay and retreating from the terminology "war on terror." Unfortunately, the military prison remains open and the "war on terror" remains part of the popular and, to some degree, the official lexicon.

2. Crenshaw (1991) is credited with introducing intersectionality as an analytics. Recent discussions include McCall 2001; Brah 2002; Knapp 2005; Phoenix and Pattynama 2006; and Yuval-Davis 2006.

3. See http://www.unwomen.org/2012/03/michelle-bachelet-highlights-quotas-to-accelerate-womens-political-participation/.

4. See Web and Video Resources listed at the end of this text for the online locations and full texts of a host of UN documents, conventions, and protocols referred to in this text, including the Beijing Platform for Action, as well as a host of videos that can supplement and deepen engagement with this text. A list of acronyms and their referents is provided at the front of this text for handy reference.

5. See http://www.unwomen.org/2012/03/michelle-bachelet-highlights-quotas-to-accelerate-womens-political-participation/.

6. On women's rights and/as human rights, see Cook 1994; Peters and Wolper 1995; Peterson and Parisi 1998; and Ackerly 2008. For critiques of this approach, see, for example, Hesford and Kozol 2005; and Hua 2011.

7. See http://www.sipri.org/media/pressreleases/2013/milex_launch.

8. See http://wilpf.org/2010MarYouGetWhatYouPayFor.

9. See Shepherd 2010 for a useful feminist IR reader with some important works, past and present.

# 2

⸺◁○▷⸺

# Gendered Lenses on World Politics

Why do lenses through which we view the world matter? How do stereo-types, dichotomies, and ideologies congeal to produce the meta-lens of the power of gender? How does the power of gender influence world politics lenses? How do feminist lenses on world politics challenge the power of gender and gendered divisions of power, violence, labor, and resources at work in world politics that precipitate global crises?

In Chapter 1, we presented an apparent contradiction. On the one hand, attention to gender inequality has expanded dramatically in the past decade, as evidenced in global activism, national and international poli-cies, and academic studies. In this sense, and especially in relation to re-positioning (some) women in world politics, gender equality appears to be taken seriously in the international community. On the other hand, what we refer to as crises of representation, insecurity, and sustainability have worsened in the past decade, evidenced not only by continued inequali-ties between and among women and men, but also by a remasculinization of global governance, international security, and global political economy (GPE). In this sense, and especially in relation to realizing a transforma-tion in gendered ideologies, practices, and structures, gender analyses ap-pear to be selectively embraced and problematically implemented. How do we make sense of this paradox?

Our answer to this question foregrounds the power of gender as an especially resilient and adaptive filtering and organizing mechanism, a meta-lens that produces particular ways of seeing, thinking, and acting in the world. Gender may feature in policymaking, women and men may be repositioned, and ideal forms of masculinity may shift, but we argue that

39

as long as the power of gender as a meta-lens continues to operate, it will produce and reproduce inequalities, injustices, and crises of global proportion. Here we make the case that feminist lenses are necessary to reveal the extent of the power of gender to produce and obscure inequalities and the global crises that ensue from and sustain inequalities.

This chapter begins with an account of how lenses work and why they matter in a general sense. Next we provide an extended discussion on what constitutes the power of gender and how it constitutes a meta-lens that structures world politics lenses. We then turn to feminist world politics lenses that challenge gendered inequalities and the power of gender as a meta-lens, or hegemonic worldview. The concluding section considers how gendered divisions of power, violence, and labor and resources (the themes of Chapters 3, 4, and 5) are crosscut by ethnicity/race, class, sexuality, and nation-based inequalities, and how the systemic reproduction of these interlocking inequalities generates global crises of representation, insecurity, and sustainability.

## HOW LENSES WORK AND WHY THEY MATTER

In simple terms, lenses focus our attention selectively. Selective attention is a necessary feature of making sense of any particular subject, practice, paradox, or social order. Because it is not physically possible for any human to see or comprehend everything at once, we rely on conceptual filters—lenses—that enable us to see some things in greater detail, with more accuracy, or in better relation to certain other things. Lenses simplify our thinking by focusing our attention on what seems most relevant. They "order" what we see and provide direction for subsequent actions. In this sense, lenses are like maps: they frame our choices, expectations, and explorations, enabling us to take advantage of knowledge already gained and, presumably, to move more effectively toward our objectives. Like maps, lenses enable us to make sense of where we are, what to expect next, and how to proceed. From the conceptual ordering systems available to us, we choose the lens we assume is most appropriate for a particular context—a lens that we expect will enable us to make sense of and act appropriately in that context.

Lenses are thus indispensable for ordering what we see and orienting our responses. But their filtering function is also problematic. Because we cannot focus on everything, any particular lens directs our attention to some features of a context, which unavoidably renders other features out of focus—filtered out—by that lens. In short, lenses both include and exclude, with important and often political implications.

By filtering our ways of thinking and ordering experience, the lenses we rely on have concrete effects. We observe this readily in the case of self-fulfilling prophecies: if, for instance, we expect hostility, our own behavior (acting superior, displaying power) may elicit responses (defensive posturing, aggression) that we then interpret as confirming our expectations. It is in this sense that we refer to lenses and "realities" as interactive, interdependent, or mutually constituted. Lenses shape who we are, what we think, and what actions we take, thus shaping the world we live in. At the same time, the world we live in ("reality") shapes which lenses are available to us, what we see through them, and the likelihood of our using them—or adjusting them—in particular contexts.

In general, as long as our lenses seem to work, we continue to rely on them. The more useful they appear to be, or the more accustomed to them we become, the more we are inclined to take them for granted and to resist making major changes in them. We forget that a particular lens is a choice among many alternatives. Instead, we tend to believe we are seeing "reality" as it *is* rather than as our language, culture, or discipline interprets reality. It is difficult and sometimes uncomfortable to reflect critically on our assumptions, to question their accuracy or desirability, and to explore the implications of shifting our vantage point by adopting a different lens.

We acquire our lenses, or learn our conceptual ordering systems, in a variety of contexts, but early childhood is especially consequential. From infancy on, we are socialized into and internalize ways of thinking and acting that enable us to perform appropriately within a particular culture. This involves acquiring an identity that constitutes subject formation—"who I am"—and assimilating cultural codes that provide meaning for "what I do." Socialization processes are embedded in wider social relations of power that determine which codes are dominant. These include familial, linguistic, cultural, economic, educational, religious, political, and legal institutions that stabilize particular symbolic and social orders and orderings. Dominant codes are infused with normative and ideological beliefs that constitute systems of meaning and valorization, and these can have significant effects on world politics. For example, in complex relationships with governmental, economic, and patriarchal power, religious institutions have historically promoted particular worldviews that guide human action in its most passionate expressions and normative investments—not least, the willingness to die and/or kill others in the name of a cause.

What we learn at an early age is psychosocially formative: the conceptual ordering system (language, cultural rules) we uncritically absorb in childhood is especially resistant to transformation. This is not simply a matter of accustomed habits but of psychic coherence and the security of "knowing" how to act appropriately and effectively in the world. Hence, we are intensely invested in identities and cultural codes learned in early childhood, and challenges to the meaning and order they afford are experienced as particularly threatening.

Of course, the world we live in, and therefore our life experiences, are constantly changing, prompting changes in our lenses as well. The modifications may be minor: from liking one type of music to liking another, from being a high school student in a small town to being a college student in an urban environment. Or the changes may be more profound: from casual dating to parenting, from the freedom of student lifestyles to the assumption of full-time job responsibilities, from Newtonian to quantum physics, from conditions of relative peace to the direct violence of war. To function effectively as reality changes, we must modify our thinking as well. This is especially the case to the extent that outdated lenses or worldviews distort our understanding of current realities, placing us in danger or leading us away from our objectives. As both early explorers and contemporary drivers know, outdated maps are inadequate, and potentially disastrous, guides.

Particularly problematic lenses through which to view the world include *stereotypes* about particular aspects or characteristics of groups of people; *dichotomies* that order our thinking in asymmetrical, either-or terms whose apparent opposition obscures how they depend on each other; and i*deologies* that are even more encompassing lenses, affording legitimacy to a wide range of beliefs and practices in support of maintaining particular social orders. It is to a further discussion of these that we now turn as they are significant building blocks of the power of gender as a meta-lens that frames our thinking and hence our realities.

## Stereotypes

"Stereotypes," which are present in all cultures and communication systems, function on one level as simple lenses: they filter our seeing, thinking, and responding. In one sense, they are like words—simply generalizations that have been stabilized—and our conceptual systems rely on such generalizations to ease the challenge of making sense of complex and constantly changing phenomena. We focus here, however, on stereotypes that produce and sustain social divisions and hierarchical social orders. We can picture them as composite images that attribute—often incorrectly and always too generally—certain characteristics to whole groups of people. In this way, groups—and individuals "perceived" to fit group stereotypes—are seen as others want or expect to see them, not necessarily as they are. Stereotypes not only foreground a negative characterization of groups; they also homogenize all members of the group, erasing the differences and complexities that actually exist within—not simply between—groups.

Studies show that we tend to see what we expect to see, and stereotypes frame how we see individuals and groups in particular ways, even—especially—when we actually know little about those groups or people. Like all lenses, the simplifying effect of stereotypes encourages us to ignore complexity and contradictory signals, which are thereby rendered out of focus. This tends to reproduce stereotypical thinking and operates to sustain status quo orderings. In the process, stereotypes become "common sense" and the particular characteristics and behaviors they project are essentialized—appearing as natural, "given," and unchanging, rather than as socially constructed, in historically specific and power-laden contexts.

By providing unquestioned and apparently unambiguous categories that prompt unreflective responses, stereotypes play a key role in legitimating discrimination and reproducing hierarchical relations of power. For example, poverty and low academic performance among poor and/or ethnically subordinated groups may be "explained" by stereotypes of their being lazy, incompetent, or irresponsible. The underrepresentation of women in political office may be "explained" by the stereotype of their being uninterested in power and politics. In this way, stereotypes "blame" individuals for their "failures" and divert attention from institutionalized practices and social structures that shape *everyone's* personal abilities, social opportunities, and realization of preferred objectives.

Because they oversimplify and overgeneralize, promote inaccurate images, and are resistant to change, stereotypes significantly affect how we see ourselves, others, and social ordering generally. Stereotypes that value some groups and devalue others are inherently political, operating to normalize (depoliticize) and thus to reproduce unequal power relations. They reproduce inequalities by being taken for granted and self-fulfilling:

if we expect certain behaviors, we may act in ways that in fact create and reinforce such behaviors. (Expecting girls to dislike mechanics and hate math affects how much encouragement we give them; without expectations of success or encouragement, girls may avoid or do poorly in these activities.) Furthermore, stereotypes depoliticize inequalities by naturalizing and essentializing negative images of subordinated groups as inferior, undesirable, or threatening. When members of such groups internalize oppressive stereotypes, they typically hold themselves—rather than social structures—responsible for undesirable outcomes. (Females are more likely to blame themselves for ineptness or poor grades rather than ask how social structures discourage girls from exploring some subjects and favor boys in regard to particular educational and career goals.) Those who believe they are acting out the inevitable are, in effect, reconciled to discriminatory treatment.

*Dichotomies*

"Dichotomies" as lenses divide concepts (terms, ideas, characteristics) into two, mutually exclusive, ontologically separate poles: paired opposites that share nothing in common because whatever qualities each depicts must belong only to one but not the other. The binary logic underpinning dichotomies results in either-or thinking, an essentializing of terms, and an exclusion of meanings (and thus awareness of ambiguity) that would otherwise complicate polarities by revealing overlaps or continuities between the terms. In this important sense, dichotomized terms are not simply "independent" concepts (A and B); they are defined in oppositional relation to each other (A and not-A). The meaning of one determines the meaning of the other, and more of one is less of the other.

The simplifying, reductionist, and parsimonious quality of dichotomized, either-or thinking is notoriously "efficient." It enables us to reduce (order) complex phenomena into discrete categories that make possible calculation and instrumental manipulation. This has played a crucial role in advancing scientific knowledge for several centuries. A contemporary example is our global—though varying—reliance on computer technologies. In effect, computerization involves the translation (reduction) of symbolic and material goods—images, data, information, designs, literature, music, machines—into a binary code of ones and zeros that can be read, manipulated, and communicated by information and communication technologies (ICTs). Digitization permits traditionally disparate and experientially dense phenomena—the textures of a tapestry, the violence of war, the multiple sensory dimensions of seduction—to be converted into binary codes available to anyone with the relevant reading capacity. Not only are these many and diverse phenomena reduced to a common, universal code, but in coded form they also are available around the world, virtually without the constraints of time and space.

As this example suggests, the application of binary thinking is not inherently pernicious, and we need not spurn dichotomized thinking in every context. As with all lenses, evaluating the outcome of their application depends on multiple factors that are specific to objectives and context. We argue, however, that in the study, analysis, and explanation of *social relations,* the structure of dichotomies severely compromises our thoughts and therefore our actions. The image of only two mutually exclusive choices keeps us locked into those—and only those—choices. Polarities (right versus wrong, rational versus emotional, strong versus weak) forestall our consideration of nonoppositional constructions (right in relation to plausible, persuasive, preferable, viable; rational in relation to consistent, instrumental, coherent, reductionist; strong in relation to effective, principled, respected, sustainable). Dichotomies thus exclude any middle, "maybe," mixing of terms, or alternative constructions. Similarly, by denying any overlap or commonalities between terms, the polarizing structure of dichotomies puts oppositional differences in focus at the expense of viewing terms *relationally.* As humans, our commonalities and even mutual interests are extensive. Differences matter and warrant analysis, but there is always a trade-off in what focus we choose. There are political consequences when we unreflectively depend on patterns of thinking that emphasize our differences—especially essentialized, stereotyped, and devalorized differences—at the expense of our commonalities and shared interests.

Because dichotomized terms are assumed to be categorically separate, their meanings appear fixed, timeless, and independent of context—as if they were givens of logic and language rather than social conventions.[1] All ambiguity, complexity, and shifts in meaning constituted by differing contexts simply disappear as they are rendered out of focus through a dichotomizing lens. In this sense, dichotomies contribute to conservative, rather than critical, analyses: they tend to essentialize either-or categories and polarized thinking (and ordering) at the expense of critical reflection on the meaning of terms and status quo hierarchies. In reality, meanings and social reality are complex, dynamic, and shaped by crosscutting variables.

Categorical oppositions misrepresent (distort) social relations by eliminating the complexity, dynamism, and interdependence of terms. They offer a "too simple" picture.

As the preceding points suggest, essentialized categories and polarized opposites present what appear to be unambiguous, inevitable, and "logical" ways of categorizing. They filter our thinking processes in ways that may be efficient for some purposes, but they severely constrain how we understand social reality. In sum, the structure of dichotomies promotes patterns of thought and action that are stunted (too reductionist, unable to acknowledge complications and consider alternatives), static (too ahistorical, unable to acknowledge or address change), dangerously oversimplified (too decontextualized, unable to accommodate the ambiguities and complexities of social reality), and politically problematic (too essentializing, reproducing oppositional ordering and disabling critical reflection).

Whereas the *structure* of dichotomies is constraining and problematic, the *status* of dichotomies in Western modernist thought poses additional problems. Although all cultures employ generalizations, categories of comparison, and patterned thinking processes, Western thought is distinctive in the extent to which binary logic (thinking in either-or oppositions) is taken for granted and privileged. This is, in large part, due to the development of scientific inquiry in the context of the rise of Western modernity, which stressed the separation of subjects from objects, facts from values, and objectivity from subjectivity. The instantiation and privileging of binary logic, however, were not confined to science. Rather, the privilege and power accorded to dualistic thinking extended to a litany of dichotomies stabilized over millennia in Western discourse, especially in dominant narratives of philosophy and political theory. Take a moment to examine and reflect on the dichotomies presented in Table 2.1, which we argue are produced by the power of gender.

Consider both how familiar these dichotomies are and how frequently they are deployed in our thinking about the world. Consider also how the essentialized oppositional meanings they constitute have become "common sense" and operate across multiple contexts. Now also reflect on how the polarized terms are not equally valorized but are hierarchical: those in the first column are typically considered desirable, admirable, and preferred whereas those in the second column are variously understood as less desirable, inferior, and/or threatening to the esteemed qualities of those in the first column. You may also notice how these dichotomies

TABLE 2.1

**Conceptual Hierarchical Dichotomies Produced by the Power of Gender**

| Subject *(Masculinized)* | Object *(Feminized)* |
|---|---|
| Knower/self/autonomy/agency | Known/other/dependence/passivity |
| Objective/rational/fact/ logical/hard | Subjective/emotional/value/ illogical/hard |
| Order/certainty/predictablity/ control over | Anarchy/uncertainty/unpredictablity/ subject to control |
| Mind/abstract/trancendence/ freedom/intellectual | Body/concrete/contingency/ necessity/manual |
| Culture/civilized/exploiter/ production/public | Nature/primitive/exploited reproduction/private |

carry gendered and racialized meanings: the first column reflects masculinist and Eurocentric qualities; the second column reflects qualities associated with femininity and subordinated groups. We return to these issues later in this chapter.

*Ideologies*

As used in this text, "ideology" refers to systems of belief—including notions of human nature and social life—that operate to justify status quo sociocultural, economic, and political arrangements. In Margaret Andersen's words, "Ideologies serve the powerful by presenting us with a definition of reality that is false [partial, self-interested] and yet orders our comprehension of the surrounding world. When ideas emerge from ideology, they operate as a form of social control by defining the status quo to be the proper state of affairs" (1983: 213).

Ideologies are thus political: they order ways of thinking about social relations and operate to legitimate particular relations of power.[2] Whereas stereotypes are essentialized expectations about certain groups of people, and dichotomies promote either-or thinking, ideologies are beliefs about the nature of social systems and the relationships among groups of people within them. They buttress the effects of stereotyping by further filtering our perceptions and actions in ways that reproduce discrimination by "naturalizing" social hierarchies. Ideologies constitute lenses that are more encompassing; they typically bring stereotypes and other differentially valorized generalizations into more systematic and apparently coherent ordering of assumptions, beliefs, and preferences. Insofar as ideologies serve the interests of the powerful, they promote political agendas that sustain the authority and power of elites and obscure the interests of others.

Political theorists have argued for millennia that ideologies are most stable and effective when most taken for granted and therefore not questioned. One of the most successful strategies for maintaining ideological stability is to draw on biological determinism, arguing that social hierarchies are the result of "natural" biological differences.[3] The classic example is social Darwinism, which emerged in the context of European developments in science, industrial capitalism, and colonial expansion. This ideology drew on aspects of the theory of natural selection to posit, in effect, narrow genetic or biological causes for complex social behaviors. In actuality, human behavior is always mediated by culture—by systems of meaning and the values they incorporate. The role that biology plays varies dramatically and can *never* be determined without reference to cultural context. Social Darwinism was used to justify the presumption of moral superiority and accumulation of wealth by powerful (European) men, while fostering a racist belief that ethnic and cultural inferiority—rather than the direct and indirect violence of imperialism—explained the subordinated status of non-Europeans. Ideological beliefs may exaggerate the role of biological factors (arguing that men's upper-body strength explains their political domination) or posit biological factors where none need be involved (arguing that because some women during part of their lives bear children, all women should be confined to mothering roles in the domestic sphere, which are deemed inconsistent with the pursuit and exercise of political power).

Reliance on biological determinism means that such ideologies tend to flourish, or be rejuvenated, in periods of disruption or transition, when uncertainties and insecurities can fuel excessive desires for stability. Partially responding to (and taking advantage of) the turbulence and uncertainty associated with dramatic changes in recent decades and, in particular, the post-9/11 environment, right-wing activists and religious fundamentalists in many countries have crusaded for a return to "traditional values." Implicitly, and sometimes explicitly, the policies they promote rely on and reproduce ahistorical stereotypes (of groups, cultures, religions, nations) and polarized thinking (right-wrong, patriots-traitors, believers-infidels). In this sense, an understandable desire for security and stability in the face of disturbing changes is translated into an incitement of essentializing and oppositional thinking that tends to exacerbate crises of insecurity.

Although they appear timeless, ideologies are context-dependent and alterable to suit the interests of those with power. For example, as conditions change, gender ideology may promote women as physically strong and capable of backbreaking work (slave women, frontier women), as dexterous and immune to boredom (electronics assembly workers), as competent to do men's work (women as industrial workers during war), or as full-time housewives and devoted mothers (postwar demands that women vacate jobs in favor of returning soldiers and focus on repopulating the nation). The point is that ideologies are often reconfigured to suit the changing interests of those in power, though rarely the interests of subordinated groups.

In sum, ideologies make the status quo appear as natural, as "the way things are," rather than as the result of human intervention and practice. Like stereotypes and dichotomies, they oversimplify what are, in fact, complex processes and obscure differences in power that serve some more than others. Insofar as elites dominate religion, myths, educational systems, advertising, and the media, these institutionalized practices are variously involved in reproducing stereotypes and ideologies that make the crises in the world we live in seem inevitable and, for some who profit from these crises, even desirable. Conditions in the world are indeed very bad, but the point here is that ideologies present only a partial and particular view of the world that favors those already enjoying disproportionate power. Most importantly, dominant ideologies obscure the reality of structural inequalities, how they impoverish the majority and threaten all of us, and how we can act to resist and change them.

### Interactions of Stereotypes, Dichotomies, and Ideologies

It is important also to consider how in the absence of critique and reflection, much of our behavior *unintentionally* reproduces status quo inequalities and oppressive ideologies. We cannot simply locate an "enemy" to blame for institutional discrimination and its many consequences. Although there are, of course, individuals who actively pursue discriminatory policies and the perpetuation of injustice, few of us positively identify with such characterizations. Most of us wish to be and think of ourselves as good family members, friends, neighbors, and citizens. Most of us express a commitment to the ideals of equality, equity, democratic principles, decreasing violence, and ensuring the sustainability of the environment.

But stereotypes, dichotomies, and ideologies play a particular role in shaping our expectations and behaviors. We begin to be socialized into dominant belief systems early in life, well before we have the capacity to reflect critically on their implications for our own or others' lives. Hence, for the most part we internalize these beliefs and do not think to question them. This is especially true of childhood socialization regarding gender, sexuality, ethnicity/race, class, and national distinctions and ordering systems. Our internalization of these belief systems subsequently disciplines our thoughts and actions, without our even being aware of this. As Allan Johnson notes, most of the time we are simply following "paths of least resistance" (2005: 80)—conforming to cultural expectations and rules that appear to be common sense. Using the example of being in a movie theater, he points out that in any particular situation there are unlimited things we *might* do (sing loudly, throw objects, light a fire), but a smaller range of things we are *likely* to do because they are the "obvious" options (sit quietly, be polite); they will encounter the "least resistance" because they are the most taken-for-granted behaviors. Typically, we follow a path of least resistance because it is the only one we are aware of or the one we consciously prefer (sitting quietly). Other times, we do so because doing otherwise would create resistance in the form of negative responses, the extent and intensity of which vary. For example, a critical remark might generate feelings of discomfort, a scolding look, a verbal rebuke, social ostracism, an arrest, or physical violence.

The point here is to recognize how, typically, our behavior is shaped by unconscious conformity to internalized "rules" and/or by conscious preference for "going along to get along," conforming simply because it is easier than not doing so. On the one hand, we cannot possibly examine every conceivable choice, and patterns in our actions are a necessary component of individual sanity and social order. On the other hand, when we follow paths of least resistance in contexts of institutionalized inequality and oppression—that is, conditions of structural violence—we effectively contribute to the reproduction of these practices, *whether intended or not*. Laughing at racist or sexist humor, assuming your audience is heterosexual, not questioning the demonization of someone or some group, perpetuating excessive consumption, failing to protest discrimination and exploitation, remaining silent or taking no action in the face of government (and other) abuses of power—all in small and large ways sustain unjust power relations. Although not the same as direct and intentional harms, taking these paths of least resistance nonetheless perpetuates harms. By "going along" we further the stabilization—rather than disruption or contestation—of beliefs, stereotypes, assumptions, privileging, orderings, marginalizations, and devalorizations that perpetuate and naturalize inequalities and oppression, that is, conditions of structural violence. In Johnson's words, "We don't have to be ruthless *people* in order to support or follow paths of least resistance that lead to behavior with ruthless *consequences*" (2006: 86). A crucial dimension of transforming systems of power—rather than perpetuating them—is that we be more consciously aware of buried assumptions, damaging stereotypes, and arrogant presumptions that have become institutionalized as "the way things are" and "how things are done."

Complicating the picture is our tendency to be unreflective about structural hierarchies and how they confer privilege—"unearned advantages"—on some people by denying it to others. Most males are privileged by gender and enjoy advantages denied to most women, though this is complicated when men are gay and hence not privileged by sexuality. Those who are identified by others as belonging to a privileged group have privilege conferred on them, whether or not they seek it or even if they are activists resisting such institutionalized privilege. For example, whites who are active against racism still enjoy the privilege of not being treated suspiciously when they enter a store to shop. It is in this sense that social hierarchies are structural—about group stereotypes and institutionalized practices—and not simply individual or idiosyncratic. Peggy McIntosh (2007) provides telling examples of how much those who enjoy privileged statuses can take for granted, how much they do not have to think about (or be angered, hurt, or impoverished by) the effects of structural hierarchies (see Box 2.1).

Being held accountable and subject to sanctions is appropriate in regard to intended and specific harms. But this addresses only the individualized aspect of the problem and tends to be counterproductive and backward looking in relation to structural oppressions and hierarchies, which are sustained less by explicit and intentional harms than by continual, unconscious, and cumulative repetition of conformity (taking the path of least resistance) to historically institutionalized practices that we inherit. Similarly, a further problem with sanctioning individual behavior is the setting up of disciplining and punishment systems that privilege coercive approaches to solving social problems. Structural oppressions and hierarchies are, by definition, the effect of institutionalized practices and social ordering and hence not reducible to individual acts or ameliorated by individual punishments.

BOX 2.1 **Illuminating Invisible Privilege**

Privilege constitutes an "invisible package of unearned assets" that can be counted on and about which the privileged are encouraged to remain oblivious. It is hard not to desire and to enjoy privilege. We are not trained to see ourselves as oppressors, as people unfairly advantaged, or as participants in damaged cultures. Hence, we often unintentionally participate in reproducing oppression simply by taking our privilege—and the culture and structures that sustain it—as "normal." The following examples suggest everyday ways in which the privileged can take for granted advantages that are denied to others. This is the nature of structural oppression: advantages to some are premised upon their denial to others.

### White/Anglo Privilege

(Many of the following apply to elite privilege more generally.)

1. I can turn on the television or read the paper and see people of my race/ethnicity widely and positively represented. I can be sure that my children will be given educational materials that testify to the existence and value of their race, and I do not have to teach them about systemic racism for their own daily protection.
2. I am never asked to speak for all the people of my racial group. I can behave in an unconventional or unattractive manner without people attributing these "faults" to my race. I am not made acutely aware that my shape, mode of dress, abilities, or body odor will be taken as a reflection on my race. When I perform well, I am not called a credit to my race.
3. I can remain oblivious to the language, customs, desires, and injuries of persons of color (who constitute the majority of the world). Within my culture, I suffer no penalty for this ignorance and insensitivity. If I do protest racism, my efforts are not disparaged as self-interested or self-seeking.
4. I can be confident that if I seek accommodation, a job, social services, legal help, or medical care, my race will not work against me.
5. I can count on the presence of English-speakers even in foreign countries, and most professional meetings I attend will be conducted in English.

### Male Privilege

1. I can watch, listen to, and read multiple media and count on most of the actors, directors, athletes, speakers, authors, teachers, politicians, scientists, religious leaders, and corporate decision-makers to represent my gender and interests. At school, I can count on learning (and my children learning) about what men find interesting, what they have said and done (mostly about and with other men) throughout history and across cultures, and how men's ideas, theories, discoveries, conquests, experiments, and conquests have determined "human" history and progress.

*(continues)*

**BOX 2.1** (*continued*)

2. I can go walking, drinking, working, and playing wherever I want to without fear of violence on the basis of my sex. I can dress as I like without being held responsible if I am harassed or attacked. If I behave assertively, aggressively, dogmatically, and/or unsympathetically, I will usually be applauded for "taking control."

3. I can attend religious services and count on celebrating the experiences, authority, power, and spiritual teachings of men. I can readily access visual and written materials that objectify women and cultivate male dominance.

4. Aside from personal relationships (and often even then), I can remain oblivious to the fantasies, life experiences, health concerns, distresses, and injuries of women (who constitute more than half the world's population). I rarely suffer any penalty for this ignorance and insensitivity. If I protest sexism, I am not dismissed as being self-interested.

5. I can choose not to participate in parenting without being branded unnatural or immoral.

6. If I am successful and single, it is assumed to be my choice rather than my inability to attract women.

**Heterosexual Privilege**

1. I can enjoy virtually all popular cultural media as a celebration of desires, humor, stories, relationships, intimacy, romance, and family life that I participate in and identify with. My children are exposed to cultural and educational materials that support our kind of family unit and do not turn them against my choice of domestic partnership. I can enjoy the taxation, legal, health insurance, adoption, and immigration benefits of being able to marry.

2. I have no difficulty finding neighborhoods, schools, jobs, recreational activities, or travel arrangements where people approve of our family unit. I can express feelings of affection for my partner in public, without fear of censure or physical attack.

3. If in my work or play I spend time with children of my sex, my motives and actions are not treated with suspicion. If I am critical of heterosexism, I am not dismissed as self-interested.

4. I, and my children, can talk about our home life or the social events of the weekend without fearing most listeners' reactions. I am not asked to deny or hide who I am, in the important sense of my sexual identity, desires, and loving relationships.

5. If the person I love does not share my citizenship, we have the option of marriage, which permits us to live together and have a family.

*Adapted from McIntosh 2007: 9–15. We have expanded and revised McIntosh's examples, in particular, to reflect our global focus.*

We emphasize two points. First, once historically in place, institution-alized hierarchies generate paths of least resistance that "automatically" reproduce structures of inequality. Hence, the perpetuation of many op-pressions is less a matter of intentionally promoting harms than unin-tentionally (unconsciously) reproducing (going along to get along) the institutions we inherit—what (unreflectively) appears to be "the way things are." Second, once in place, structural privilege confers power on those with privilege, whether desired or not. Hence, privileged individuals are not to blame for (inherited) institutional hierarchies, but the privileged in every hierarchy have greater power *and therefore greater responsibility* for transforming those and related hierarchies. Rather than be caught up in blaming and its defensive responses, we wish to increase awareness of these opaque issues and promote less *unintentional* participation in repro-ducing inequalities and structural oppressions, that is, taking paths of least resistance, when these are actually part of the problem.

Oppressive hierarchies are not in fact inevitable. If we are to change the world, we must change ourselves, as well as the social structures that both produce and are produced by those selves. We cannot change either without changing how we think. In that regard, understanding the role of stereotypes, dichotomies, and ideologies is crucial. We turn next to how these interact to constitute the power of gender.

## THE POWER OF GENDER

We make numerous claims about the power of gender as a meta-lens be-cause it involves numerous dimensions, most of which are so taken for granted (normalized) that they operate below a conscious level. We argue that the constellation of these interactive dimensions (our meta-lens) has become a hegemonic worldview that is rarely acknowledged, therefore not analytically or critically addressed, and hence often unintentionally repro-duced. In this section we "unpack" these dimensions to bring into sharper focus the many ways in which gender operates to normalize hierarchical thinking and ordering and effectively disable more complex intersectional analyses that are crucial to "seeing" and addressing crises of representa-tion, insecurity, and sustainability.

The questions we address in this section include these: How does gen-der become so deeply internalized, so taken for granted, and so embedded in social relations? How are gendered identities constructed so that we are deeply invested in them and enact them pervasively in social life? How are stereotypes and dichotomized thinking gendered in ways that deepen the normalization and unreflective reproduction of the power of gender? How has the power of gender become so pervasive and potent yet so invisible and marginalized in accounts of world politics?

To clarify the power of gender as a meta-lens requires mapping the multilayered social construction of gender and gendered hierarchies. We do so by examining gender as an ordering power that undergirds hierarchical dichotomies and as powering the devalorization of feminized "others." In the context of gender as an ordering power, we consider the formation of gendered identities (subjectivities) and internalization of hierarchical gender coding, the operation of gender coding throughout social relations, and the institutionalization and reproduction of gendered social structures. These entail discussions of how individuals are socialized into (taught to internalize) culturally appropriate gendered ways of identifying, thinking, and acting and how these gendered ways of identifying, thinking, and acting are kept in place structurally through systems of control that generate conformity and compliance. In brief, we argue that gender coding shapes and is shaped by dominant conceptual ordering systems that become institutionalized through the favoring of some practices over others. Families, schools, media, and religious institutions are important sources of gender socialization. As individuals participate in these institutions, the power of gender coding and hierarchies tend to be reproduced, not least because doing so constitutes a path of least resistance. Moral and intellectual control is effected through the privileging of certain belief systems (masculinism, myth, religion, rationalism, science) so that gender becomes pervasive in social life. More direct social control is effected through job markets, laws, governance, and physical coercion, which tend to reproduce gendered hierarchies and sustain elite power at the expense of obscuring its costs to the majority or identifying alternative ways of thinking and acting.

In the context of gender as powering the devalorization of feminized "others," we explore how gender coding is extended to further justify, naturalize, and institutionalize all manner of social dichotomies and hierarchies. Although the power of gender is only one among many ordering systems that structure and normalize power relations, we argue that it is not independent of other ordering systems and plays an important and even necessary role in deeply legitimating multiple forms of domination.

*Gender as an Ordering Power*

We begin with the earliest socialization that individuals encounter: their emergence into the world as an effect of biological reproduction. We rarely question the need to reproduce social members, but under what conditions, how many, and to what purpose are perennially vexing questions. Actual practices of biological reproduction are shaped by cultural norms, economic conditions, demographic dynamics, reproductive health and technologies, and disciplinary regimes in regard to sex/affective relations.[4] Patriarchal belief systems (which essentialize heterosexual families) and institutionalization of patriarchal ordering (positioning males as heads of households, as citizens, and as religious, military, and political authorities) have over millennia become normalized in virtually all social formations. Hence, heterosexism (belief in heterosexuality as the only "normal" mode of sexual orientation, family life, and social relations) is currently the hegemonic model worldwide. Heteronormative ideology assumes a binary construction of (hetero)sexual difference, some form of heterosexual union, and heterosexual patriarchal families as "givens." Critics challenge the adequacy of this assumption, which is increasingly belied by actual arrangements.[5] Sexual relations and family structures have taken diverse forms in the past, and contemporary sex/gender identities, sexual practices, and family forms are undergoing continual change. The point here is that conventional representations of social reproduction are selective, projecting (hetero)sexual identities, heteronormative families, and (hetero)sexual reproduction as simply given and natural. But they in fact are embedded in and (literally) embody particular sociocultural, economic, and political relations.

Procreation is a starting point for thinking about gender, but the reproductive choices, practices, and strategies in which procreation occurs are already embedded in social formations with their particular gender codes and patterned expectations. In this sense, socialization precedes and shapes the birth of individuals and how their arrival will be experienced. For many reasons, some are more welcomed than others. However welcomed, the arrival of infants launches socialization processes for that infant. Binary sex differentiation is key: if newborns are not unambiguously male or female, this poses difficulties that may be variously addressed (depending on cultural contexts and prevailing practices) but will not go unnoticed. Establishing the "sex" of newborns constitutes a basis for responding to and socializing infants, which at the same time shapes the gender-differentiated subject formation processes that infants undergo. Gender identities that subsequently develop are crosscut by other axes of difference, but our earliest sex-differentiated gender identifications constitute particularly defining elements of "who we are" throughout life. In this sense, the essentialized binary of sex difference (which appears across cultures) is both internalized as a defining "core" of individual identity and materialized in the production of embodied, gendered individuals.[6] And in a larger sense, the subjective internalization of gender difference and historical normalization of gendered and heteronormative social ordering become deeply embedded, stabilized, institutionalized patterns in how we identify, think, and act.

From birth on, the way we are treated depends on our gender assignment, and we learn in multiple ways how to adopt gender-appropriate behaviors (as these are shaped by age, race, class, nationality, etc.). There are few occasions or interactions where our gender is truly irrelevant: our names, clothes, hairstyles, toys, games, rewards, threats and punishments, the attention we get, the activities we are encouraged to engage in, the roles we are expected to assume, the subjects we study, the knowledge claims we make, the jobs we work at, and the power we have are all profoundly shaped by gendered expectations. As individuals, we differ considerably in the extent to which we conform to cultural expectations. But none of us escapes gender socialization. "Everyone is born into a *culture—a set of shared ideas* about the nature of reality, the nature of right and wrong, *evaluation of what is good and desirable,* and the nature of the good and desirable versus the bad and nondesirable. As totally dependent infants we are *socialized*—taught the rules, roles and relationships of the social world. In the process we learn to think, act, and feel as we are 'supposed to'" (Richardson and Taylor 1983: 1).

As noted earlier, political theorists recognize that the most effective way to maintain systems of rule is not through direct violence but through ideology: persuading those who are subordinated that inequalities and social hierarchy are natural, therefore inevitable, and even desirable. When people believe that differences in status and power are part of the "natural order of things," they are less likely to see or challenge how society is organized to benefit some more than others. Such people do not require constant external policing because they have internalized their own policing in terms of selective perceptions and lowered expectations. As a consequence, they internalize an acceptance of their own unequal positioning and status quo inequalities between groups. In short, our early socialization into hierarchically ordered systems plays a crucial role in reproducing inequalities and undercutting—though not precluding—resistance. The gender socialization we encounter in early childhood is reinforced by gendered stereotypes, dichotomies, and ordering systems that are present in all cultures. Gender stereotypes pervade the fairy-tales, myths, and stories we tell children; the cultural representations they are exposed to (in schoolbooks, religious training, popular media); and the ubiquitous advertising that is now present worldwide. What these communications typically share is a message conveying categorical (essentialized) distinctions between boys and girls, men and women. In many of the world's cultures, dominant, idealized gender stereotypes depict men/masculinity as strong, independent, worldly, assertive, rational, tough, and "in control"; women/femininity are portrayed as the opposite: weak, dependent, naive, peaceful, emotional, gentle, and often unpredictable. This exemplifies the binary structure of gender: constructing man/masculinity and woman/femininity as two poles of a dichotomy—as mutually exclusive or oppositions—that define each other. Not all men (perhaps very few) will meet the normative standards of the hegemonic model of masculinity, but all reap a patriarchal dividend: "the advantage men in general gain from the overall subordination of women" (Connell 1995: 79).

In short, the heteronormative dichotomy or polarization of gender insists (1) that sex difference is ontologically binary, essentializing males and females as unambiguously distinguishable; (2) that there are different scripts (ways of identifying, acting, and knowing) for males and females; (3) that sex difference is important enough to shape diverse spheres of activity (leisure, work, governance); and (4) that persons deviating from sex-appropriate scripts are problematic (suspect as "unnatural" or "immoral"). Hence, heteronormativity insists on unambiguous distinctions between males/masculinity and females/femininity and cultivates *gendered* stereotypes, dichotomies, practices, and institutions in virtually all cultures. This gendering is structurally maintained not only through masculinist myths and narratives, but also through customs, policies, and legislation that impose heteronormative marriage and family arrangements, androcentric (male-as-norm) political institutions, masculinist security arrangements, and sex-differentiated labor markets.

Like dichotomized thinking more generally, putting so much weight on the differences between men/masculinity and women/femininity ensures that what we share is obscured and that any blurring of gender boundaries—and concomitant erosion of masculinism/heterosexism—feels uncomfortable or threatening (it is a path that encounters negativity/resistance) and is typically avoided. The gender dichotomy (and heteronormative denial of ambiguities) highlights distinctions between groups rather than differences within them or commonalities between them. For example, in reality not all males are engaged in "productive" labor, nor do all females bear children, and no female bears them throughout her lifetime. But the dichotomy pitting men as performing productive labor (working for wages, creating ideas and products) against women as performing reproductive labor (maintaining the household, bearing and caring for children) masks this variation among females and commonality between males and many females.

Dichotomized thinking is both habitual and political: its structure constitutes "man" as not simply a different category than "woman" (A and B) but in a relationship of hierarchical opposition (A and not-A); this structure thus reproduces either-or thinking and privileges some qualities and interests over others. Much is at stake, and it takes a great deal of power to maintain categorical boundaries between masculinity and femininity.[7] Gender stereotypes and dichotomies play a key role. Consider depictions of males and females in popular culture and media: How often is there a physically "rough" or politically powerful girl or woman, especially one who is likable? Or a boy or man who is nurturing and sensual as a constant way of being, not just in certain circumstances? Most telling, why are there so few media images of gender-neutral individuals—people whose gender status is not immediately and unequivocally apparent? Why are we so uncomfortable with gender ambiguities, virtually insisting that individuals be patently *either* men/masculine *or* women/feminine?

Our discomfort reflects two important points. First, gender ambiguity is uncomfortable because we simply do not know how to respond. That is, our expectations and behavior regarding gender are so taken for granted that when we are confronted with ambiguous gender signals, we become confused; we literally do not know how to act. When deeply programmed expectations of gender performance are disrupted—forcing us to think consciously about how to act or respond—we realize how much they (unconsciously) shape our habitual behavior. Second, and relatedly, we typically resent the discomfort and confusion. This reveals how significant our unacknowledged commitments to gender are. That is, when people confront us with gender ambiguity, we resent both not knowing how to act *and* the questions that our confusion raises. If gender identities are not reliable and stable, what does this mean for our own identities? Because gender identification is so important for "knowing who we are" and how to act, and for securing self-esteem when we "do gender well," confusion about gender identification can feel very threatening.

In the context of masculinist/heteronormative culture, insecurity about gender identity is especially acute for males and arguably a lifelong preoccupation. Because femininity is devalued and male expressions of femininity render men's masculinity suspect, males face tremendous pressures to establish that they are "real men," and being a "real man" requires that gender distinctions are unambiguous. Given the high stakes, it is not surprising that men consistently demonstrate greater discomfort with gender ambiguities than women do. For example, men are much more likely to express homophobia (the abhorrence of homosexuality), in part because homosexuality disrupts conventional gender distinctions and raises questions about what it means to be a real man. Quite simply, in masculinist/heteronormative cultures, men are motivated to enhance and exaggerate their masculinity by denying any commonality between themselves and women or gay men.

The point to notice here is how completely fabricated—and thus ultimately fragile and unstable—gender is. It is constructed rather than natural, obvious, or unchanging, and men are never sufficiently masculine simply because they have the appropriate genitalia. Establishing masculinity is never a done deal: males face relentless pressures to demonstrate they are real men by exhibiting unequivocally masculine qualities and distancing themselves from what is defined as feminine (Kimmel 2008). This may involve avoidance of body decorations, bright colors, ballet, quiche, flowers, child care, gentleness, and asking directions. It may involve fear of acknowledging emotion, needs, vulnerabilities, and desires for affection/intimacy. It may involve a man exaggerating his rationality, competitiveness, and power or feeling obliged to engage in assertive, tough, and even violent behaviors. It may involve a preference for hard liquor, hard-hitting sports, heavy metal or rap music, militarized video games, or risk-taking exploits.

These examples suggest how cultural codes of gender come to pervade all aspects of social life because "appropriate" gender performance is not only expected but also demanded by social ordering. We are thus deeply invested in gendered identities and performances because demonstrating that we are real men and real women matters emotionally and materially; there are a variety of costs—from mild to deadly—for not conforming to gender stereotypes. Because biological criteria alone do not establish our status as real men and real women, we must continually "perform" (demonstrate, act out) gender attitudes and behaviors to "prove" our gender identification. Doing so makes all social life a test of our performance: Gender comes to matter in what we wear, eat, and drink; how we talk, laugh, and gesticulate; what entertainment and activities we prefer; how we approach risk-taking and dependence; and how we measure intelligence, courage, and leadership.

In sum, the acting out of gender—and the importance we put on doing so appropriately—demonstrates (1) how gender is not biologically determined but socially constructed, expected, and performed throughout life; (2) how we become deeply invested in oppositional gendered identities and the appropriate performance of gender; and (3) how polarized gendered identities and their corollary performances then reproduce gender-differentiated identities, behaviors, and, ultimately, inequalities. At the same time, the preceding points suggest the fragility of gender, how easily it can be disrupted and altered, how complex and differentiated our gendered lives actually are, and how much power it takes to sustain categorical gender distinctions and project the "superiority" of masculinity over femininity.

From yet another angle of vision, dichotomized gender is not only hierarchical (privileging the first term over the second) but also *androcentric* (assuming a male-as-norm point of view). This androcentrism has three interacting effects. First, because the primary term (A) is androcentric and privileged, masculinist values are effectively elevated over those of the secondary (not-A) term. Thus, reason, control, and culture are associated with maleness and are privileged over affect, uncertainty, and nature. Second and closely related, characteristics and activities associated with femaleness are deemed not only less important but also unworthy or undesirable because they appear to threaten the values represented by the primary term. Thus, emotion, relationality, reproduction, and caretaking are given less attention and often disparaged.[8] At the same time, reason, rationality, and rational agency are withheld from those feminized, reducing their thoughts, actions, and very beings to "instinctual" or "cultural" explanations. Moreover, rationality is reduced to only instrumental rationality put into the service of control.

Third, androcentrism assumes that (elite) men are the most important actors and the substance of their lives the most important topic to know about. As long as the realities of women, nonelite men, and children are treated as secondary to the main story—as the background that is never important enough to warrant being spotlighted—we, as collective knowledge seekers, are made unaware of what the background actually is and what relationship it actually has to the main story. What we are unaware of we cannot understand or analyze. Nor can we understand to what extent and in what ways the main story depends on background that is made invisible or silenced by focusing illumination and attention elsewhere. Rendering the experiences or realities of "others" invisible tends to present the main story, which often rests upon unexamined or naturalized assumptions about "others," as real and authoritative, as if it were all that we needed to know to understand what is going on. In all three cases, assumptions of privilege and importance encourage an attitude of superiority and dismissal or fear of what constitutes the background. From the lofty heights, contrasting experiences and alternative perspectives are invisible and hence effectively excluded or silenced. Certain questions cannot even be asked or concerns expressed.

## Gender as Powering Devalorizations of Feminized "Others"

We have argued that gendered coding and ideologies present in all social formations normalize and privilege masculinist ways of identifying, thinking, and acting. At the same time, stereotypes, dichotomies, and hierarchical ordering are present in all social formations, sustaining narratives of mutually exclusive, oppositional difference and legitimating the domination of some over "others." Although masculinism most obviously operates to devalue women and reproduce unequal positionings of men and women, it operates across hierarchies of ethnicity/race, class, nation, and sexuality as well. In this section we shift attention from men and women to ways in which ideological manipulation of gender coding and gendered differences produce and "justify" divisions and hierarchies.

The central point is that the symbolic, discursive, and cultural *privileging of masculinity does not privilege only men or all men.* Rather, privileging who and what is masculinized is inextricable from devaluing who and what is feminized. It is recognizing the interdependence of masculinity and femininity as oppositional but reciprocally defined terms—one "requires" the other—that provides analytical and political leverage. The claim is then that gender—with its lauded masculinity and denigrated femininity—pervades language and cultural codes, with systemic effects on how we take for granted (normalize and effectively depoliticize) the devalorization of all feminized statuses (e.g., "lazy migrants," "primitive natives," "effeminate gays"). Romanticizing femininity often appears to privilege it,

2. Gendered Lenses on World Politics  63

but never empowers it. We argue instead that the more an individual or a social category is feminized, the more likely (although not invariably) its categorical difference and devaluation are assumed or presumed to be "explained." These claims advance intersectional analysis by enabling us to see how diverse hierarchies are linked and ideologically naturalized by the feminizing of individuals and subordinated social categories.

There are several interactive moves here that require closer inspection. In one sense, casting the subordinated as feminine devalorizes not only women but also sexually, racially, culturally, and economically marginalized men. Underpinning this claim is the observation that, although structural hierarchies vary by reference to the "differences" emphasized and the disparate modalities of power involved, they typically share a common feature: their denigration of feminized qualities attributed to those who are subordinated (lacking reason, control, etc.). Because the "natural" inferiority of the feminine is so taken for granted, invoking it plays a powerful —though not exhaustive—role in "legitimating" these hierarchies. In a second sense, not only subjects (women and marginalized men) but also concepts, desires, tastes, styles, ways of knowing, cultural expressions (art, music), roles, practices, work, and nature can be feminized. This effectively reduces their legitimacy, status, and value and fuels stereotypical characterizations that can be deployed to depoliticize unequal valorizations. In both senses, devalorization powerfully normalizes—with the effect of legitimating—the subordination, exploitation of, and various forms of violence against feminized concepts, skills, activities, and persons.

As intersectional analysts argue, oppressions differ, and so do attempts to explain and/or justify them. Feminization is then only one among a number of normalizing ideologies. To be clear, we are not arguing that gender hierarchy is the primary oppression or the most salient or powerful hierarchy in any particular context. As Nira Yuval-Davis notes, "In specific historical situations and in relation to specific people . . . some social divisions . . . are more important than others" (2006: 203). At the same time, some social divisions (e.g., age, gender, ethnicity/race, class) "tend to shape people's lives in most social locations," whereas other divisions (e.g., castes, status as indigenous or refugee persons) profoundly affect those subject to them but "tend to affect fewer people globally" (Yuval-Davis 2006: 203). Nor is our objective to prioritize the subordination of women or deny the different organizing logics or modalities of power operating in racism, classism, nationalism, and so on. It is rather to note that even as social divisions have different ontological bases, they are not historically independent of each other and gender is an important linkage among them, especially with reference to the political project of normalizing, hence depoliticizing, hierarchical valorizations.

Our central point is that what distinguishes feminization—and renders it so potent an aspect of the power of gender—is the unique extent to which it invokes the deeply embedded, internalized, and naturalized binary of sex difference and gender dichotomy. Ambiguities of sex and gender may be increasingly visible to some, but most people most of the time take "sex difference" completely for granted—as biologically "given," reproductively necessary, and psychosocially "obvious." We have argued, however, that sex difference is a (mistakenly) essentialized binary that (falsely) "grounds" gender as a system of difference construction and hierarchical dichotomy production. In this sense, the symbolic coding of gender differentiation and material manifestations of gendered hierarchies are mutually constituted and mutually reinforcing. To repeat: the naturalness of sex difference naturalizes dichotomized gender differentiations (pervading all social life) and thinking in hierarchical, categorical oppositions more generally. Insofar as these naturalizations and masculinist (not necessarily male) privilege become common sense, their ideological power is then "available" (through cultural coding of reason, agency, governing and protecting, etc., as masculine and irrationality, dependence, being governed and protected, etc., as feminine) for legitimating other forms of domination (e.g., racism, imperialism, militarism, homophobia, economic exploitation).

The power of gender produces a common sense of privileging the masculine and devaluing the feminine that is culturally and collectively internalized to such an extent that we are all variously complicit in its reproduction. It is also implicitly and explicitly manipulated to reproduce inequalities as if they were natural and inevitable, thus undercutting critique and resistance. In these ways, devalorizing through feminizing produces even as it obscures vast inequalities of power, authority, and resource distribution.

## THE POWER OF GENDER
## AS A META-LENS IN WORLD POLITICS

Whatever their institutional forms, parenting practices are embedded in and reinscribe power relations because infants are helpless and children are variously dependent. Family life is where we first learn about and observe gender differentiation, its respective identities, and its divisions of labor. It is also where we begin to internalize beliefs about race/ethnicity, age, sexuality, class, religion, nationality, and other axes of difference. Historically sedimented conventions of masculinist language, religion, and worldview inscribe the heteronormative gender order as foundational and nonnegotiable, while predominately heterosexual family life ensures that heterosexual identities, roles, and practices are the only apparent options. The effects of this ordering system, and psychic acceptance of it, are manifested throughout social relations, not simply contained in early childhood or family dynamics. Rather we are exposed to, and typically internalize, the dichotomizing and ordering power of gender from infancy onward, which enhance its apparent "given-ness" and make resistance to it especially difficult. It is the power of gender to pervasively and potently naturalize dichotomous or binary thinking and invisibly uphold hierarchical relations between and among the polarized opposites gender constructs or co-constructs that makes it, for us, a "meta-lens." Meta-lenses structure thought and action in ways that are relatively immune to critical reflection and intervention because they are so deeply productive of and embedded in what is assumed to be the natural order of things. We argue here that IR inquiry and the understandings of and priorities in world politics promoted by its dominant perspectives have not been immune to the power of gender as a meta-lens. The taken-for-granted status of dichotomized thinking and hierarchical order that the meta-lens power of gender inculcates has rendered difficult the dislodging of it at the center of IR inquiry.

There are many lenses (or theoretical perspectives, explanatory frameworks) through which world politics has been viewed in history and in the contemporary context (idealism, liberalism, realism, and so on). How to label lenses is always controversial, and most lenses are continually changing in response to both analytical debates and real-world developments. Most at the center of IR inquiry have been (neo)realist lenses that bring the conflictual behavior of states to the fore as well as (neo)liberal lenses that focus attention on interstate cooperation and organization. More at the margins of IR inquiry, but gaining increasing attention and use, have been a host of older and newer lenses that are critical of the inadequacies of (neo)realist and (neo)liberal lenses to understand how power works in the international system. (Neo-)Marxist lenses direct our gaze to class inequalities and conflicts within and across states, and postcolonial lenses call attention to racial inequalities, nationalist identities and conflicts, and imperialist practices within and across states. Constructivists foreground the interaction of agency and structure and include ideas and culture in IR theorizing. Poststructuralists emphasize the politics of symbolic ordering, language, and discursive practices to illuminate how power operates in knowledge production. Feminists focus on gender and its relation to other inequalities and the political nature and effects of masculinist and other inequality-producing orders. Most recently, queer theorists and transgender theorists in IR, many of whom are feminist, have directed greater attention to the implications of heteronormativity and gender conformity not only for sexual and gender minorities, but also for further disruption of binaries in IR. As is discussed at more length later in this chapter when we turn specifically to feminist lenses in world politics, feminist IR scholars partake of all these "critical" lenses in their work, but too often other "critical" researchers still fail to include feminist, queer, and transgender lenses in theirs. This is yet another consequence, we argue, of the power of gender to render masculinist and heteronormative orders and commitments invisible in even "critical" research.

As in all academic inquiry, differing world politics theoretical lenses direct our attention and orient our research in particular ways. World politics lenses shape, for example, our assumptions about who are the significant actors (states, transnational corporations, social movements), what are their attributes (rationality, self-interest, power, activism), how are social processes categorized (conflict, cooperation, division), and what are desirable outcomes (national security, wealth accumulation, welfare provisioning, global equity). Thus, world politics lenses have world political consequences. Critics of lenses at the center of IR inquiry argue that these must be "decentered" because they perpetuate unjust consequences for much of the world's people:

> First, IR focuses primarily on and legitimizes the actions and decisions of the US and the global North/West. Second, IR privileges certain political projects, such as neoliberal economic policies, state-centrism, and Northern/Western liberal democracy. Third, IR legitimizes the most privileged socio-political players and institutions, in both the Global North/West and the Global South, to produce knowledge and make decisions about the rest of the world, thus replicating or maintaining certain unequal power relationships. Finally, IR examines certain understandings of political concepts (such as sovereignty) and particular narratives that can elide, distort, or completely miss multiple ways of understanding and living in the world. (Nayak and Selbin 2010: 2)

Indeed, it is no accident that the majority of IR scholars who engage (neo)realist and (neo)liberal lenses at the center of IR inquiry are primarily US/Western-based, white, heterosexual, and male. It is also no accident that many critics of these lenses are either non-US/non-Western-based, of color, nonheterosexual, or female (or some combination of these). Those in IR who occupy the most privileged social locations tend to evince a top-down preoccupation with elite governance, international militarism, and corporate profits while rendering everything that underpins and enables these activities—and their power—irrelevant. Those in IR who do not occupy one or more privileged social locations tend to be more interested in and sensitive to the underside of elite power and militarized power projections and bottom-up resistances to social injustice. But there are also deeper forces at work that center noncritical lenses at the expense of critical ones.

## Ontologies, Epistemologies, and Dichotomous Thinking

When considering different theoretical lenses and how some are deemed more central than others, we find it helpful to distinguish between *what* objects (variables, topics, issues, levels of analysis) are focused on and *how* knowledge/truth about those objects is produced (empirically, analytically, comparatively, intuitively). Stated another way, the former refers to *ontology* (the nature of "being," i.e., *what* is reality?) and the latter to *epistemology* (the study of truth claims, i.e., *how* do we know?), and they are always intertwined because claims about what $x$ is are necessarily also claims about how we know what $x$ is.

Epistemological preferences cut across both normative/political commitments and substantive foci (objects of inquiry), though such preferences often go unacknowledged. As a starting point, the most salient epistemological distinction in world politics lenses is between *positivist* (sometimes called modernist, Enlightenment, rationalist, empiricist) and *postpositivist* orientations (including critical, interpretive, reflexive, postcolonial, poststructuralist, queer, transgendered, all feminist forms of these as well as some constructivist perspectives).[9] We simplify the discussion by noting two assumptions associated with positivist orientation: First, through the application of scientific method, facts can be separated from values; second, subjects (knowers, observers) and objects (the known, the observed) can also be categorically separated. Hence, positivists assume that the subject/knower is independent of—can stand "outside of"—the reality being observed, and that the observer can see this reality objectively (separating fact from value) by employing the scientific method to control for bias or other emotional investments. Similarly, positivists assume that social reality is "given" (separate from the knower) and is the product of identifiable "laws" of (human and physical) nature and rational action.

A key point is the extent to which positivists assume a referential view of language, understanding it as a neutral, transparent medium that corresponds to, and therefore simply reflects or refers to, the "objective" world "as it is." The claim here is that objects (horses, trees, rights, power) have some central essence or timeless form that can be captured and conveyed linguistically in a word, or signifier, that simply refers to that essence. This orientation tends to essentialize—to understand as timeless, unchanging, and independent of context—the meaning of terms (power, rationality, human nature) and hence what they refer to (capacity to enforce compliance; logically determined relationships; atomistic, self-interested, acquisitive). It assumes that the meanings of and the differences between terms can be clearly specified and will remain constant across contexts, thus suggesting order, continuity, and stability.

In contrast, postpositivists argue that "reality" is *socially constructed* in the sense that humans/subjects create meaning and intelligibility through the mutual constitution of symbols, languages, identities, practices, and social structures. This is decisively *not* to argue that the physical world does not exist independent of humans/subjects, but rather that it has no social meaning independent of what is constructed through human thought and interaction. In other words, there is no presocial or prediscursive meaning (or essence) to things, only the meanings produced by social subjects inevitably reflecting their specific contexts, interests, and objectives. Recall the discussion of lenses: humans depend on selective attention to make sense of and act in the world. Lenses are drawn from the conceptual ordering systems and languages available to us, and these do not predate culture and social relations but instead are produced by them. The conditions of human existence and the successful reproduction of social formations *require* some stable ordering—of meaning systems *and* of social practices. Yet we often forget that the conceptual systems, social identities, and institutionalized practices that humans have constructed are historically specific and contingent. They "lack any essence, and their regularities merely consist of the relative and precarious forms of fixation [stabilization, normalization] which accompany the establishment of a certain order" (Laclau and Mouffe 1985: 98). Moreover, power relations operating in all historical contexts have shaped which and whose ordering preferences dominate. Those who have more access to and control over symbolic and material resources have more opportunities and capabilities for stabilizing and institutionalizing particular symbols, meanings, lenses, norms, rules, and practices. In this sense, elites draw on particular lenses to construct more encompassing belief systems—or ideologies—to normalize, legitimate, and reproduce their privileged positions. As with all lenses, these reflect selective attention and interests that entail devaluing, marginalizing, or excluding alternatives.

The key point, and one to which we subscribe, is that knowers cannot stand outside of the reality they observe because their participation in that reality is a necessary condition for the object observed to have any meaning; both subject and object gain their meaning and intelligibility by reference to their locations in a system of meaning (language, discourse, norms, rules) that encompasses them both. In this view, subjects and objects are not categorically separate, but rather exist in a relationship and in a historically specific context that shape what we wish to know (what questions we ask, etc.), how we go about knowing (what methods we use, etc.), and whose knowledge counts (whose truth claims are included or excluded). When we as knowledge seekers question the positivist lens, we rethink objectivity, we see the centrality of the relationship between power and knowledge, and we understand that language is political insofar as it constitutes the meaning system of intelligibility and order.

Accepting that knowledge is socially situated and thus productive of, at best, only partial accounts of reality does not entail a position of absolute relativism—that "anything goes" or that no criteria for comparative assessments can be substantiated. That conclusion reflects a positivist lens of we have *either* "real truth" *or* complete relativism. But the either-or cage is rejected by postpositivists, who insist on thinking not oppositionally but relationally. Sandra Harding proposes an alternative lens: practicing "strong objectivity" that permits one "to abandon notions of perfect, mirror-like representations of the world, the self as a defended fortress, and 'the truly scientific' as disinterested with regard to morals and politics, yet still apply rational standards to sorting less from more partial and distorted belief" (1991: 159). In other words, we must give up pursuit of an Archimedean standpoint, the "God's-eye view," or the illusion that certainty is attainable, and recognize instead that all perspectives, problems, and methods are context-specific and value-laden (shaped by power and commitments). This does not mean that they are all equally valid or that we cannot comparatively assess them. It does mean that all claims must be situated and therefore that any absolute, transcendent, universal claims—because they deny context and the politics of their making—are inherently suspect and politically problematic. Because inquiry is a social practice and so is always value-laden, it is incumbent on inquirers to critically examine their social locations and the values that arise from them. In this way, the normative commitments that underlie inquiry are made visible and can become the subject of political debate about what values inquiry should advance.

By denying the categorical separations (fact from value and subject from object) that are assumed by positivists, then, postpositivists—and especially poststructuralists—challenge conventional claims about scientific objectivity and spurn either-or thinking (dichotomies) as a distortion of social reality. But as we now argue, postpositivists who do not take the power of gender as a meta-lens seriously miss links between dichotomized gender and the status of dichotomized thinking in modernist, positivist orientations that remain present and dominant in the field of IR. The basic argument is that the essentialized binary of sex difference (which grounds and generates the dichotomy of gender differentiation) and the privileged status of dichotomies (which grounds rationality and objectivity claims) are *mutually reinforcing*. As a consequence, both are further naturalized (taken for granted), become constitutive elements of the power of gender, and operate systemically to shape conceptual and social orderings hierarchically. Exposing how this power operates to effectively move beyond it is necessary for any critical agenda that purports to be concerned with social justice.

On the one hand, poststructuralists and postcolonialists criticize the structure and status of dichotomized thinking that pervades modernist, positivist thought. They argue that dichotomies *structure* our thinking in ways that are stunted (reductionist), static (ahistorical), simplistic (decontextualized), and politically problematic (essentializing, disabling critical reflection). And the privileged *status* of modernist, positivist orientations sustains dichotomized thinking as a taken-for-granted and desirable outcome, obscures how dichotomies structure thought in extremely limited ways, and resists critical reflection on the politics of dichotomies and their divisive effects. As constitutive elements of ideological thinking, dichotomies essentialize particular group identities in oppositional, hierarchical terms; amplify and privilege the interests of elites at the expense of stereotyped "others"; and obscure the commonalities and possible shared interests of larger collectivities and longer-term objectives.

On the other hand, feminists and other critics of heteronormativity have exposed the assumption of binary sex difference as stunted (reducing "sex" to paired opposites, precluding alternatives and commonalities), static (neglecting historical shifts in how "sex" is "seen" and responded to), simplistic (obscuring the complexity of "sex" and its relationship to gender), and politically problematic (unreflectively essentializing what is historically situated and socially constructed). Feminist research has additionally documented the deeply sedimented normalization of dichotomized gender (generated by essentializing sex as a binary) as a governing code valorizing what is privileged as masculine at the expense of what is stigmatized as feminine. Gendered socialization and social control mechanisms amplify individual and collective internalization of, and investments in, reproducing gendered orderings. Here we argue that more adequate analyses of power require attending to and integrating the critical insights of poststructuralist, postcolonial, and feminist lenses. In particular, to comprehend the resilience of hierarchical thinking and its reproduction of divisions and inequalities requires making sense of the power of gender as a hegemonic and pernicious but typically unacknowledged worldview.

Stated simply and based on preceding arguments, the "naturalness" of sex difference becomes indistinguishable from the "naturalness" of dichotomized and hierarchical gender differentiation that we reproduce, consciously and unconsciously, as we act out gender in all areas of social life. Because of this interaction, gendered stereotypes have political significance far beyond their role in male-female relations. First, gender normalizes dichotomized thought as a deeply embedded practice reproduced throughout social orders. Second, the gender dichotomy is so taken as given that it lends authority to the binary logic that "naturally" divides terms and identity groups into polarized opposites. The naturalness of dichotomized gender then becomes indistinguishable from—and lends credibility and authority to—the naturalness of dichotomized thinking. Third, the normalization of dichotomized thinking reproduces not only gender hierarchy but also other relations of inequality as dichotomies are taken for granted and effectively legitimate hierarchical ordering.

At the same time and as we argued earlier, the binary logic of positivist orientations normalizes and privileges thinking in dichotomies. The elevated status of this logic lends credibility and authority to the practice of essentializing categories as paired opposites, valuing one over the "other" term, and normalizing domination of whatever and whoever is "othered." In this sense, the normalization of dichotomies in modernist thought lends credibility and authority to the binary of sex and dichotomy of gender. Insofar as other familiar dichotomies have gendered connotations (culture-nature, reason-emotion, autonomy-dependency, public-private), when they are deployed in modernist thought, they buttress the stereotypes of masculine and feminine.

This is what we mean by mutually reinforcing: the dichotomy of gender gains its naturalness by being grounded in the assumption of essentialized sex difference; gendered orderings are normalized by being reproduced throughout social life; dichotomies gain their taken-for-granted and even desirable status by being privileged in modernist thought and acquiring credibility through the "reality" of pervasive gendered differentiation. The mutually reinforcing interplay of essentializing sex, dichotomizing gender, and the binary logic of positivism generates the constellation of dimensions we refer to as a meta-lens. Recognizing the power of these coding and filtering devices is crucial for improving our ability to see beyond essentialized identities and oppositional "wholes." Thus, feminists argue that dichotomized thinking cannot be adequately understood, critiqued, or effectively transformed without addressing how sex-differentiated gender grounds, naturalizes, and reproduces binary thinking.

These points are crucial to the arguments of this text because the perpetuation of dichotomized thinking and its gendered normalizations reproduces hierarchical divisions and hence antagonistic relations between groups. What we referred to in Chapter 1 as remasculinization of world politics involves reprivileging (elite) men as political and military leaders and media commentators, new forms of hegemonic masculinities, the manipulation of women's and feminist issues to support masculinist projects, and the manipulation of even the concept of gender equality to privilege some women over other women and some men over other men. The power of gender here operates to obscure intersectionality—how we have multiple identities carrying different forms and degrees of privilege that operate within as well as across groups. When the power of gender focuses attention on essentialized notions of gender—masculinity and femininity—we fail to see these as constructed and crosscutting dimensions operating within any particular group and across groups. Similarly, when essentialized notions of group identities erase the differentiations within them, we fail to see the complexity of social orders and how inequalities are often sustained by pitting subordinated groups against each other. In the process, we lose sight of the potential for coalitions and more comprehensive resistances to unjust social and world political orders. Deploying intersectional analysis facilitates a more comprehensive notion of gender equality that is indivisible from racial, class, and sexual equality and equality among nations. It encourages us to ask not just "Where are the women?" but also "Which women?" and "Where are the men and which men?"

## FEMINIST WORLD POLITICS LENSES

Masculinism is arguably the dominant mode of gender ideology: valuing what is characterized as masculine at the expense of what is feminine, with the material effect of elevating the positioning of men in general above and at the expense of the positioning of women in general. But masculinism also operates to materially exclude or marginalize all those who are feminized, whether women, men, or other genders, as well as intellectual and political commitments that are concerned with social justice. Understood as a key "move" in producing, reproducing, and naturalizing gender hierarchy, masculinism and masculinist lenses are political and deeply implicated in exclusionary practices.

Feminism, in contrast, is a more complicated and contested term. There are, in fact, many forms of feminism. Here we suggest that the common thread among feminisms is an orientation valuing women's diverse experiences and taking seriously women's interests in and capacities for bringing about social and political change for social justice. (Because ideologies are not given biologically but are socioculturally and politically constructed, we note here that masculinist perspectives can be held by women and feminist perspectives can be held by men.) As an aspect of making change, many feminists advocate shifting attention away from men and their activities so that women and their lives come into clearer focus. The objective is to increase awareness of and take more seriously women's diverse ways of identifying, acting, and knowing—and especially—women's agency. This may involve revaluing feminized characteristics—affect, connectedness, sensitivity to others and the self—that have traditionally (through masculinist lenses) been romanticized, trivialized, or deemed inferior. But we note here that the ultimate objective is not a simplistic role reversal in which women gain power over men or femininity becomes more valued than masculinity. Rather, a range of feminist individuals, organizations, perspectives, practices, and institutions seek an end to social relations of gender inequality in recognition that class, race, sexuality, and national origin inequalities exist among women and men and between them. Such recognition arose from the question of which men women want to be equal to given the many inequalities among men. This, in turn, prompted the understanding that economically and racially privileged women can oppress less economically and racially privileged (or feminized) men. Thus, gender equality has been rethought to entail transforming the stereotypes and polarization of gender identities and contesting how masculinity is privileged in concepts, practices, and institutions. For us, this also entails transforming the masculinist and imperialist ways of thinking and acting that produce global crises of representation, insecurity, and sustainability. Doing so requires feminist lenses that reveal not only the (re)positionings of women in relation to men but also how the power of gender operates to reposition some women at the expense of other women and to continually disempower the majority of men—and women.

More than three decades of feminist scholarship have repositioned gender on the agenda of academic disciplines. Both within and outside IR, feminist critiques have altered disciplinary givens, challenged conventional explanations, and expanded the reach of intellectual inquiry. As noted earlier, feminists share a commitment to investigating gendered inequalities and to improving the conditions of women's lives. But neither feminists nor women constitute a homogeneous category, and there is no single meaning of feminism. Like theoretical lenses or perspectives in IR, feminist approaches vary and have been characterized in a number of ways.[10] Most importantly, endless mixing is the rule, not the exception, so assuming that lenses constitute discrete "boxes" misrepresents the diversity, the range, and especially the extensive overlap among many perspectives. Individuals make assumptions that may be common to various lenses, they may make different assumptions when focusing on different substantive topics or normative issues, and how assumptions are mixed is an effect of learning, objectives, experience, and context. With these thoughts in mind, we present in this section a very brief introduction to feminist lenses, especially those developed in the context of IR work, though transgressing the boundaries of it.

Compared with other fields of inquiry, for a variety of reasons feminist interventions in the disciplines of IR (and economics) emerged only in the late 1980s and hence in the midst of debates throughout the academy regarding the nature and politics of knowledge claims. Their critiques of rationalism as masculinist positioned feminists as some of the earliest and most telling critics of modernist, positivist epistemologies. In IR, the "problems and pitfalls of positivism" featured in what has been called the discipline's "fourth debate" (Steans 2006: 22). As noted earlier, positivism is criticized for its dichotomizing assumptions (separating subject from object, fact from value), its essentializing (ahistorical and reductionist) tendencies, and how these generate an unreflective (acritical) attitude and hence conservative effects.

Feminist IR scholars adopt a wide range of positions and research orientations, but most identify with postpositivist epistemologies, in part because these permit a wider range of questions and afford more space for critical reflection on world-politics-as-usual. Like the work of feminists in other disciplines, early efforts tended to focus on revealing how masculinist bias operated in, and hence distorted, the discipline's knowledge claims. This involved exposing androcentrism in fundamental categories, empirical studies, and theoretical perspectives; asking "Where are the women?" and making them visible; documenting mainstream constructions of abstract "woman" as deviant from or deficient in respect to male-as-norm criteria; and incorporating women's activities, experience, and understanding into the study of world politics. These inquiries tended to rely on gender as an empirical category—in effect, as a reference to embodied sex difference—that permitted researchers to "add women" to existing scholarship. They also tended to reflect existing feminist lenses, which we briefly characterize here.

*Feminist Lenses in Relation and Tension*

Figure 2.1 offers a schematic of the lenses that inform contemporary gender and sexuality theorizing, especially as applied in feminist IR and transnational feminist inquiry. All of them in some sense are feminist in orientation in terms of political commitments to thoroughgoing social justice, but not all of them are "feminist" in the sense that they give primacy to "women." The figure does not show any particular direction, progression, or hierarchy. Feminist lenses, even as they appeared at different points in time, are currently employed in mixed fashion by feminist scholars who understand that there are both relations and tensions among perspectives. Mixing them reveals how each uses elements of the others but also how they interrogate each other for what is foregrounded and backgrounded, made visible and invisible, and voiced and silenced. Feminist lenses differentially foreground identity categories (middle-class women, working-class women, racialized women in the North and South,

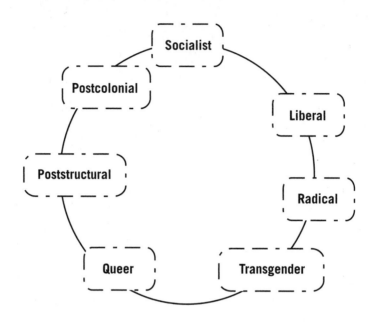

FIGURE 2.1　Feminist Lenses for Intersectional and Transnational Theorizing: Both in Relation and in Tension

sexual minorities, transgendered people) for political purposes, but some are more mindful than others of how socially constructed, nonessentialist, nonuniversal, and provisional identities are even though the material and symbolic orders that produce and marginalize those identities are quite "real."

Liberal feminisms gained formal expression in the context of Europe's bourgeois revolutions that advocated equality but limited its application to (propertied) males. Built upon Enlightenment claims and shaped by its historical context, liberal feminisms tend toward positivist inclinations, decrying the exclusion of women from, and promoting their "addition to," male-dominated activities and power structures. Socialist feminisms draw on Marxist traditions to foreground economic inequalities between women and men. They link capitalism and patriarchy to expose how gender hierarchy operates in the workplace *and* the home, and thus these feminisms challenge categorical boundaries between public and private spheres. Radical feminisms problematize the cultural denigration of femininity and link this to masculinist violence across all levels of analysis.

They expose how experiences and activities associated with women and female bodies are devalued, how sexual violence is a form of social control of women, and how heterosexism reproduces the objectification of and violence against women (and feminized men).

Asking initially "Where are the women?" and subsequently "adding women"—and comparing their positions to those of men—were and remain productive orientations. They make embodied women (and men) visible in our picture of world politics, illuminate how women and men are differently engaged with and affected by international politics, and reveal women as agents and activists, as well as victims of sociocultural, economic, and political oppressions. But adding women to existing paradigms also raised deeper questions by exposing how the conceptual structures themselves presuppose masculine experience and perspective. For example, women/femininity cannot simply be added to constructions that are constituted as masculine: the public sphere, rationality, political identity, objectivity, "economic man." Either women as feminine cannot be added (e.g., women must become like men) or the constructions themselves are transformed (e.g., adding women as feminine alters the masculine premise of the constructions and changes their meaning). In this sense, the exclusions of femininity are not accidental or coincidental but rather are required for the analytical consistency of reigning explanatory frameworks.

The lesson that emerges from these studies is that we cannot systemically add women without rethinking gender—recognizing it not only as an empirical category or variable but also as an analytical category and governing code. Doing so requires acknowledging the constitutive power of language, which is most effectively addressed through a poststructuralist (sometimes referred to as postmodern) lens. This redirects our attention from adding women and deploying sex as a variable to analyzing gender as a category of mental ordering that produces masculinity and femininity as hierarchical power relations. In effect, examining "the woman question" leads us to examine "the man question," which in this text we argue leads us to examine questions of "race," "class," "sexuality," and "nationality" as well. Doing so requires acknowledging intersectionality, derived from antiracist and postcolonial feminist thought, as a necessary analytic, which is also further illuminated through poststructuralist lenses. As used in this text, poststructuralist lenses in general reject essentialized categories, unitary meanings, sovereign claims, universalizing solutions, and presumptions of (foundational) objectivity associated with positivist and modernist commitments. Moreover, feminist poststructuralists criticize the residual essentialism that haunts references to "women" and other "identity-based" groups, rendering them homogeneous, undifferentiated wholes and erasing hierarchies within as well as across all groups.

As in other disciplines, we have seen that diversity among women has forced feminists in IR to reflect critically (and uncomfortably) on the meaning of feminism, definitions of "woman," the politics of representation, and the dangers of universalizing claims. "Sisterhood" aspirations have always been in tension with differences of ethnicity, race, class, age, physical ability, sexuality, and nationality and are especially fraught in a global context marked by stark inequalities among women. Intersectionality approaches attempt to address these issues by rejecting ahistorical and essentialist identities and recognizing "complex or hybrid subjects" (Grewal and Kaplan 2001: 669). These lenses owe much to women of color in the North, women of the global South, and postcolonial critics.

Postcolonial feminists criticize the presumption and privilege of Western feminists and insist on the importance of local and "Third World" agency in identifying problems and negotiating remedies (Mohanty 2003; Chowdhury and Nair 2002). They expose how the ideologies of racism and imperialism continue to reproduce the subjugation and exploitation of "women of color" worldwide. They draw attention to the economic, political, and sociocultural forces of contemporary recolonizations and to nationalist and/or religious fundamentalisms that are dominated by men and deployed to discipline women. When viewed through a postcolonial feminist lens, globalization is both a continuation of colonizing practices that span centuries and, through neoliberal capitalism, an intensification of the exploitation of women in the global South (which includes poor and migrant women in the North). Feminist postcolonial critics challenge the binary "othering" that Eurocentric discourse invokes as a perpetual explanation for and justification of hierarchical power in world politics. They put into sharp relief how gender, race, class, nationalist, and imperialist hierarchies are interwoven in ways that particularly undermine the lives of women (and men) in the global South—physically, politically, economically, and culturally.

Most recently, queer and transgender theorizing has emerged, both out of feminism and in some tension with it. Queer theorists and researchers expose how heteronormativity operates to pathologize sexual minorities and reduce their life chances throughout much of the world where political, or state-sponsored, homophobia is fomented by (neo)conservative elites to deny rights and even life in some places to them. Queer lenses (which are generally poststructuralist in orientation but also employ postcolonial and other critical analysis) have also shown how sexual minorities, particularly among the poor, people of color, and people from the global South, are rendered invisible by economic and social development, entitlement, and immigration programs that are designed only for supporting heteronormative families. As a result, these lenses challenge the heteronormative family as the foundation of the state and seek to enable other family and social arrangements for human intimacy, care, and welfare to emerge. In doing so, queer lenses disrupt even further the dichotomizing power of gender and further shift feminism from a focus on "women" to a focus on resisting gender and sexual normativities that disallow or constrain multiplicitous social formations and relations. They have also countered moralizing approaches to sexuality and sexual expression that can be found in some feminist work, particularly in relation to sex trafficking, calling instead for a "sex-positive" orientation in feminist thought and activist agendas that foregrounds multiple forms of sexual agency and pleasure for women and men. And they have also critiqued homonormative approaches that advocate "conservative" strategies for "fitting into" the heteronormative order through, for example, traditional marriage rather than countering that order for everyone. Transgender theorizing (sometimes referred to more broadly as trans theorizing) challenges both feminist and queer theory to go beyond the dichotomies of male/female and heterosexual/homosexual that still infect those lenses. Taking seriously the lived experiences of transgendered people who are uncomfortable with their assigned sex and/or gender (or, in the case of intersex people who wish to remain so, comfortable with the ambiguous sex organs with which they were born), transgender theorizing argues that sex and gender are not just social constructions, but neither are they fixed or reducible to male/female and masculine/feminine polarities. Instead, transgender theory directs us to "gender diversity," intersex bodies and identities, and the ability to actually change gender and/or sex assignments, sometimes surgically,[11] in ways that do not line up with "sex as a dichotomy" (Sjoberg 2012: 341). This has implications for breaking down not only dichotomized identities but also dichotomized thought.

*Feminist IR Methodologies*

As feminist IR lenses have shifted, combined, and recombined through a greater multiplicity of theoretical voices and orientations—creating their own productive tensions—subjects of feminist IR inquiry have also shifted. Ann Tickner (2006) expresses this in generational terms: first-generation feminist IR scholars tended to focus on deconstructing key concepts in IR—sovereignty, the state, security, development, and the economy—exposing or unpacking their masculinist bias and underpinnings. Through these openings that put gender inquiry on the IR map, second-generation scholars have applied gender analysis—often in more intersectional ways—to a range of world politics topics both familiar (alliance constructions, state militaries, peacekeeping, peace agreements, trade agreements, UN conventions) and unfamiliar (sex tourism and sex work, homework and domestic service, migration, social movements, and even world art and the cruise industry).[12] In doing so, these scholars have not only greatly expanded what world politics inquiry entails but also have rethought earlier approaches to gender theorizing in IR. At the same time, they have multiplied the methodologies used in world politics inquiry in order to get at the multiple ways in which world politics is gendered. In contrast to conventional positivist IR research, feminist IR scholars (and other transnational feminist scholars who engage with and contribute to feminist IR thought) have often utilized such qualitative approaches as ethnographic fieldwork to learn about the lives of the nonelite, social action research through participant observation of social movements, and discourse analysis of classic IR texts, world leaders' pronouncements, (inter)governmental policies and documents, NGO campaigns, and local group articulations of social problems. They also plumb cultural sources, such as popular culture images on the airwaves and the Internet and even literature, art, and poetry, to find expressions over time and space of resistance to world-politics-as-usual in unusual places (Ackerly, Stern, and True 2006).

Such practices seek to reveal the underside of world politics, simultaneously exposing the gendered dynamics that underlie and infect the thought, language, structures, and practices of it and privileging dissident and alternative voices about how it might be rethought, rearticulated, and rearranged. These practices also require reflexivity about the power relations between the researcher and the researched. In cases of "studying down"—such as working with nonelite actors—feminist IR scholars aim to be cognizant of their privilege and thus their responsibility to allow such actors to represent themselves in their own ways so as not to impose Eurocentric/Orientalist, heteronormative, or classist interpretations on the motivations, nature, and outcomes of their struggles. When "studying up"—or dealing with elite or more privileged actors—feminist IR scholars aim to be cognizant of how such actors limit access to researchers engaged in critical scholarship and mystify their power through bureaucratic language. Discourse analysis is thus especially productive when studying up because it enables reading between the lines and catching how the powerful consistently represent themselves and how they consistently represent "others" to justify their policies and actions. In these ways, feminist IR scholarship itself seeks to counter the crisis of representation both in the field of IR, in which the study of people and especially nonelite people has historically been absent, and in world politics, which has historically operated as if people and especially nonelite people did not matter.

In sum, as we move across the array of feminist IR lenses and the array of actors and subjects they reveal as operative in world politics, attention focuses less on women as an empirical variable and more on gender as an analytical category and the power of gender as a meta-lens that (re)produces positivist presumptions and systemic difference construction. In subsequent chapters we employ a range of feminist IR lenses to examine repositionings of women and men and the power of gender in world politics, drawing from the extensive and variant feminist IR and transnational feminist literature that now exists. The very extent and diversity of contemporary feminist IR work reveal that it is not engaged in static, monological, or universalizing analyses that deflect debate. Due to our explicitly critical and intersectional commitments, in this text poststructural and especially postcolonial orientations inform our analysis. These feminist lenses share a critique of positivism's essentialized and homogeneous categories, oppositional dichotomies, and universalizing narratives. But postcolonial lenses emphasize as well how earlier and continuing imperialist practices produce the racialization of "others"; the marginalization, devalorization, and even elimination of alternative visions and voices; and the presumption of Eurocentric superiority in moral, political, military, and economic terms. In Chapter 6 we return to these issues as we imagine degendering as a transformative response, particularly informed by a range of feminist, queer, and transgendered perspectives in IR, to global crises of representation, security, and sustainability.

## GLOBAL GENDERED DIVISIONS OF POWER, VIOLENCE, LABOR, AND RESOURCES

In this final section we introduce the issue areas examined in the subsequent chapters and begin to expose—bring into focus—how the power of gender operates to shape conventional accounts of IR and produces and reproduces crises of representation, insecurity, and sustainability.

### Politics and Power

Masculinism pervades politics. Wendy Brown writes, "More than any other kind of human activity, politics has historically borne an explicitly masculine identity. It has been more exclusively limited to men than any other realm of endeavor and has been more intensely, self-consciously masculine than most other social practices" (1988: 4).

In IR, as in political science, power is usually defined as "power over," specifically, the ability to get someone to do what you want. It is usually measured by control of resources, especially those supporting physical coercion. The appropriate analogy might be power understood as tools: if you have them, you can use them to get certain things done if and when you choose, and some have more of these tools than others. This definition assumes measurable capacities, privileges instrumental rationality, and emphasizes separation and competition: Those who have power use it (or its threat) to keep from securing enough to threaten them. The emphasis on material resources and coercive ability deflects attention from the fact that power reckoning is embedded in dominant conceptual orders, value systems, disciplinary practices, and institutional dynamics.

In IR the concept of "political actor"—the legitimate wielder of society's power—is derived from classical political theory. Common to constructions of "political man"—from Plato and Aristotle to Hobbes, Locke, and Rousseau—is the privileging of man's capacity for reason. Rationality ostensibly distinguishes man from other animals and explains his pursuit of freedom—from nature and "necessity" as well as from tyranny. Feminist scholarship has exposed how models of human nature presupposed in constructions of political man are not in fact gender-neutral but are androcentric, based on exclusively male (especially elite male) experience and perspective. "Political man" also presupposed "civilizational" status: early Greek texts excluded "barbarians" and Persians; premodern European texts excluded "primitives" and racialized "others" within Europe and outside it as colonization proceeded.

With reference to gender divisions of power, "woman" is excluded conceptually from political power by denying her the rationality that marks "man" as the highest animal. Substantively, women have historically been excluded from political power by states' limiting citizenship to those who perform military duty and/or are property owners. Under these conditions, most women are structurally excluded from formal politics, even though individual women in exceptional circumstances have wielded considerable political power. Women worldwide have largely won the battle for the vote, though definitions of citizenship continue to limit women's access to public power and women's political power is circumscribed by a variety of indirect means (discussed elsewhere in this text). Most obvious are the continued effects of the dichotomy of public-private that privileges men's productive and "political" activities over women's reproductive and "personal/familial" activities.

With reference to gender*ed* divisions of power, historically men and women of various "othered" groups have been excluded from political power by various means: barred on the basis of property claims, denied leadership in their own lands by colonial domination, displaced to other lands and denied power through slavery and debt bondage, and more generally excluded from citizenship rights based on criteria related to birth location, "appropriate" documentation, or "economic" status. Today most people have a "right" to political participation, but the most powerful decision-makers in world politics are those occupying positions of power in national and international governmental institutions and transnational corporations. Occupants of these positions continue to reflect privileged statuses, especially of national and economic power, which are also marked by ethnicity/race, gender, and sexuality.

These conventional constructions—of power, political man, citizenship, public-private, and so on—reproduce masculinist, androcentric, and heteronormative assumptions. For example, sovereign man and sovereign states are defined not by connection or relationships but by (masculinist) autonomy in decision-making and putative freedom from interdependence and collective responsibilities. Security is understood not in terms of producing and sustaining life but of acquiring sufficient power to protect "one's own" and keep "others" at bay. The androcentrism of Hobbesian claims is revealed when we ask how helpless infants ever become adults if human nature is universally competitive and hostile. Through a lens on child-rearing practices—necessary for life everywhere—it makes more sense to argue that humans are naturally cooperative, for without the cooperation required to nurture children, there would be no men or women. And although Aristotle acknowledged that the public sphere depends upon the (re)production of life's necessities in the private sphere, he denied the interdependence that this implies in articulating political theory. In the modern era, colonialism racialized and sexualized divisions of power, justifying the conquest of "others" by coding Europeans as uniquely moral and "respectable" as well as racially superior.

Divisions of power in today's world politics suggest a crisis of representation and equity. "Democracy" is strategically promoted while its radical promise is undermined by fraudulent elections, political machinations, and imperial impositions. As we address in greater detail in Chapter 3, "global governance" sounds good and is presumably desirable in some form, but its current form obscures the predominantly nondemocratic and unaccountable forms of international rule. Behind this friendly face, the diffuse power of neoliberal governmentality effectively disciplines us all by securing our consent to disciplining ourselves and—through acquiescence to surveillance, fear, and oppositional politics—each other.

In these senses, analyzing divisions of power requires greater attention to political, economic, and sociocultural forces below and above the level of the state, thereby revealing the greater complexity of global politics, which cannot be reduced to the actions of state elites and their international organizations or the top-down "problem-solving" orientation they advocate. Such a lens would highlight the diffusion of disciplinary techniques and how their micropolitical effects individualize responsibility and undermine collective solidarities. It would reveal inequalities as a source of conflict in world politics and illuminate divisions within groups—as well as linkages among groups—not only along national lines but also along gender, race, class, sexuality, and culture lines. The corollary of this is that many people are resisting world-politics-as-usual by finding common cause with each other across national boundaries and "identity politics" and thus creating a different kind of international relations, or world politics, from that of elite policymakers.

Given their interest in stability, elite power-wielders in world politics (and many who study them) act to maintain current divisions of power and their corollary forms of (nondemocratic) political representation. Nonelites around the world (and most who study them) focus on divisions of power that are created in the name of stability but undermine democracy and accountability and compromise the security of the global majority. People around the world struggling against the tyrannies of sexism, homophobia, racism, classism, militarism, and/or imperialism seek justice, which requires upsetting the status quo. The danger is that even when people struggle for social change, the power of gender typically prevents them from seeing beyond particular interests and oppositional politics to the collective interests of all planetary inhabitants and the complex politics of social justice. It thus (re)produces a crisis of representation by (re)producing global gendered, racialized, and sexualized divisions of power.

## Security and Violence

Essentializing claims about men's superior strength are favored justifications for gender hierarchy. But such claims are misleading. On the one hand, men's strength varies cross-culturally and within cultures, and a considerable number of women are in fact stronger than men. On the other hand, why do we consider men's upper-body muscular strength more significant than women's burden-carrying strength and greater endurance? Decades ago Ashley Montagu undertook a comprehensive review of scientific literature and concluded that "the female is *constitutionally* stronger than the male": she has greater stamina, lives longer, fights disease better, and endures "all sorts of devitalizing conditions better than men: starvation, exposure, fatigue, shock, illness and the like" (1974: 61–62).

Historically, the upper-body strength of (some) males was presumably an important factor when the success of hunting large game or the outcome of conflicts depended on this particular strength. Modern technologies, however, have dramatically altered the relationship of muscular strength to success in battle or in the workplace. Yet a cultural preoccupation with power and strength defined in masculine terms endures. With reference to sports, Mariah Nelson (1994) acknowledges that typical men's and women's bodies differ in terms of athletic qualities (oxygen-carrying capacity, muscle mass, flexibility, etc.) and the advantages of each depend on what sporting event is featured. Dominant media worldwide, however, overwhelmingly privilege sports that favor male bodies, thus reproducing the invisibility of women's particular strengths and sustaining the illusion of men's "supremacy."[13]

With reference to gender divisions of violence, stereotypes of superior male strength are inextricable from hegemonic constructions of masculinity that cultivate male arrogance and overweening power. Most models of masculinity, historically and presently, include elements of courage, competition, assertiveness, and ambition that are difficult to disassociate from physical aggression and even violence, especially when males are systematically placed in situations where proving their manhood involves aggressive behavior. Willingness to engage in violence is then easily mobilized, whether against feminized intimates (lovers, wives) or feminized "others" (opponents, enemies). As one effect, across national contexts men (especially of particular ages) engage in violent behaviors more frequently and with more systemically destructive effect than do women.

With reference to gender*ed* divisions of imperialist violence, Europeans manipulated ideologies of superior (masculinist) "strength" to justify colonial wars and obscure their racist, economic, and heteronormative dynamics.[14] What surfaces repeatedly are characterizations of the colonized as feminine: weak, passive, irrational, disorderly, unpredictable, and lacking self-control. This afforded European power-wielders (not only men or all men) a justification for military interventions by casting themselves in favorable masculinist terms: as uniquely rational, sexually and morally respectable, and more advanced economically and politically. In colonial wars and geopolitical "othering," civilization became a code word for European heteronormative masculine superiority. Through this lens, imperial violence was perhaps a regrettable but nonetheless necessary component of "enlightening" and "civilizing" primitive, unruly, feminine "others." As Zillah Eisenstein observes, although Europeans extolled the virtues of reason as a progressive force, they positioned rationality "against savagery (natives), emotionality (women), and sexuality (racialized others)" (2004: 75).

At the same time—and complicating simplistic models of gender—the development of European nationalisms and normalization of bourgeois respectability produced an idealized model of (bourgeois) femininity: passive, pure, dutiful, maternal. This superficial valorization of femininity did less to empower women than it did to render them perpetual dependents, as feminine virtue and morality were best assured by confining these qualities and "good women" to a private sphere of domesticity and assigning men the public-sphere responsibility of defending and protecting feminized dependents. The patronizing and protectionist logic of bourgeois norms provided imperial governments a moral—as well as rational—justification for militarized colonization: the barbarity of "other" men was proven by their (allegedly) oppressive treatment of women, and this *called for* the rescue of victimized females by honorable, civilized men. In short, the defense of idealized femininity—to paraphrase Gayatri Spivak's (1988) apt analysis—justified wars by white men to "save" brown women from brown men.[15] This protectionist and crusading rhetoric obscured exploitative agendas and appeared to legitimate militarized violence. As we discuss in Chapter 4, it resurfaces, with particular vengeance and new complexities, in contemporary global security practices, including militarization—the extension of military thinking and practices into civilian life—and imperialist projects.

The US-led "war on terror" exemplifies gendered divisions of violence and how a crisis of (in)security escalates when masculinist arrogance spurs imperial strategies. Some argue that George W. Bush's "forceful" response to the 9/11 bombings involved not only his outrage and claim to military leadership but also his desire to establish a hypermasculine image—of himself *and* the United States.[16] For many, US identity and power had been feminized by the nation's defeat in Vietnam, made more humiliating by losing to a people stereotyped as ethnically/racially inferior. Feminization anxiety was also fueled by the increasing visibility of women in politics and the workplace and the growing strength of LGBTQ social movements in the United States. Given these conditions, a yearning to remasculinize the nation (Jeffords 1989) was easily tapped by Bush and his neoconservative advisers.

*[margin note: disagree]*

Like earlier imperial powers, Bush used the gendered logic of crusading protectionism to justify his warring agenda, claiming instead to be liberating the women of Afghanistan and Iraq. Silencing any alternative interpretation, the war story he broadcast featured monstrous terrorists inexplicably committed to destroying freedom and democracy by extremes of violence; enemies this irrational and unpredictable could only be defeated by drawing an absolute line between good and evil and eliminating the latter. The power of gender operates here to vilify (feminized) enemies as so categorically different from and absolutely opposed to "us" that the only viable strategy is their annihilation. In a parallel move, those who were skeptical, fearful, or actively opposed these strategies were rendered unequivocally suspect—as unpatriotic, anti-American, naively (irrationally) out of touch, or quite simply *unmanly* (lacking the guts to do what must be done) (Peterson 2007). Feminization here vilifies dissenters and denies absolutely the rationality of any critique. Dissenters are simply and irredeemably discredited: unwilling to stand up for their country, ungratefully abandoning the United States and freeloading on its military power, and/or failing to grasp real-world politics. In the former president's imperial words, "Those who are not with us are against us." And as enemies, those who are against us lose any claim to inclusion, respect, or (apparently) rights. *This is all author's opinion / Trying to make a case for feminism where their is none*

Today's crisis of insecurity is also revealed when we look beyond direct to indirect or structural violence, exemplified by increased health risks to families and the poorest when war-making undermines access to safe water, food, and medical attention. Neoliberal globalization erodes state authority, welfare provisioning, and employment security, whereas global militarization increases violence and amplifies the need for legitimate and stable authority, social welfare programs, and survival resources. Neoliberal austerity measures instituted now in the global North since the recent financial crisis and in the face of debts racked up by runaway "defense" spending for the "war on terror" are impoverishing greater swaths of people while income inequality grows. Structural violence disproportionately affects women and groups subordinated by cultural markers and economic inequalities, and when we ignore this fact, we ignore the (in)security of the planet's majority.

The power of gender produces a crisis of violence and global insecurity. It constructs a world shaped by hostile forces and naturalizes war against all who are feminized. In a self-perpetuating cycle, threats (real or fictive) increase preparations for defense and/or retaliation that are inextricable from conditions of structural violence. An essentializing, oppositional lens magnifies and legitimates self-other, us-them, aggressive-passive, soldier-victim, masculine-feminine, and protector-protected dichotomies. These exemplify how the binary terms are interdependent and call forth each other problematically: assuming the "other" is threatening justifies preemptive or confrontational behavior; assuming women are weak (or victims) justifies pumping up real men who "must" protect them. Neoliberal capitalism, which has made a comeback undaunted by the recent financial crisis, and global militarization, which while abating some is still substantial, continue to merge in today's Empire, as inequalities between groups provide motives for conflict and fuel militarization and wars provide profit-making opportunities for some that delay the resolution of conflicts and deepen the crisis of insecurity for all.

## Labor

Divisions of labor and resources within households and the global workforce are shaped by masculinist and capitalist ideologies, both of which entail relations of inequality and exploitative dynamics. Gender divisions of labor are particularly visible through a lens on how "work" is defined and "counted," what kinds of work are most valued, who does what work, and how much—if anything—they are paid. Stereotypes of women and femininity here interact powerfully with dichotomies of public-private, productive-reproductive, and mental-manual to generate quite rigid labor patterns between men and women, rich and poor individuals, "skilled" and "unskilled" workers, and nations of the global North and South. Just as the public is seen as (politically) more important than the private, (ostensibly less skilled) reproductive and manual labor is monetarily devalued, accorded less status, and rendered less visible, even though it constitutes the structural underpinning of what "more important" workers—especially elite men—do.

As we examine in greater detail in Chapter 5, for the past several decades geopolitical elites have promoted neoliberal policies that effectively restructured production and financial arrangements worldwide. Deregulation has favored private capital at the expense of public provisioning and shifted risks and responsibilities from the collective to the individual. Increasing "flexibilization" of work arrangements has dramatically repositioned men and women in relation to paid, safe, and secure ("formal," long-term, with benefits) forms of employment. With reference to gender*ed* divisions of labor, male workers in general face increasing un- and underemployment (work "below" their skill level), and the poorest workers in the global North and South face declining prospects for any "meaningful" work or income sufficient to escape poverty. Greater numbers of men and women are on the move globally in search of work, and these racialized flows alter identity politics and heighten immigration "issues." Women virtually everywhere are increasingly entering the workforce, but for the vast majority, they find work only in low-status and poorly paid jobs.

The power of gender operates here to (re)position women primarily in services, especially in taking care of the emotional (counseling, nursing), "entertainment" (performing arts, sex industries), production (word processing, assembly-line jobs), and maintenance (cleaning, clerical, child care) needs of men as individuals and the masculinist social system generally. It also operates as well to continue the concentration of jobs that assume low technologies and minimal skills—and/or that are physically demanding, unsafe, and risky—in poorer and racially marked groups and in the nations of the global South. And it operates in a pervasive sense to devalorize all jobs—and the men as well as women doing them—associated with or sharing the stereotypical characteristics of "women's work": unskilled, informal, reproductive. This devalorization is manifested conceptually (affecting self-esteem and status) and materially (affecting wages and physical well-being). In these senses, the feminization of work raises a host of issues regarding gendered divisions of labor and potential fore-closure of traditional masculinities. The feminization and flexibilization of employment does favor some women and some workers, but this is most often at the expense of "decent" or "secure" employment more generally and entails a deterioration in working conditions and real wages for most of the world's workers.

Although women often seek paid work because males in the household are un- or underemployed, the division of labor in the household is rarely transformed when women (re)position themselves in the workplace. Rather, studies worldwide confirm that women who work for pay rarely do less unpaid work at home because even when men are unemployed, they resist doing "women's work" in the home. One effect is a global trend of women doing more work than ever: still carrying the primary responsi-bility for child care, the emotional and physical well-being of family mem-bers, and everyday household maintenance, but now also earning income for the family and often being called upon to nurture community survival networks in the face of worsening socioeconomic conditions.

The power of gender operates here to perpetuate categorical distinc-tions between what "real men" and "real women" do, which encourages men to avoid feminized activities even when participating would benefit loved ones. And it operates to sustain expectations that women, consis-tent with the stereotype of femininity and ideology of patriarchal house-holds, work to serve others—both at home and in the workplace. In this sense, women are seen to work "for love" or as secondary income earners to sustain families, rather than primarily for income or status as most cul-tures expect men to do. When economic conditions deteriorate, women are expected to take up the slack—working in whatever capacity to keep the family/household going no matter what sacrifices of self are necessary. Of course, the trade-offs for women who do this work vary tremendously. Nor do *all* men seek or benefit equally from the exploitation of women's labor. But as a generalization, men in the aggregate do benefit in various ways from the systemic masculinism that treats women's energies, lives, skills, intellects, demands, and needs as secondary to those of men.

The larger problem, however, is not simply a failure of men to "do their share" but the structural contradictions of neoliberal capitalism and crisis of social reproduction they constitute. In the context of deteriorating eco-nomic conditions and reduced public support, there are ultimately lim-its to how far and how long women can "stretch" their energy and labor to meet survival needs and ensure the daily reproduction of social life. Isabella Bakker and Stephen Gill refer to "a global contradiction between the extended power of capital (and its protection by the state) and not only sustainable but also progressive forms of social reproduction for the majority of the world's population" (2003: 4). In short, neoliberal restructuring is undermining the viability of social reproduction, upon which all productive processes, indeed human life, depend. The crisis of social reproduction in daily life and the household is thus inextricable from a crisis of sustainability borne of gendered divisions of resources and environmental degradation.

That a crisis of social reproduction and its implications remain largely invisible in mainstream accounts of economics and world politics reflects the power of gender as well. Quite simply, women's work and economics within the family/household are deemed unimportant compared with men's work, formal, productive economic activities, and male-dominated financial arrangements. Economic vision is further compromised by adopting methods of inquiry that discount subjective, qualitative, and cultural dimensions of social life. Mainstream IR scholars draw on neoclassical economic theory both as a methodological preference and as a means to study the global economy. Most endorse neoliberalism as the optimal strategy not only for pursuing economic growth and prosperity but also for promoting "democracy" worldwide. Until the recent financial crisis, neoliberal commitments to deregulation and liberalization were assumed to be the most efficient and therefore most desirable approach to national and international economic relations. Through this lens, an expanding world economy would provide an ever-larger pie and, through a process of "trickle down," ever-bigger pies would translate into larger slices, theoretically, even for those with few initial resources. Even before the current economic crisis, cumulative data indicated that resource inequalities within and between nations had not declined but had become more polarized under neoliberal policies. Tragically, the crisis in social reproduction and environmental sustainability that feminists have long foreseen merged during and since the recent financial crisis that critical economists also foresaw but that its perpetrators still find "surprising," leading to mostly more of the same in the post-financial-crisis period.

On the face of it, advocates of traditional approaches tend to reproduce, rather than challenge, the status quo because the questions they frame result in answers that confirm the assumptions upon which the questions are based. The power of gender is presupposed in the dichotomies favored by economic analysis: paid-unpaid work, formal-informal, providers-dependents, production-reproduction, and "autonomy" in the marketplace versus interdependence. Just as women are deemed feminine by their dependence within the family, "less developed" nations and their people are "unmanned" by their position of dependence in the global economy. Finally, trickle-down theories tend to benefit those who control the most resources by promoting the continued growth that delivers the biggest pieces of pie to those in power. Many argue that not only do the poorest never see trickle-down benefits, but also even if they get marginally larger pieces, the proportional distribution of the pie does not improve—in fact, the proportion going to a very small elite has increased. And not least, today's ecological crises (which hurt the poorest the most) challenge the entire premise of ever-expanding growth.

## Resources

Through conventional lenses, IR scholars distinguish the "high" politics of state-centric security from the "low" politics of economic relations, and they effectively discredit environmental concerns as "soft politics." More recently, the seriousness of environmental degradation, an emerging consensus on global warming, and the deadly politics of oil have prompted a shift in focus, though not a transformation in this paradigm (explored more fully in Chapter 5). Taking environmental issues seriously would entail a critical analysis of how resources are used, distributed, and controlled, and this exercise would reveal the disproportionate and, to a large extent, irresponsible consumption of resources on the part of the global minority/North that so exacerbates resource depletion.

Ecological irresponsibility is spurred by multiple factors: inflated desires, ill-conceived projects, short-range planning, greedy consumerism and profit-seeking, unrealistic expectations, and unintended consequences. The "success" of industrialization fueled growth-is-always-good and technology-can-fix-it mentalities and exploitative, wasteful practices. Poor and nonindustrialized peoples rarely have the luxury of operating on a throwaway mentality, and without the illusion of constant growth, many live in a symbiotic relationship with their environment. Population expansion in environments often made resource-poor through colonization, war, and the like, however, increasingly forces people to secure their everyday subsistence by depleting the very resources they depend upon. Water, food, and fuel for domestic use are essential for life, but the acquisition and consumption of these goods in the short term often conflict with long-term ecological planning and resources. Many economic development policies (securing foreign currency through the sale of timber, building an industrial base with fossil-fuel-driven factories, creating even greater dependence on the dirtiest fossil fuels) have costly ecological consequences. The choices for developing (or underdeveloped) countries are especially stark, but many overdeveloped nations deny their historical role in creating these stark choices and decry the desire of "others" to industrialize in ways that exacerbate environmental degradation.

Gender divisions of ecological resources are problematically revealed when we consider how women are assigned primary responsibility for social reproduction, which requires basic resources, but they have little control over how local and global resources are used, distributed, and controlled. Gender*ed* divisions are institutionalized with the growth of science and industrial technologies in service to capitalist and colonial projects. At the core, the modernist, Eurocentric ideology of limitless growth presupposes a belief in (white, Western) "man's" dominion over nature (promoted, for example, in Christian and capitalist belief systems) and the desirability of (white, Western) "man's" exploiting nature to further his own ends. Conquering nature, digging out "her" treasure and secrets, proving (white, Western) man's superiority through control over and manipulation of nature—these are familiar and currently deadly refrains. The identification of nature as female is not an accident but a historical development that is visible in justifications by elites for territorial and intellectual expansion. Exploitation is most readily legitimated by objectifying who or what is exploited. Understanding people or nature as "objects" denies them agency, purpose, feelings, intelligence, a right to exist and/or to warrant respect. Through the lens of (white, Western) man's dominion, it is taken for granted that natural resources are there for humans to exploit and control: no questions asked; such resources are "there for the taking." In various ways throughout history, aboriginal peoples, women, colonies, and the earth's bounty have all been treated as such natural resources (Mies, Bennholdt-Thomsen, and von Werlhof 1988). The gendered dichotomies of culture-nature, mind-body, subject-object, control-uncertainty, exploiter-exploited, and dominator-dominated variously shape how we think about and hence treat what is objectified. But we are learning at great cost that (white, Western) "man's dominion/domination" over feminized (and racialized) nature is neither morally acceptable nor environmentally sustainable.

Gendered divisions are revealed in terms of who has access to what resources, who controls resources and to what ends, who suffers most from environmental degradation, and how masculinist lenses normalize irresponsible resource use. Worldwide, but particularly in the global South, females are more dramatically affected by environmental degradation than are males. As food providers, women find their workload increases when water, food, and fuel resources deteriorate; as last and least fed, they suffer most from starvation and malnutrition; and as caretakers, they have to work harder when economic, health, and environmental conditions deteriorate and when families and communities are victims of environmental disasters. Economically and ethnically marginalized populations are also more directly affected and more starkly than elites. As the poorest, they lack resources and power, and they are least able to quit jobs, acquire adequate health care, purchase safer products, move away from toxic environments, or prevail against those who seek to dispose of toxic waste in "their backyard." As the most politically marginalized and devalorized groups, they are less visible when they protest, are silenced (or seen as "overreacting") in what debates do take place, their neighborhood and community claims are disregarded, and they are subject to being seen as "disposable" themselves.

In these multiple senses, divisions of labor and resources—and the inequalities and crises they generate—expose starkly who and what is valued and who and what is not. The power of gender operates to privilege and (over)valorize skills, workers, and "production" associated with hegemonically masculine identities and activities; and these identities and activities presuppose (white) man's dominion over females and nature, as well as capitalist commitments to growth. In complex ways, these patterns of devalorization determine the world's winners and losers and, specifically, those consigned to what Giorgio Agamben (1998) characterizes as "bare life": an exceptionally abject and materially precarious condition.

We suggest here how the gendered divisions of power, violence, and labor and resources constitute crises of representation and equity, insecurity and violence, social reproduction and environmental sustainability. We argue throughout this text, and document in subsequent chapters, how the power of gender is not simply an aspect of these crises but is productive of them. Consider how the premise of "disposability" is built into currently dominant ways of thinking and acting in world politics: top-down governance by elites and experts, imperial violence as how to settle differences, commodification as a cultural logic, and growth as a capitalist imperative.

2. Gendered Lenses on World Politics

These lenses variously presuppose that inequalities of authority, power, and resources are inevitable, and that therefore some individuals, peoples, and natural resources will necessarily (though perhaps regrettably) be "wasted." Once disposability is built into expectations and operating rules, it raises the question of who shall be disposed. The power of gender operates both to produce the necessity of the question and to provide (or at least guide) the answer. On the one hand, it underpins these lenses by normalizing masculinist, objectivist, and modernist modes of instrumental rationality and Eurocentric moralizing, which assume superiority and categorically preclude alternative visions or even alternative questions. On the other hand, the power of gender "answers" the question by normalizing categorical and hierarchical oppositions, essentialized "othering," and devalorization of the feminine, which operate simultaneously to identify who is most disposable and to justify that disposal.

Crises produced by gendered divisions of power, violence, and labor and resources, and the power of gender that sustains them, cannot be addressed without degendering world politics, the topic of our concluding chapter.

### Notes

1. English-language training exacerbates this tendency by teaching word meanings as opposites. Learning antonyms forces us to think in apparently unchanging oppositions: right-wrong, hot-cold, friend-foe, boy-girl, night-day, us-them. Dichotomized or dualistic thinking is criticized from diverse perspectives, but especially from those identified as postpositivist, poststructuralist, or postmodernist.

2. References to ideologies do not always emphasize their role in justifying inequalities, but that is our focus here.

3. See McCaughey (2008) for an accessible critique of how evolutionary theory is today increasingly used to render stereotypes of male desire, sexuality, and violence—the caveman mystique—as natural.

4. "The conceptual category sex/affective production is a way of understanding the social organization of labor and the exchange of services that occur between men and women in the production of children, affection, and sexuality" (Ferguson 1984: 154; also 1989). In the present book, sex/affective relations include exchanges between men and between women as well as in heteronormative couples. Links to the state include marriage and family law, antihomosexuality legislation, sex and reproductive education, maternal health and parental support policies, domestic and international politics of reproductive health, and population politics.

5. Even though heterosexual intercourse was—until recently—a necessary condition of biological reproduction, this biological demand did not require the

normalization of heterosexist/patriarchal families as the exclusive basis of intimacy and group reproduction.

6. Some cultures afford space for more than two genders or for more complex constructions of gender. See, for example, Nanda 1998; Roscoe 2000; and Fausto-Sterling 2000.

7. Enloe's (1989) early treatment starkly exposed how much power it takes to keep gender in place in world politics and to keep world politics gendered. This remains an eye-opening and especially teachable text.

8. Consider how mainstream media and academic studies highlight issues and activities that are masculinist or male-dominated: competitive sports, sexual pursuits and conquests, male bonding, crime and espionage, fighting and killing, war-making, risk-taking, public figures and events, making money, national and international politics. In comparison, media and academic studies, except those that have been influenced by feminist perspectives, rarely focus on issues and activities associated with women's lives: cooperative and care-taking activities, building interpersonal and community relations, poverty and physical victimization (assault, rape, homicide), reproducing everyday life and activities—in the home, family, workplace—and, especially, reproductive issues involving women's mental and physical health and when, whether, and under what circumstances to bear children.

9. In the interests of brevity and accessibility, we often rely on this oversimplified contrast between positivist and postpositivist orientations in this text.

10. For feminist lenses in IR, see, for example, Tickner 2001; Steans 2006; and Squires and Weldes 2007.

11. Transgender analysis argues that among "cisgender" or gender-normative privileges is a certain abhorrence among some feminists of surgical procedures performed on the "female" body, thereby unjustly vilifying desired transsexual surgeries and upholding naturalistic constructs of sex and gender.

12. See multiple issues of the *International Feminist Journal of Politics,* the journal devoted to feminist IR scholarship and emerging from the Feminist Theory and Gender Studies Section of the International Studies Association.

13. The title of Nelson's (1994) book contends that "the stronger women get, the more men love football." As women gain some measure of equality and erode men's athletic claims to superior bodies, men become more ardent fans of those sports—gridiron football, baseball, basketball, ice hockey—that appear to sustain the illusion of unequivocal male superiority.

14. Key works include Said 1979, 1993; Spivak 1987; McClintock 1995; and Eisenstein 2004.

15. Cultural generalizations of enemy groups or nations typically feminized them, and European notions of ethnic/racial hierarchies permitted selective valorization of men identified with "martial races" and "warrior" cultures. Without conceding any sense of their military superiority, imperial governments selectively allied with soldiers of particular cultural identities to advance colonial interests. The British, for example, recruited Nepali Ghurkas to fight their wars and now recruit Fijian men. In the "war on terror," the Bush administration selectively allied with ethnically and religiously differentiated groups—without exception extremely masculinist—that

best served its short-term military objectives, with little attention to the hierarchies—especially of gender and sexuality—these exacerbate.

16. Zine captures succinctly the political work this war story does: "The archetypal image of the deprived and debased Muslim woman was resurrected to perform her duty as a signifier of the abject difference of Muslims; the barbarity and anti-modernism of Islam and its essential repression of women; and most importantly as camouflage for US military interventions" (2006: 34). Many feminists criticized these wars (Hawthorne and Winter 2002; Joseph and Sharma 2003; Eisenstein 2004; Hunt and Rygiel 2006; Alexander and Hawkesworth 2008; Eisenstein 2009) and Bush's co-optation of feminist discourse, especially given his history of antifeminist policies (e.g., showing indifference to Taliban practices preinvasion, cutting domestic programs that benefit women, restricting access to contraception at home and abroad).

# 3

─────────────────◄○►─────────────────

# Gender and Global Governance

How does the power of gender affect "who rules the world"? What do gendered divisions of power tell us about how the world is ordered and for what purposes? How are women and men positioned and repositioned in and by global power structures and with what effects? What is the new global politics of gender equality, and why did it arise? How has neoliberal governmentality captured and depoliticized feminist politics for gender equality?

In this chapter, we look at the relationship between gendered inequalities and global governance. Although there is no world government, and much conventional IR thinking continues to see states as the central actors in world politics, in recent years the term *global governance* has come to refer to a constellation of global actors including states; IGOs such as the UN bodies and agencies, the World Bank, the International Monetary Fund (IMF), and the World Trade Organization (WTO); regional governments such as the European Union and regional IGOs such as organizations of African, American, and Asian states and free-trade regimes like the North American Free Trade Agreement; global market actors such as transnational corporations and transnational NGOs (Rai 2008: 22). States make up IGOs, and the wealthiest and most militarily powerful states hold primacy in them. At the same time, states are variously subordinated to IGO rules made by state representatives (with increasing input by NGO actors), which range from international laws and regulations to agreed-upon norms. Thus, although we especially focus on the *power of gender* to shape the meaning of state power in world politics and the relative positionings of women and men as state actors in world politics, we also look at other gendered institutions at the global level and the new gender rules that are emanating from some of them and that are having impacts on states and the *repositionings of women and men*. We conclude, however, that these new rules associated with the new global politics of gender equality do not necessarily disrupt gendered divisions of power and leave intact the power of gender and the *crisis of representation* it sustains.

Before examining the gender distribution of global power, we begin with the gendered nature of the idea of "power" itself. The definition of power conventionally favored in IR, as in political science generally, is one of "power-over." Power-over is captured in Robert Dahl's (1961) classic definition: the ability of A to get B to do something that B would not otherwise do. Defining power in this way emphasizes control of material—especially military—resources and a willingness to use them in order to enforce one's preferences. It is power-over in the sense of being top-down (those on top, where the most resources are concentrated, are determined to have the most power) and coercive (the ability to force compliance is presumed to be the surest sign of power). When we use only this narrow definition of power to study world politics, however, we neglect investigating how other dimensions of social reality—moral commitments, religious beliefs, ethnic allegiances, disciplinary practices, sociopolitical ideologies—shape how power works and who rules the world. Finally, and singularly relevant to our thesis, this definition of power is masculinist when it presupposes androcentric notions of strength, competition, aggression, and coercion and because it focuses on power understood only in terms of public-sphere activities dominated by elite men who embody these traits and exercise power-over strategies that are assumed, particularly in realist thinking, as endemic to states.

One aim in this chapter is to examine where women are positioned relative to men as political elites in formal global power structures. In doing so, we address the following questions: Where are the women who wield power in global governance? Why have women and gender issues been so underrepresented in global power structures, how may this be changing, why, and with what effects? This chapter further demonstrates how the power of gender remains systematically at work through an apparent paradox. On the one hand, women gaining positions of power challenges gender stereotypes that portray women as uninterested in or unfit for political leadership, and greater attention to gender equality in global governance could be read as a success story. On the other hand, gains in women's power positions in global governance do not eradicate gender stereotypes, and gender-oriented policies are more an effect of neoliberal restructuring and governmentality than of commitments to gender justice. These realities preclude fundamental change in the conduct of world politics and its priorities. The gendered concept of power as power-over—accompanied by the co-optive power of neoliberalism—maintains gender, race, class, sexual, and national hierarchical dichotomies (gendered divisions of power) that continue to be productive of world crises even as more women are represented in, and gender equality gets on the agenda of, global power structures.

As intimated in the last chapter, these *gendered divisions of power* include dichotomies of political-apolitical, reason-emotion, public-private, leaders-followers, active-passive, and freedom-necessity (see Table 3.1). Those who are feminized—including most women and many men—are generally denied the status of independent and rational agency and leadership qualities in the public sphere and are reduced to the ground upon which real men act, thus enabling political man to be released from and unmindful of the necessities of everyday life. At the same time, these divisions narrowly define rationality as instrumentalism in the service of power-over and control, disregard the intertwining of private life with public life and domestic politics with international politics, and mistake acting together (or interdependent action) and refraining from harmful actions as signs of weakness, passivity, and lack of autonomy. Autonomy (or reactionary individualism devoid of affective relationships and concern) becomes privileged as the "true" meaning of freedom, which sets in motion a zero-sum game. The overall effect of the power of gender to dichotomize thinking about power and privilege power-over identities and actions is a crisis of representation whereby large numbers of people, peoples, identities, and perspectives remain un- or underrepresented in formal and informal positions of power, and those who supposedly speak for "others" misrepresent them, their issues, and their aspirations in service to the priorities and desires of the few at the top of whatever hierarchical structure. This crisis of representation, in turn, feeds crises of insecurity and sustainability that, in turn, silence or marginalize alternative or engaging dissident voices, all of which sustains the crisis of representation. This vicious cycle sets up the dynamic of reducing responses to bureaucratic "problem-solving" rather than efforts toward transformation of the cycle itself. Thus, the power of gender remains relatively undisturbed even as there are some shifts in the gendered divisions of power.

TABLE 3.1
**Gendered Divisions of Power Productive of the Crisis of Representation**

| *Masculinized* | *Feminized* |
| --- | --- |
| Political | Apolitical |
| Reason | Emotion |
| Public | Private |
| Leaders | Followers |
| Active | Passive |
| Elite | Nonelite |
| Power-Over | Power-To |
| High Politics | Low Politics |
| Hard Politics | Soft Politics |

## FEMINIST APPROACHES TO POLITICS

Prior to the rise of feminist IR, feminist interventions had been made in a host of disciplines, primarily in the humanities and social sciences, since at least the 1960s. The general trajectory of these interventions was also to initially ask, "Where are the women?" The women first identified as missing were "women worthies" (Harding 1986), or those women whose outstanding contributions to literature, art, history, and social, political, and economic thought were overlooked or hidden because they were produced by women in patriarchal societies that could not imagine women as capable of great things. In political science more generally, this meant recovering histories of women political thinkers and leaders (Smith and Carroll 2000) to make the case that women have always been fit for politics and have generated significant and original political thought, despite ideologies to the contrary. This was an important insight, but it still did not yield significant change in women's representation in political office or significantly increase women's access to and participation in formal politics more generally. Such a focus on "women worthies" also limited feminist interventions to getting relatively few women into relatively few positions of formal power. This led feminist political theorists to question the very definition of politics and the standards by which political behavior is judged.[1]

That public-sphere, formal politics is only one form of politics was revealed by showing how the private sphere and everyday life are shot through with power relations and negotiations ("the personal is political"). This drew attention as well to ways in which women engaged in nonformal political action to turn practices assumed to be natural and unchangeable (such as rape and domestic violence) into "political" (and thus changeable) "issues." Feminist political theorizing also revealed that formal politics was defined and political behavior judged on the basis of (hegemonic) male norms that privileged notions of politics as winner-take-all affairs, effectively necessitating individualist and aggressive traits to be successful in such politics. This problem is magnified in the case of international politics, which could be defined as hypermasculinist when compared with masculinist domestic politics. Feminists have also shown that domestic politics, as not only national but also local, household, and interpersonal politics, is not separate from international politics, arguing that "the personal is international."

These points suggest how this shift in analysis, in turn, shifted strategies: from "adding women" to formal power structures to valorizing feminine traits in order to redefine politics from "power-over" to "power-to" (also known as "power-with" or enabling power) and change the standards of political behavior in favor of interdependence and cooperation. Still, this left intact a lingering and limiting referent to "women" that did not dehomogenize the category to recognize power differentials among women and the power some women hold over some men. It also left intact the association of embodied women with feminine values, which, on the one hand, led to essentialist assumptions about women as cure-alls for social (and global) ills and, on the other hand, positioned certain embodied men (largely non-Western, nonwhite, and/or lower class) as the villains of the piece. In the process, attention is deflected from the complicity of both women and men—particularly those with the most power and privilege—in contributing to global ills. It also misrepresents feminist politics as exclusively about women rather than about resisting gender and gendered hierarchies and the ills they cause globally. This is not to say that raising the status of women and other subjugated people—in politics and other facets of life—is not necessary to increase formal representation and better equalize voice, but to note that it is insufficient if there is no attendant ideological shift away from politics as power-over to politics that enables resistance to and transformation of world-politics-as-usual, which the power of gender sustains.

In this chapter we follow the general trajectory of "adding women," to disturbing gender and gendered assumptions, to complicating gender, and, finally, to expanding feminist politics beyond the issue of women in politics. This brings us to the matter of resisting the contemporary world political force of neoliberal governmentality, which has the capacity to manage or depoliticize feminist critiques and resistances. As we conclude, the antidote to this is repoliticizing such demands for change.

## WOMEN ACTORS IN GLOBAL GOVERNANCE

### State and National Leaders

Heads of states and/or governments are among the world's most powerful political actors, and a number of women have held these powerful positions over the past century and into the current one. Heads of state are key executive decision-makers and policy implementers within the nations they lead. At the same time, their power within the state has external, international consequences to the extent that the military, political, economic, and cultural priorities they establish extend beyond territorial borders. Additionally, heads of government "represent" their states culturally as well as politically: In varying ways, such leaders come to symbolize the values of the country they represent. Female heads of state and government are no exception.

Individual elite women have, throughout history, wielded considerable political power and influence. Consider such legendary hereditary rulers as Cleopatra, Queen Elizabeth I, and Catherine the Great and such well-known twentieth-century leaders as Indira Gandhi, Golda Meir, and Margaret Thatcher. However, they have so far proved to be more the exception than the rule when we recognize that in 2011 only twenty women beyond seven ceremonial monarchs and governors-general were serving as prime ministers, presidents, or chancellors (Hawkesworth 2012: 27). The fact that women have led states on most continents over time suggests, however, that women can achieve such power across a range of political systems and cultures. Still, as Gunhild Hoogensen and Bruce Solheim note, certain patterns do persist—namely, the continued importance of dynastic political family ties that enable women to play on their names to downplay their gender, the continued paucity of women leaders at the top in most of the most powerful countries in the West and the global North compared with the global South, and the contemporary trend of more women coming to power in conflict or postconflict areas of the global South (with the exception of much of the Middle East), where women leaders "might be perceived as being less corruptible, mother figures, and often tap into the power of martyred husbands and fathers" (2006: 16, 128–132, 129).

This latter trend can particularly be seen in parliamentary statistics on women assembled by the Inter-Parliamentary Union (IPU).[2] As of 2013, postconflict Rwanda still tops the world in the percentage of women elected to parliament, standing at 53 percent women members of parliament, after becoming the first country in the world with more women than men in a national legislative body in 2008. Thirty other countries have reached or transcended the minimal threshold of 30 percent women in national legislatures called for in the 1995 Beijing Platform for Action. These include the Nordic countries, which were among the first to do so, as well as much of western Europe. But Andorra has now reached parity (50–50); Cuba, the Seychelles, Senegal, South Africa, and Nicaragua are all at more than 40 percent; and a host of other Latin American, African, Caribbean, and Asian states, interspersed with western and eastern European states as well as New Zealand, are at or above the 30 percent threshold. Compare these with the United States, which continues to fall in the ranks, standing at 78 out of the 145 countries ranked with only 17.8 percent women in its national legislature as of 2013. UNIFEM's *Progress of the World's Women Report 2008/2009* observed that women's representation in national assemblies had been greatly accelerating since 1995 (2008: 21). UNIFEM accounted for this relatively dramatic rise by pointing primarily to the increased use of legally required or voluntary quota systems and proportional representation (PR) electoral systems, practices that in some cases were stimulated by gender equality advocates working at international and national levels who have used the BPA for leverage and by the adoption in 2000 of the United Nations Millennium Development Goals (MDGs), which include Goal 3 promoting gender equality and women's empowerment (UNIFEM 2008: 20). (These advances are discussed in more detail later in this chapter.)

As reported in the most recent *Progress of the World's Women Report 2011–2012*,[3] produced by the United Nations Entity for Gender Equality and the Empowerment of Women (known as UN Women), the vast majority of countries with 30 percent or more women represented use some form of legal or voluntary quota system (2011: 119). Moreover, as quantitative research conducted to account for the rise of women's representation in national legislatures between 1945 and 2006 has found, quotas, whether the commonly used voluntary quotas or the less often used compulsory party quotas or reserved-seat quotas, are among the most statistically significant predictors of increased women's representation and tend to be "contagious" within regions—once one country in a region adopts one kind of quota system, others tend to follow (Thames and Williams 2013: 126–128).

Hoogensen and Solheim note one other particularly significant feature shared by those countries with the highest proportions of women in national legislatures: a strong separation between church and state (2006: 17). According to UNIFEM's 2008–2009 report, other strategies that appear to promote women's numerical representation in national public officeholding include (1) seeking parity in executive positions in political parties (such as in the rare case of Costa Rica); (2) further developing women's parties that have existed in such countries as Iceland, Sweden, the Philippines, and now Afghanistan and that circumvent mainstream parties to bring gender equality issues to the fore; (3) reforming campaign finance to provide equitable public financing and tying it to developing or sustaining party quota systems; (4) having more women's political action committees that raise money for women candidates; and (5) combating sexism in media coverage of women candidates (2008: 23–26). Indeed, as Frank Thames and Margaret Williams find in their statistical study, there is no substitute for women's active engagement in politics as voters, office seekers, and activists to increase their political representation (2013: 131). Thus, women's unprecedented but still relatively low gains overall, as 20 percent of the world's legislatures in 2013, are in jeopardy should there be any letup in efforts on any of these scores. Moreover, the gendered divisions of power that portray—and internalize in women—the sense that women are unfit for politics, the masculinist construction of power as aggression and confrontation, and the separation between public and private that leaves women leaders (most of whom are mothers) responsible for the family on top of their governing jobs remain strong countervailing forces (UNIFEM 2008: 22). These and other barriers to women's representation are discussed more fully later.

Gains have also been seen in the percentage of women in national cabinets. According to the 2012 Women in Politics map compiled jointly by

UN Women and the IPU,[4] twenty-six countries have reached the goal of women occupying 30 percent of their ministerial positions, with Norway, Sweden, and Finland having more female ministers than male ministers and Iceland having reached female/male parity. Following the Nordic countries with the highest representations of women ministers (on average 48 percent) are the Americas, sub-Saharan Africa, Europe as a whole (ranging between 21 to 15 percent), trailed most by Pacific, Asian, and Arab states (ranging from 11 to 7 percent). Cabinet ministers are appointed and thus not subject to quota systems for parliamentarians that some countries have adopted, but Thames and Williams find that the existence of parliamentary quotas of all types does increase the likelihood that more women will gain executive power (2013: 128). In the absence of quotas but sometimes even with them, increases in this area must rely on enlightened heads of state and government backed up by gender equality advocates within and outside government. Despite some notable gains in this area (including three female US secretaries of state since the 1990s, one of whom was African American), cabinet appointments that go to women still tend to be clustered in domestic-focused social welfare agencies, while men far more routinely head foreign affairs, military defense, and finance ministries that have far more influence internationally, as evidenced by the UN Women/IPU 2012 Women in Politics map.

### UN and Other IGO Officials

As IGOs have become more significant actors in global governance, more attention has been given to women's representation in these bodies. In 1985 the UN committed itself to increasing the number of women on its professional staff to 30 percent by 1990, which it achieved in 1991. In 1998 the General Assembly further committed to the 50/50 goal of gender parity in all posts in the UN system (UN 2000: 167), but this is far from being achieved. As of 2006 women remained concentrated in the lowest levels of the UN professional staff, and it was primarily UN agencies that have social welfare portfolios and/or that have been headed by women (such as UNITAR, UNFPA, UNESCO, UNICEF, FAO, UNHCR, UNAIDS, WHO, and UNDP) that had reached the "parity zone'" of 40 percent women on professional staffs (UNIFEM 2008: 104–105). According to the UN Secretariat's Department of Social and Economic Affairs in its report "The World's Women 2010: Trends and Statistics,"[5] women still hold only about 20 percent of senior positions in the UN. However, in response to the need identified by NGOs and IGOs with gender equality portfolios for a more coordinated UN response to gender inequality in the world and in its ranks, UN Women was formed in July 2010, merging under its banner the following UN agencies: Office of the Special Adviser on Gender Issues (OSAGI), the United Nations Development Fund for Women (UNIFEM), the United Nations Division for the Advancement of Women (UNDAW), and the United Nations International Research and Training Institute for the Advancement of Women (UN-INSTRAW). With a current budget of about US$500 million, UN Women was charged in 2012 with overseeing the new UN-SWAP (or United Nations System-Wide Action Plan) for gender equality and women's empowerment to mainstream gender perspectives across all UN bodies and activities through standardizing and measuring performance indicators of progress being made (or not) on instituting gender equality in representation and as a matter of substantive concern in relation to all UN-sponsored events, agreements, and issue areas.[6]

Member state performance with respect to women's representation of their countries as permanent representatives at the UN has been particularly poor considering that in 2004, only 3 percent of those serving as such in New York were women,[7] although that percentage has been increasing since then. Many more women have served as ambassadors to other countries, practicing the art of diplomacy that is well recognized as a dimension of effective international relations. However, because women's numbers still remain comparatively small in diplomatic and foreign policy circles, women have organized lobbying and policy groups (such as the Associates of the American Foreign Service Worldwide and Women in International Security [WIIS]) that both expose and influence gender dynamics in ministries, departments, and committees dealing with foreign affairs. Of special note, however, is a recent proliferation of special rapporteurs and envoys for women's issues representing states and regional commissions and within UN agencies. For example, the Obama administration created the Office of Global Women's Issues in the US State Department in 2009 when the first US ambassador-at-large for global women's issues was appointed.

What has been most problematic until very recently was the relative lack of women in IGOs that have real enforcement power. Three women are now (2013) serving as judges on the International Court of Justice (ICJ), constituting 20 percent of this judicial branch of the UN that adjudicates state behavior; however, the more recently formed International Criminal Court (ICC), which tries individuals for crimes against humanity, including genocide and war crimes such as sexual assault, when national courts fail to do so, now has ten women, constituting 58 percent of ICC judges. What remains more disconcerting is the relative paucity of women on the governance boards of international financial institutions (IFIs), including the World Bank, the IMF, and the WTO, which have much say in the workings of the global economy. Still, it is notable that Christine LaGarde, former minister of finance for France, became the first woman director of the IMF in 2011, succeeding Dominique Strauss-Kahn, who became the subject of a sexual assault scandal involving a hotel maid that tarnished his reputation even though he was eventually acquitted. Also of note is that women make up the majority of the top leadership of the International Trade Center, a joint agency of the WTO and the UN for promoting the economic competitiveness of developing countries through small and medium-sized business exports as part of meeting the UN MDGs.

## The Global Market and NGO Actors

Many observers of the global political economy see global market actors such as TNCs as rivaling state power on the world stage, particularly since the 1990s. But just as women are heavily underrepresented in economic decision-making within state and IGO bodies, so, too, are they poorly represented in the top echelons of global business entities. As of 2013, women constituted only a little more than 4 percent of the chief executive officers of Fortune 500 and Fortune 1000 companies,[8] and in 2009 in only three European countries did women constitute at least 10 percent of board chairs for top companies (UN Secretariat Department of Social and Economic Affairs 2010: 124–125). Norway is among those countries—it mandated in 2002 that state-owned companies and in 2006 that private companies have at least 40 percent women on their boards, which increased female board membership to 42 percent by 2009 (UN Secretariat Department of Social and Economic Affairs 2010: 123–124). Although such radical action does not appear in the offing elsewhere except Spain, which introduced board quotas in 2007, for a period immediately following the 2008 financial crisis the world's corporations began to take notice of studies that linked high risk and volatile trading with men and more careful and even financial management of stocks by women. Still, women were not represented on the G20 expert committees that attempted to deal with that crisis and avoid future ones through new regulations (Marchand and Runyan 2011: 246). Nevertheless, the World Economic Forum (WEF), a Swiss-based independent forum of worldwide business, government, and civil society leaders who gather periodically to shape global economic agendas, has developed an interest in closing the global gender gap as a matter of economic efficiency and competitiveness, issuing annual reports on the Global Gender Gap Index since 2006. Its 2012 report found that despite narrowing gaps primarily in education and health and secondarily in economic participation in many countries, the least progress has been made in empowering women politically overall.[9]

At the other end of the spectrum of women's representation in global governance are transnational NGOs. Few formal statistics exist on women's participation in NGOs, but it is estimated that women constitute the majority of members of NGOs, particularly at the local, grassroots level, but also through the transnational level given that they have much more access to and voice in them when compared with their prospects for participating in formal political officeholding and decision-making. Although women constitute the majority of rank-and-file members of most NGOs, particularly those concerned with human rights, labor, social justice, and environmental causes but also more conservative issues, women exercise the most NGO leadership in women's NGOs. Although women's transnational NGOs have a long history (consider, for example, women from warring countries gathering at The Hague during World War I to form the still-extant Women's International League for Peace and Freedom), most contemporary women's transnational NGOs, sometimes referred to as transnational feminist networks (TFNs), began forming during the UN Decade for Women and proliferated particularly in the 1990s. Margaret Keck and Karen Sikkink (1998) hypothesize that such TFNs are part of a generalized rise of transnational social networks that emerged in response to their causes being blocked at the state level and the UN providing (through conferences, consultations, and so on) the political opportunity structure that enabled them to air their issues at the international level to pressure states to act. Valentine Moghadam (2005) divides up TFNs that have been most active and influential in international forums and policymaking contexts into five issue areas: women's human rights; peace, antimilitarism, and conflict resolution; ending of violence against women; reproductive health and rights; and economic critique and justice. We also add environmental protection and sustainability. TFNs also tend to interconnect these issue areas (discussed in subsequent chapters). But our main point here is that women participate most in global governance through these channels, albeit exercising little masculinist power-over but significant power-with, a feminist conception of power that stresses shared, collective, bottom-up empowerment.

## BARRIERS TO WOMEN'S PARTICIPATION
## IN GLOBAL GOVERNANCE

As can be seen from this brief review of women's contemporary numerical representation in global governance, women's recent, highly uneven, and fragile gains in this area have been largely due to the institutionalization of particular gender equality measures at international and national levels advocated primarily by TFNs and national women's movements. Such measures as gender quotas were advocated to address persistent and otherwise intractable barriers to women's political participation at almost all levels, but particularly the highest, and in all arenas of government and governance. Factors such as "the level of development within a country, the existence or absence of a tradition of political participation and labor force participation by women, the type of electoral or selection system, the characteristics of the institution, and [political] ideology all have strong and significant effects" on the level of women's representation (Thames and Williams 2013: 130). But two other conclusions have emerged repeatedly from the extensive research done on women's political participation and slow progress on this. First, women do not lack interest in or motivation for political action: studies of women's participation in grassroots organizing, community politics, election campaigns, and political organizations suggest that "women are as likely (if not more likely) to work for political causes or candidates as are men" (Lips 1991: 91). Second, a point related to the first, women's underrepresentation in political office and leadership positions is linked to gender-differentiated patterns still pervasive in today's world. Gender socialization, situational constraints, structural obstacles, and institutional impediments interact in favoring men and discriminating against women as formal political actors (Randall 1987: 83–94; Henderson and Jeydel 2010: 12–22).

*Gender Socialization*

Early studies tended to focus on the effects of sex-role stereotyping—that is, on the enduring consequences of childhood socialization of girls and boys into mutually exclusive gender roles. Presumably, socialization into appropriate "feminine" behavior makes women less likely than men to pursue traditionally defined political activities. For example, feminine identity formation is inextricable from cultural expectations that motherhood is the primary role of women, that women's domestic role is antithetical to public-sphere activities, and that traits associated with political efficacy (ambition, aggression, competitiveness, authority) are distinctly unfeminine. To the extent that women internalize these stereotypical norms, then, they are less likely to perceive themselves as political actors or aspire to public office.

As a corollary, socialization into appropriate "masculine" behavior makes men more likely than women to identify with political activities. Just as important, gender stereotypes, because they are held by men and women, create a climate that encourages male participation while discouraging female participation in politics. Thus, individual women who seek leadership positions must struggle not only with their own internalized stereotypes but also with the fact that gender stereotyping in general fuels resistance to women as political actors. Finally, for women who do achieve positions of power, expectations of appropriately "feminine" behavior are often in conflict with qualities required for successful leadership. In short, gender stereotypes suggest that appropriately feminine women (passive, dependent, domestic, engaged in meeting private, familial needs) are by definition inappropriate political agents (active, autonomous, public-oriented, engaged in meeting collective, not personal needs).

This picture is further complicated by men's and women's positions in relation to race/ethnicity, religion, sexual orientation, ability, age, and so on. Masculinities and femininities vary along these dimensions, and not all men are socialized to desire or expect political participation or leadership. These variations matter significantly in terms of who actually enters and/or succeeds in politics. But despite hierarchies among men, the consistency of gender stereotypes is so strong that within particular groups more men than women will be associated with public-sphere activities, political participation, and corporate power.

## Situational Constraints

Gender socialization produces different male and female orientations toward political participation. Also, gender stereotyping produces behavioral patterns that result in different concrete living situations for women and men that also constrain women's participation. Hence, we are better able to explain gendered political participation if we look at the *interaction* of stereotypes (for example, how women are assigned domestic and mothering responsibilities) and gender-differentiated living situations (for example, how the gendered division of labor limits women's involvement in traditional or formal politics). In masculinist societies, it is women who confront the time and energy demands of having primary responsibility for family and home care—what UN Women (2011) now refers to as "time poverty." Family care includes child-rearing and/or care of the elderly or infirm as well as the emotional maintenance work required to sustain intimate and extended family relationships—responsibilities that disproportionally fall on women regardless of their sexuality or the family form in which they live. Worldwide, home care involves ensuring that food is secured and prepared for all and that the household is physically maintained. For millions of women, the latter entails arduous efforts to secure water and fuel. For most women, it means responsibility for cleaning, laundry, upkeep, and adequate performance of household functions. Even for affluent women, it means a great deal of shopping, scheduling, and transporting family members. Not surprisingly, because these demands are placed on women more than men, women are constrained in terms of how much time and energy they have for political participation, especially the pursuit of political office. When this reproductive work is coupled with productive work for an income that most women in most of the world perform, whether in formal or informal sectors, women's energy and time are further constrained. It is not simply the double workload of reproductive and productive labor that inhibits women's participation in politics; it is also women's lack of control over when they will be available and whether (or how) family obligations will interfere with political pursuits. These problems persist once women hold political office because "national capitals are often quite far away from people's homes, the hours are unorthodox, and there are often no on-site daycare options" (Henderson and Jeydel 2010: 21).

Men are typically not forced to make these choices because their political activities are considered separate from their domestic relations. Women, in contrast, are so closely identified with the domestic sphere that when they take on political activities, this is considered in combination with, not separable from, their role in the family. It is also important to note that globalization or global economic restructuring (see Chapter 5) for the most part exacerbates this gender imbalance. Men increasingly confront un- and underemployment. But this change in their workday still rarely translates into their making greater contributions to family and home care. At the same time, withdrawal of social and welfare services by the state disproportionally hurts women, who (in their role of family and home caretakers) are assigned responsibility for "taking up the slack."

Decreased public spending on education, health, and food subsidies means that increased costs must be borne by women, who work longer hours, look for less expensive food, spend more resources on basic health care, make difficult choices about which children will get an education and which will work to sustain the family economy, and face lower wages or fewer job opportunities as the wages in female-dominated industries decline or as the returns to agricultural labor are not sustained (Chowdhury and Nelson et al. 1994: 6).

Hence, insofar as political participation requires time, resources, and control over them, capitalist and masculinist conditions make women's participation exceedingly difficult. For women of nondominant race/ethnicity and of subordinate classes, the obstacles are multiplied.

## Structural Obstacles

Clearly, stereotypes and situational constraints shape the gender of political activism, but the recurring differences in women's and men's participation must also be examined in relation to large-scale, interacting, and enduring social structures. Here we refer broadly to sets of power relations and/or social-cultural institutions that determine the boundaries of individual behavior. Understanding why so few women hold political power requires understanding how social structures and their interaction make it much more difficult for most women (than for most men) to seek and secure political office. Although primary gender socialization occurs in childhood, the hierarchical dichotomy of masculine-feminine is enforced throughout our lives. The gender dimensions of multiple social structures interact and in effect "discipline" individual behavior to conform to stereotypes.

For example, traditional religious belief systems and institutions play an important role in perpetuating images of women that deny them leadership positions. All too frequently, women are portrayed as either the source of evil (the uncontrollably sexual whore) or the model of saintliness (the self-sacrificing virgin). Neither is an appropriate identity for political leadership. In addition, the vast majority of religious institutions themselves exclude women from top leadership roles. No matter how this exclusionary practice is legitimized, it in fact sends a clear and unequivocal message that reinforces gender stereotypes: that women are not equal to men and that they cannot be trusted with or lack the qualifications for positions of authority and power.

Religious beliefs interact with and may reinforce other cultural sources of gender stereotyping. This is generally the case in regard to identifying the home/family as woman's sphere and the public/politics as man's sphere. It can also be quite explicit, as in the seclusion of women (*purdah*) practiced in many Islamic countries or in Western ones where neoconservative policies (sometimes inspired by Christian fundamentalism) seek to return women to the home and to reconstructed patriarchal and heteronormative families. The point is that the structural separation of public and private has gendered consequences. Religious, educational, and judicial institutions tend to reproduce the ideological—and gendered—division of public and private. And both informal and formal public-private separations affect women's political participation negatively by identifying women exclusively with the private sphere.

Thus, our expectations of different behaviors for men (appropriate for politics) and for women (inappropriate for politics) make it difficult, first, for women to see themselves comfortably in conventionally defined political roles and, second, for men and women generally to see and accept women as political agents. Attitudinal changes are occurring, however, with younger generations showing more acceptance of women in politics, and women within younger generations the most likely to advocate for women's increased representation (Henderson and Jeydel 2010: 21). But to the extent that the stereotype of "a woman's place is in the home" (or in the bedroom) is held, women will be seen as "out of place" in political office.

The horizontal and vertical segregation of both men and women in the workforce affects women's access to political power. Horizontally, women are concentrated in fewer occupations than men and in jobs where women are the majority of workers—clerical work, elementary teaching, domestic maintenance, daycare, nursing, waitressing. Moreover, these are not occupations from which political candidates are traditionally recruited. In general, the work women do for pay is an extension of the feminine role assigned to women (and feminized others) and replicates work that women, according to both gender and heterosexual norms, are expected to do as mothers and wives: caring for dependents, serving the needs of others, providing social and physical necessities, and being docile, flexible, emotionally supportive, and sexually attractive (Macdonald and Sirianni 1996). Not only are women (and feminized others) clustered in certain jobs, but they are also expected to be "feminine" in whatever job they hold.

The workplace is also segregated vertically, with women concentrated in pink-collar jobs (men in blue-collar ones), in domestic services (men in protective services), and in light industry (men in heavy industry). Vertical gender segregation (the higher, the fewer) occurs both within and across industries: Women generally are concentrated in part-time, temporary, nonorganized, lower-status, lower-paying, and less powerful positions (Henderson and Jeydel 2010: 106). As a result, women earn less money, have less secure jobs, and rarely climb into powerful executive ranks. Race, ethnicity, and class discrimination interact with gender discrimination to exacerbate the self-perpetuating cycle of elite males holding onto power at the expense of all other groups.

Gendered divisions of labor affect women's political participation in multiple ways. Most obviously, women's structural disadvantage in the labor market translates into their having fewer resources, less status, and less experience wielding power when competing with men for political office. And when it comes to recruiting and promoting people for political office, educational and occupational structures interact to exacerbate women's disadvantage. Women receive not only a different education from what men get but also, until very recently, a good deal less education than men. Because education is so closely related to occupational opportunities, lack of educational training fuels the gender segregation of the workforce and its negative consequences for women. Moreover, certain professions have historically been associated with or appear particularly compatible with achieving and maintaining political power: law, military, career civil service, big business. It remains the case that women are underrepresented in most of these occupational areas and are especially few in number at the top levels from which political leaders are often recruited.

Other obstacles to women's political participation are direct and indirect legal barriers. It is only in the past century that most women secured the rights to vote and to hold political office, which are prerequisites to seeking formal power. Women in some of the Arab world as well as some women (and men) elsewhere continue to be denied these rights, either due to their gender, race or ethnicity, or sexuality. Military experience has also been a traditional path to power not only in authoritarian states but also in democracies such as the United States. To the degree that women remain small percentages of state militaries, are legally prevented from holding combat roles, and/or are excluded from being in such militaries because of their sexuality or ethnicity, this avenue is effectively blocked. Moreover, as long as military experience is perceived as a requisite criterion of manliness for high political office, women may be pressured to "out-macho" their male counterparts and sublimate any "feminine" concerns that they might bring to high office.

For women who do gain power as the result of family connections and, specifically, the death of a father or husband who is in office or in the midst or wake of a conflict situation where symbols of unity, compromise, or conciliation are sought, being a woman and expressing traditional femininity can be an advantage. But when women act "like women," even though they are at the helm of national governments, the traditional picture of gender is not disturbed. Similarly, when women assume national leadership as a result of their success in grassroots activism, their association with "soft issues" (the environment, peace, feminism) can reinforce the traditional disassociation of women with "hard issues" (national security, economic competition) and the masculine traits assumed necessary for dealing with them (fearlessness, calculative reason). It is not surprising, then, that women who achieve national-level leadership positions "on their own" are often identified as especially masculine, but this also brands them as "deviant or abnormal" (Henderson and Jeydel 2010: 20).

The overall picture remains one of continued gender dichotomies creating no-win situations: Women succeed through their identification as "traditional" (feminine) women facilitating male-defined projects, as trivialized "soft leaders," or as perversely manlike leaders by playing down any association with feminine "weakness." As long as female political actors are perceived either as traditional (or "hypervisible") women or "invisible women" (because they are acting "like men"), hierarchical gender expectations are not really disrupted. Paradoxically, even when women wield the highest state power, by continuing to behave in gender-stereotypical ways, they often reinforce, rather than challenge, the politics of gender. Even though the power of gender is at work here (shaping pathways to and the exercise of power), it remains "invisible" to observers of world politics. In other words, by appearing as traditional women or honorary men, and often rejecting any identification with feminism or the history of the feminist struggles that often paved the way for them (Hawkesworth 2012: 204), female politicians do not challenge the categorical distinction between femininity and masculinity and do not politicize this gender dichotomy. Their conformity to traditional gender stereotypes in fact works to reproduce them.

The pervasive bias of androcentrism in political science and international relations operates to produce this no-win situation. One effect of this bias is the assumption that political actors are men. Another is the narrow definition of politics as exclusively public-sphere or governmental activities. Yet a third effect is the narrow definition of power as the capacity to enforce one's will (power-over in contrast to an alternative feminist conceptualization of power, namely, empowerment or power-to).

These effects are not simply an academic concern, because the definitions they take for granted are promoted outside of academic disciplines as well. Consider the focus of television news on "spectacular" (rather than everyday) events: wars, weapons, violence, crises, men as leaders/legislators/protectors, and women as dependents/victims. The leaders we see tend to be heads of government of countries that are geopolitically powerful or significant at the level of foreign policy. Otherwise, international news is almost exclusively viewed through the lens of various crises: seemingly hopeless extremities of governmental, military, economic, refugee, population, health, food, water, fuel, and/or ecological breakdown, all seemingly emanating from the global South. Such images sustain gender, race, class, and nationality stereotypes, denying political agency to women and people of the global South and the roles of men and the global North in precipitating such crises.

In these accounts, gender operates but remains invisible in various ways. Attention to wars and spectacles is at the expense of everyday maintenance activities that in fact are a precondition of the world's continuing to function. The latter are largely ignored, yet they are the activities occupying women's—indeed most people's—lives. To the extent that women appear in depictions of politics, they tend to be acting "like men" (paradigmatically Margaret Thatcher) or functioning in supporting roles to the main/male actors (for instance, as wives, secretaries). Although there are increasing exceptions to this among women leaders who identify with feminist principles and thus see a greater repertoire for women's behavior and action in politics, such as Michelle Bachelet, who was an active supporter of women's rights when she was president of Chile and who just stepped down as the first head of UN Women, gender conformity in positions of power remains the rule. In depictions of crises, women (or what Cynthia Enloe [1990] terms "womenandchildren") remain the ever-present victims in need of protection by men or through male-defined programs. Not inconsistent with the crisis picture, women occasionally appear as saints and crusaders (Mother Theresa, Princess Diana, Angelina Jolie), whose model of sacrifice and commitment spurs men on to greater feats of protection (or competitive performance), thereby strengthening male roles.

Again, not only are women and their activities depicted as secondary to (or merely in support of) men's public-sphere pursuits, but also the way in which women make an appearance tends to reinforce, rather than challenge, conventional gender stereotypes. From manner of dress and demeanor to lifestyle and sexual orientation, we rarely observe any blurring of rigid gender boundaries in the mainstream media. Left in place are androcentric accounts that obscure women as powerful actors and leaders across a spectrum of political activities, that deny the politics and societal importance of ostensibly private-sphere activities, and that mystify the role of masculinism (ideologically and structurally) in the continued subordination of women and perpetuation of multiple social hierarchies. In short, the gender dynamics of politics—especially international politics—remain in place yet invisible as long as women "appear" only when they adopt masculine principles or epitomize feminine ones.

### Institutional Impediments

From another angle of vision, political institutions themselves can be seen to impede women's participation. Over two decades ago, Vicky Randall identified three institutional barriers to political recruitment and promotion that still hold true today (1987: 92–94). First, at each level, political advancement requires "appropriate" political, leadership, educational, and/or occupational experience: As already noted, these criteria discriminate against women who are structurally likely to have different and fewer resources and/or who start later in their pursuit of office. They also ensure that women's campaigns are typically far less financed than men's (Henderson and Jeydel 2010: 13).

Second, the institutions associated with politics and power and the norms and practices of these institutions are those of "a man's world." Exclusively male until recently and still dominated by men, they are hegemonically masculinist in the following senses: behavior traits deemed suitable, sometimes essential, for political success are stereotypically masculine (ambition, leadership, rationality, competitiveness, authority, toughness); meeting times and locations as well as socializing (networking) activities are, in practice, convenient for men's (not women's) schedules and geographical mobility; and issues of central importance are not those most immediately relevant to most women's lives ("women's issues" have been treated as peripheral to conventional politics until very recently) (Henderson and Jeydel 2010: 17, 20–21).

Third, there is outright prejudice and discrimination against women. Forms of discrimination in the workplace vary, but the presence of gender hierarchy and sexism (complicated further by racism and/or heterosexism for women in racial and sexual minorities) creates a less favorable environment for women, who must then struggle harder than their male counterparts to be successful. As long as the workplace and political office are identified as "male terrain," women constantly confront and must deal with resentment of their unwanted presence. Women are most frequently reminded of their outsider status when they are viewed not as colleagues but through their gender and sexuality. Subtle and not-so-subtle references to women and sexuality produce an atmosphere of male dominance in which women must either become "like men" or become invisible. These are not trivial aspects of power. The pervasiveness of masculinist assumptions, of androcentric worldviews, and of sexist and heterosexist humor poses formidable obstacles. Because we are so saturated with gendered assumptions, these obstacles typically go unrecognized or are not taken seriously as the pillars holding up male privilege and power—at the expense of women's participation.

Such obstacles continue when women do achieve high political office. Study after study has found that women across polities have proven to be just as effective as men as legislators and leaders, and are, in fact, more effective, particularly when it comes to working across parties and putting social welfare generally and gender equality measures more specifically on the legislative and policy agenda. However, their often-greater efforts not only to become state actors but also to serve constituencies-at-large as well as to "substantively" represent women through greater attention to so-called women's or gender issues are met with resistance at every stage. Androcentric norms and outright hostility to women as undeserving political interlopers translate into lack of party and male counterpart support for women's legislative proposals, trivialization of any gender-based reforms, and paternalistic or sexualized treatment of women officeholders by their male counterparts (Hawkesworth 2012: 206–214).

In sum, long-entrenched gender stereotypes and the interaction of situational constraints; domestic responsibilities; religious, educational, economic, legal, and military structures; and institutional impediments have so discriminated against women's political participation and, especially, their access to and room to maneuver in high political office and global power structures that feminists have long concluded that major policy interventions must be launched even to hope to level the playing field.

## INSTITUTIONALIZING
## GLOBAL GENDER EQUALITY

As indicated earlier, the 1995 BPA arising out of the UN Fourth World Conference on Women, which was unanimously supported by UN member states, provided a major impetus for the widespread adoption of a range of gender equality policies and measures at national and international levels. These include not only gender quotas, but also the institution of women's policy agencies, the practice of gender mainstreaming, the inclusion of women's empowerment in the MDGs, and the creation of a host of global measurement systems to track gender (in)equality and rank states on the basis of them. Prior to these instruments, the Convention on the Elimination of All Forms of Discrimination Against Women was adopted. It is binding on the vast majority of states that have ratified it (180 as of 2010, with the still notable exception of the United States). CEDAW's objective is, among other things, to ensure that gender equality, as defined by CEDAW, is enshrined in and enforced through state constitutions and laws to achieve equality outcomes. Far fewer countries have signed onto the CEDAW Optional Protocol that makes them liable for complaints made to the CEDAW committee (of which there have so far been very few formal ones), and many countries ratified CEDAW with reservations that reduce its intent and enforceability (UNIFEM 2008: 74–75). However, CEDAW has also been the basis of an international women's human rights movement that has added to the definition of human rights certain previously unrecognized rights, such as reproductive rights, sexual rights, and rights to be free from domestic and sexual violence. Although such women's human rights are unevenly accepted by states, they are reflected in the BPA as a norm-setting document.

These are significant developments that bear testimony to the success of the power-with strategies of national women's movements and TFNs working in concert with UN women's agencies to hold the international community accountable for gender equality. However, as we address in our review of these measures, institutionalization carries not only rewards but also risks in terms of uneven implementation, co-optation, and deepening divisions among women. It can also maintain the power of gender by institutionalizing gender difference while depoliticizing it, shifting attention away from a broader feminist critique of gendered power relations that uphold world-politics-as-usual in favor of simply increasing women's (and only certain women's) participation in those politics.

*Gender Quotas*

A quota is typically seen as an affirmative action measure designed to redress to some degree (ranging from setting minimum numbers or thresholds to creating representative balance) the political underrepresentation of a particular group, which can include women, ethnic minorities, indigenous peoples, and even geographical groups. Drude Dahlerup distinguishes among three major types of quota systems currently in use that target an increase in women's political participation: quotas enlarging the candidate pool that are usually determined voluntarily by political parties; candidate quotas for party lists, which may be voluntary party quotas or legal or constitutional quotas mandating that all parties comply; and reserved-seat quotas that require by law, the constitution, or ruler edict that a certain number of seats must be occupied by the target group. There are also so-called "soft" quotas that involve recommended targets set by political parties and governments (2006b: 19–21). Party quotas were first adopted in the Nordic countries of Western Europe by leftist political parties in the late 1970s and early 1980s, but only after women had secured between 20 to 30 percent of parliamentary seats, in part due to robust feminist movements, political cultures oriented to social welfare values, and PR systems. These party quota systems have remained voluntary and representative of what is called an "incrementalist" approach to women's empowerment (Friedenwall, Dahlerup, and Skjeie 2006: 49–50). Even though Nordic countries have not used legal or constitutional quotas to reach consistently high numbers of women in political office, the Scandinavian case has been cited as an example of what can be achieved with some form of quota system, especially a more "fast-track" one that is legally or constitutionally mandated. This is particularly the case in those countries where women's share of political power has been persistently low and incrementalist change is unlikely to alter that anytime soon.

Feminists have long made the argument that getting more women into political office is not only a matter of fairness but also crucial for having any true democracy. The quota argument gained significant traction in the 1990s when a range of countries were undergoing transitions to some form of democracy and entering into the rising global capitalist economy. This was the same period in which UN agencies and IFIs began to take up the argument that gender equality was necessary as part of democratization and of a modern market economy and good governance. The conflation by IGO actors of gender equality with democratization and mature market-based economies accelerated the top-down institution of legal or constitutional gender quota systems, particularly in the South. The assumption was that such commitments to gender equality would help to legitimize the countries that adopted them as modern, democratic, and market-oriented (Matland 2006: 277; Squires 2007: 29). At the same time, most older democratic nations have tended to resist legal quotas on the assumption that they have already achieved democracy, regardless of the current statistics on women's representation.

Thus, of the ninety or so countries with some kind of party or legal gender quota system as of 2006, most of the forty with legal quotas (heavily concentrated in Latin America and sub-Saharan Africa but also including countries such as Afghanistan, Iraq, and Nepal) are not part of the Organization for Economic Cooperation and Development (OECD), to which mostly Western democracies belong. Moreover, most legal quotas (including reserved-seat systems that can be found in parts of the Middle East, Africa, and Asia) were adopted after the Beijing women's conference in 1995 or in the wake of the institution of MDGs in 2000. In contrast, voluntary party quotas are more typical in OECD countries with parliamentary systems that include social democratic or other left-leaning parties. The United States has remained hostile to quotas (with the exception of their use by the Democratic Party in the early 1970s), although the two major political parties are mindful of the need for some women's (and racial minority) representation and thus exercise informal, or soft, quotas (Squires 2007: 26–28). Democratizing eastern and central European countries have been more resistant to gender quotas, which are seen as smacking of old forms of central control (Dahlerup 2006a: 197–198), despite the postcommunist downward plunge in women's relatively high formal political representation (albeit not in the most powerful echelons) during the communist period. Of notable exception, however, are the states that emerged from the violent breakup of the former Yugoslavia, with a number of them adopting gender quotas in recent years.

Tunisia is also among the countries that have recently adopted mandatory electoral list quotas for women, requiring parity in the numbers of women and men on those lists. Thus, the Arab Spring that cut across wide swaths of the Middle East and Northern Africa and most notably brought down dictators in Tunisia, Yemen, and Egypt in 2011 through massive popular protest by men and women (as opposed to armed conflict as in Libya the same year) is another factor in the increase of gender quotas, although Tunisia is alone in adopting them so far. Such recent cases arising from political upheaval, the regional diffusion (or "contagion") effect of quotas, and the documented success of quotas for fast-tracking women into high office have brought the number of countries adopting some form of gender quota system to 111 as of 2011 (Hawkesworth 2012: 43).

## Women's Policy Agencies

It was following the UN First World Conference on Women, held in Mexico City in 1975, which called for the adoption of state machineries to advance the status of women, that the first women's policy agencies were instituted. Since that time, as a result of continued TFN lobbying using CEDAW and UN women's conference documents as leverage coupled with pressure from UN women's agencies, 165 countries had created some form of national women's policy agency by 2004 (Squires 2007: 33). These range from "stand-alone government ministries" and "offices within the head of state's department" to "quasi-autonomous state agencies such as national commissions or divisions for gender equality within ministries for labour, social welfare or national development, parliamentary commissions and delegations" (Squires 2007: 34). Women's policy and gender equality units have also been formed within regional and supranational entities, such as the EU and its constituent executive, legislative, and judicial bodies. Although these units vary considerably in terms of resources and functions (ranging from policy formation or input to mere reporting) and thus influence, they have been productive of what is termed "state feminism," with insider "femocrats" working to advance women's representation and issues not only in elective arenas, but also in bureaucratic ones (Squires 2007: 33).

In the midst of the initially laudable and rapid institutionalization of women's policy agencies, feminist "outsiders" have questioned to whom femocrats are really accountable (typically governments rather than women's movements), how they can effectively represent diverse women (as they are largely elite women), and what women's issues they tend to advocate (typically those that are digestible by a government in power, leaving more radical demands by the wayside) (Squires 2007: 119). At the same time, economic restructuring pressures, particularly during the last decade, have led to some defunding and privatization of these entities, which are then essentially reduced to NGOs without state support (Hawkesworth 2012: 227). Moreover, since the mid-1990s, those agencies that remain have been charged with the advocacy of gender mainstreaming, which shifts attention away from women, women's movements, and women's issues. Instead, the focus is on what is seen as a more expert-based, bureaucratic exercise that has been adopted, like gender quotas and women's policy agencies, less because of any commitment to gender equality and more because of states' desires to appear more modern and market-oriented.

## Gender Mainstreaming

Although the BPA calls upon governments to engage in gender mainstreaming, it is largely a creation of IGOs. Conceptually developed by the World Bank and the UNDP in the early 1990s, gender mainstreaming has been globalized through its adoption by the UN, the OECD, Northern development agencies (which also disseminate it to the South), and, especially, the EU since 1995 (Squires 2007: 41–42). Somewhat differing UN and EU definitions of gender mainstreaming share the following in common: the goal of integrating the experiences, needs, and concerns of both women and men into the design, planning, implementation, monitoring, and evaluation of all policies (economic, political, and social) with the aim of achieving gender equality (Squires 2007: 39–40).

At first blush, gender mainstreaming constitutes a significant improvement in how to bring about gender equality in that it attempts to decenter the male norm upon which policymaking has rested and within which women have to fit. Moreover, it represents a more thoroughgoing application of gender equality norms into all spheres of policymaking and makes all government agencies accountable for this application. Gender mainstreaming need not await parity in women's political representation that is still a long way off, nor is it the sole responsibility of typically under-resourced and more lowly women's policy agencies. Plus, its focus on gender moves away from constructing "women" as the problem toward tackling the problems that have arisen as a result of gender inequalities, such as poverty and violence. Thus, TFNs and femocrats in state and UN agencies have supported it.

However, studies have found that the rapid adoption of gender mainstreaming by states and IGOs appears to be yet another attempt to conform to "favoured international norms such as modernization and good governance" rather than a desire for "gender justice" (Squires 2007: 48). As a result, not only is it quite unevenly enforced where it has been adopted, but also it is most often engaged in through an "expert-bureaucratic model" rather than a "participative-democratic model," thereby cutting out consultations with and accountability to social movements and relying on femocrats (Squires 2007: 41). It has also had the effect of pulling back commitments to women's policy agencies on the assumption they are less needed under this diffused approach and reducing a transformational political struggle for gender equality to a management technique whereby gender audits and assessments are performed through largely quantitative approaches that are seen to adhere to the social science ideals of objective truth and rationality (which are also most associated with masculinity and masculinist commitments to positivism) (Squires 2007: 143). Those social movements and NGOs that do not present their claims through such language and filters are dismissed. This has spawned cadres of NGO gender experts, typically at the transnational level, who can speak in the language of gender mainstreaming bureaucracies at the cost of being further separated from the struggles of the movements they claim to represent (Squires 2007: 145–154).

*Gender Equality Indices*

There has been a veritable explosion in the creation of, tracking of, and reporting on gender equality indices. Beginning in 1995, the annual UNDP's *Human Development Report* began issuing Gender-Related Development Index (GDI) and Gender Empowerment Measure (GEM) statistics by country. The GDI was an adjustment of how countries rank on the Human Development Index based on gender differentials in life expectancy, adult literacy, and primary, secondary, and tertiary education. GEM measured opportunities by gender based on relative numbers of women in parliament, official and managerial positions, and professional and technical work, as well as women's earned income relative to men's. But amid criticisms of these tools for insufficiently capturing gender differences in quality of life and improvements in this in low-income countries, in 2010 the UNDP introduced the Gender Inequality Index (GII), which determines how much is lost in terms of achieving full labor force, education, and political participation as well as reducing teenage fertility and maternal mortality as a result of gender inequality in countries and regions. The aforementioned WEF Global Gender Gap Index measures gaps between women and men in terms of health, education, and economic and political participation gleaned from UN statistics, while the World Bank and a number of other UN agencies use similar, other, or additional indices to track gender (in)equality in relation to a range of issue areas. What emerges from the plethora of these statistical measurements and the annual reports that are spawned by them is some commonality in results: OECD countries, particularly Nordic ones, rank the highest in gender equality and gain the most from this economically and socially, and Arab states rank the lowest and lose the most from this. As indicated earlier, UN Women is also now charged with introducing and monitoring more standard indices across the UN system to track gender (in)equality and mainstream gender equality in all UN activities.

On the one hand, the gathering of such data on the relative "female friendliness" of states and the seriousness with which it is now taken by forming these global indices are welcome. On the other hand, such measurements are representative of the kind of quantitative policy world to which gender equality politics has been reduced. Similarly, even though these indices have no doubt facilitated the contagion of states institutionalizing gender quotas, women's agencies, and gender mainstreaming, they also tend to set up gender equality as a feature of modern progress and development rather than as a matter of gender justice. Finally, although such statistical rankings are helpful to social movement and NGO actors seeking leverage to advance gender equality, they can also be used by powerful states and IFIs to punish less powerful states, through, for example, decreased aid or trade on the basis of their gender equality failings. At the same time, more powerful Western states that underperform on gender measures relative to expectations and resources (like the United States, which keeps falling relative to other OECD states and even a number of global South states on some indices) are not subject to such "discipline." These latter two concerns also relate to the MDGs that constitute "the new aid agenda" (Antrobus 2006: 39).

## Millennium Development Goals

The UN General Assembly approved the UN Millennium Declaration in 2000, which sets out the following eight MDGs as the basis of the international development agenda ideally to be achieved for the most part by 2015:

1. Eradicate extreme poverty and hunger.
2. Achieve universal primary education.
3. Promote gender equality and empower women.
4. Reduce child mortality.
5. Improve maternal health.
6. Combat HIV/AIDS, malaria, and other diseases.
7. Ensure environmental sustainability.
8. Create a global partnership for development
   (UNIFEM 2008: 118).

So central are these seen to women's well-being that they are now either the centerpiece of or of significance in almost all UN reports, particularly those of UN Women.

Progress on these goals is measured and monitored by the UN (based on statistics provided by states) in relation to particular quantitative targets set over time within each of the goals, such as cutting in half by 2015 the proportion of people with incomes of less than $1.25 per day and suffering from hunger, as well as the more recent target of achieving full employment in decent work for all people by that date to reach Goal 1 (UNIFEM 2008: 118). Not all data so far are sex-disaggregated, so the "good news" that the overarching target of Goal 1, to halve those in extreme poverty, was met in 2010, was met five years ahead of schedule, does not tell us how many women were lifted above $1.25 per day, only that this was due largely to advances in China and India. The "bad news," according to UN Women, is that women's unemployment rose dramatically between 2007 and 2010 in the wake of the 2008 economic crisis, and given that women are the majority of those in vulnerable work, women still are disproportionally the poorest of the poor, and food insecurity is rising, making for more hungry people in the world (UN Women 2011: 106). Other data on MDG goals are discussed in later chapters, but here we turn to Goal 3 as it is most focused on the issue of women's political representation.

Goal 3 is the one goal that specifically targets women in general (not just mothers as in the case of maternal health) and promotes gender equality even though all the other goals, as we can see from the preceding discussion, relate to the multiple conditions that (dis)empower women. This MDG uses such indicators as women's educational attainment relative to men's as well as women's share of wage labor (in nonagricultural work) and women's representation in national parliaments. Even though gender parity in primary education has been achieved ahead of schedule in most regions and the gender gap in secondary education is closing in much of the world, poor girls have far less access than wealthier ones (UN Women 2011: 108), a pattern that continues with respect to higher education. The attainment of these educational targets in many cases does not tell us anything about the quality of education enjoyed (or not enjoyed) by women relative to men, nor do they address fields of study pursued (or tracked into) that can also divide women from men and account for continuing occupational segregation and higher rates of women's unemployment. Women's wage work has only increased by 5 percent since 1990, and women constitute 53 percent of those in vulnerable employment globally and 80 percent of vulnerable workers in South Asia and sub-Saharan Africa (UN Women 2011: 108). Meanwhile, despite the quota contagion, women's representation in parliaments worldwide has not gotten over 20 percent, while many women have little decision-making power within their own homes, where they remain subject to high levels of domestic violence (UN Women 2011: 108).

Although the MDGs as quantitative indicators are reductionist tools that fail to capture the richness and complexity of social reality, they do represent a seeming shift in global priorities. As we discuss in Chapter 5, the dominant approach to development since World War II and throughout most of the twentieth century focused on economic development to the exclusion of social or human development. Large-scale, capital-intensive, and high-technology projects that privileged male actors, from decision-makers to workers, were systematically promoted and funded by the World Bank to "modernize" (read: Westernize) the infrastructure and economies of the so-called developing countries. Gross domestic product (GDP)—a measurement of the output of domestic goods and services by a nation—does not measure human well-being and in fact externalizes (or does not take into account) the costs of human misery and environmental destruction, yet it became the central indicator of "growth," and economic growth, in the dominant model, was to be pursued at any human and environmental cost.

Beginning in the 1970s, feminists focusing on development began pointing out that women were being left out of and even harmed by these modernizing ventures, leading to, first, a women in development (WID) model that was unevenly taken up by some Northern development aid agencies to "integrate" women into development. The insufficiencies of this model, which saw women integrated only at the margins of economic development through separate, small-scale, "income-generating projects" and the like, gave way to a gender and development (GAD) approach in the 1980s. GAD not only focused on attending to gender relations that needed to be shifted for women to have a say in concert with men on what forms of development would most benefit them and their communities, but it also focused attention more generally on development "with a human face." Various economic shocks occurred from the 1970s through 1990s that particularly hit the global South, ranging from the debt crisis and IMF-imposed structural adjustment programs (SAPs) to the "transition" to liberal capitalist democracy undergone primarily by Eastern bloc and Latin American countries (a transition often referred to then as going through "shock therapy"). At the same time, the rise of globalization was shifting production from North to South in search of cheap labor and reducing social welfare commitments by states. In the process, human immiseration was becoming increasingly evident and tied in with the very economic development policies of the World Bank and the IMF. By the mid-1990s, the World Bank had undergone an "ideological shift" that "entailed the increased acceptance of policy intervention to temper market excesses and heightened emphasis on participation, empowerment, and poverty alleviation" (Squires 2007: 45). Not coincidentally, this occurred at the same time as the Beijing women's conference, which called for similar priorities in the BPA arising from it. This brief history and the BPA are also the backdrop for the MDGs, but as Peggy Antrobus argues, the BPA is much more comprehensive than the MDGs, has much more legitimacy among the women's movements that worked on it, is far more political than "technical," and is less captured by the "neoliberalism, religious fundamentalism, and male backlash" that served to limit what the MDGs entail and what they measured when they were generated in 2000 (2006: 48–49). Although Antrobus recognizes the MDGs are here to stay and can still be used as leverage, she recommends that "when others talk MDG, we must think BPA" (2006: 48–49).

It is particularly essential to think BPA because the MDGs imagine development, albeit far better conceived than in the recent past, as separate from security issues, whereas the BPA includes the effects of armed conflict on women and human development. As we discuss in the next chapter, the very resources needed to reach the remaining and relatively modest MDG goals even by the end of this century (as all concede the 2015 date is utopian for most goals) are steadily eaten up by military expenditures, and militarized violence continues to produce human degradation and environmental destruction. Human development, despite all the rhetorical and statistical attention given to it at the international level, continues to be feminized and deprioritized as "low" or "soft" politics in relation to the masculinized "high" and "hard" politics of state security. At the same time, masculinist neoliberal constructions of and commitments to the global capitalist economy have loosened little in the wake of the MDGs, which do not call for a transformation of global economic structures controlled primarily by the North, particularly the West. Under such circumstances, MDGs, which ideally are goals that all countries should work to achieve through cooperation and a massive redistribution of resources not just within but also across countries, can also be used as "conditionalities" to withhold the distribution of aid more in the interests of power politics than of social justice. Relatedly, as we discuss next, gender equality itself can be used as a pawn of power politics, sustaining both neoliberalism (covered in the next section) and neocolonialism or (neo)imperialism (covered in the next chapter).

## NEOLIBERAL GOVERNMENTALITY AND THE NEW GLOBAL POLITICS OF GENDER EQUALITY

As indicated by the preceding analysis, the recent gains made in women's representation in global governance and global governance attention to gender equality have been cause for some celebration but also significant suspicion among feminists. Postcolonial feminists in particular have pointed to these advances as the "neoliberal governmentalization" of gender equality. This refers not just to the co-optation (and attendant depoliticization) of gender equality by global governance bodies, but, more significantly, also to the way in which gender equality (and more generally women's human rights) has been made coterminous with neoliberalism. In this view, it is no accident that gender equality becomes (at least a rhetorical) priority in global governance precisely at the time that neoliberal ideology is globalized.

This critique stems from another conceptualization of power put forth by Michel Foucault (1991), who coined the term "governmentality" to refer to how individuals and populations "could now be controlled, administrated, empowered, or disciplined through certain governmental techniques" (Woehl 2008: 69). Governmentality pertains not only to state and suprastate bureaucratic apparatuses and policies but also to civil society institutions (including NGOs) that enable governing on the basis of rational, scientific, and statistical calculations and produce human subjectivities that are amenable to being "managed" or "regulated" and even participate in self-management or self-regulation in conformance with rationalized approaches to "problem-solving," now associated with "good governance" (Woehl 2008: 65–66). Power in this sense is more diffuse and both repressive and enabling, but it rests upon "hegemony," or the inculcation of "the right order" that brooks no deviation. Neoliberal governmentality refers to the ascendance of the global capitalist economy and "economic rationality" as "the sole criteria for governance" (Woehl 2008: 69). Under neoliberal governmentality, the state is reduced primarily to the promotion of the "free market," leading to the privatization of social welfare and the "marketization" of political and social life, whereby populations are to be "free, self-managing, and self-enterprising individuals in different spheres of life—health, education, bureaucracy, the professions, and so on. The neoliberal subject is therefore not a citizen with claims on the state but a self-enterprising citizen-subject who is obligated to become an 'entrepreneur of himself or herself,'" (Ong 2006: 14). In this scenario, gender equality becomes the technique to "free" women to be these free-market actors, taking care of their own needs without resort to the state for their welfare. The male (and class-based) norm of free-market actors, devoid of dependents and interdependencies, and an androcentric construction of states as not responsible for the welfare of their citizenries are strengthened by this reduction of gender equality to the production of "economic woman" in the form of "economic man."

Thus, the traction that gender equality has gained in the context of global governance can be read more critically and most cynically as just a neoliberal strategy, with NGOs, TFNs, and femocrats being turned into agents of neoliberal governmentality. Indeed, the very proliferation of these NGOs and TFNs can be seen as a feature of neoliberal governmentality, taking on roles of states to "manage" (depoliticize) populations and their problems and even providing services, albeit in far more underresourced ways, that states used to provide. This has implications as well for women gaining public office in states, for if the reigning ideology is that states are to withhold public service in favor of privatization that makes individuals solely responsible for their own welfare, then it is difficult to mount more expansive public commitments and garner more public resources for changing negative conditions for women (as well as children, nonelite men, and even the planet).

There is little question that IGOs and, especially, IFIs frame gender equality as a matter of modern economic efficiency. States have been most responsive to this framing, and TFNs have often made their own arguments in relation to it. However, it is also the case that local, grassroots, and national women's movements have drawn on these instruments of neoliberal governmentality to make claims on states, although NGOs, TFNs, and state feminists, to varying degrees, continue to critique the insufficiencies of governmental responses. Thus, there are contradictions in this process that open up opportunities for resistance to neoliberal governmentality and for more radical demands than it typically allows (which we note next and address more in Chapter 6).

However, just as neoliberal governmentality circumscribes how (global) gender issues are framed, the presence of women in global governance is no guarantee that these issues will be acted upon or reframed in social justice terms.

## WOMEN IN POLITICS
## VERSUS FEMINIST POLITICS

There is no one-to-one relationship between the presence of women in politics and the extent of feminist politics. Women cut across the political spectrum and can just as easily hold antifeminist views or very narrow feminist commitments that justify the opening of doors for women like themselves to be in power but do not translate into supporting policies that improve conditions for all women or "other" women. Nevertheless, in its 2008–2009 report on the progress of the world's women, UNIFEM reported on several international and national studies finding that women in public office (1) tend to raise and give priority to "women's issues," (2) tend to encourage women in civil society to engage more in the political process, and (3) have some relationship to diminishing political corruption (2008: 26–27). These trends and their relative strengths, however, are also predicated on the numbers of women in a particular governing body (the BPA calls for at least 30 percent), the presence and resourcing of women's caucuses and machineries within government, and the transparency of the governing body within which they serve (UNIFEM 2008: 27–28). Other studies show that unless women in government are tied strongly to women's movements, whatever women-centered policies they raise will not be successful (Lovenduski 2005). Moreover, a study on the effects of the much-heralded women's majority in the Rwandan parliament shows that, although they have put such issues as HIV/AIDS and women's property rights on the political agenda, have built some solidarity among themselves (and with men) through collaborative work, maintained some contact with grassroots women's groups, and created a more "normalized" environment for women in politics, they have had no real success in the area of policy outcomes (Devlin and Elgie 2008). Thus, states and governments, as masculinist (and increasingly neoliberal) formations, continue to be resistant to substantive change on so-called women's issues despite advocates, and even large numbers of them, on the inside.

At the same time, feminists themselves have begun to question the very notion of some universalist construction of "women's issues" or "women's interests" or even "women's human rights," especially in light of the co-optation of such concepts by neoliberal governmentality (Chappell and Hill 2006; Hesford and Kozol 2005). Jennifer Chan-Tiberghien (2004) expresses this as the tension between the "gender boom" in transnational feminist organizing and "gender skepticism" in postmodern or poststructural feminist thought. The latter sees dangers in essentialist assumptions about the nature and very category of "women." Negative and even valorized constructions of "women" as some kind of undifferentiated group seen only in relation to the undifferentiated category of "men" sustain a "gender hegemony" or meta-lens (which we refer to as the power of gender) that entraps, conforms, excludes, and manipulates human subjectivities and actions. The key to resisting this is to resist rigid categorizations of "women" and "gender" altogether, seeing them rather as fluid and unstable signifiers that cannot be pinned down and thus not subject to control. From another angle, as we have repeatedly pointed out, postcolonial feminists argue that universalist categorizations of "women" and "gender" obscure differences and, more importantly, power relations among women who are differentiated by race, class, sexuality, nationality, physical ability, age, and so on (which are productive of what we call gendered divisions not only between women and men but also among women and men) and that these categorizations fail to recognize that women (and men), in fact, have a range of "genders" as a result of these other infinitely varied combinations of social locations and identities. When these multiple genders go unrecognized, policies made in the name of women or gender tend to be based on a particular hegemonic construction of women (e.g., racially privileged, Western, heterosexual, middle class, able-bodied, and so on) and their interests. At the same time, "other" women are lumped together (often statistically) under various "victim categories" within which women constitute the majority—such as the poor, the diseased, refugees, the hungry, and the raped and battered in war and peace—and targeted as problems to be solved through outside intervention and rescue (whether by Western-dominated IGOs or NGOs), thereby not according women in these categories agency themselves. These are important critiques, but gender skepticism carries the danger of undercutting political claims made by and for women, whether by movements, NGOs, or state feminists, even though such claims are necessarily based on a fluid and unstable category.

As Chan-Tiberghien observes, one effect of not seeing women as a highly diverse category at the level of global governance is that the 1965 International Convention on the Elimination of All Forms of Racial Discrimination (ICERD) has long been seen as separate from CEDAW, as if racial discrimination had nothing to do with gender discrimination (2004: 465). This has been changing since the 2001 UN World Conference Against Racism (WCAR) where UNIFEM and women's NGOs made this link in official ways, getting reference to gender into "forty-one paragraphs of the NGO outcome documents and sixteen in the IGO documents" as well as additional references to "multiple forms of discrimination" and even "intersectionality" in these documents (Chan-Tiberghien 2004: 468–469). "Sexual orientation," even though also prominent in NGO documents, was excised in IGO documents (Chan-Tiberghien 2004: 469).

While IGOs in general continued to prefer "adding women" and to resist more radical and complex notions of gender beyond a male-female sex binary, what emerged especially from the Women's Caucus in the NGO Forum held alongside the WCAR was an insistence that "women's issues" be expanded to include "globalization, colonialism, slavery, foreign occupation, caste, HIV/AIDS, etc., in addition to the theme of intersectionality of gender, sexuality, and race" (Chan-Tiberghien 2004: 468). Yet states and IGOs continue to be silent on many of these because they consider them improper women's issues (Chan-Tiberghien 2004: 467). This "gender in intersectionality approach," as Chan-Tiberghien terms it, has also affected how women's NGOs and TFNs are using CEDAW to highlight the conditions of ethnic minority women (including undocumented migrants) who are typically left outside of narrow gender policymaking (2004: 477–478). Judith Squires also reports that at least within the EU there is now some attention being given to "diversity mainstreaming" to address race and disability as well as gender discrimination (2007: 163–164). However, progress on this has been slow and contested (Prügl and Thiel 2009), and the additive approach of IGOs continues to pit gender inequality against race inequality in terms of which should get priority and resources, as if many women did not experience both (Squires 2007: 165). Meanwhile, class inequalities continue to most divide women not only on the ground but also in global governance insofar as only the most privileged from North and South can participate most directly in it (Chan-Tiberghien 2004: 468), albeit still in numerically fewer, more marginal, and subordinated ways. Although such divides among women within countries are increasingly statistically tracked, widening inequalities between rich and poor associated with poor regulation of capitalist accumulation remain largely unaddressed in state and IGO constructs of diversity under neoliberal governmentality,

Discrimination against sexual minorities and nonnormative gender identities has only recently become a part of the global governance agenda. In 2011, after years of organizing by such NGOs as the International Gay and Lesbian Human Rights Commission (IGLHRC) and the International Lesbian, Gay, Bisexual, Trans, and Intersex Association (ILGA), the UN Human Rights Council passed the first resolution identifying discrimination on the basis of sexual orientation and gender identity as a human rights violation.[10] Notably, the United States was among the forty-one cosponsors of the resolution, a direct result of the Obama administration's support for LGBTQ rights and, most recently, same-sex marriage, constituting a major reversal from the previous administration's positions on these. CEDAW remains unratified under Obama; however, the election and reelection of an African American man, who is multinational, multicultural, and liberal or progressive (and liberal feminist) in US political terms, speaks to the continued enormous symbolic and material importance of working to diversify political leadership in terms of race/ethnicity, gender, class, culture, nationality, and, most importantly, ideology—particularly in the most powerful states—to bring about political change. It is also notable that in 2009 Johanna Sigurdardottir, prime minister of Iceland, became the first openly lesbian head of government worldwide. Nevertheless, the actual illegalization of nonnormative sexual and gender identities bars many more women, men, and other sexes/genders from public power and can even cost them their lives. As of 2012, same-sex relations were illegal in seventy-eight countries and punishable by death in all or parts of seven countries, fifty-two countries banned employment discrimination on the basis of sexual orientation but only eighteen banned this on the basis of gender identity, and only ten countries allowed same-sex marriage (now standing at fourteen with such additions as France and the United Kingdom [UK] in 2013) (ILGA 2012: 11–21).

Thus, the meta-lens of the power of gender continues to operate in terms of sorely limiting whether women, and which women (and men and others), can gain power in global governance, in what contexts do "women's" or "gender" issues get attention and why, how such issues are framed and through what mechanisms, and how they are acted upon (if at all). Despite recent progress of the type we have detailed here—mostly as a result of considerable "insider" and "outsider" feminist organizing—the continued power of gender largely keeps gendered divisions of power intact, which, as discussed in subsequent chapters, also leaves relatively undisturbed gendered divisions of violence and labor and resources. These all contribute to the crisis of representation that un-, under-, and misrepresents citizens as well as noncitizens, including those defined as stateless. According to the UN High Commission on Refugees,[11] as of 2012, 10.4 million people were refugees, representing a slight downward trend; however, internally displaced people (IDPs) numbered 28.8 million, a figure that continues to grow, most recently as a result of the new conflict in Syria and the ongoing one in the Democratic Republic of Congo (DRC). The power of gender also ensures that when formal representation is achieved, it is circumscribed and often co-opted by neoliberal governmentality (Caglar, Prügl, and Zwingel 2012). Nevertheless, these processes are being countered through feminist struggles to deepen democratization within global civil society upon which democratization of formal politics depends. This includes democratizing feminist movements through the hard work of forging shared interests through politics, which, at its best, is an open process for debate and the expression of differences and dissent through which shared and conflicting interests can be declared, worked through, and aggregated to make change (Vickers 2006: 32–33). As Mary Ann Tetreault and Ronnie Lipschutz (2005) remind us, politics, understood in this way, is the opposite of and the foil to neoliberal governmentality. As they put it:

> "Too political" is code for the creation of a space of appearance in which people can engage in politics and practice. People experience what is possible in these spaces, and they learn that action is a form of productive power. . . . Politics challenges the very basis of governmentality. It challenges exactly those principles, practices, and policies that seek to "manage" the problem by managing populations in a way that keeps people out of the process. Speech and action offer a different way to build a life, one that grows out of association, coming together to engage in common enterprise. (2005: 184, 185)

As we argue throughout the text, but particularly in our concluding chapter, repoliticization is key to resisting the crisis of representation and its related crises.

**Notes**

1. For examples of early and influential contemporary challenges by feminist political theorists to conventional constructions of politics and political actors, see, for example, Okin 1979; Jagger 1983; Benhabib and Cornell 1987; Pateman 1988; W. Brown 1988; and Phillips 1991.

2. See http://www.ipu.org/wmn-e/classif.htm.

3. See http://progress.unwomen.org/pdfs/EN-Report-Progress.pdf.

4. See http://www.ipu.org/pdf/publications/wmnmap12_en.pdf.

5. See http://unstats.un.org/unsd/demographic/products/Worldswomen/WW_full%20report_color.pdf.

6. See http://www.unwomen.org/2012/04/un-women-welcomes-a-landmark-action-plan-to-measure-gender-equality-across-the-un-system/.

7. See http://www.americanambassadors.org/index.cfm?fuseaction=Publications.article&articleid=69.

8. See http://www.catalyst.org/knowledge/women-ceos-fortune-1000.

9. See http://www3.weforum.org/docs/WEF_GenderGap_Report_2012.pdf.

10. See http://www.iglhrc.org/content/historic-decision-united-nations.

11. See http://www.unhcr.org/pages/49c3646c11.html.

# 4

$\cdots\cdots\cdots\cdots\cdots\cdots\cdots\cdots\cdots\cdots\cdots\cdots\cdots\cdots\cdots$◄○►$\cdots\cdots\cdots\cdots\cdots\cdots\cdots\cdots\cdots\cdots\cdots\cdots\cdots\cdots\cdots\cdots$

# Gender and
# Global Security

What is security, and how is it obtained? Whose security are we talking about? At what expense and at whose expense are national security and global security pursued? How are men, women, and even feminism militarized? How are peacemaking, peacekeeping, and peace-building gendered? Can security be disarmed?

Chapter 3 examined how gendered divisions of power marginalize women's (and other feminized people's) status in conventionally defined politics as well as how the power of gender sustains the crisis of representation even in the face of recent gender policies aimed at increasing women's formal representation and attention to gender inequality as a source of world political problems. This chapter examines how *gendered divisions of violence (security)* and the *power of gender* that produces them construct and reproduce massive insecurities, or the *crisis of insecurity*. To organize the discussion, we identify three interacting components: (1) the gendered security ideology at work (its underlying assumptions and expectations), (2) the differential effects of this ideology on differing men and women (the roles they are assigned in relation particularly to militaries), and (3) the systemic consequences of these intersectional gender dichotomies (exacerbating global insecurities even as the frequency of wars has diminished and violence against women and women's exclusion from peacemaking, peacekeeping, and peace-building have been identified as major impediments to peace and security). The patterns we identify through the examples we offer (which are, by no means, exhaustive) paint an overwhelmingly negative picture of the gendered effects of violence pursued in the name of security. However, it is necessary to understand the highly negative impacts of the gendered divisions of violence and put them in relation to the negative impacts of the gendered divisions of labor and resources that we cover in Chapter 5 in order to appreciate the varied struggles against these interrelated processes that we document in Chapter 6.

To review, what we mean by the gendered divisions of violence are the hierarchical dichotomies of self-other, us-them, aggressive-passive, soldier-victim, and protector-protected that divide the world into masculinized offenders and defenders and feminized populations over which they fight and seek to conquer or defend (see Table 4.1). This has long been the main story of IR, although only recently has this been understood in gender terms within IR. Moreover, although IR was founded ostensibly to address how to end war, its masculinist bias and imperialist commitments—born of its creation initially by elite, Eurocentric men who made it a useful tool for elite, Eurocentric statesmen—have made it less about ending war and more about controlling it and using it more effectively in the interests of those in power. Given the masculinist construction of politics as aggressive and combative power-over practices, it was an easy leap to argue, as Carl von Clausewitz (2004) did in the nineteenth century, that war is the extension of politics by other means.

However, if, as we argued in the last chapter, politics is seen as enabling power, then politics is the opposite of war, which shuts down debate in the face of the raw power of might makes right. Similarly, for war to be contemplated and waged "effectively," those against whom it is waged must be dehumanized (typically through feminization and racialization) in order for aggressors to feel superior and righteous in their actions. At the same time, both offenders and defenders need to justify their actions by waging war in the name of those who cannot fight and thus are in need of and worthy of protection (typically, a nation's or group's "own women-andchildren"). Such rationales for war are disturbed by the realities that "womenandchildren" are now rarely protected from direct violence in most contemporary wars and that the structural violence of homelessness, hunger, disease, and so on visited by war, particularly in the global South, and war spending affects especially civilian populations the world over. These inconvenient truths also redirect attention to the most historically frequent reasons for war and conquest—namely, the colonizing practices of the extraction of wealth and resources through the brutalization of populations in order to destroy communities and thus the will to resist such extraction. But the power of gender covers up this inconvenient

**TABLE 4.1**
**Gendered Divisions of Violence Productive of the Crisis of Insecurity**

| *Masculinized* | *Feminized* |
| --- | --- |
| Self | Other |
| Us | Them |
| Aggressive | Passive |
| Protector | Protected |
| Soldier | Civilian victim |
| Life-Taker | Life-Giver |
| Battlefront | Home front |
| Violence | Nonviolence |

(and currently politically unpalatable) truth and sets up the dynamics, in the forms of the gendered divisions of violence, that justify war and other forms of violence with which it is connected.

There have long been critiques of and resistances to war by women for the harm it does—ranging from the (male-authored) fifth-century BCE fictional play *Lysistrata*, which (comically) portrays women withholding sexual servicing from men until they stopped fighting, to such an actual action by Iroquois women in the seventeenth century, which opened the way for the long peace of the Iroquois Federation and to the writings of pacifist women (such as Christine de Pizan, Bertha von Suttner, and Virginia Woolf) from the Middle Ages through the world wars (and to the present day). But it was only in the past few centuries that there has been organized resistance to war in the form of peace movements. We argue, however, that the association of peace with the (hyper)feminine and the association of war with the (hyper)masculine have disadvantaged and marginalized calls for and analyses of how to bring about peace, not only as the absence of war and other forms of direct violence but also as an end of structural violence. Only by addressing both direct and structural violence can the crisis of insecurity be reversed.

## FEMINIST APPROACHES TO SECURITY

Feminist IR approaches to war and violence and peace and security have their roots especially in the thinking of nineteenth- and early-twentieth-century women peace theorists and activists. Many of these early thinkers and activists based their arguments against war on women's maternalist desires to protect their children from the ravages of war, neither wanting their sons to become cannon fodder nor their daughters to suffer from the destruction of families and communities (Pierson 1987). For those who were steeped in the biological determinism characteristic of nineteenth- and early-twentieth-century thought, these maternalist desires were seen as innate, making women "natural" peace supporters and peacemakers. Maternalist arguments continued through the Cold War, when women's peace organizations sought to protect future generations from the threat of nuclear war, and into the present day, but more contemporary feminist peace researchers and activists have argued that maternalism is not innate but rather the result of women being made largely responsible for "maternalist practices" or caring work, whether or not they have children (Ruddick 1984). This makes them more likely to have empathy for "others" and the world's children and to be against war and its destructive power.

Other contemporary feminists, however, have pointed out that women have historically supported wars (both imperialist wars and wars of national liberation) and fought in them, often in the name of maternalism. Sending sons and daughters to war can be seen as a patriotic motherly duty, and fighting in wars can be seen as a form of motherly protection of the homeland (Elshtain 1987). At the same time, many women have become soldiers out of economic necessity or sought gender equality in soldiering as a ticket to full citizenship and a path to public power for women. Thus, the idea that women are either naturally or socially geared for peace has been put in question and even seen as an impediment to women seeking gender equality because it bars them from or marginalizes them in militaries that control significant resources and are particularly valorized in the stories of nations and the fabric of national life. This produces a "gendered nationalism" in which only men who forged a nation in blood get to define what that nation is, regardless of whether women spilled blood for it or on its altar as (fewer) combatants or (many) noncombatants, and regardless of the many other contributions that women make to (re)producing and sustaining the life of a nation (Enloe 1989: 63).

When women are seen only as the symbols and the reproducers of the nation, not as agents in its narratives, then they become subject to an array of controls over their bodies and their beings by men of the nation (Kaufman and Williams 2007: 16–18; Yuval-Davis 1997).

Nevertheless, still other contemporary feminists have shown that there is a relationship between international violence and domestic violence, which gives women particular interests in resisting warfare and war preparedness because it produces men who do not visit violence only on the "enemy" but also on their own wives, partners, and children. But men, too, feminists have argued, can develop interests in resisting war because of the harm it does to their bodies and psyches, leading to the destruction of their loved ones and their own selves. What keeps more men—particularly those in subordinate military positions whose bodies are most on the line—from developing such interests is the valorization of war as the penultimate masculine activity through which men can prove they are "real men" (Whitworth 2008). As we have pointed out, heteronormative masculinity is an extraordinarily fragile and unstable construct and identity that leaves men having to prove repeatedly that they have "it." They are put in constant fear and anxiety that they will be dubbed less than "real men" and therefore be demoted down the gender hierarchy and be subject to greater violence by other, higher men.

But even though there are high costs for subordinated men who participate in or who resist war, feminists have particularly focused on the fact that women pay high prices for its valorization and conduct. Militarized violence makes them more subject to gender violence (whether they are combatants or noncombatants) in the forms of militarized domestic violence, rape, and prostitution and more subject to the structural violence of dislocation, poverty, and disease that war leaves in its wake. Military spending also extracts resources needed for social welfare, shredding social safety nets, which leads to the violence of desperation. But even beyond this, postcolonial feminists in particular point to the costs of women's and subordinated men's support of imperial warfare and violence, typically in the name of national security and increasingly global security (Eisenstein 2007). As long as wars of extraction, most typically waged on the soil of the South, are cloaked as "civilizing," "pacifying," and "liberating" missions to protect national and global security, women and subordinated men in states with imperialist ambitions can be drawn in to support them and do the work of violence associated with them. This is at the expense of forming solidarities among women and less privileged men across North and South to resist war and the violence that most harms them. Such solidarities can be built on the recognition that exclusivist and violent ethnic nationalisms (whether of the imperialist or anti-imperialist variety) are "'integral' to globalizing processes," with "opportunistic" nationalist movements "seeking statehood in some instances" while not being able to legitimately provide for the welfare of citizens under globalization and others "sustaining their power through the market economy" (Giles and Hyndman 2004: 18).

We argue in this chapter that the power of gender obscures and militates against the potential alliances between women and men and among them across borders to resist war and other forms of violence. In the process, we problematize dominant constructions of security, examine the strategy of "adding women" to security structures and policies, destabilize assumptions undergirding the gendered divisions of violence, and take on the question of Empire, which keeps the world enthralled in violence but which still can be resisted. We are critical of "solutions" that put peace-making and peace-building solely on the backs of poorly resourced and marginalized women and vilify only certain men to deflect attention away from elites (including some women) who promote militarism and war in the name of security. But we also see some value in what has been called "strategic essentialism" (Spivak 1987), which refers to the way groups of people like "women," who are in reality nonhomogeneous, have diverse experiences, and have multiple and even conflicting interests, can still make political claims as a group on the basis of what they perceive as their shared perspectives and conditions on the understanding that the commonalities they identify and strategically mobilize to make political demands for change are not timeless or the result of innate traits. As such, strategic essentialism constitutes a political strategy for women to articulate interests in and paths to peace and act together (with supportive men) to bring about disarmed security.

## GENDERED SECURITY

War—its causes and effects—animated and has long dominated the study of IR. Since the Cold War period, war has been studied in IR under the rubric of "security" studies. In (neo)realist security studies, the maintenance of security is understood as controlling and containing, but not eliminating, direct violence between state militaries through balances of military power and nuclear terror as well as collective security measures that rely on sustaining both credible threats to use force and the actual use of force. Ironically and problematically, this ensures the continued growth of militaries and the continuation of war to promote security—but only the security of the state, not necessarily of people within or across states and certainly not of the planet.

The early post–Cold War period of the 1990s brought more interest within the discipline in wider definitions of security, ranging from economic to human, environmental, and even food security. These redefinitions occurred in the face of new "threats" to state security (such as globalization and global warming, discussed in the next chapter), but also newly recognized notions of security arising from critical perspectives (including feminist ones) entering the field, which pointed out that state security often compromised the welfare of people and the planet. Nevertheless, conventional security studies have enjoyed somewhat of a resurgence in the post-9/11 period because decisions to engage in interstate and intrastate conflict and the globalized "war on terror" once again spiked militarized violence. The resurgent interest in direct violence has once again been at the expense of attending to structural violence and the insecurities generated by structural inequalities. We must be mindful that direct and indirect (structural) violence are not separate but interdependent. The inequalities of the latter shape the expression of the former. As dire as are the effects of direct violence, indirect violence shapes the lives of all of us all of the time—and especially injures women and other subordinated and marginalized people.

Hence, feminists argue that to understand violence and insecurities, we must look not only within particular "levels" but also at the linkages among them. According to Ann Tickner, "Feminist perspectives on security would assume that violence, whether it be in the international, national, or family realm, is interconnected. Family violence must be seen in the context of wider power relations; it occurs within a gendered society in which male power dominates at all levels. . . . Any feminist definition of security must therefore include the elimination of all types of violence, including violence produced by gender relations of domination and subordination" (1993: 58).

We add that gender in combination with racialized, sexualized, and class violence also reveals the interconnections between relations of domination and subordination that are present across all levels and constitute the conditions (structural violence) and goads for war (direct violence) as well as the effects of war or militarized conflict. Unless these are taken seriously, even rival notions of (nondisaggregated) human security to state security will fail to recognize all the sources of insecurity (bred of the injustices of structural violence) and their differential effects.

At the same time, we share the more poststructural feminist view that security is always "elusive and partial" because the quest for absolute security is in itself productive of violence: it relies on the eradication of all threats, real or imagined, and thus sets up a never-ending defensive and offensive posture (Tickner 2001: 62). Such a posture is emblematic of the "sovereign man" (Ashley 1989), who, like the sovereign state that is fashioned upon this construct of hegemonic masculinity, thwarts connection and interdependence in fear of engagement with difference that might break down walls between the sovereign "self" and the "other" on whom is projected all that one denies in oneself (Eisenstein 2007: 13).

On this point, Susan Faludi's *The Terror Dream* (2007) is quite instructive. Not only does this work document the resurgence in the United States of a state security discourse proffered across the airwaves, almost exclusively by military men (to the almost absolute exclusion of female and particularly feminist voices representing alternative views), in the first few years of the post-9/11 period, but it also analyzes the resurgence of older sexist and racist mythologies from America's past called up to cover up the chink in the sovereign man's armor. Whether it was the lionizing of male rescue workers at "ground zero" (and the attendant silencing of female rescue workers long discriminated against, as well as widows who questioned the US military response, because neither conformed with adulating male protection and security at any cost), the ersatz "rescue" of US soldier Jessica Lynch supposedly from rapacious Iraqi captors (who turned out to be caring medical personnel), or overblown (and in most cases untrue) claims about women opting out of the workplace to return home to raise babies and become "security moms" in support of war, Faludi argues that these convenient "fictions" have roots in earlier frontier stories, captivity narratives, and Cold War hysterias. These get trotted out whenever there are fears of "masculine insufficiency" because hegemonic masculinity cannot countenance "vulnerability" (2007: 280).

When we look more closely at the events behind these earlier narratives, we find that white male frontiersmen (such as Daniel Boone) were in fact undistinguished as providers or protectors and more often relied on the provisioning and protective skills of their wives, children, and indigenous peoples to survive, and the majority of white women taken captive by indigenous peoples either preferred to stay with their newfound families into which they were adopted or won their release from their captors on their own (Faludi 2007: 256–262, 212). Nevertheless, Faludi argues, insecure times in patriarchal cultures ratchet up the need for elaborate mythologies that "measure national male strength by female peril," requiring that "women be saved from more and more gruesome violation to prove their saviors' valor" (2007: 262). In the US white patriarchal cultural imagination, that peril is limited to concerns for white women and symbolized most by racialized men, whether they be indigenous "captors" of old, the new Iraqi ones, the "yellow" and "Hun" hordes of World War II, or the "red" communist threat of the Cold War. In each case, fears of "alien" invasion required the "securing of American domesticity," which conjured images of (white) women (re)confined to the home front, obsessions with "women's sexuality purity" supposedly at risk from racialized men, and a summoning of "John Wayne and his avenging brethren" (Faludi 2007: 282–283, 286). As Faludi concludes, the constant replaying of this "security myth" (currently evoked by obsessions with "homeland security") disables an alternative response that "involves learning to live with insecurity, finding accommodation with—even drawing strength from—an awareness of vulnerability" (2007: 286) in order not to create sacrificial altars, but instead to create space for multiple voices and ways of acting and being.

The too easy devolution of security into continual justifications for violence also makes us wary of new processes of "securitization" associated with a widening security agenda. On the one hand, the application of the term *security* to an issue elevates it to a matter of "high politics," as security (matters of war and peace) has traditionally held pride of place in IR theory and practice. Thus, relatively new conceptions of human security and environmental security, and even more recently, food, water, energy, and health security, have brought welcome international attention to sources of structural violence that undermine the well-being of people and the planet. On the other hand, there is also a tendency to reduce these once again to state security matters to be handled not through more collective and more nonviolent means, but more typically through war or some approximation of it. Resource wars, wars on terror, wars on AIDS, wars on drugs, and so on all follow a similar logic. As Zillah Eisenstein argues, the logic of war of any kind is "opposition, differentiation, and the othering of peoples" (2007: 25). Thus, gendering, racialization, classing, and sexualizing go on unabated (and become even more pronounced) in order to affix blame and control, contain, and quarantine these "new" threats. For example, racial profiling becomes a weapon in the "war on terror," targeting sexual minorities and sex workers becomes the focus of the war on AIDS, and peasant farmers become casualties of the war on drugs.

The logic of war also entails resort to military means, and as more and more issues are securitized, more and more of daily life is militarized. As Cynthia Enloe (2007) points out, anyone, any group or institution, and anything can be militarized. "To be militarized is to adopt militaristic values (e.g., a belief in hierarchy, obedience, and the use of force) and priorities as one's own, to see military solutions as particularly effective, to see the world as a dangerous place best approached with militaristic attitudes" (2007: 4). Thus, militaries are only a small part of the actual "security" apparatus. They rely on wider civilian cultures to enact militarized values, whether in the form of wearing "fashionable" camouflage clothing, joining militaries, working for defense industries, supporting national security over civil liberties, calling for closed borders and more prisons, and so on (Enloe 2007: 4–5). As a result, although "security," perhaps more than any other activity, has been constructed as "men's" business, its logic and enactment must be shared widely to shore up the elevation of militaries as the pinnacle of masculine endeavor. As we shall see in the following sections, the price of this elevation is too high for both women and men and for the planet.

## WOMEN, MILITARIES, AND POLITICAL VIOLENCE

Although it is often assumed that women serving in militaries is a relatively recent, "modern" phenomenon, throughout history women have fought in wars. In *Women Warriors: A History,* David Jones provides an account "of the female martial tradition in a pan-historical and global perspective" (1997: xiv). He documents how women warriors have had an important presence across cultures and throughout history. They have led armies, constituted women's battalions, passed themselves off as male soldiers, rallied the troops as symbolic leaders, defended family and community structures in the absence of men, and exhibited the same courage, loyalty, steadfastness, heroism, and even bloodthirstiness that we associate with male warriors. Jones argues that "from the beginning women shared the qualitative experience of the warrior; everything men have ever done in warfare, women have also done, and, in many instances, they have done it better" (1997: xiii). Despite such evidence and the fact that even in the United States it is increasingly more commonplace to hear references to "men and women" in the armed forces and the gender-neutral term "troops", there is still discomfort with—and even a desire to reject—the image and, indeed, the reality of *women warriors*. Still lingering and still powerful gendered divisions of violence account for this.

*Gendered Divisions of Violence at Work*

With modern state-making, gendered divisions became codified in particular ways. Liberalism in political theory favored divisions of power into public-private, government-household, whereas capitalism in economic theory favored divisions of labor into paid-unpaid, productive-reproductive. Interacting with these developments, modern state-making promoted particular divisions of violence. Masculinity involved not only heading the household and earning a "family wage" but also being prepared to defend "home and country." As Jean Bethke Elshtain notes, "War is the means to attain recognition, to pass, in a sense, the definitive test of political manhood. . . . The man becomes what he in some sense is meant to be by being absorbed in the larger stream of life: war and the state" (1992: 143). Femininity involved not only bearing and rearing children and maintaining the home front, but also serving, symbolically and literally, as the object that required protection. Whereas men served their country in combat as "life-takers," women served their country as mothers, as "life-givers" (Elshtain 1987).

In recent centuries, most male-dominated societies have constructed elaborate sanctions and even taboos against women as warriors, especially against women bearing arms and initiating violence. As a result, men have gained almost exclusive control over the means of destruction worldwide, often in the name of protecting women (and children), who are either discouraged from or not allowed to take up arms to protect themselves or to be warriors protecting others. It is therefore not surprising that war—which remains the centerpiece of IR—is seen as *men's* deadly business. We argue, however, that war has always involved women as well as the power of gender to promote masculine characteristics—typically, as we already noted, at the expense of cooperation, interdependence, and conflict resolution (Grant 1994). Moreover, the identification of war with men and peace with women completely unravels in the face of war practices over time in which civilians, not just combatants, have been subject to a significant direct violence and even more to structural violence.

As life-givers, women are not only prevented from engaging in combat but are also expected to restore "life" after a death-dealing war is over. Women are expected to mourn dutifully the loved ones who fell in war and then to produce new lives for the nation to replace its lost members. Thus, after the devastation, they must "pick up the pieces" and create the conditions for repopulating society. These conditions include creating more men, who too often serve as soldiers, and more women, who bear sons only to lose them too often through war. The work of men as life-takers thus creates perpetual work for women as life-givers.

In this sense, women are not separate from either the production or the consequences of war, even though they are often prevented from engaging in direct combat. Yet in spite of their participation, women remain associated with war's opposite—peace. By denying the historical construction of gender stereotypes, the characterization of "woman" as passive and submissive is often translated into the idea that women are pacifist by nature. This reinforces the stereotype of women as life-givers and portrays them as insufficiently fit or motivated to be life-takers. The assumption that women have a natural revulsion against war also makes them undesirable partners in combat: How can women be trusted on the battleground if they are unwilling to fight and kill? Men, in contrast, are stereotyped as naturally aggressive and competitive, which presumably prepares them to kill or be killed. In addition, through heteronormative lenses, it is assumed that the presence of women on the battlefield will distract men from fighting successfully, perhaps by turning their aggressions away from fighting and toward sexual conquest or by tying them down to protect "weaker" female comrades, thereby endangering the pursuit of body counts. In this view, men might lose the war by pursuing or protecting women on the battlefield rather than fighting successfully to protect women at home.

After the battle, women are expected to take care of returning soldiers, salving their wounds and psyches as well as meeting needs—for food, clothing, and shelter—previously met by the military. When the "boys come home," women are expected to serve them and to do so with gratitude for those who fought and took life on behalf of their women and their nation. If women fail in these duties, then male protectors are often given tacit approval to "discipline" their women, through physical violence if necessary. Such physical violence is learned on the playground when boys "play" war in preparation for their adult roles as potential soldiers. The role is honed when men are actually trained by militaries and participate in "real" wars. Life-takers have no responsibility for "unlearning" these skills when they leave the war front; global statistics on domestic violence suggest that men may use these skills against the women and children they protected in wartime if the latter do not please them in the home. Thus, those who are denied access to the means of destruction to protect themselves during wartime also have little protection against the wartime protectors who may turn violent in the home (Sharoni 1995: 127; Nikolic-Ristanovic 1996).

As Faludi's (2007) study of the continuation of the security myth previously discussed shows, gender dichotomies such as the following are still powerfully at work in reproducing ever-expanding variations on the gendered division of violence: soldiers-mothers, protectors-protected, aggressive-passive, battlefront-home front, batterers-victims. However, it is becoming harder to sustain these dichotomies in the face of women's greater visibility in armed forces and their activities as perpetrators of political violence (that is, sanctioned or extralegal violence against or in the name of the state) in recent years. These still constitute in relative terms what Elshtain (1987) refers to as the "ferocious few," but they nevertheless challenge the old story to a degree.

## Military Women

Just as conforming to rising UN-sponsored gender equality norms (at least in terms of rhetoric and formal policy if not in terms of actual enforcement and results) is motivated by states' desires to appear modern, the presence of women in a state's armed forces is increasingly seen as another mark of modernity. By 1994 there were more than 500,000 female soldiers serving in regular and irregular armed forces (Smith 1997: 64), but women still typically made up less than 10 percent of state militaries as a whole, with many militaries still excluding them altogether. There have been some increases, however, in those countries with the highest percentages in the mid-1990s. By 2005, the United States went from 12 to 15 percent; Canada, from 12 to 16.3 percent; and New Zealand, from 14 to 15 percent, with others holding relatively steady, such as Australia at 13 percent and Russia at 11 percent. Israel, Latvia, and South Africa have the highest percentages of women in the military, at 37, 23, and 22 percent, respectively (Enloe 2007: 70; Seager 2009: 103). By 2010, New Zealand and Australia increased to 16.5 and 15.7 percent, respectively, but Canada was down to 14.5 percent (Mathers 2013), indicating that upward progress is not only slow, but also can be reversed. The vast majority of countries disallow or substantially limit women in combat, although, significantly, the United States ended its policy of combat exclusion in 2013, opening up as many as 200,000 more positions for women in the US military. Also, other than most western and central European countries, as well as Canada, Australia, New Zealand, Japan, South Africa, Israel, Russia, Taiwan, Argentina, Uruguay, and the United States as of 2011, many countries still ban lesbians and gays from their militaries. In addition to the still relatively low rates of female participation in state militaries worldwide that speak to the continuing masculinization of military jobs, Enloe (2007) reminds us that increases in women's soldiering must be analyzed very carefully. On the surface, they may appear to be the product of "'postsexist' enlightenment" and modernity, but underneath there are different stories (Enloe 2007). The unprecedented South African case represents the results of a postapartheid debate (that included feminists) about the need to create more democratic armed forces in terms of both race and gender, but the Israeli case reveals a more cynical approach that relies on conscripting Israeli women to make them complicit in the occupation of Palestine while portraying Israeli female solders as sexual appendages to and assigning them more domestic duties in the army to keep them in their place (Enloe 2007: 73, 75).

Most often it is for such unenlightened reasons that women are included in state militaries. For example, when African American women were most needed to fill the ranks of the all-volunteer US military prior to 9/11, they constituted 46 percent of all women in the armed services, while African American men constituted 25 percent of enlisted men. Yet by 2007, four years into the Iraq War, they dropped to 38 percent of enlisted women, while Latinas were up only 5 percentage points (Enloe 2010: 166–167). Presumably, there were enough other recruits to reduce the military's dependency on black women. Moreover, during 1993–2011 when the US "Don't Ask, Don't Tell" policy was in force, 13,000 people were dismissed from the services for being gay, with lesbians accounting for about one-third of those (and thus a disproportionate amount relative to the low numbers of women in the military) and the majority of those dismissed in the air force in 2008.[1] Far from simply yielding to feminist and other demands for democratization, the US military has traditionally sought, even in high wartime, to preserve "its racist, androcentric, and heterocentric foundations" (D'Amico 1997: 200).

These foundations have been responsible for other forms of discrimination against women in the military. Despite the fact that women have "routinely been assigned to combat operations" (Enloe 2007: 66) in the US wars in Afghanistan and Iraq, where 99,467 women soldiers and 37,925 women reservists and National Guard members had been deployed by the United States by 2006 (Enloe 2007: 89), formal combat exclusions, only recently lifted, disabled most women from claiming the combat experience that has often served as a prerequisite or a test of leadership skills for those seeking high political office. Moreover, when we consider that as of 2012, worldwide military spending reached $1.583 trillion, with the United States accounting for 41 percent of that, followed distantly by Asia and Europe,[2] the considerable resources devoted to war-making end up in overwhelmingly male (and mostly Western) hands. These huge political and material consequences for women of men dominating the means of destruction are sustained by keeping women's numbers down in militaries and by creating elaborate prohibitions on and punishments of women who do get into militaries.

Although women enter militaries for many of the same reasons as men (including out of patriotism or nationalism), in the United States they report most often that it is for education, jobs, and career training (Eisenstein 2007: 21). However, because militaries are first and foremost about maintaining masculine (typically along with racial majority and class) privilege, women must enter them on certain terms—those that conform to "gender differentiation" (Eisenstein 2007: 6) while at the same time adopting masculinist militarist values. While the film version of *GI Jane* (1997) had her become a "man" to fit into the culture of an elite commando unit and thereby end the sexual harassment she was subjected to by her comrades-in-arms,[3] the more typical reality for women soldiers is they are expected to remain "women" and put up and shut up about sexual harassment and assault, which has reached "epidemic" proportions today, despite revelations about it over the past two decades that supposedly were being addressed by military hierarchies.

From the 1991 Navy Tailhook Convention and the 1996 US Army Proving Ground scandals to the 2012 Lackland Air Base case and the egregious and worsening statistics on sexual assault released in 2013 by the US Department of Defense (DOD), evidence continues to pile up that sexual harassment and assault are rife within all US military branches. Just prior to the release of the latest report on military sexual assault within the ranks,[4] which found that reported sexual assaults had increased from 3,192 in 2011 to 3,374 in 2012 and an estimated 26,000 assaults occur each year (an average of 70 per day), the Academy Award–nominated documentary *The Invisible War* (2012) was aired. It detailed the stories of multiple female and male survivors of sexual assault in the military from the 1970s on, the punishments they received for reporting their rapes, and the damage done to their mental health and their careers not just by their rapists, but also at the hands of the military chain of command and its anemic and victim-blaming approaches to dealing with the rampant problem. The film, building on the organizing work of the Service Women's Action Network, had already triggered congressional hearings to upbraid the military for its poor response and for structural perversities that forced victims to report their rapes to their superior officers, even when these were their rapists or friends of their rapists, and allowed superior officers to overturn rape convictions adjudicated in military courts. The DOD's latest report, coupled with allegations that at least two officers charged with overseeing sexual assault response and prevention had committed sexual assault and domestic violence, redoubled the efforts of congresswomen to introduce bills to take sexual assault and harassment reporting and adjudication out of the hands of the chain of command.

What the film and the latest report reveal is that (largely heterosexual) men, given their far greater numbers in the military, are most often the targets of other (almost exclusively heterosexual) men's sexual abuse. However, women constitute the vast majority of those who report sexual harassment and assault, leading to only 160 convictions that resulted in court-martial in 2012. Thus, while military officialdom primarily in the West now tracks sexual crimes, it is only after some highly visible incident or event that a more serious response is demanded. Heretofore, keeping the lid on sexual assault in the military has typically been driven by the fear of undermining male soldier morale (and recruiting) by reducing the sexual privileges that heterosexual male soldiers expect to go along with the job. At the same time, women have been discouraged from reporting such incidents because they are rarely acted on except to punish those who do report (and who are also threatened with retaliation, including death, by perpetrators for reporting), but also in the name of protecting (male) military morale to which they are expected to kowtow. Revelations about the extent of heterosexual-male-on-heterosexual-male sexual assault have catapulted concerns about the cost of this to military readiness, which are driving current attempts to bring about legislative and policy reforms. What is not discussed is how an institution that is organized for "sanctioned" masculinist violence can eradicate newly "unsanctioned" masculinist violence.

In addition to suffering physical violence at the hands of their own comrades-in-arms, women in the US military are discriminated against in a host of other ways that, in the United States, are tracked by the Women's Research and Education Institute (WREI), which also gathers data on discrimination against women in other Western militaries. The litany has remained the same year after year: "exclusion from combat jobs, sexual harassment, antilesbian 'witchhunts,' discrimination in promotion evaluations, and neglect of employment and health needs of the growing number of women veterans" (Enloe 2007: 86). Although combat and sexual orientation exclusions have lessened recently, the other patterns are worsening. Such circumstances mirror the experiences of civilian women in other male-dominated occupations, but there are deadlier twists in the case of the military, which is a far more captive and dangerous environment for military women (and feminized men), who are at more risk from their own militaries than from foreign ones, even as female casualties have mounted on the battlefield.

Feminists who question whether it is possible to democratize the military tend also to question democratizing moves by the military insofar as an increased presence of women serves to legitimize the institution by giving it a façade of egalitarianism. When women accept the "warrior mystique," they soften the image of the military as an agent of coercion/ destruction and help promote the image of the military as a democratic institution, an "equal opportunity employer" like any other, without reference to its essential purpose. In this sense, they serve as what Zillah Eisenstein (2007) refers to as "sexual" or "gender decoys" (and in the case of women of color, "race" as well as gender decoys). Such decoys "camouflage" and distract attention from any actual evaluation of the efficacy of militaries and the consequences of militarist values. If the symbol of modernity is the equal participation of women in acts of torture, such as those perpetrated at the Abu Ghraib prison in Iraq by US women soldiers, then gender equality based on women conforming to masculinist and racist norms becomes not a significant source for reducing structural and direct violence but rather a basis for furthering it.

## Women's Political Violence

Despite the seemingly more commonplace event of seeing women in militaries, the image of them as actual killers and purveyors of other forms of direct violence, rather than simply "support" personnel who happen to carry weapons, still remains unsettling under the gendered division of violence. It is particularly unsettling when that violence is "proscribed violence," or violence that violates laws within and between states, including torture, genocide, and terrorism. As Laura Sjoberg and Caron Gentry (2007) argue, women who commit such violence are reduced to mothers, monsters, or whores (or all three) to explain their behaviors because they are not accorded rational political motivations for their crimes. The association of aberrant violence with aberrant womanhood has a long pedigree. As Kelly Oliver points out, motherhood is constructed as Janus-faced in patriarchal culture—at one and the same time the source of life-giving and the source of death (through the power of withholding nourishment from infants and the symbol of mother earth to which the dead return) (2007: 21). Female sexuality is also constructed as intoxicating, beguiling, and more treacherous than anything men can deploy, and women's bodies themselves are seen as sources of concealment and dangerous fluids (Oliver 2007: 31, 38). Thus, it is a fine line in these imaginings between women's natural passivity and womanhood gone mad if not properly restrained. This supposed dual nature of women is used not only to justify their control but also to explain their behavior. But as Oliver also chronicles, this mythology has been "rationally" deployed in calculated ways to make women's bodies weapons in the "war on terror." Detainees at Guantánamo Bay were smeared with (fake) menstrual blood by US interrogators, and all-female teams of interrogators practiced "sexual lechery" on the most "troublesome" inmates to break them (2007: 28–29).

Such images have now found their way into popular culture. Consider the film *Zero Dark Thirty* (2012), in which the protagonist, a CIA (Central Intelligence Agency) operative named Maya recruited right out of high school who is single-mindedly tracking down Osama bin Laden as the instigator of the 9/11 attack on the United States, is totally complicit with torture conducted in CIA black sites in such countries as Poland, Israel, and Pakistan, where "enemy combatants" were sent secretly under rendition by the US government after 9/11. A young, lily-white, red-haired beauty, Maya is glorified for her unexpected toughness, tenacity, and defiance against the CIA male hierarchy as she gazes steely-eyed at the genitals of Arab detainees to humiliate them, relentlessly combs through torture videos for credible intelligence gathered from what was euphemistically called "harsh interrogations" by the Bush administration, and ferociously demands of commandos getting ready to raid the compound where Bin Laden is in hiding to "find and kill bin Laden *for me!*"

Thus, in an age of terror, women are constituted as the most ruthless and terrorizing when unleashed. This then accounts for the particular horror many found in the real-world images of US women soldiers sexually terrorizing inmates at Abu Ghraib because it evoked deep patriarchal (and heteronormative) fears (Peterson 2007; Puar 2007). These acts were also dismaying to those feminists who held out some faith in women as being more peaceful and potentially tempering of military excesses. But in the uproar over the (un)naturalness of women torturers, attention was deflected from what we now know was state-sponsored torture and terrorism, not just the work of a few bad girls and boys.

As Sjoberg and Gentry (2007, 2011) chronicle, women have long engaged in state and (both left- and right-wing) insurgency terrorism most often in logistical support roles, but also as perpetrators of direct violence. However, it is in the twenty-first century that women have become highly visible as torturers, suicide bombers, hijackers, kidnappers, and genocidaires. During much of the twentieth century, some women, primarily in the West, gained some notoriety for their involvement (including playing leadership roles) in the Ku Klux Klan and the Weather Underground in the US, the Baader-Meinhoff gang in Germany, the Red Brigades in Italy, the Irish Republican Army in Northern Ireland, and the like. The focus of Western counterterrorist policymakers today is trained on the rise in non-Western (primarily Islamic) women's terrorist acts, particularly in the form of suicide bombings (or martyrdom operations as they are referred to in the Middle East), 26 percent of which had been attributed to women by 2007 (Brown 2011: 194). Seeing this rise as evidence of the increasing uncontrollability of insurgents and a measure of their desperation, security policymakers construct women, especially in the Islamic world, as particularly dangerous security threats (Sjoberg, Cooke, and Neal 2011: 5). That al-Qaeda began recruiting women to conduct suicide bombings as a strategic move and a way to swell its ranks with both women and men has heightened the state security lens through which women in the Islamic world are now being scrutinized, demonized, and pathologized (Brown 2011). Rather than seeing women who commit insurgent terrorist violence as willing actors responding to political crises and resisting, as a matter of nationalist and/or religious duty, the insecurities they experience, the securitized (and Orientalist) lens on female suicide bombers, whether they be members of the Tamil Tigers in Sri Lanka, the Chechen rebels in Russia, Hamas in Palestine, or al-Qaeda in Iraq, portrays them as vengeful mothers, brainwashed dupes of Islam, or monsters. Such a lens deflects attention away from the political claims of their movements and the role state terrorism has played in producing insurgent movements.

State terrorists include such genocidaires as Biljana Plavšić of Serbia and Pauline Nyiramasuhuko of Rwanda, both of whom have been tried by the International Criminal Tribunals for Yugoslavia and Rwanda, respectively, for their roles in fomenting genocide and genocidal rape in those countries in the 1990s. To attempt to excuse their actions, they fell back on gender stereotypes, constructing themselves as avenging or protective mothers of the nation, while being portrayed as madwomen by others (Sjoberg and Gentry 2007: 155, 165, 152, 167). Such stereotypes denied that both were highly educated, highly placed political women who used their political power to perpetrate political genocide, not victims of maternalism gone awry. As long as the latter is foregrounded, then genocide as a political act of which anyone is capable given the means, ideologies, and contexts is backgrounded. Similarly, as long as women are constructed only as victims, brutal treatment of them will be invited in times of war and "peace."

In short, violence can be "resexed," in Eisenstein's (2007) words, as long as it does not disturb the power of gender to valorize violence, militarism, and war. Moreover, femininity can be militarized without threatening male privilege and can even bolster it as long as women play "idealized militarized femininity" roles as "capable" but "sanitized" and supportive "Just Warriors" who retain the "innocence" and "vulnerability" of "Beautiful Souls" (Sjoberg and Gentry 2007: 86).

## MEN, MILITARIES, AND GENDER VIOLENCE

In societies where masculinity is associated with power-over and violence, men are under constant pressure to prove their manhood by being tough, adversarial, and aggressive. There are, of course, a variety of forms of male aggression that have been deemed unacceptable or illegitimate within civil societies (such as murder, assault, gang warfare, and, at least in terms of the laws of some countries, wife battering and child abuse). However, in one highly legitimated and organized institution within most societies, men not only can but also—to be successful—must prove their masculinity through violence: the military.

State militaries serve many functions. According to world politics wisdom of the (neo)realist variety, militaries serve to protect the borders of states and the citizens within them from outside aggression, inevitable given the anarchic interstate system, which is based on power politics, not the rule of law. In this view, militaries are deemed necessary for the maintenance of national security, either as deterrents to would-be aggressors or as effective fighting machines capable of vanquishing actual aggressors.

More critical world politics perspectives see militaries serving other less laudable functions, such as protecting repressive state elites from rebellion by their own people. This is often described as maintaining the internal security of states at the expense of nonelite citizens. Also, militaries are implicated in maintaining permanent war economies arising from the infamous "military-industrial complex," which organizes a state's economy around producing weapons rather than civilian goods. Under such conditions, the military can become one of the few sites for "employment," not only for the poor and least educated who turn to soldiering or working in weapons plants but also for large numbers of middle-class voters engaged in, for example, research and development activities. More recently, there have been references to the "security-industrial complex" that has arisen since 9/11 in which private industries are organized around producing and purveying intelligence, surveillance, and control systems as extensions of the state and even providing private armies for the state, such as the infamous Blackwater operation in Iraq. Like the "prison-industrial complex" that has arisen alongside this and in which inmates are used as captive slave labor to produce goods for private industries and are surveilled and controlled at ever higher levels in increasingly private prisons and increasingly worldwide (Sudbury 2005), the security-industrial complex organizes not only the economy but also much of life around the dictates of security at the expense of human rights and welfare.

Still less appreciated or analyzed, even by many critical world politics observers, is the role that the military plays in producing and reproducing masculinity. As Enloe argues, militaries need men to act as "men"—that is, to be willing to kill and die on behalf of the state (or rivals to it) to prove their "manhood" (1983: 212). This remains the linchpin for sustaining vast coercive apparatuses and practices.

## Militarized Masculinity

As a social construct, masculinity is not a given but rather is made. Moreover, as we pointed out earlier, there are multiple masculinities, most typically divided up between hegemonic masculinity (associated with elite, Western, upper-class, race-privileged, and heterosexual men) and subordinate masculinities (associated with racial minority or global South, lower-class, and sexual minority men). But the nature of hegemonic masculinity also shifts over time as well as across cultures. According to Charlotte Hooper, there have been at least four forms of Western hegemonic masculinity historically: the "Greek citizen-warrior," the "patriarchal Judeo-Christian model," the "honor-patronage" form, and the "Protestant, bourgeois-rationalist" man (2001: 64). She hypothesizes that in the 1990s a new "globalization" man was emerging, particularly in the Anglo-American context. These differing formations, although emerging over time, never cancel each other out. Rather, each morphs from the last so that each model retains elements of previous ones adapted to maintain hegemony in the face of changing socioeconomic, geopolitical, and even technological contexts (Hooper 2001: 65). Thus, although the homosocial martial qualities of the Greek citizen-warrior and the military heroism and risk-taking adventurism bound up in the European aristocratic ideal of the honor-patronage system are downplayed in the more modern bourgeois-rational man—who is all about the "reason and self-control or self-denial" needed to command capitalism rather than armies—aggression and power-over remain common threads (Hooper 2001: 65). They are simply rechanneled for new arenas of power. The captains of industry and the titans of finance who followed in the age of globalization speak in martial terms, wield economic and technological weapons, and aspire to ruthless takeovers. Such men no longer need hard bodies and physical strength to play out their martial identities, but they carry on the ideal of militarized masculinity nonetheless.

Even though actual military service as the ultimate test of manhood has been somewhat displaced as hegemonic masculinity came to be expressed in other forums, for most men without the highest class privilege and in patriarchal culture more generally, it retains pride of place as the most masculine activity. It also enjoyed somewhat of a renaissance in the post-9/11 period with the heavy reenactment of the security myth that has re- and hypervalorized male military protection and rescue. As the titans of finance faltered in the face of the economic crisis of their own making, globalization man gave way to some extent to "security man." As we saw previously, modern militaries actively preserve the association between masculinity and militaries by limiting the participation of women and effeminate or feminized (gay) men. But they also actively construct militarized masculinity through the making of soldiers. As Sandra Whitworth chronicles, this involves a whole range of grueling, humiliating, and degrading techniques from boot camp on to break down men's (and a smaller number of women's) sense of individuality and inhibitions about violence and then to build up conformity, "toughness, obedience, discipline, patriotism, lack of squeamishness; avoidance of certain emotions such as fear, sadness, uncertainty, guilt, remorse and grief, and heterosexual competency" (2008: 114). To make a militarized man means "killing the woman" in him (Whitworth 2008: 114), but as Aaron Belkin (2012) argues, it more accurately entails being forced to live out the contradictions, in a world based on hierarchical gender dichotomies, of being simultaneously masculinized and demasculinized. As he puts it, "The U.S. military has compelled the troops to embody masculinity and femininity" by requiring them to dwell in the "filth" of combat training and combat while kowtowing to the military's obsession with "cleanliness" (e.g., being hygienic and free of sexual disease contamination); to be both "impenetrable" as a predominantly heterosexual male fighting force protecting the homeland and "penetrable" in a military culture rife with routinized heterosexual-male-on-heterosexual-male rape; to be both "dominant" over those invaded and "subordinate" to the chain of command; and to uphold "civilization" as a "noble institution" through "barbarism" against those deemed uncivilized (2012: 173).

Thus, alongside and underneath the norms and façade of militarized masculinity (or hypermasculinity) lie deeply feminizing processes in an institution based on relations of domination and subordination. Such relations not only are normalized by the institution, but also structure a military masculinity that requires servicemen in particular to embody both domination and subordination while disavowing feminine weaknesses. Internalizing these contradictions makes militarized men particularly susceptible to obedience to a military that demands they conform to this schizoid structure of military masculinity, but it also ensures that they rarely report the sexual assault and the post-traumatic stress disorder (PTSD) that are pandemic in the military. Previously referred to as shell shock during the world wars, the more clinical diagnosis of PTSD was applied during the Vietnam War, and it was later found that 30 percent of male Vietnam veterans suffered from it (Whitworth 2008: 115). The particularly high rates of it for soldiers coming out of Iraq and Afghanistan, partially as a result of continuous redeployments, endanger the mystique of the warrior brotherhood and its invincibility. Thus, male soldiers are discouraged from reporting their symptoms and censor themselves for fear of seeming weak and unmanly. Indeed, the Pentagon disallowed US soldiers with PTSD, numbering approximately 300,000 in 2009, from receiving the Purple Heart in honor of their sacrifice (Alvarez and Eckholm 2009: A1), further pushing sufferers in the closet. Left untreated, the symptoms of "anxiety, fear of death, anger, depression, nightmares" and "hypervigilance" from reliving battlefield memories can also result in "unemployment, alcoholism, and even suicide," as well as divorce, domestic violence, and even murder (Whitworth 2008: 116).

Contemporary military efforts to play down the vulnerability of the male psyche are matched by current military efforts to compensate for the vulnerability of the male body. Armoring military men is not new, but Cristina Masters (2008) argues that the modifications and extensions of the male body have reached new heights, creating a "cyborg soldier" who will never die and will be willing to kill without remorse. The extreme technologicalization of postmodern warfare, now most symbolized by the Obama administration's reliance on drone warfare, seeks to circumvent the comparatively weaker male body, inserting it within machineries of command and control both in and highly distant from the battlefield that are "stronger, faster, more agile, and have much more staying power" (Masters 2008: 95). This displacement of militarized masculinity onto machineries enables such masculinity ideologically to survive the maimings and deaths of flesh-and-blood male bodies, assuring that militarized conflict will not be slowed down by the failings of male bodies and that the maiming and killing of "other" flesh-and-blood bodies will not be seen as other than "blips on radar screens, infrared images, precision-guided targets and numbers and codes on computer screens" (Masters 2008: 99). Thus, militaries are able to retain the mystique of militarized masculinity by disembodying it even as they still rely on male bodies to represent them and do much of their work.

Of course, the reality is that male warriors still die and are maimed psychologically and physically in great numbers because they make up the vast majority of the world's fighters—"the militant many" (Elshtain 1987). According to Joshua Goldstein, the twentieth century, possibly the "bloodiest relative to population" on record, produced approximately 110 million war dead from both direct and indirect violence (such as "war-induced famines and epidemics") (2011: 36–37). Combatants made up two-thirds of those killed by direct violence, while civilians made up two-thirds of those killed by indirect and direct violence. Direct violence is most often perpetrated by males on other males, but the "collateral damage" is much greater for noncombatants, although who among noncombatants suffer most depends on the conflict and the nature of it at any given time. Estimates of civilian deaths from violence in the Iraq War between 2003 and 2013 range from 112,017 to 122,438 compared with 39,900 fatalities suffered by all combatants, and it appears that the great majority of civilians killed in that war have been men performing police and neighborhood and private security work.[5] In the case of the war in Afghanistan, civilian deaths (estimated at 14,728 between 2007 and 2012) have also been much greater than US and coalition forces fatalities (3,315 between 2001 and 2013, albeit with an additional 17,674 US combatants wounded since 2001).[6] Although civilian deaths and injuries declined some from a high in 2011, the number of female civilians killed and wounded increased by 20 percent.[7] These costs of war do not count the millions of refugees and IDPs and the amount of food, shelter, and health insecurities produced or worsened by these two twenty-first-century conflicts alone. Thus, male combatants pay a heavy price in terms of their lives, their psyches, their bodies, and even their humanity; however, civilians of all genders bear the largest brunt of past and contemporary armed conflicts, which goes well beyond dying in them.

## Gender Violence

"Gender violence" typically refers to acts of domestic and sexual violence directed at maintaining gender hierarchies and punishing femininities. It most often means male violence against women, ranging from battering and burning to sexual harassment, assault, mutilation, slavery, trafficking, and torture as well as forced pregnancy and sterilization. However, men also visit gender violence on other men, and women, too, can commit gender violence against other women and men. Women's gender violence occurs less frequently, and because it often involves fewer weapons, it often produces less physical harm; however, armed women and women who have the power to use men as proxies to perform their gender violence can exact considerable harm. Gender violence also can refer to violence visited upon gays, lesbians, bisexuals, and transgendered peoples targeted for their sexuality (and gender). Although notoriously underreported in national and UN statistics, gender violence is acknowledged by the UN as epidemic throughout much of the world and across cultures, ethnicities, and classes. It is a regular feature of civilian life in heteronormative patriarchal societies, but it is especially rife in military settings. As we have seen, military women suffer gender violence most frequently at the hands of their male comrades, and this is the largest cause of PTSD (increasingly referred to as military sexual trauma, or MST) suffered by women soldiers (Whitworth 2008: 120). Military wives and girlfriends experience domestic violence at the hands of their male partners at three to five times the rate that women in civilian relationships do, and men "who have been in combat are four times more likely to be physically abusive" (Eisenstein 2007: 24). In the United States, rates of domestic and sexual abuse in military families particularly escalated since 9/11 (Eisenstein 2007: 24).

Even though widespread gender violence by "friendly" forces against their own is unsanctioned in theory, militaries actually institutionalize gender violence against "allied" and "enemy" women. According to Enloe, there are "three 'types' of institutionalized militarized rape: 'recreational rape'—the assumption that soldiers need constant access to sexual outlets; 'national security rape'—when police forces and armies use rape to bolster the state's control over a population; and systematic mass rape as an instrument of open warfare" (quoted in Seager 1997: 116). Although recreational rape is a feature of most state militaries, it is particularly associated with the US military, in part because the United States maintains the largest number of foreign military bases. This aspect of the US military gained worldwide attention in September 1995 when two marines and a navy seaman gang-raped a twelve-year-old Japanese girl in Okinawa (Seager 1997: 116). The storm of protest and anti–US military feelings on the part of the Japanese that this case evoked have not stopped military bases from also being deeply implicated in the business of prostitution.

Many military men have come to expect sexual servicing not as a perk but as a right and even a necessity during their stints overseas. Given that recreational rape can unleash protest against a foreign military presence (as in the Okinawan case), providing military men access to legitimate sex (with prostitutes) has been a policy of the US government. As part of Status of Forces Agreements (SOFAs) between the US government and its allies that codify the conditions under which US forces can be stationed in a host territory (Enloe 2000: 92), there are R&R agreements that detail the conditions for permitting and controlling the sexual servicing of the US military (Enloe 1993: 154). Perhaps the most notorious site was Subic Bay Naval Base in the Philippines. In the late 1980s, Filipino feminist organizations reported that as a result of high unemployment and extreme poverty, more than 20,000 Filipino women and about 10,000 Filipino children regularly acted as prostitutes for US servicemen at Subic Bay (Enloe 1989: 66). This situation contributed not only to the spread of HIV/AIDS but also to racial tensions and nationalist fervor: Filipinas/os denounced militarized prostitution as a symbol of their compromised sovereignty. The Subic Bay base was closed in 1991 when the Philippine government revoked its lease, but the nexus between military bases and prostitution and other forms of sex work continues elsewhere.

Katharine Moon's study of the SOFAs between the United States and South Korea since the Korean War finds that the numerous "camptowns" that grew up around US troops stationed there, particularly between the 1950s and 1970s, constituted a "GI's Heaven" where "20,000 registered prostitutes were available to 'service' approximately 62,000 US soldiers by the late 1960's" for as little as $2 for a half-hour sexual encounter (1997: 30). In the face of rising venereal disease, HIV/AIDS, and racial tensions born of Korean women's disinclination to service military men of color, US and Korean military officials engaged in elaborate measures to "clean up" the camptowns. These efforts were not designed to protect sex workers or to change the postwar economy that left so many primarily rural women, as well as men and children, scrambling to provide "entertainment" for GIs, but rather to make them safer for GIs to continue to be sexually serviced with less fear of disease and racial discrimination. As Moon argues, in this way the US–South Korean alliance was preserved on the backs of women literally on their backs.[8]

The Gulf wars in the Middle East have required a different approach to alliance building. In cultural and religious deference to such hosts as Saudi Arabia, the United States issued a "no-prostitution-allowed" policy, but there is evidence that soldiers returning home or redeployed stop along the way for sexual servicing in other ports of call, particularly in Southeast Asia (Enloe 2000: 72). There is no evidence that prostitution or no-prostitution agreements reduce rape. Richard Rayner (1997) finds that even after the shocking and genocidal rapes in Europe and Africa in the early 1990s that were documented and censured, many US military officials and experts continued to accept that rape is a "necessary corollary" to the military's main function—killing.

"Genocidal rape" refers to a systematic program of raping women and girls (and forcing captured "enemy" men and boys to rape each other) to humiliate (feminize) the enemy and to dilute it as a (biological) nation through the impregnation of the enemy's women (Hague 1997: 56). It gained worldwide attention when reports surfaced that during the war in Bosnia-Herzegovina that began in 1992, up to 60,000 women (most of them Bosnian) had been raped by 1993, largely by Serb forces (Bunch and Reilly 1994: 36). The massacres and countermassacres engaged in by the Tutsi and Hutu ethnic groups that began in Burundi in 1993 and in Rwanda in 1994 left well over 1 million people dead, and estimates put the number of women raped in the Rwandan conflict as high as 500,000 (Leatherman 2011: 41). The Sierra Leone civil war (1991–2001) subjected 64,000 female IDPs to rape, and the war that has been staged in all or parts of the Democratic Republic of Congo (DRC) between 1998 and 2013 has been associated with high degrees of brutal gang rapes of women by combatants at the war's height in the mid-2000s and especially in the eastern Congo since (Leatherman 2011: 2, 118–119, 128–129). Some call the war in the DRC Africa's "world war" because it began as a spillover from the Rwandan conflict and escalated as armies and militias within the DRC and from neighboring countries scrambled to profit from illicit trade in the DRC's mineral resources, with the complicity of Western TNCs.

Although rape has been a feature of all wars, its current visibility and more targeted and mass nature are attributed to the changing nature of war in the post–Cold War era. There has been a startling decline in wars and war deaths, with "90 percent fewer people each year" killed in armed conflicts in the twenty-first century than were killed "in the average conflict in the 1950s" (Leatherman 2011: 23). The reasons for this decline are multiple: more intrastate than interstate warfare, greater reliance on smaller armies and small arms, more "geographically limited war zones," more "precision" bombing and other "technological" warfare, improved public health services, and a greater amount and efficacy of humanitarian aid (Leatherman 2011: 22–23). Reductions in the resort to war and to some scourges of war are also associated with "spreading norms about peace and human rights," which are also seen as related to increasing numbers of NGOs and women in politics (Goldstein 2011: 15).

But as Janie Leatherman argues (2011: 34), what particularly characterizes the so-called "new wars" in the post–Cold War period in which rape has been most visibly used as a significant and calculated tactic of war are "runaway norms," or the fomenting (often by elites for political and economic gain) of hate of the "other" that is so extreme and boundless that it precipitates and prolongs a cascade of social harms. What particularly sets up runaway norms and are signals that a conflict is being generated include nationalist discourses that polarize gender and ethnic identities, demonize sexual minorities, and extol hypermasculinity (Leatherman 2011: 80–83). Runaway norms in recent (and some notable past) armed conflicts have fostered the widening of who commits rape (men, women, and children) and the specific targeting of who is raped (females or males, children or elderly) for particular strategic purposes, which frequently breaks peacetime taboos as to who is rapeable, as well as increasing the ferocity of sexual violence (including gang rapes and sexual torture and mutilations). Runaway norms also justify the veritable imprisonment by military commanders and combatants of women and children primarily through "forced" incest, marriage, prostitution "or survival sex," trafficking, and child soldiering. Finally, these norms ensure that there is no "safe" or "neutral" space for civilians, whether inhabitants, aid workers, or peacekeepers, to live, work, or attempt to mediate conflict, a condition that is made even worse by the fact that aid workers and peacekeepers have also been implicated in perpetrating gender violence against local women (Leatherman 2011: 42–61, 104–107). Thus, while war has decreased in its frequency and lethality, it has become more thoroughgoing in the brutality exacted on and through civilians and civil society, leaving deep wounds and continued gender violence well after the conflict is officially ended. Although sexual assaults have been defined as crimes of war since the 1940s, it was not until recently that rape has been prosecuted as a crime of genocide and against humanity (Oosterveld 2005). However, as we address later, this has had little effect on rape as a continuing tool of war.

Although gender violence is most associated with direct violence, it involves considerable structural violence. The sheer costs of military spending ensure that money is not available for meeting the human needs for which women are most responsible and that they are most denied. Despite dramatic post–Cold War declines in interstate warfare and even a precipitous drop in the nuclear arsenals of Russia and the United States (down from 60,000 to 14,000), as Goldstein observes, state officials responsible for military budgets have not gotten this memo (2011: 19). As noted in Chapter 1, worldwide military spending reached Cold War levels again in the first decade of the new millennium and there was only a miniscule reduction in this in 2012, driven not by the new realities of war but by budget austerity measures in the wake of the 2008 economic crisis. During the height of military spending in the post-9/11 era (just slightly more than today), it was estimated that only "one third of the world's military spending would satisfy budgetary needs for addressing any and all global problems, from deforestation to HIV and AIDS, from clean water to illiteracy" (WCC 2005: 2). Instead, countries in the global South were underspending on basic services such as education and health, devoting on average only 12 to 14 percent of their national budgets to these (WCC 2005: 18), whereas countries in the global North, especially the United States, continued to overspend on means of destruction. The largest arms dealers in the world were and remain the permanent members of the UN Security Council (the United States, Russia, France, China, and the UK), which sell primarily to the global South, including countries they have officially deemed human rights violators (WCC 2005: 22–23). At least one-fifth of the global South's debt has been attributable to its import of arms, and small arms or light weapons are by far the most traded as they are easily used in civil wars where interstate rules of war are least observed, for gender violence, and by child soldiers, including girls, who are pressed into fighting, raping, and being raped (WCC 2005: 24).

Given that at the same time, it was estimated that females made up 70 percent of the world's approximately 1.3 billion people living in absolute poverty (making less than $2 per day), two-thirds of the world's 800 million illiterates, and the majority of the world's refugees, HIV/AIDS sufferers, land-mine casualties, and sex trafficking, rape, and domestic violence victims (NCRW 2006), military largesse translates into massive structural as well as direct gender violence, enormously affecting women in the global South. Worldwide women's movements and NGOs have long made the connection between war and militarization and the compromising of women's security. Their efforts to bring this to world attention started during the UN Decade for Women, when women first held their own tribunals for crimes against women, followed by their promotion of women's human rights at the World Conference on Human Rights in Vienna in 1993 and the codification of the connection between armed conflict and gender violence as a violation of women's human rights at the 1995 Fourth World Conference on Women in Beijing (Joachim 2007). Amnesty International and Human Rights Watch also began monitoring and reporting on gender violence in the 1990s, ever since making it a major focus of their human rights campaigns (Joachim 2007: 128), and the genocidal rape in Bosnia and Rwanda also catapulted gender violence and its relationship to armed conflict onto the UN agenda. As explored in the following section, although UN action on this has been unprecedented, it has been weak at best, largely upholding gendered divisions of violence, gender violence, and especially the power of gender to privilege militarization and neocolonial or (neo)imperial relations.

## GENDERED PEACEMAKING,
## PEACEKEEPING, AND PEACE-BUILDING

Although part of a longer and wider struggle for women's security from militarized violence, the NGO Working Group on Women and International Peace and Security, consisting of the century-old WILPF, the Women's Caucus for Gender Justice, Amnesty International, International Alert, the Women's Commission for Refugee Women and Children, and the Hague Appeal for Peace in collaboration with UNIFEM, is credited with the final push to have the UN Security Council pass Resolution 1325 in 2000 (Cohn 2008: 187). Although nonbinding, 1325 "calls on" the UN and member countries to do the following: protect women from gender-based violence in war zones and include women (and gender perspectives) in peace negotiations, support their peacemaking initiatives in addition to providing gender-sensitive training to peacekeepers, and engage in gender mainstreaming through UN monitoring of and reporting on the gender dimensions of conflict and conflict resolution, including the impact of armed conflict on women and girls and the roles of women in peacemaking.

This landmark document and the activism that spawned it and continues since have also found expression in popular culture in the form of a five-part documentary series *Women, War & Peace* initially aired on US PBS stations in fall 2011. The series heralds the (mostly untold) stories of local women who survived the "new wars" of the late twentieth and early twenty-first centuries in Bosnia, Liberia, Afghanistan, and Colombia and who were and continue to be instrumental in pressing for peace negotiations, reconciliation, accountability for war crimes, and postconflict reconstruction, as well as a formal place for women in those processes to place women's and human rights more generally at the center of them. Although the women's stories are as complex and context-dependent as they are heroic, the narrative overlay (provided by Hollywood stars) of the series, which also features, for example, former US Secretary of State Hilary Clinton, former US Ambassador-at-Large for Global Women's Issues Melanne Verveer, and a special women's unit of the US military engaging in humanitarian (and intelligence) activities in Afghanistan to gain access to and the trust of Afghan women, is that women are an undertapped resource for peace and security that 1325 should remedy.

However, the effects of 1325 have been muted at best. Widespread rapes in the DRC conflict as well as in the Darfur genocide in Sudan and increased reports of rape by peacekeeping forces were featured in subsequent UN secretary-general studies and reports on women, peace, and security that were mandated by 1325. This acknowledgment of worsening gender violence in war led to the passage of additional UN Security Council resolutions (1820 in 2008, 1888 and 1889 in 2009, and 1860 and 1983 in 2010) that codify sexual violence as a matter of peace and security, call for the development and strengthening of measures to address sexual violence and to have more women present in peace operations and negotiations, mandate tracking of the implementation of 1325 and documenting of "credibly suspected" perpetrators of sexual violence in armed conflicts, and make HIV/AIDS resulting from sexual violence in armed conflicts a focus in peacekeeping and peace-building processes (DeLargy 2013).

These resolutions, which have been the first to address women and, most notably, women as security actors rather than only as victims in the history of the Security Council (Enloe 2007: 129), were preceded by the formation of international criminal tribunals for the former Yugoslavia (ICTY) and Rwanda (ICTR) in 1993 and 1994, respectively. Rape was first prosecuted by a World War II military tribunal that found several Japanese commanders responsible for systematic rapes in Nanking, and the 1946 Fourth Geneva Convention and 1974 UN Declaration on the Protection of Women and Children in Emergency and Armed Conflict speak amorphously to protecting women from war violence (Oosterveld 2005: 68–69). However, the ICTY and ICTR were the first tribunals to begin developing international case law and precedents that spell out a wide range of gender violence (including gender violence perpetrated against men) that is prosecutable as a crime of war and a tool of genocide (Oosterveld 2005: 79).[9] By 1998, these were codified in the Rome Statute of the International Criminal Court (ICC), which recognizes multiple forms of gender violence in armed conflict as crimes against humanity and war crimes and requires gender-sensitive judges and court proceedings that do not retraumatize victims (Oosterveld 2005: 67).

These are significant gender gains in the struggle against gendered insecurities, but they remain problematic on a number of scores. With respect to 1325 and its successors, there has been great resistance to including women in peace negotiations on the part of the male establishments of warring parties, international donors, and conflict resolution specialists, and the few who are included are typically proxies for those male establishments, having no political base of women to whom they are accountable, and/or having been left out of "real" backroom negotiations

(DeLargy 2013). Moreover, in 1325 and related resolutions since, gender violence is reduced to sexual violence against women and only in the context of armed conflicts, ignoring that it is just as rife before and even worse after conflicts (True 2012: 137). There is no mention in these resolutions of a central need to address hegemonic/militarized masculinity or of the critical relationship between sexual violence and the global economic interests that have driven armed conflicts, ranging from the trade in illicit blood diamonds as in Sierra Leone and minerals as in the DRC to the licit small arms trade (Leatherman 2011: 164). Similarly unaddressed are the gendered economic harms that arise from the neoliberal economic restructuring that is often imposed after conflicts, including far greater resources given by international donors, and reflected in postconflict national budgets, to security apparatuses (including the disarmament, demobilization, and reintegration of combatants—or DDR programs) as opposed to basic needs, much less gender equality, which makes it very difficult for resource-poor women to perform peace-building in their societies (True 2012: 151, 146–147). Moreover, under the gendered division of violence that assumes women are peaceful, DDR programs have also failed to pay attention to female combatants and their special problems with reintegration into still patriarchal societies (Leatherman 2011: 169). Ultimately, these resolutions reproduce very narrow constructions of gender and gender violence that do not disturb and in fact reinforce the international order that is productive of gender harms (Shepherd 2008).

With respect to the question of holding perpetrators accountable for sexual violence, which is now part of the successor resolutions to 1325, although women now constitute the majority of judges on the ICC, those states that are not signatories to the Rome Statute, such as the United States, are exempt from having their officials and troops prosecuted by the ICC; much individual military peacekeeper gender violence cannot be proven to rise to the level of crimes against humanity in nongenocidal contexts; SOFAs typically keep peacekeepers as well as militaries immune to prosecution in the host country, and they are rarely, if ever tried in their home countries; and civilians and private contractors serving as military or peacekeeping extensions are also immune (Bedont 2005). Finally, there is no international jurisdiction for gender violence perpetrated against a soldier's own comrades-in-arms.

Thus, beneath the failures of these formal mechanisms lie a range of insidious processes that the following discussion of peacekeeping connects. Peacekeeping remains a male bastion, with women constituting barely

4 percent of the military experts, troops, and police who carry out peace-keeping missions (Cohn and Jacobson 2013). As feminist IR experts have pointed out (Enloe 1993; Whitworth 2004), donning a "blue beret" sets up contradictions for the military men who become peacekeepers. Military training that inculcates militarized masculinity neither prepares peace-keeping troops for the humanitarian work they are expected to perform nor encourages them to embrace the light weapons they carry or the force restraint they must observe. Peacekeeping can also breed male resentment for "missing the 'main' show—conflict and warfare" (Whitworth 2004: 150), but it also ensures that peacekeepers (from both the global North and the global South) expect the same perks as other military men, as they "run brothels, assault local women, and kill local citizens" (Whitworth 2004: 152).

On the other side of the coin, as Whitworth (2004) argues based on her study of Canadian peacekeeping operations, the UN's new interest in "add-ing women and stirring" simply grafts on (essentialist) gender analysis, which assumes women will just ease and assist the already predetermined business of peacekeeping and peace negotiations by bringing information on women and "women's issues" into these activities. This predetermined business disregards any considerations of militarized masculinity as a ma-jor source of prolonged conflict or such sources of structural violence as neocolonial economic and political relationships and neoliberal economic restructuring that may lie at the heart of the conflict (Whitworth 2004: 133, 137). Instead, this business focuses on "when the fighting broke out" and how to control, if not cease, it (Whitworth 2004: 133). Thus, rather than causing a rethinking of peacekeeping and peace negotiations, "anal-yses of women and of gender thus become part of the 'programmatic solutions' that form the UN repertoire of responding to conflict and inse-curity around the world, and, in this way, confirm the appropriateness of the repertoire" (Whitworth 2004: 137). In this sense, like gender equality that is subsumed under neoliberal governmentality, gender perspectives on international peace and security are subsumed under a kind of secu-rity governmentality. Whitworth concludes that the issue is not so much adding more women to peacekeeping and peacemaking operations as it is questioning the sole reliance on militaries to do the job of peacekeeping and, by extension, on military leaders and civilian defense elites to do the job of peacemaking (2004: 183).

Even more problematic, Whitworth (2004) points out that peace-keeping itself is a colonial practice. Given that fourteen of the thirty

UN peacekeeping operations launched between 1988 and 2005 were in Africa (Hudson 2005), with almost all the rest in the South as well, contemporary peacekeeping "comes from an understanding of the places in which those conflicts occur, 'conflict-prone third world countries,' which are defined by what they lack: the institutions, the liberalism, the rationality, and the order of Western states. Peacekeeping, as part of the contemporary '*mission civilatrice*,' is the means by which that 'lack' can be addressed, bringing meaning and order where there are none. Peacekeeping is, in short, part of the 'subject constituting project' of the colonial encounter" (Whitworth 2004: 185).

Beyond the irony that the weapons the West sells to the South enable and increase brutal conflict there, the colonizing dimensions of peacekeeping not only invite greater militarization of peacekeeping and the conflicts it seeks to quell, but also undermine the peace-building efforts of "local" women (and their male allies), who are ignored or discounted and underresourced.

## (DE)MILITARIZING FEMINISM

Given that all "*genders lose in war,* although they lose in somewhat different ways" (Goldstein 2001: 402), we still confront the problem of dealing with the recurring linkages identifying masculinity with aggression and war and femininity with passivity and peace that shore up militarization. Judith Hicks Stiehm (1989) argues that achieving gender parity in the US armed forces might ultimately force an acknowledgment that war is not "manly" and that women can protect themselves. In this view, women's equal participation might destabilize the ways in which the gendered division of violence and the gender inequality upon which it rests contribute to militarization. However, given the historical patterns, gender parity seems an unlikely development in any state military. Moreover, as the jobs of militaries and even peacekeeping forces are increasingly privatized into the hands of essentially paid mercenary forces like Blackwater (now known as Xe Services), such contracting ensures that the "real" business of war will be kept largely in male hands and remain "manly," regardless of some "resexing" of state militaries.

Other feminists have pointed out that, although comparatively few women are or will be soldiers on the battlefront, many more serve the military on the home front, working (typically at the lowest levels) for defense and related industries. We could argue that this labor contributes more to life-taking than do individual male and female soldiers on the battlefront. At the same time, as we have seen, women's political violence has become more visible as women gain more political power and enter the ranks of militaries and "terrorist" groups, even though their violence is typically not represented as political violence. And images and realities of military men's vulnerability are becoming harder to hide and contain, even though there continue to be herculean efforts to do so.

Still other feminists point out that in times of violent conflict, gender dichotomies are not only rigidified but also can lose their rigidity. In contrast to the post-9/11 response in the United States that brought a particularly virulent restaging of gender (and race) binaries and asymmetries, Simona Sharoni (1998) finds that in cases such as "the troubles" in Northern Ireland and the Israeli-Palestinian conflict, women under British and Israeli occupation became significant political actors as patriarchal taboos were lifted in the midst of conflict. This has also occurred in a range of especially Latin American guerrilla or armed national liberation movements against repressive authoritarian governments in which women have been involved in large numbers as politicized and often explicitly feminist actors and combatants (Kampwirth 2002). At the same time, some men, such as imprisoned Irish Republican Army (IRA) members, have developed new understandings of their own vulnerabilities as a result of their prison experiences. As Sharoni (1998) recounts, captured IRA members incarcerated in British prisons learned to protest their treatment in prison out of vulnerability. For example, in resistance to being marked as criminals rather than as political prisoners, they refused to wear prison-issue clothing for more than four years, choosing to be naked instead and using only blankets to cover themselves. This is the opposite of and in opposition to the armored man. They also gained new appreciation of feminist perspectives on conflict and peace as a result of working with feminist educators and supporters on the outside who backed their protests. By coming to recognize the interconnections among gender, sexuality, race, class, nationality, and international violence, they thereby learned to eschew militarized masculinity on the understanding that it gets in the way of broad and inclusive struggles for justice and peace that are more nonviolent than violent.

This example brings us to an important distinction: imperialist violence versus resistance to it, whether nonviolent or violent. Since 9/11, feminist debates have shifted to grapple with the militarization of feminism (particularly Western, but especially US feminism) through its appropriation by the Bush administration. In Ann Russo's (2006) analysis of the US Feminist Majority Foundation's (FMF) campaign to stop "gender apartheid" in Afghanistan, she argues that beyond the well-known claim by the Bush administration that the war against Afghanistan was at least partially about liberating Afghan women from the male oppressors of the Taliban, thus using feminist rhetoric as a stimulus for war, the FMF also actively enabled, supported, and partook in this rhetoric at the expense of Afghan women and women's movements. Although the FMF's pre-9/11 campaign against gender violence could be seen as "counterhegemonic," this campaign ended up colluding with the "project of US imperialism and retaliatory violence as a method of maintaining US power" (Russo 2006: 558). The reasons for this, according to Russo (2006), include the FMF's desire to be taken seriously on the foreign policy stage by pointing to the success of its impact on the Bush administration; its ahistorical reading of the causes of gender violence in Afghanistan, including the Soviet invasion of it and the subsequent US arming of the Taliban; its myopic focus on lifting the burka and on "freeing" that nation's women, which led the FMF to support the war without consideration of the greater costs that war would visit on Afghan women; and its participation in colonialist and Orientalist thinking. As we pointed out earlier, Orientalism assumes Western superiority and constructs the West as the source of rescue and salvation for the rest, which has justified over the centuries invasions and colonizations that have caused the havoc from which "others" must be saved. The FMF's alliance with the US State Department in support of the Afghanistan War caused a split between the FMF and the Revolutionary Association of Women in Afghanistan (RAWA), which rejected the invasion and the postinvasion installation of more gender-violence-producing patriarchs in the form of the Northern Alliance, a development that the association had warned would be the result of the invasion (Russo 2006: 574). Western, particularly US, LGBTQ activists have also been implicated in shoring up bellicose US foreign policy when they have protested "state homophobia" in selective parts of the global South, such as Iran, thereby providing further ammunition for invasion talk when it suits US policymakers (Nayak and Selbin 2010: 80).

Many other feminists and queers in the West, as well as more generally in the global North and South, have condemned the war in Afghanistan and the "war on terror" more generally (Hawthorne and Winter 2002; Joseph and Sharma 2003; Hunt and Rygiel 2006; Puar 2007; Alexander and Hawkesworth 2008; Butler 2010). Many US feminists also have chronicled the relentless "war on women" at home and abroad by the Bush administration (Flanders 2004; Finlay 2006), which belied its claims to feminist motivations and put into serious question assumptions about the relationship between Western modernity and support for gender equality. In contrast, those who do practice "imperial feminism" and imperial "global gay" politics, which imposes Western approaches to gay liberation on other cultures in ways that make it difficult for sexual minorities in them to engage in their own struggles while also demonizing global South countries for their homophobia (Alexander 2005), militate against transnational solidarity to resist war and militarism.

As a range of feminist historical scholarship has shown, imperial feminism is not new. Whether operating in the context of British, Dutch, French, or other empires (McClintock 1995; Midgley 1998; Clancy-Smith and Gouda 1998; Levine 2004), it has been implicated in the imperial, masculinist, racist, heteronormative, and homonormative project of white(ned) men saving white women from racialized men. Contemporary imperial feminism and global gay imperialism help to construct, buy into, and represent the imperial, racist, heteronormative, and homonormative project of white(ned) women/Western gays saving "brown women [and brown sexual minorities] from brown men" and brown homophobes (Spivak 1988: 297), and thus further contribute to continued imperialist militarism.

Most recently, feminist scholars, along with other critical world politics scholars, have focused their attention not only on US empire, in the form of the military and political unilateralism that the Bush administration in particular enacted (Eisenstein 2004), but also on Empire as the current expression of global capitalism, which while most championed by the United States subsumes even it and the IGOs it dominates under processes of neoliberal governmentality (Hardt and Negri 2000). Although US-fostered securitization of borders and movements of peoples seems in contradiction to the open borders that global capitalism requires, the combination of security regimes or globalized militarization with global capitalism allows greater exploitation and oppression. This is not only because globalized militarization causes greater desperation and thus more and more at-risk or captive and thus cheapened and quiescent labor—as well as a way for private industry to reap enormous profits from war industries—but also because the "war on terror" and global capitalism have been constructed as *the* way to "democracy" and therefore are not to be questioned.[10] Thus,

Empire partially accepts feminists and other social movement actors (as well as some resexing of male-dominated militaries and occupations) who do not question these twin pillars, for they lend the veneer of democracy to these projects.

Thus, feminists transnationally who do not accept this arrangement, which deradicalizes feminism and other social movements seeking to reduce human insecurities and planetary destruction, have turned their attention to linking and building solidarity against these twin pillars that actually undermine democratization. To resist Empire is to disrupt the gendered division of violence, not by claiming equality to do imperial violence but rather by challenging the power of gender to valorize it. As Arundhati Roy puts it:

> Our strategy should be not only to confront Empire, but to lay siege to it. To deprive it of oxygen. To shame it. To mock it. With our art, our music, our literature, our stubbornness, our joy, our brilliance, our sheer relentlessness—our ability to tell our own stories. Stories that are different from the ones we're being brainwashed to believe.
>
> The corporate revolution will collapse if we refuse to buy what they are selling—their ideas, their version of history, their weapons, their notions of inevitability.
>
> Remember this. We be many and they be few. They need us more than we need them. (2003: 112)

## DISARMING SECURITY

As we indicated at the outset of this chapter, security is always elusive and partial. This does not undercut our argument for the need to confront the crisis of insecurity, which is born of the pursuit of absolute security. The desire for absolute security is the product of hardened masculinist identities that imagine themselves and the world as a series of armed camps set up to preserve their respective autonomies. Whether security can be completely detached from this imagining is an open question, but security has come to mean far more than that (Sutton, Morgen, and Novkov 2008), and it can be pursued without compromising the security of "others" by resisting "othering" itself and recognizing that processes that compromise the security of others compromise the security of a reimagined "self" in solidarity with others.

The newfound attention of "security" IGOs to the compromising of women's security through armed conflict is, on the one hand, welcome, but, on the other hand, has reproduced gender ideologies that construct women as "natural" victims and peace proponents. This sets up women to carry the burden of peacemaking and peace-building while lacking the material resources and political representation and sway to do so. It also deflects attention from the continued and overwhelming prerogatives of elites, states, and markets to make war and unjust peace. Even the new prosecutions of gender violence in war can have nonhumanitarian effects, including providing additional "fuel for nationalist fervor" and thereby resulting in reprisals against women who testify and the sustaining of conflict (Giles and Hyndman 2004: 13). As we have seen, peacekeeping is also more of a colonizing practice than a peaceful one, and refugees and internally displaced persons are far from safe from combatants as well as peacekeepers and aid workers. Thus, humanitarian efforts are increasingly being exposed by feminists as part of the "security myth."

Although there are many good reasons to disconnect peace from women (as well as war from men), there remains some value in Gayatri Spivak's concept of strategic essentialism to resist war and other forms of violence. The notion that women, especially as mothers, are more peaceful has been thoroughly problematized, but the fact remains that women continue to mobilize against war based in part on this very notion. Once into such struggles, they may shift their political identities and recognize that homogenizing notions of womanhood or motherhood are not enough for, and may stand in the way of, transcending or working through political differences and economic and social inequalities. But however women become politicized to resist war together, in doing so they "reject the prevalent relationship to the state (and sometimes with their spouses and partners) and redefine it" (Kaufman and Williams 2007: 30). Thus, identity "myths" can be useful for peace and justice mobilizations as long as they are seen as provisional and political, not foundational or natural.

## Notes

1. See http://www.nbcnews.com/id/33230836/ns/us_news-military/t/lesbians -more-likely-be-kicked-out-military/.

2. See http://armscontrolcenter.org/issues/securityspending/articles/2012_topline _global_defense_spending/.

3. All films cited in this text are referenced in the Web and Video Resources at the end of the text, which also includes many more film and video resources.

4. See http://www.sapr.mil.

5. See http://www.iraqbodycount.org/analysis/numbers/ten-years/.

6. See http://icasualties.org/OEF/Index.aspx.

7. See http://unama.unmissions.org/Default.aspx?tabid=12254&ctl=Details&mid=15756&ItemID=36445&language=en-US.

8. Recently, former sex workers in South Korea have sought an apology and compensation from their government for its role in serving as "one big pimp" for the American military, likening their case to that of the "comfort women" who were pressed into serving as prostitutes for the Japanese military during World War II and who also have sought an apology and compensation from the Japanese government (Sang-Hun 2009).

9. See Henry 2011 for accounts of these tribunals.

10. See Grewal for an analysis of how security has become the dominant mode of governmentality, using race and gender to "produce figures of risk" who must be disciplined and must adopt self-discipline in order not to threaten the "'security,' happiness and freedom" of those who determine who is "risk-producing" and "at risk" (2005: 202).

# 5

⋯⋯⋯⋯⋯⋯⋯⋯⋯⋯⋯⋯⋯⋯⋯⋯⋯⋯◄○►⋯⋯⋯⋯⋯⋯⋯⋯⋯⋯⋯⋯⋯⋯⋯⋯⋯⋯

# Gender and
# Global Political Economy

How are women and men positioned and repositioned in and by global economic processes and with what effects? What do gendered divisions of labor tell us about how work is defined, valued, and distributed? How does the power of gender affect who has access to and control over symbolic, economic, and environmental resources? How has neoliberal globalization undermined social reproduction and environmental protection as well as produced apolitical, market-based responses that leave structural inequalities intact?

There is tremendous variation in how economic processes work in households, rural and urban communities, nations, and geographic regions. In this chapter, we look at the relationship between gendered inequalities and global political economy (GPE).[1] We put globalization, a process that we describe at length later in this chapter and that is most often associated with the rise of and spread of neoliberal "global capitalism," at the center of this examination and argue that it is a gendering and gendered process that reflects both continuity and change. We also continue to consider the contemporary paradox between the *repositioning of* (some) *women* and (some) *men,* this time in the context of the GPE, and the *power of gender* to undermine broader economic justice and breed the economic and ecological *crisis of sustainability*. On the one hand, more women worldwide are seeking and gaining employment, thus becoming income earners and presumably benefiting from the enhanced self-esteem and economic empowerment that formal work affords. On the other hand, the feminization of employment has done little to alter expectations regarding gender divisions of labor or valorizations of masculinized work

181

over women's work or to enable women in the aggregate to significantly increase their control over economic decision-making or environmental resource use. Although gender mainstreaming now features in the World Bank's and other international agencies' economic development policies, the objective is to integrate women into markets rather than to promote social justice by altering hierarchical gender relations. The power of gender here operates to reproduce divisions of labor and responsibility in social reproduction and formal production that favor short-term neoliberal objectives and sustain commitments to competition and growth—but at the price of long-term crises of social reproduction and environmental sustainability.

With reference to owning economic resources and wielding economic authority, at first glance the positioning of men and women suggests more continuity than change. Gender stereotypes persist in assigning men the primary responsibility for generating income in households worldwide, and men in aggregate still hold higher-paying and more secure jobs than do women. Men—especially those who are economically, ethnically, racially, and geopolitically privileged—continue to control power-wielding and decision-making authority in economic development planning, corporate investment strategies, and IFIs. These patterns relate to what we have called the *gendered division of labor*: paid-unpaid work, providers-dependents, production-reproduction, and independence versus dependence in the marketplace. We address this in concert and as interrelated with the *gendered division of resources* (culture-nature, active-passive, subject-object, users-resources, advanced-primitive, and exploitation versus stewardship) in this chapter (see Table 5.1). And as we continue to show here, the *power of gender* persists through masculinist, racist, classist, and heteronormative assumptions and objectives in economic and geopolitical thinking and practice (despite some economic attention to women, particularly in the early wake of the 2008 financial crisis). This is most visible when we observe how policymaking remains largely top-down, formulaic, and overreliant on growth and quantifiable indicators, often at the expense of being focused on provisioning, human well-being, and social and environmental sustainability, contributing to what we refer to generally as the *crisis of sustainability*.

But we also note how globalization is disrupting familiar gender patterns and repositioning women and men by altering assumptions, roles, identities, and livelihoods worldwide. These disruptions are especially visible in relation to economics, in part because gender is so key to unequal

TABLE 5.1

**Gendered Divisions of Labor and Resources
Productive of the Crisis of Sustainabilty**

| *Masculinized* | *Feminized* |
| --- | --- |
| Paid work | Unpaid Work |
| Providers | Dependents |
| Production | Reproduction |
| Independence in market | Dependence in market |
| Developed | Undeveloped |
| Culture | Nature |
| Active | Passive |
| Subject | Object |
| Users | (Disposable) resources |
| Advanced | Primitive |
| Finance | Consumption |
| Exploitation | Stewardship |

divisions of labor and their valorizations, and in part because new technologies are so profoundly altering what is produced, how, where, and by whom worldwide. Some changes are small and incremental, whereas others challenge our deepest assumptions (male breadwinner roles) and most established institutions (patriarchal families where male heads of household are the primary "providers"). The effects of these repositionings and disruptions are complex and defy easy generalizations. As more women enter the paid workforce—some by traveling great distances—this both empowers some women and complicates expectations of hegemonic masculinity for most men. The geographical unevenness of employment opportunities spurs internal and external migrations that alter "traditional" household formations, and diasporas reconfigure ethnic/racialized identifications and alignments. Neoliberal policies have also imposed new disciplining practices that shape the expectations, options, and responses of workers worldwide.

Neoliberal economic approaches to poverty abatement (and those things that attend poverty, such as HIV/AIDS, maternal mortality, and susceptibility to human and sex trafficking), primarily in the global South, have spawned not only top-down measures such as the MDGs, but also the shifting of responsibilities for this abatement to the NGO sector and to an individualistic donor culture, primarily in the West. This culture is produced by NGO and corporate campaigns adorned with celebrity spokespeople who exhort the power of humanitarian giving, sometimes by just consuming charitable items. *Half the Sky* is emblematic of this approach to poor women's economic empowerment. While on the one hand this approach democratizes aid and connects people to laudable causes beyond themselves, on the other hand it is associated with "poverty capitalism" (Roy 2010), a term that refers to the capitalist industry that has grown up around private and privatizing antipoverty campaigns. As we address later in this chapter, such an approach fails to address the more massive and equitable redistribution of economic resources to serve the worldwide public good and human well-being, which would require structural reforms in the GPE. Such an approach also encourages consumption as a solution to poverty, unmindful of the exploitative work conditions under which items for sale for charity are too often made by the very women antipoverty campaigns are supposed to help. As we also address at more length in this chapter, the encouragement of (over)consumption also has severe environmental effects.

Relatedly, the growth imperative of "disaster capitalism," in which the private sector profits from reconstructing places devastated by "natural" disasters (typically precipitated by man-made pollutants) and most often in ways that do not benefit the poor, exacerbates old and produces new environmental degradations (Klein 2007). We also address this phenomenon more in this chapter, but suffice it to say here that it is part of the overvalorization of masculinized activities—literally at the expense of feminized activities and feminized workers—which continues to reproduce gendered inequalities and intensifies a polarization of (masculinized) haves and (feminized) have-nots, manifested as well in the masculinized North dumping its disproportionate waste on the feminized South. These stark economic inequalities constitute structural violence and global insecurities, including the insecurity of environmental conditions upon which all else depends. Neoliberal responses to environmental harms, particularly climate change experienced globally but falling the hardest on the most economically vulnerable, have too often constituted "climate capitalism" (Parr 2013) under which the environment is simultaneously commodified and feminized and the only way in which presumably it can be saved, or at least managed, is through owning it and consuming it, albeit in supposedly "greener" ways.

When we examine how globalization is repositioning women and men in the GPE, we gain a contemporary picture of what work is available, where and under what conditions, and who does it as well as who controls and who is impoverished in economic systems. When we examine how the power of gender operates, we advance our understanding of how "work" is defined, accounted for, and differentially valorized; how technologies are transforming production, marketing, distribution, and consumption in gendered ways; how stereotypes of gender, sexuality, and race shape whose bodies and services are sought and "consumed" in pleasure-seeking and care-based industries and whose bodies are disposable; and how gendered economic priorities and practices produce and sustain the crisis of sustainability. In general, our focus on GPE reveals starkly how the power of gender constitutes not only a sexual division of labor that exploits women (and feminized "others"), but also a gendered, polarized valorization of skills, activities, work, workers, and bodies under gendered economic presumptions that serve to "naturalize" the exploitation of most of the earth's population and the planet itself.

## FEMINIST APPROACHES TO GLOBAL POLITICAL ECONOMY

Economic and work issues raised by feminists include how the gendered division of labor positions men and women differently; how women's domestic, reproductive, and caring labor is deemed marginal to "production" and analyses of it; and how orthodox models and methods presuppose male-dominated activities (paid work, the formal economy) and masculinized characteristics (autonomous, objective, rational, instrumental, competitive). In effect, the extensive (feminized) labor involved in social reproduction and upon which all else ultimately depends is treated not only as noneconomic but also as coincidental, as if the rest of the social system could survive without it. As a corollary, "women's work" and feminized qualities are devalued: deemed economically irrelevant (done "for love" not for money); characterized as subjective, "voluntary," "natural," and "unskilled"; and either poorly paid or not paid at all. At the same time, feminists criticize mainstream assumptions that all caring labor and social reproduction occur through heteronormative families and nonconflictual intrahousehold dynamics. Through a mainstream lens—whether academic or policymaking—alternative household forms and the rising percentage of female-headed and otherwise unconventional households are rendered deviant or invisible.[2]

How feminists address and attempt to correct these biases and omissions, which they have found are characteristic of androcentric and masculinist political economies in the global North and South, has varied over time and along numerous dimensions. Once again, many begin by "adding women," which invariably prompts new questions regarding what counts as relevant data (marriage patterns, family budgets), appropriate sources (family and community records, personal diaries), and germane topics (caring labor, shopping, food preparation, sex work). Attention shifts from a (masculinist) focus on "the main story" of men's activities to the "background" story that underpins and enables men's activities.

Early feminist studies on the GPE that "added women" focused on women in "Third World" economic development, which we explore later in this chapter. In the early 1970s, for example, Esther Boserup (1970) studied the effects of modernization policies on women in nonindustrialized countries. Paying attention to women's experiences exposed the often deleterious effects of modernization and undercut orthodox claims that development benefited everyone. As we noted earlier, subsequent WID (women in development) research documented both how policies and practices marginalized women and how women's exclusion jeopardized development objectives.

With its focus on "empirical" gender, WID scholarship initially sought more effective *inclusion* of women in the practices and presumed benefits of development. This orientation was important and productive for revealing inequalities of positioning among women and men. Cumulative research suggested, however, that simply "adding women" did not address significant problems: the devaluation of feminized labor, the structural privileging of men and masculinity, or the increasing pressure on women to work a triple shift (in familial, informal, and formal activities) to ensure family survival during economic crises. In response, feminists increasingly asked how the power of gender was shaping underlying assumptions, expectations, and even rules of the game. For many researchers, the liberal, modernist inclinations of WID approaches were gradually displaced, as we also noted earlier, by the more constructivist, critical starting points of gender and development orientations.[3] GAD (gender and development) scholars problematized the meaning and desirability of development (especially as modernization) imposed by Western development experts and agencies, interrogated the definition of work and productive activity generally and how to "count" that activity, and exposed the masculinism of men's reluctance to "help" in the household even as women were in or entering the labor force. These scholars also challenged some Western liberal constructions of feminism that imagined women's economic independence as necessarily freeing; investigated intersections of sexualization, racialization, and neocolonialism that enabled hyperexploitation of labor; and criticized narratives of victimization that particularly denied agency to poor and racialized women. These studies marked an opening up of questions, an expansion of research foci, and a complication of analyses more consonant with investigating gendered divisions of labor among women and men.[4]

In the new millennium, feminists have broadened their focus beyond development to the GPE writ-large, including ideologies that underpin its workings. Their expanded inquiries have encompassed matters of aid, trade, and finance and the regional and global institutions, interstate and private, that orchestrate these, as well as the processes of global restructuring that are reconfiguring national and local economies, polities, and cultures in complex ways. In the process, these scholars have continued to expose masculinist bias and its effects and expanded the evidence corroborating early feminist critiques while also complicating those critiques through intersectional lenses, particularly by bringing postcolonial and queer perspectives to the fore. They have deepened the interrogation of foundational constructs (rationality, work, production, capital, value, development) and the critique of neoliberal globalization as masculinist, racist, heterosexist, and imperialist,[5] making the link between globalization and militarization. They have extended their research from more obviously gender-differentiated effects of microeconomic phenomena and national budgets to the less direct effects of macroeconomic policies, including how gender operates even in the abstracted realm of financial markets.[6] The activism of women in the global South raised the profile of women's knowledge and agency, and feminists more generally engaged in rethinking economic "givens" and generating alternative visions of economics based on a more relevant and responsible model of "social provisioning."[7]

In the following sections, we detail some of the findings over the past several decades of feminist research on the GPE, identifying gendered impacts of larger and shifting economic processes. As in previous chapters, we note that feminists have had some success in shifting the attention of global policymakers (and ordinary citizens) toward ameliorating the socioeconomic conditions of women as central to achieving any real development, both economic and human. However, we argue that responses have been not only too little, but also highly problematic as they fail to disrupt both the gendered divisions of labor and the power of gender to privilege capitalist accumulation by the few at the expense of the many.

## WOMEN, GENDER, AND DEVELOPMENT

Gender stereotypes are promulgated by dichotomized categories favored in economic analysis: paid-unpaid work, production-reproduction, skilled-unskilled, formal-informal. These interact with other gendered dichotomies that shape how we think about and valorize work: men's work-women's work, labor for profit–labor for love, working-caretaking, breadwinner-housewife, and so on. We note here that for the most part, these divisions are recent in world history. Prior to modern state-making, colonization, and industrial capitalism, rigid dichotomies were less familiar because all able-bodied family and community members were expected to contribute. Work was therefore a more communal activity, and divisions between public and private spheres, paid and unpaid labor, were not yet institutionalized. Although specific tasks might be gender coded, the particular coding varied greatly over time and across cultures, and activities in general were valued as necessary and complementary contributions to sustaining families and households. Processes of colonization and industrialization were key to constituting more rigid, less equal, and thus less complementary conceptions of how labor should be divided between and among sexes, classes, and nations.

### Colonization and Industrialization

This Western gendered division of labor was imposed on many cultures in the Americas, Asia, and Africa beginning in the fifteenth century.[8] In many instances, the economic status and well-being of women in diverse cultures were diminished by the patriarchal and political ideologies imposed by colonizers. For example, farming in many African countries was almost exclusively women's work, and men were responsible for clearing fields, hunting, and engaging in warfare. Because Western colonizers assumed land should be "owned" and men should be the "heads of households" and hence the primary earners, they transferred land rights to men (away from women under communal systems) and ensured that men (rather than women) received agricultural training and technological supports as well as access to cash and credit. Giving some men titles to small plots of land not expropriated by Europeans for plantation agriculture or other uses, and turning men as well as women into farm laborers—either as slaves or minimally paid workers—did not mean empowerment (enhanced capacity) for most colonized men. It favored men's positioning relative to women's, but not relative to those who gained from European colonization. As Gita Sen and Caren Grown observe, "The colonial period created and accentuated inequalities both 'among' nations, and between classes and genders (also castes, ethnic communities, races, etc.) 'within' nations" (1987: 24).

These gendered effects of the imposition of Western "modernity" were extended with the rise of "industrial capitalism" from the late eighteenth century on.[9] Industrialization drove a significant wedge between the home and the workplace, which were more or less melded in agricultural economies. As caste divisions (aristocrats versus peasants/indentured servants versus slaves) slowly and unevenly (and still not completely) shifted to class divisions (upper versus middle versus lower class) in the industrializing West, certain women (those in upper and rising middle classes and of European descent) were to be confined to the home to provide a "safe haven" for male industrialists. European-born and immigrant poor and working-class women (and children) of European descent were a part of the Western industrial workforce in some (especially textile) industries, constituting preferred "cheap" and "controllable" labor in the form of factory and piecework performed at home for a time. However, male labor increasingly became preferred (in part as a result of social reforms to relieve women and children from the most exploitative factory labor as well as the rise of male-led unions), and the ideal of the heteronormative family supported by a male wage earner became a norm (if not a reality) even for the working classes. Women of African descent, even after slavery was legally abolished throughout the West, remained in the fields or as maids for white(ned) women in the rising middle classes who were expected to remain at home. In the still colonized or newly "independent" parts of the global South still subject to neocolonial relations with their former colonizers, resource extraction to fuel the industrial revolution occurred on the backs of men and women, although it was men who were brought more into wage labor (in the mines and increasingly mechanized fields owned by former colonizers), while women were left to engage in subsistence farming on what land remained to poor families, too often held under men's names as sole owners.

### Development as Modernization

Western development strategies launched in the mid-twentieth century to "modernize" (essentially industrialize) the "Third World" (to allow the expansion of Western manufacturing, to create new markets for Western-manufactured goods, and to gain allies in the global South during the Cold War) exacerbated this pattern of leaving women out of landowning, wage labor, and support from Western development agencies. Western aid, loans, and technical assistance favored landowning men as recipients of assistance, thus disregarding women's vital role in food production and in many cases worsening the conditions of female farmers, which led to malnutrition for families dependent on subsistence crops. Moreover, large-scale, highly mechanized farming to produce crops for export undermined the female farming systems central to the maintenance of food self-sufficiency in many countries of the South. It was this pattern that feminists studying development first identified and responded to by agitating for WID and later GAD programs within development agencies. Such agencies were more amenable to WID and GAD strategies as they moved to a new focus on "development with a human face" that foregrounded fighting poverty and "including" those most marginalized under modernization approaches to economic development.

Since then, the greater focus on food insecurity represented by the first MDG goal—to eradicate extreme poverty and hunger (revisit the full list of MDG goals in Chapter 3)—has brought more focus to women's roles in food production. Despite, however, the introduction of more gender-sensitive tools for use by development planners and workers and the primary focus of the MDGs on income and food insecurity, according to UN Women (2011: 104), the numbers of undernourished people went up from 827 million in the early 1990s to 906 million in 2010. Had women really been provided equal access to agricultural inputs such as seeds and tools, it is estimated that hunger would have gone down by 150 million as women still constitute the majority of farmers in sub-Saharan Africa and South Asia, where extreme poverty is concentrated, and a significant number of farmers in the global South generally (UN Women 2011: 105). But there are much wider problems that account for the increase in food insecurity, and these have to do with the power of gender to devalue the lives and health of the poor, of which women and children make up the majority.

For example, most food is grown not for local or even national consumption but for the now global network of food circulation, which is problematic in terms of local health and larger environmental concerns. Crops have also been diverted from providing food to being used as alternative fuel sources, primarily in the West. Moreover, the steady decline of value attributed to agricultural and other (nonoil) primary commodities is devastating for individuals and countries that depend on the sale of primary goods for their economic well-being. Individuals and countries find themselves without sufficient cash for purchasing food and other goods to meet even basic human needs. Top-down and arguably masculinist responses feature accelerating food production through large-scale mechanization, widespread use of chemical fertilizers, and even genetic modification of seeds, plants, and livestock. This strengthens corporate control over food production, further distancing local farmers, particularly women farmers, from the means to adequately and safely feed their families, communities, and nations.

*Neoliberal Development*

As noted earlier, (nonsecurity-related) development has always been greatly underfunded by almost all donor nations relative to their GDPs, and so, as our discussion next on the rise of neoliberal globalization indicates, development became more "marketized" since the 1980s as countries in the global South were expected by IFIs to open their economies to global market forces to improve the lives of their citizens. Whereas WID and GAD approaches tended to focus on small income-generating development projects for poor women, the globalization of global South economies brought great numbers of poor women into light industrial work for export, particularly in export-processing zones (EPZs)—a development referred to as the "feminization of labor." Similar to early industrialization patterns in the West, poor, young, and unmarried women without children were designated as a source of "cheap" and "docile" labor. Even though such light industrial work gave women more income than they could have made in agricultural labor as that sector continued to decline, superexploitative and highly dangerous labor practices have been documented by feminists and protested by women workers since the onset of this marketized "development" strategy.[10] The recent physical collapse of a Bangladesh textile plant, which serviced major US clothing retailers, killed hundreds of women workers, underscoring how poor the conditions remain for female factory workers, particularly in the global South. Although poor women continue to be the preferred labor force in textile/clothing industries, their employment has declined more recently in other industries overall and/or relative to men's. When production shifts either to other countries in the relentless corporate search for cheaper labor or toward more automation, women lose their jobs. Relatedly, as men's income sources have declined under globalization, they have become more amenable to taking "feminized" (poorly paid, unregulated, nonunionized) jobs. Moreover, as already noted, women's unemployment in all sectors has increased substantially since the 2008 economic crisis, and of those who still have wages, too many have little say in how they are spent (UN Women 2011: 105). Thus, there is nothing secure or necessarily uplifting or poverty abating about this marketized strategy for development.

In the new millennium and on the faulty assumption that increasing women's wage work alone, especially given how little poor and working-class women in the formal economy actually earn, would address poverty in the global South, development agencies began to look at poor men as the problem. Deciding that poor men were keeping poor women in heteropatriarchal households from their income-generating potential by failing to assist with domestic responsibilities in the home, perpetrating domestic violence against women who attempt to work outside the home, and controlling and wasting the money that women do earn, the World Bank in particular began to pursue a development policy that would encourage men "to care better" in order to release women "to work more" for incomes (Bedford 2009: 22). Even though there is much evidence of such heteropatriarchal constraints on poor women and, in fact, on women across the socioeconomic spectrum in the global South and North, such a policy targets and demonizes poor, racialized men in the global South rather than holding more structural factors in the GPE responsible, such as maldistributions of wealth and power among nations, socioeconomic classes, and races that have their roots in heteropatriarchal (neo)colonizing and modernizing practices. This policy also constitutes a form of social engineering engaged in by IFIs that Kate Bedford (2009) identifies as a global-level attempt to govern intimate relations for the purpose of aligning private life with the needs of the global economy, rather than aligning economies to enable the social provisioning necessary for more equitable and just, as well as less violent, familial (and other) relations. What such a policy also ignores is that some poor women are either single or sexual minorities who do not live in heteropatriarchal households (Lind 2010). The heteronormative lens of development ensures that female-headed and lesbian-headed households are either marginalized or unseen and therefore significantly excluded from development assistance.

What has also occurred in the new millennium is a "financialization of development" (Roy 2010: 31), to which we return after our discussion on the rise, gendered nature, and other gendered effects of neoliberal globalization. Suffice it to say here, and in light of the foregoing, that despite greater attention to women and gender relations, contemporary development approaches have done little to alter the gendered divisions of labor or stem poverty and have instead reinforced a range of power relations in the GPE that we associate with the power of gender.

## ANATOMIES OF NEOLIBERAL GLOBALIZATION

Since approximately the 1970s, globalization has been driven primarily by neoliberal economic policies favored by geopolitical elites (mostly men), especially economists trained in the global North and acting as policymakers in international economic institutions (IMF, World Bank, WTO). Advocates of neoliberalism—also known as supply-side economics, the Washington Consensus, or market fundamentalism—draw on neoclassical economic theory to argue that markets function most efficiently and productively, and generate the greatest overall prosperity, when they are unfettered by government regulation. Many advocates also claim that unconstrained markets "naturally" foster liberty, democracy, and more peaceful societies. From these assumptions, neoliberal advocates promote a combination of restructuring policies aimed at achieving "freedom" from state-imposed restrictions and opening national borders to create a "world" economy.

The code word of neoliberal capitalism is *liberalization:* ensuring a free-market economy by removing governmental interference in and impediments to the "free" flow of money, goods, services, and capital (financial assets). Policy reforms are variously aimed at eliminating such restrictions (while continuing to constrain the movement of workers). *Deregulation* refers to relaxing or removing existing state controls, for example, on wages, prices, and foreign exchange rates, and reducing state regulatory functions, for example, in regard to protecting workers' rights and the environment. *Privatization* refers to replacing the "inefficiencies" of public ownership and control by reducing state ownership and management of enterprises (often those providing public goods and services, such as electricity, transportation, security) in favor of the private sector. Complementing these supply-side reforms are fiscal and monetary *stabilization policies* to reduce government spending, deficits, and aggregate demand; these involve fewer public-sector jobs and a decrease in state expenditures on social programs (welfare, education, health). Finally, *specialization* in economic activities is promoted—based on the assumption of comparative advantage—and export-oriented policies are favored in pursuit of economic development and growth.

### Structural Adjustment and Restructuring

One widely noted effect of neoliberal policies has been the imposition by the IMF of structural adjustment programs (SAPs) in many developing countries in the wake of a series of debt crises produced by Northern financial markets in the 1980s. Unfortunately, these programs have eroded whatever gains were made earlier in getting public and private development lending agencies to recognize the importance of women's work and gender issues to successful economic development. Until recently, most critiques of neoliberal restructuring focused on the effects of SAPs in the South, where the costs have been starkly visible (Joekes and Weston 1995; *World Development* 1995; Rai 2002; Eisenstein 2009). Many of these countries seek foreign currency loans to finance continued or new debt obligations, and to secure such loans, they must accept a variety of neoliberal conditions imposed by World Bank structural adjustment or IMF stabilization programs. Yassine Fall provides a succinct description:

> Structural adjustment policies are meant to sustain and reinforce conditions that will invite foreign investors to exploit either the labor or natural resources of a country to produce foreign currency for balance of payments purposes and to repay national debt. They encourage the use of a country's resources for export development rather than for domestic development (again to produce foreign currency to repay debt). They encourage the privatization of services, which reduces the autonomy of local governments and often generates massive unemployment. They encourage cuts in health, education, and social welfare budgets for the purpose of reducing

deficits, leaving people, especially women and children who are already impoverished and disadvantaged, in desperate and life-threatening situations.
(2001: 71)[11]

Because of their initial interest in women and development, feminists have generated the most extensive research on the effects of SAPs.
Although there are important differences among countries subject to restructuring, cumulative studies reveal patterns: the enormous social costs
of adjustment, increases in income inequality, tendencies toward social
polarization that aggravate conflicts, shifts in control over resources, and
the "existence of class, gender and ethnic biases in the adjustment process"
(Benería 1995: 1844).

Neoliberal globalization has been operating to produce similar patterns in "developed" economies, particularly since the end of the Cold
War. Former Soviet bloc countries instituted, also under pressure from
Western governments and lending agencies, "shock therapy" programs
designed by Western economists to quickly turn socialist economies into
capitalist ones. These programs drastically cut and/or privatized government services while also privatizing production to increase productivity,
exports, and foreign direct investment. In these countries, working-class
women have been disproportionately bearing the costs and economic
inequalities are expanding, as unemployment grows and socialized benefits, welfare supports, and medical services that were formerly available
are no longer assured. Western countries, to greater and lesser degrees,
have also been steadily self-imposing the privatization and diminution of
public services, particularly under neoconservative governments. Since
the 2008 economic crisis, this "austerity" approach has widened and accelerated, particularly in Europe and the United States but also throughout
the West and under a range of political regimes. The establishment of the
Eurozone, which created a common currency for most members of the
EU, meant that the subsequent debt crises, again produced by Northern
financial markets, hitting a number of southern European countries en-
dangered the Eurozone itself. So as a condition of bailouts provided by
the European Central Bank as well as the IMF and European Commission
and brokered by the richest members of the EU, these countries have also
had to undergo SAP-like restructuring to the detriment of their peoples
(including their middle classes) and their democracies. The United States
bailed out banks and large corporations that were "too big to fail" during
the financial crisis, but while they are now running record profits and Wall

Street is booming, ordinary people continue to suffer. As a result of a weak stimulus program coupled with largely stymied regulations of financial capital and little relief for home owners facing home foreclosures arising from the mortgage crisis, which was among the factors that precipitated the financial crisis, large swaths of working and middle-class people have been facing high unemployment and underemployment and stagnant or reduced wages. This has led them to default on their (mostly unadjusted) mortgage loans for houses worth less after the crisis, thereby losing a great deal of their assets. At a time when up to half of the US population is poor or nearly poor (Smiley and West 2012), services for the poor, the vast majority of whom work, have also been slashed through an across-the-board budget-cutting measure known as "sequestration."

The production of a huge cadre of the working poor is associated with the "Walmartization" of the US economy, or the business model of retail giant Walmart, taken up and globalized by almost all others, including high-tech firms such as Apple. This model relies on global supply chains of cheap labor and goods, which drive down wages, unions, and employee benefits in the deindustrialized North and superexploit workers in the South. The working poor in the North become reliant on the cheap goods produced in the South (especially China) for Walmart and others. To make up, if possible, for poverty-level wages and for a lack of health, retirement, and other social welfare benefits withheld by these huge and obscenely profitable conglomerates, these workers must supplement their incomes with a host of government programs, such as food stamps. Cuts in these programs translate into even greater food, housing, and health insecurities. These processes have been well chronicled in popular culture, beginning with such box office films as *Roger and Me* (1989), which follows the economic and social ravages that ensued from the deindustrialization of Flint, Michigan, as the auto industry outsourced, to the recent Home Box Office (HBO) documentary *American Winter* (2013), which takes viewers into the precarious lives of the working poor and nearly poor, who are, for the most part, just like viewers themselves, most of whom are one step away from the poverty that would result if they lost all or even part of an income or if a health care crisis occurred and some of whom are already in poverty.

Such now truly "global" restructuring is most visibly gendered when we look at its effects on welfare provisioning, which is key to the reproduction of social groups. In large part due to feminist interventions, economic policy analysts and critics now recognize that, while the effects of restructuring have been most severe in the global South, there are parallel racialized gender and class effects in the North, where cutbacks in public welfare also have their greatest impact on feminized populations: women and the (working) poor, but particularly (working) poor women.[12]

*Producing Consent and Crisis*

The advent and eventual institutionalization of neoliberal principles marked a turn away from dominant economic policymaking in the post–World War II era. We therefore need to consider how neoliberal ideology and practice became so taken for granted as "the way things are" in recent decades. In the first place, late-twentieth-century electronic and computer technologies dramatically enhanced the global and real-time circulation of information, and deregulation policies enabled unprecedented concentration of media power and control in very few national and transnational agencies and corporations. The result is that private capital and primarily business interests dominate the most powerful media worldwide, with crucial political implications for what news, issues, knowledge, stories, and advertising are circulated. Although the Internet greatly complicates claims regarding the dominance of conventional media and there are still alternative press and independent filmmaking, the vast majority of the world's people get their information about and develop their understanding of national and global "realities" through the selective lens of these powerful media giants. And the lens they necessarily prefer is profit-oriented and for the most part is aligned with neoliberal capitalism. Hence, what most of us "know" beyond our personal experience and local realities emerges from exposure to an intentionally selective and narrow range of information that is shaped not only by commercial interests (they also dominate the Internet, which is further controlled by state censors in various parts of the world) but also, inevitably, by the race, gender, sexual, and national interests embodied in those who decide what to publicize.

In the second place, business interests increasingly dominate even the most powerful and ostensibly democratic states, with crucial implications for what policies, programs, and national projects are funded and who the eventual winners and losers will be. On the one hand, the growing influence of business on governance is the result of state officials internalizing neoliberal principles and ceding public, political authority to private, market-based decision-making. On the other hand, capitalism enables the concentration of resources in a minority of elite "haves" who typically want to have more, and they have more to contribute to the campaigns and lobbying efforts of those who share this agenda. Money is then translated into political power, undercutting democratic principles and further marginalizing have-nots. When election outcomes, legislation, and priorities are increasingly determined by the rich, citizens effectively get the "best government that money can buy" and the policies that "best" reproduce concentrations of wealth.

Moreover, as we noted in Chapter 3, neoliberal governmentality merges global capitalism with "economic rationality" and instrumental logic as the appropriate criteria for governance. When corporate interests dominate the media, and moneyed interests dominate governance, people have a dangerously narrow understanding of "reality" and democratic processes have little chance of flourishing. A major consequence—in spite of long-standing critiques and alternative visions by feminists and others—is that dominant economic and political interests have imposed and to a large extent "normalized" the logic of corporate capitalism as cultural common sense, and they have ensured the widespread acceptance of neoliberal ideology and policies as both desirable ("growth provides more for all") and anyway inevitable ("there is no alternative"). This is another way in which economics and politics interact—and in their dominant modalities today—generate entwined global crises.

Once in place, the hegemonic rules of the neoliberal game effectively compel all nations to act like corporate businesses: competing globally with each other for credit, resources, and markets and "cutting costs" to enhance their competitive position. Governments cut costs by cutting back on public expenditures (especially in regard to supporting health, welfare, education, and training programs and maintaining occupational safety and environmental protections, but rarely in regard to militarization), by eroding or prohibiting the power of organized labor and weakening workers' rights, and by restructuring the workforce to produce a lean and mean management system, a smaller core of permanent, secure employees, and a vast pool of informalized and flexibilized workers who are disproportionately women and other economically marginalized groups. One effect of slashing social services is that women's reproductive labor is made even more demanding because they must take on caretaking tasks for which the public sector is abandoning responsibility. As another effect, when public welfare is cut, those most in need of food, medical, and educational assistance—not least to secure employment in the restructured economy—are further marginalized. The general pattern is that neoliberal rules favor private capital and corporate shareholders (embodied primarily in elite males) at the expense of social reproduction, public welfare, and citizen stakeholders, while the growth imperative of neoliberal capitalism favors accumulation of wealth (for some) over social reproduction and environmental sustainability for all.

When the neoliberal model becomes operative, the market logic of global competition effectively compels all workers to identify with corporate interests. In other words, it becomes rational (within the logic of the system) for workers to effectively "discipline" themselves by accommodating cost-cutting measures and limiting labor demands in hopes of preventing business closures or the movement of jobs to other sites and even overseas. As workers internalize this logic, resistance appears futile; survival requires submission to market dictates and acceptance of ruthless competition as the only apparent choice when playing the only game in town. This is not to say that there are no resistances. There, in fact, have been many and highly visible protests against the effects of neoliberal globalization across the world, some of which we identify in our concluding chapter. But this diffuse discipline is still effective as mainstream media ensure that workers everywhere are aware of global competition and systemic economic insecurities, and this awareness generates fearful and too often accommodating responses. At the same time, the cultural logic of profit-making respects no boundaries, as marketization penetrates even intimate spheres of social life: bodily functions, sexual relations, biological reproduction. Activities previously considered noncommercial, private, and even sacrosanct are increasingly commodified and drawn into circuits of capital accumulation. Reproductive ova and sperm, infants, human organs, sexualized bodies, intimate caring, sensual pleasures, and spiritual salvation are all for sale.

These developments may be rhetorically "reduced" to instances of "commodification," but they actually constitute enormously complex and ethically fraught quandaries that defy simplistic answers. How are questions of ownership, rights, and responsibilities resolved as private commercial interests transgress formerly "natural" boundaries (of bodies and sexual intimacies), expropriate indigenous knowledge (of plants and societies), and claim dominion over public goods (air, water, outer space)? How does democracy fare as neoliberalism erodes the regulatory capacity and public accountability of states in favor of unaccountable decentralized markets, international agencies, and private interest networks? The emerging questions and unfolding crises confront us with multiple challenges, and there are no easy answers. But as systemic insecurities mount and disturbing outcomes accumulate, we must avoid the familiar and too-easy response of blaming problems on marginalized or "suspect" groups: "irresponsible mothers," "drug-ridden (racialized) inner-city gangs," "job-stealing migrants," "unpatriotic dissidents," "anti-American foreigners," "Muslim extremists," and the faceless—but always also racialized—poor.

To conclude this section, we note that the cumulative effects of neoliberal restructuring and capitalism as a cultural logic are complex, uneven, and controversial. Not all women or historically marginalized groups are disadvantaged by economic restructuring processes. Some individuals with the appropriate skills, training, knowledge, experience, management style, access to credit, and/or social class (as well as racial privilege) are able to do well in the restructured global economy. And in some countries of the South, an accelerated ICT sector has generated economic benefits to those with technical and language skills employed by transnational corporations, for instance, in telemarketing operations and computer support services. Nevertheless, we argue here, and demonstrate in the remainder of the chapter, that the overall trends and cumulative effects of neoliberal policies and the cultural logic of capitalism are not conducive to ameliorating economic inequalities, promoting social justice, or improving the environmental health of the planet.

## WOMEN, GENDER, AND NEOLIBERAL GLOBALIZATION

As all aspects of life, not just economic relations, have been marketized under neoliberal globalization, gendered divisions of labor have taken new turns (including returning to old forms) even as they have remained relatively in place. Here we detail a range of gendered economic trends and activities that are particularly associated with the rise of neoliberal globalization. We have already raised the feminization of formal (wage) labor as industrialization globalized in the latter part of the twentieth century. Concomitant with this has been a rise in (im)migrant labor (both documented and undocumented) and informal labor (both licit and illicit) in which women figure prominently. But before we turn to these, we want to discuss the most enduring form of labor women have been expected to perform—reproductive labor—and how it is increasingly organized for *and* undermined by neoliberal globalization.

*Reproductive Labor*

Dominant accounts of GPE focus almost exclusively on market-based "productive" activities and the financial arrangements that fuel the economy. Conventional and continuing neglect of reproductive activities exemplifies the power of gender to bias our knowledge of economics by valorizing the (masculinized) public sphere of power and formal (paid) work at the expense of the marginalized (feminized) family/private sphere of emotional, domestic, and caring (unpaid) labor. Yet all social life and economic production ultimately depend on reproductive activities, which therefore warrant much closer attention.

Socialization involves teaching infants how to behave according to the codes (meaning systems) of a particular culture; it is indispensable for the survival of individuals and groups and for the reproduction of the economic order. It teaches us—and we internalize—beliefs regarding gendered identities, roles, and divisions of labor, as well as rules regarding what constitutes "work," who does what work, and how different kinds of work are valued. These lessons are not only about gender but also inextricably about race/ethnicity, age, class, religion, nationality, and other axes of difference and differential valorization.

Effective socialization and social reproduction matter structurally for economics because they produce individuals who are ultimately able to "work," and this unpaid reproductive labor still done primarily by women the world over (UN Women 2011: 105) saves capital the costs of producing key inputs. In this way, capitalism benefits from the patriarchal ideology of states, religions, and heteronormative families that locates women in the home as loving caregivers and assigns them primary responsibility for social reproduction and for sustaining the emotional and physical health of family members. Capitalism also benefits from socialization that ensures workers accept as "natural" the hierarchical divisions of labor, differential valorizations of workers and what work they do, and workers' subordination to managers and market-based objectives. In spite of relying on reproductive labor that produces workers, and family relations that relieve work-generated pressures, neoliberal globalization reduces the emotional, cultural, and material resources necessary for the well-being of most women and families. This is key to what we mean by a global "crisis in social reproduction," as women with less time, fewer options, decreased resources, and reduced social services are expected to meet increased labor and nurturing demands, cope with mounting insecurities, and ensure their own and the survival of dependent family members in the context of deepening structural violence (Ehrenreich and Hochschild 2002a; Bakker and Gill 2003; Bakker 2007).

### (Im)Migrant Labor

As economic conditions deteriorate under neoliberal restructuring, people seek work wherever they can find it, fueling internal and external labor migrations: to urban areas, EPZs, seasonal agricultural sites, tourism locales, and anywhere jobs are presumed to exist. People are often "pushed" to move by neocolonial and capitalist processes that disrupt or destroy former livelihoods. For example, recall that Eurocentric development strategies favor building large-scale industrial and urban infrastructures, often at the expense of small-scale and subsistence farming. Until recently, this generated primarily poor and working-class male migrations, especially to urban areas, mining or oil field sites, and even distant locations (in other countries) where low- or semiskilled jobs (typically in agriculture and construction) are available. These migrations alter distributions of labor and resources within families, often leaving women full responsibility for agricultural tasks and household survival or driving them to seek other sources of income. Too often, men attempting to find work and survive in distant cities or foreign countries eventually abandon their families, pushing many women into ever-more-constrained economic choices.[13]

But with the rise of neoliberal globalization, poor and working-class women from the global South are now migrating beyond borders as much as men are for economic survival, very often to perform traditionally "feminine" and "feminized" jobs—domestic work (including housekeeping and child care) and nursing (including home care of the elderly)—in the global North (and some wealthy areas of the global South). In some countries, such as the Philippines, women are encouraged and assisted to migrate as "guest workers" to perform such "care" labor as a matter of state development policy because the remittances they send home from the comparatively higher wages they can make abroad help to sustain families and communities at home, effectively subsidizing the national economy. Remittances sent home by (im)migrant laborers worldwide reached an estimated $305 billion in 2008, and although declining the following year to $290 billion in the wake of the economic crisis, they still dwarf "official development aid and private capital flows" (Bach 2011: 133). But as we discuss when we turn to domestic labor, there are high costs to (im)migrant women and their families for propping up developing economies and cheaply servicing developed ones.[14] Moreover, many migrant women, like many migrant men, are increasingly forced to migrate as undocumented workers as states in the global North have tightened borders and immigration requirements in the wake of 9/11. This heightens the exploitation of migrant workers and puts them at far greater risk from punitive actions by the host state, including arrest and deportation, but also denial of access to health (including reproductive health) care, education, domestic violence programs, and a whole range of other social services.[15]

Still, there remain significant "pulls" for (im)migrant labor in the contemporary GPE. As we have already noted, women especially are sought as preferred workers (as a source of cheap and supposedly more accommodating labor) where export manufacturing has been established (shaped by colonial histories, uneven capitalist development, and selective foreign direct investment) and in particular industries such as clothing production, whether in factories in the global South or sweatshops in the global North. Such employment for women tends to be precarious and short-lived due to industrial preference for very young women, the arduous and less protected work conditions, and high turnover rates. Moreover, as industry develops, labor-intensive processes decline in favor of capital-and-technology-intensive production that generates fewer, and male-dominated, jobs. The overall effect is un- and underemployment, further pushing women and men to seek whatever income they can wherever they can. The "care deficit" in the global North created by the need to have dual-income earners to sustain families, the rise in aging populations, and declines in publicly supported social safety nets also continues to pull (im)migrant women into domestic and other caring work at low wages.

Historical inequalities shape whose vulnerability renders them subject to economic migration, what education and training they have received, and what forms of relatively devalorized labor they can access. Consistent with structural vulnerabilities and the nature of "unskilled" jobs available (cleaning, harvesting, domestic service, sex work), these workers tend to be marked (in combination with class) by ethnicity, race, and gender, and the work they find tends to be informal and feminized. In the context of neoliberal globalization, recent migration flows tend to reflect polarized opportunities: at the (masculinized) top is an elite pool of highly skilled professionals and technicians (linked to transnational corporatist opportunities and the "brain drain" from developing countries), and at the (feminized) bottom is a much larger and generally devalorized pool of semi- or unskilled workers who take whatever work is available (linked to urban areas, corporate agriculture, global cities, and the care deficit in the global North).

Being on the move affects personal and collective identities and cultural reproduction, creating new opportunities for some and new problems for others. Traditional family forms and divisions of labor are disrupted, destabilizing men's and women's identities and gender relations more generally. This is particularly true when we consider that women now constitute half of all (im)migrants, and where demand is greatest for personal service providers, care work, and domestic labor, women often outnumber men. The enormous care deficit affects household reproduction transnationally because as women leave their own families to provide care for richer families, divisions of labor are also reconfigured. (Im)migrants encounter unfamiliar and often hostile environments, especially where anti-immigrant fervor is whipped up. Poor female migrants are especially targeted for their supposedly uncontrolled fertility, constituting a particular drain on the social services of host nations, which then seek to withhold them despite evidence that migrating women are seeking employment *and* contraceptives to better enable them to work and contribute to the host nation's coffers through taxes for the very services they are denied (O'Leary and Valdéz-Garcia 2013). Anti(im)migrant identity-based politics also feeds into the militarization of borders, demanding more state resources at the expense of social services, drawing more (mostly working-class) men into border control security apparatuses, and endangering the lives of migrants, who are subjected to more physical and sexual violence as they attempt to cross borders, sometimes with the aid of unscrupulous guides through remote areas with no access to water or food, and deal with militarized border guards (Lind and Williams 2013).

As Jacqui True notes, "Few countries have ratified the international conventions that extend citizenship and labor rights to migrant workers" (2012: 58), such as the most recent International Convention on the Protection of the Rights of all Migrant Workers and Members of Their Families (1990), which has been ratified by only 17 percent of states. States' lack of interest in protecting migrant labor relates to the key role it plays in the informalization of work that is a central feature of neoliberal globalization.

### Informalization of Work

The destabilization of national economies under globalizing forces that has put so many people on the move to look for work is also implicated in the rise of the informalization of economies in which work is less subject to state regulation, national accounting, and formal, long-term employer-employee contracts. What are conventionally referred to as "productive" economic activities are the most familiar because economists focus on them as "formal" economic activities—those that typically include earning wages or salaries and in most contexts are recorded by agencies and are in some way regulated and/or taxed by governments. Traditional economic framing distinguishes primary (natural resource, agricultural), secondary (industrial, manufacturing), and tertiary (services, information) production, but these distinctions are increasingly inadequate, especially as ICTs alter what is produced and how.

Changes in primary production are especially marked by technological developments and the steady decline in world prices of and demand for (nonoil) primary products and raw materials. "Declining terms of trade" (lower for primary, sustained or higher for manufactured and high-value-added commodities) are particularly devastating to (feminized) nations where manufacturing capacity is underdeveloped and/or primary production dominates. To compete for credit and markets, states may advertise the availability of "cheap" and/or docile (feminized) labor and nonunionized, environmentally unregulated worksites, or they may encourage out-migration of workers in hopes of easing unemployment pressures and securing foreign remittances.

Secondary production is being transformed by "deindustrialization." This involves two shifts: first, from material-based and more often unionized factory manufacturing to knowledge-based manufacturing (e.g., computer games), and second, from well-paying, relatively skilled, and secure (masculinized) jobs to low-paying, semi- or unskilled, and insecure (feminized) jobs. The point here is that manufacturing remains important but declines in value relative to the higher status and earnings of ICT-based work, which reflects a larger global trend in production and employment: from manufacturing to services. Because service jobs tend to be either skilled high-wage (professional-managerial; read: "masculinized") jobs or semi-, unskilled, and poorly paid (personal, cleaning, retail, and clerical; read: "feminized") jobs, this shift amplifies existing income inequalities between males and females, skilled and unskilled workers, and developed and developing nations.

In order to be more competitive by cutting costs (especially of labor), firms and nations take measures to render their operations more flexible. "Flexibilization" in general refers to shifts in production processes: to more spatially dispersed networks and decentralized control (the global assembly line, subcontracting); to increasingly casualized (nonpermanent, part-time) and informalized (unregulated, noncontractual) jobs; to small-batch, "just-in-time" (short-term rather than long-term) production planning; and to avoidance or prohibition of organized labor. At the core of flexibilization are efforts to deregulate production processes and labor markets—hence, increasing freedom for management—ostensibly to eliminate inefficient rigidities imposed by regulation and to ensure that the "freedom of the market" is unconstrained. Here the discourse of neoliberalism invokes flexibility as essential for competitive success and as an inherently positive practice and orientation. In contrast, critics argue that flexibilization erodes hard-won workers' rights and constitutes a retreat from the progressive agenda of achieving what the International Labour Organization (ILO) characterizes as "decent work" for all workers.

Cutting back on the workforce is most visible as loss of employment for significant numbers of workers, especially those holding what were previously regarded as full-time, permanent, protected, or secure positions. But a more apt generalization refers not simply to unemployment per se but also to the polarization of available employment, with increasing opportunities for those who "fit" the demands of postindustrial or informational capitalism. At the top end are valorized (masculinized and primarily elite male) workers sought for their technical, informational, and knowledge-based skills. At the bottom are those in demand as semi- or unskilled workers: they are valuable to employers and to the accumulation of global capital but are devalorized by their location in feminized jobs. In fact, we argue that flexibilization constitutes *feminization* of employment, understood simultaneously as a material, embodied transformation of labor markets (increasing proportion of women, deteriorating work conditions for men), a conceptual characterization of deteriorated and devalorized labor conditions (less desirable, meaningful, safe, or secure), and a reconfiguration of worker identities (feminized managers, female breadwinners). As the proliferation of lower-end jobs requires fewer skills and flexibilization becomes the norm, employers seek workers who are perceived to be undemanding (unorganized), docile but reliable, available for part-time and temporary work, and willing to accept low wages. Migrant workers, especially undocumented ones, are particularly positioned to have to accept such precarious employment, but gender stereotypes depict women more generally as most suitable for these jobs, and gender inequalities render women especially desperate for access to income. In short, as more jobs are casual, irregular, flexible, and precarious (read: feminized), more women—and feminized men—are doing them.

Although neoliberal policies have the effect of decreasing formal—especially permanent, secure, decent—employment, they spur phenomenal growth in "informal"—unregulated, unprotected, and insecure—economic activities. Until recently, conventional accounts paid little attention to informal activities, which were trivialized as remnants of "incomplete modernization" associated with "traditional" (read: non-European) societies. But economists are increasingly aware that informal activities are inextricable from and indeed make possible the "productive" economy, in part because they are based on flexibilization: the outsourcing and subcontracting processes of flexibilization shift production toward less formal, regularized, and regulated work conditions; the erosion of labor power accompanying flexibilization exacerbates the decline in family income, which "pushes" more people into informal work; and flexibilization reduces tax revenues, which exacerbates the decline in welfare provisioning and spurs informal work to compensate in part for this loss.

How to define and measure informal activities is controversial, but all observers agree that the value and extent of these activities have increased dramatically in recent decades and that this phenomenal growth poses a variety of economic, analytical, and normative challenges.[16] Women especially rely on informal activities as a survival strategy to ensure social reproduction: they are overrepresented in informal activities worldwide, the informal economy is the primary source of earnings for women in most developing countries, women are the majority of part-time informal workers in rich countries, and the gender gap that persists globally is even wider in the informal than in the formal economy.[17] Homework, domestic work and sex work, to which we now turn, are "old" forms of informal labor most associated with women, but they have become growing features of and major enterprises in the new, postindustrial global economy, becoming almost emblematic of it.

*Homework and Domestic Work*

The practice of subcontracting or outsourcing as key to flexibilized production has generated explosive growth in "homework," or home-based production.[18] Homework is not a residual form of production but is in fact integral to industrialization and current restructuring processes: it exposes the blurred boundaries between unpaid housework, paid informal work, and formal waged labor. Global growth in homeworking is attributable to several factors: corporate desires to cut labor and overhead costs by outsourcing production tasks (e.g., sewing, light assembly work) that can be performed by subcontracted laborers in their homes anywhere in the world, large pools of migrant and immigrant workers who are drawn into homework because of racist and sexist discrimination and restrictive immigration laws that prevent them from working in the formal sector, and increasing pressures on women to generate income in support of household survival. These same factors are also associated with the reappearance of sweatshops in the North as well as the South, where (immigrant) women and children toil at sewing machines, typically under unsafe and "hidden" conditions, to produce designer clothing and niche market commodities as part of just-in-time production. Women especially are sought for homework because they are considered available and reliable, and their below-subsistence earnings are justified as merely "supplemental" income. Employers may also promote homework as a means of gaining more control over labor by decentralizing and thus undercutting traditional sites of unionization and the development of solidarity among workers (Benería 2003). Subcontracting to (female) homeworkers can reap the additional benefit of controlling workers through masculinist ideologies and practices. Like informal activities more generally, homework is very poorly paid, and this is justified by characterizing homework as an extension of (unpaid) housework or as merely supplementary income. The increasing reliance of the formal economy on the informal economy to produce goods and services under poor working conditions and at extremely low pay rates begins to explain why it is that at a time when women are entering the formal workforce in record numbers, the global phenomenon of the feminization of poverty is increasing.

In addition to homework, another burgeoning transnational economy of a "domestic" nature is the "maid-trade" (Chin 1998; Anderson 2000; Ehrenreich and Hochschild 2002a; Benería 2003; True 2012), in which gender is not only pervasive but also clearly racialized. Domestic work is called that because it presumably occurs in a private location—"behind closed doors"—typically a family household or the "temporary home" afforded by commercial accommodations when people are on the move. In addition to the unpaid domestic work of most women in their own homes, class-privileged women and families often seek domestic workers to maintain their homes and care for their children. This transference of domestic labor may be due to employment by the "woman of the house" that precludes her doing it or to sufficient resources that she need not do it herself.

In a less familial but still domestic sense, tourist hotels, conference facilities, training and research institutions, and global cities depend on a large number of maids, cooks, and cleaning workers, as well as other service providers.

Domestic work is a rapidly growing global business involving vast networks of people and agencies that facilitate transnational flows, such as moneylenders, airlines, hotels, translation services, training institutions, and banks. It is important to note that payments for domestic work, especially caregiving work related to a health provision, constitute an important source of foreign remittances for countries of origin and reduce labor costs in receiver countries. In spite of providing socially necessary labor, domestic workers typically reap few benefits and face multiple hardships—especially women who migrate for these jobs. Gender stereotypes associate cleaning and caretaking as women's work; domestic work is understood to be unskilled; it attracts women who need paid work, have little (valued) training, may require housing accommodation, and/or seek work where citizenship status is not monitored. Not surprisingly, domestic workers in private households are often immigrant women. As noncitizens, and even nonnative speakers, they are particularly vulnerable to employer intimidation and abuse occurring in spaces that are understood to be separate from the public gaze and state regulation. Domestic workers who "live in" are especially subject to a variety of exploitative practices: they work long hours and may even be considered "on call" twenty-four hours a day, they are typically paid very poorly and may have few resources or time for venturing beyond the household, their activities and personal behavior are closely scrutinized, and their live-in status makes them especially vulnerable to sexual exploitation or to being construed as "promiscuous or exotic" due to racialized stereotypes (Pettman 1996: 192).

Wives and mothers who pay other (often racialized and migrant) women to do "their" domestic work avoid disrupting gendered divisions of labor within the household, but at the expense of exacerbating class (and often racial and national) divisions among women. Even though the hiring of domestic workers ostensibly "frees" women who employ such workers from household chores, it also effectively relieves pressure on men to do their share of caring labor and relieves pressure on states to provide child care and support social reproduction. These dynamics are further complicated by the fact that many—perhaps most—domestic workers are themselves married women with children, many of whom face the stark choice of either living with their children in poverty or earning desperately needed money by living away from them (Ehrenreich and Hochschild 2002b: 2; Young 2001: 57; Barber 2011). Who hires and who serves may reflect colonial histories (black maids of white madams in South Africa) or newer hierarchies of international debt and employment opportunities (Filipino maids in Saudi Arabia). But in all cases it appears that cultural and racial stereotyping occurs in terms of preferred—"suitable" or "trusted"—domestic workers. As Bridget Anderson observes, "Racist stereotypes intersect with issues of citizenship, and result in a racist hierarchy which uses skin color, religion, and nationality to construct some women as being more suitable for domestic work than others" (2000: 2).

Such conditions and concerted efforts by domestic workers, feminist and labor union supporters, and remittance-dependent countries have led to the landmark ILO Domestic Workers Convention adopted in 2012 and ratified so far by only two countries, including the Philippines, but enough to put it in force. Compliance, however, is another thing, and such a convention, while bringing domestic work and workers out of the shadows, institutionalizes a system of carework performed by mostly poor, (im)migrant women that does nothing to reorient global or national economic priorities toward social provisioning or to widen who is responsible for carework.

Ehrenreich and Hochschild argue that migration for domestic work is part of a "worldwide gender revolution": as men are increasingly unable to meet traditional breadwinner roles, women are compelled to work outside of the home, which generates the larger question of "who will take care of the children, the sick, the elderly? Who will make dinner and clean house?" (2002b: 3). Domestic work exemplifies the socially necessary labor upon which all else depends. But it is hard to measure objectively, and the commodification of personal, private, and intimate services is also socially and morally controversial. Whether commodified or not, the intangible, emotional aspects of caring labor elude conventional economic theory but are crucial to domestic work—and to paid labor and the economic order more generally. These subjective and cultural aspects extend into an even more controversial regime of labor intimacy: the international political economy of sex.

## International Sex Work

There is tremendous variation in how, why, and in what form women (and men and other genders) participate in "sex work" (the commercialization of sex).[19] Participation may be on a temporary or part-time basis, as a weekend or full-time job, or intermittently in the many ways made possible by ICTs and especially the Internet. In contrast to the conventional, narrow meaning of "prostitution," sex workers engage in a wide range of activities: as escorts, strippers, exotic dancers, erotic entertainers, people engaging in sexual practices, or people being observed in sexual performance. Pornographic videos are tremendously popular and profitable, but prostitution and the trafficking of women and children for that purpose feature more prominently in international accounts of sex work.[20] Prostitution is the most frequently studied—and the most sensationalized—version of sex work; as an international industry, it particularly exposes linkages among private fantasies, gender and other sexual stereotypes, economic stratifications, and global markets. It is also linked to militarization, as those countries in Southeast and East Asia where it constitutes a significant proportion of GDP (2–14 percent) experienced the establishment of "prostitution systems on a scale and with a precision which is industrial" as a result of the occupation of them by US and Japanese militaries (Jeffreys 2009: 4).

To analyze the international political economy of sex is, however, to enter treacherous terrain: conceptually, for the ethical and political issues at stake, and materially, for the bodies and underground economies involved. The conceptual difficulties center on our discomfort and ambivalence regarding sex as a public topic, whether in terms of research, regulation, or commercialization. Like the commodification of caring and domestic labor, sex for purchase is controversial, and analyzing sex work is particularly problematic for feminists. On the one hand, due to heteropatriarchal identities, ideologies, and practices, it is *female* bodies that are most objectified, manipulated, violated, and physically harmed. This makes the sex industry—including advertising, pornography, videos, prostitution, and trafficking—a particular concern to critics of women's subordination. On the other hand, sex is a profoundly personal and intimate realm of human activity, which cautions against simplistic and moralizing pronouncements regarding appropriate, desirable, or despicable sexual conduct. Moreover, (typically conservative) sexual mores and moralizing judgments feed directly into pathologizing and criminalizing nonnormative sexual behaviors, whether for profit or not, stigmatizing and even imprisoning not only sex workers but also, for example, LGBTQ persons. So whereas the violence entailed in coercing sexual activities or trafficking people for such purposes must be condemned, evaluating the array of sexual activities a person might voluntarily engage in—commercially or otherwise—is problematic.

Of further concern is how sensationalized sex trafficking has become when it, in fact, constitutes only a part of the much larger problem of human trafficking for all kinds of coerced labor. Although few countries have ratified UN conventions for protecting the rights of migrants, at least 100 have signed onto the 2000 UN Protocol to Prevent, Suppress, and Punish the Trafficking in Persons. Partially accounting for this has been the concerted efforts of "abolitionist" or "prohibitionist" feminists and some strange bedfellows—religious conservatives particularly associated with the US Christian Right—working in global arenas to end "sex slavery." Although this protocol signaled international recognition of sex trafficking, it and the national legislations it has spawned against sex trafficking are more motivated by "securing" states against unwanted migrants, including criminal and criminalized elements associated with the sex trade. Moreover, because the focus is on punishment, it is a "securitizing" approach to anti–sex trafficking that fails to address the economic pushes and pulls of all trafficking in persons and does little to assist those trafficked, whose agency is denied and who are frequently revictimized by punitive state actions (Kamrani and Gentile 2013). This approach also militates against the decriminalization or legalization of sex work that is advocated by "prosex" or "sex-positive" feminists and that has been found to be a necessary step for enabling sex workers to articulate their own needs (including through labor unions they form) and generally improving their working conditions (Goodyear and Weitzer 2011).

The "moral panic" that has privileged sex trafficking over other forms of human trafficking as a matter of international and national concern also operates to either demonize "prostitutes" (more so than their pimps and procurers) or to reduce them to helpless victims in need of "rescue" by more enlightened Western or Western-supported actors. These points are cogently made by Laura Maria Agustín (2007) in her recent study of migrant sex workers and the European social workers and activists dedicated to "helping them." In particular, she exposes the self-importance of middle-class women (normalized by Eurocentric imperialism), their presumption of moral clarity and cultural superiority, and their denial of voice and agency to non-European women while claiming to aid them through rescue. The neocolonial basis of rescue missions becomes even more visible when we consider the actions of Western-based evangelical NGOs such as the International Justice Mission, which is lauded in *Half the Sky* and which storms brothels in the global South to "free" girls, who typically return to brothels because underlying ideologies and socioeconomic structures remain untouched.

An ideology that particularly puts sex workers in a no-win situation is the masculinist and frequently racist dichotomy that pits good/moral/ upright/marriageable women against bad/immoral/fallen/"usable" women. "Rescuers" reproduce this dichotomy in their efforts to turn what they see as the latter into the former so that the moral order can be restored. The sex industry also exacerbates hierarchies among women. Racially, there is a hierarchy among prostitutes reflecting which women are constructed as "sexually appealing" (Asian women represented as exotic and "hospitable") and which are valued as comfortably "European" (women from transitional economies represented as culturally "European," feminine but not feminist). Seiko Hanochi also notes hierarchies among sex workers themselves, based on countries of origin and types and "class" of sexual work (2001: 144). More starkly, Jan Jindy Pettman reports that, although Australian sex workers are likely to insist on condom use, Australian brothels promote their Asian sex workers as available to customers without this protection (1997: 103). These examples reveal that it is not only poverty but also masculinist ideologies filtered through stereotypes of race, culture, and nationality that constrain women's economic choices, construe women as sexual servicers, and construct some women as more attractive and some as more disposable than others.

The supply side of the sex industry primarily involves women in need of income-generating opportunities, typically in the context of limited employment options, deteriorating economic conditions, and increasing pressures to earn money for themselves or their families. Some sex workers view their participation as a positive choice, others situate their choice in the context of realistic and limited options, others apparently have very little freedom of choice, and at the extreme are women and children literally coerced into sex work and sometimes trafficked far from home. Definitions of trafficking vary from literally abducting women to intentionally misleading women who are seeking work and then coercing them into the sex trade by threats of violence against them (or family members), actual violence, and psychological intimidation. Trafficked individuals are subject to many forms of direct and indirect violence, and even for those who escape, returning home may no longer be an option: families may not welcome a "fallen woman," and marriage prospects may be nonexistent. For most sex workers, there is little public sympathy or assistance; they are stereotyped as "immoral" and held responsible for sex scandals and even the violence committed against them.

As in studies of the international drug trade and illegal immigration, the demand side of the sex industry is rarely questioned or investigated. Masculinist ideologies construct men as naturally eager for and often in pursuit of sex so that "demand" for women's sexual services—from hospitality hostesses and erotic entertainment to temporary or permanent rights over a woman's body—and a sense of entitlement to women's bodies are taken for granted as the way things are.[21] Prostitutes face a number of risks, yet the men (and some women) who seek them out and typically exacerbate those risks are rarely arrested or even stigmatized for their role in the demand side of the sex industry. Sex workers are especially vulnerable if they lack citizenship or are working where "prostitution" is illegal. Pimps, of course, take advantage of these vulnerabilities to threaten and manipulate sex workers, to maintain their sense of insecurity and reliance on pimps, and to reap maximum profits off their labor. Such patterns are also operant for sexual minorities in the sex trade. Like heterosexual sex tourism, global gay tourism rests on a sense of entitlement that Western gay men (and sometimes Western lesbian women) have to the "exotic" bodies of (often racialized) sexual minorities (who may not define themselves as such but nevertheless cater to comparatively affluent sexual minorities), particularly in the global South.

Prostitution and sex work more generally exist worldwide. They appear, however, to be increasing as economic conditions deteriorate, ICTs afford novel and elusive activities, and geopolitical developments alter migration flows. Who buys and who sells may vary, but similar to domestic work, in all cases it appears that cultural and racial stereotyping occurs in terms of preferred—desirable, exotic, submissive—sex workers. Barbara Ehrenreich and Arlie Hochschild offer this explanation:

> Immigrant women may seem desirable sexual partners for the same reason that First World employers believe them to be especially gifted as caregivers: they are thought to embody the traditional feminine qualities of nurturance, docility, and eagerness to please. Some men feel nostalgic for these qualities, which they associate with a bygone way of life. Even as many wage-earning Western women assimilate to the competitive culture of "male" work and ask respect for making it in a man's world, some men seek in the "exotic Orient" or "hot-blooded tropics" a woman from the imagined past. (2002b: 9–10)

In sum, interpreting gendered shifts in formal and to informal work associated with neoliberal globalization is controversial. Some individuals prosper in a less regulated environment, for example, in microenterprises (favored by neoliberal development agencies to which we turn next) that may offer new opportunities, in developing countries (and increasingly in developed ones) where informal activities are crucial for income generation, and in illicit activities that are big business worldwide. Critics argue that flexibilization and informalization favor capital over labor and hence exacerbate economic inequalities and, more generally, that avoidance of regulations is directly and indirectly bad for wages, workers, the environment, and long-term prospects for societal and global well-being. Feminists expose how these shifts reproduce women and feminized "others" as cheap labor, drive women and feminized "others" to informal and precarious work as a survival strategy, and exacerbate inequalities among women and among men as well as between rich and poor states. Many feminists are also critical of antitrafficking policies that fail to distinguish between sex work and trafficking; are steeped in moralizing, rescue, and punishment discourses; root the problem in the actions of only "bad" men of the global South; and leave "rescued" women still subject to the neoliberal economic processes that impoverish them and circumscribe their choices.

## GENDERED FINANCIALIZATION

For three decades, neoliberal policies have been altering not only production processes and the value of "work," but also financial arrangements and the value of "money." In brief, and necessarily oversimplified, deregulation enabled tremendous expansion of cross-border capital flows—of bonds, loans, currencies, equities, and so on. This afforded new opportunities to create profits ("wealth") not through the real economy of production, commodities, consumption, and trade, but through trade in capital (financial) assets—in effect making money from money. What matters is that these processes of wealth creation are based less on exchanges in the "real" economy of goods and services than on *perceptions*—primarily in the minds of male traders and financial investors—of expected revenues and potential risks. Although the bubble of inflated perceptions generates mind-boggling wealth for some for a while, when it bursts, it has devastating effects on the many.

Because this wealth is not generated in the real economy and does not conform to conventional economic expectations, the "credit" market" is in an important sense out of sync with the "commodity" market. But this does not mean that the real economy (of goods and services, prices and wages) is insulated from the dynamics of global finance. Rather, prices "set" in financial markets, especially through interest and exchange rates (whether these are high, low, or unstable), have effects throughout the socioeconomic order. They shape, for example, whether investments are directed toward trade, financial instruments, or human resources; whether production is labor-intensive or capital- and technology-intensive; and how labor markets are structured (what types of labor, where located, with what compensation, and under what conditions). When financial matters assume priority, status and decision-making power within businesses, governments, and IGOs shift to those who "manage money" and "know" how to invest. Access to credit becomes decisive for individuals and states and is deeply structured by familiar hierarchies: women, the poor, and those who are un- and underemployed face much greater obstacles when credit is sought. Financial markets thus have pervasive effects, and when they are free of governmental regulation, these effects are primarily to enhance concentrations of wealth among elites.

The point to notice here is that the allure of financial trading shifts attention and funding from long-term investments in industry, infrastructure, and human (social) capital and thus exacerbates the conditions of extreme inequality and crises of social reproduction and sustainability we identify in this text. As the recent instability of financial markets has shown, increased risks taken by the financial industry are socialized—hurting public welfare because the collectivity pays rather than those who inflated the bubble and variously profited from it. Examining the generation of crises and their effects reveals the power of gender in operation. First, women and gender-sensitive analyses are absent—or at best marginalized—in the decision-making processes and analytical assessments of the financial order. Women are underrepresented in the institutions of global finance, a model of elite agency and (instrumental) economic "efficiency" is deemed common sense, and the masculinism of financial players and their practices is presumed (despite a brief questioning of this in the immediate aftermath of the 2008 financial crisis). Second, these exclusions and blinders filter what elite analysts are able—or willing—to "see," especially the dangers of short-term greed and the arrogance of power. They particularly obscure the gendered costs of crises: loss of secure jobs and earning capacity due to women's concentration in precarious forms of employment, length-ened work hours for women as they cushion the impact on household income, decreased participation of girls in education and deteriorated health conditions for women, increased child labor and women's licit and illicit informal activities, and increased structural violence as well as direct violence against women.[22] These costs have important long-term effects: girls and women are less able to participate as full members of society and have fewer skills required for safe and secure income generation, and the intensification of women's work with fewer resources imperils social re-production more generally. At the same time, entire societies are affected as deteriorating conditions of social reproduction, health, and education have ongoing consequences.

## Women, Microcredit, and the Financialization of Development

As finance capital became a favored macroeconomic sector under neolib-eral globalization, microfinance was embraced by development agencies and has been popularized as a new, initially women-centered way to abate poverty. As part of the financialization of development or finance capi-tal for the "bottom billion" (Roy 2010), microfinance or microcredit proj-ects disburse small loans to a group of borrowers who collectively share responsibility for repayment. Access to the credit (US$50–200) rotates among members, who use it to jump-start or advance entrepreneurial activities, the success of which enables increased earnings, repayment of the loan, and further reinvestment and accumulation in an upward and out-of-poverty spiral. This strategy especially targets poor rural women precisely because their lack of any conventional collateral excludes them from access to credit, without which they have no hope of jump-starting a small business, of achieving their entrepreneurial potential, and of break-ing out of the cycle of poverty. Women are also targeted because they are presumed to be better at forging social networks and sustaining the trust necessary for group success, and because their presumed fear of letting the group down will ensure they make an optimal effort toward repayment (Bergeron 2003: 166–167). Finally, women are targeted because of the ex-pectation, and considerable evidence, that they are more likely than men are to use resources in support of family well-being (health, school fees).

Although there is growing evidence that this strategy is not reducing poverty and/or empowering women, it remains widely endorsed as a tool for alleviating poverty that is now being extended to poor men (Roy 2010). Some feminists initially saw microcredit projects as useful for directing attention to poor rural women who face limited options and who may be able to realize entrepreneurial benefits from access to these loans. By widening their focus to include issues of social status and the world's poorest women, development agencies draw attention to women as clients of development and provide openings for addressing related gender issues and mobilizing resources (Keck and Sikkink 1998). And in contrast to conventional narratives of devalorization, enthusiasts for microcredit promote positive representations of women's capacities and "traditional" community values. These shifts provide new opportunities because they target women as agents and beneficiaries, but these opportunities are proving to have considerable undersides.

A growing number of feminist critics of microcredit initiatives (Goetz and Gupta 1996; Poster and Salime 2002; Bergeron 2003; Roy 2010) have identified several problematic assumptions on which they rest. Such initiatives presume that the "solution" for ending poverty is to integrate the poor into commercial market activity by ensuring access to financial credit—what Gayatri Spivak characterizes as "credit-baiting without infrastructural reform" (1999: 418); that poor people can be quickly and easily "rescued" by making small amounts of money available to them; and that poor people have the entrepreneurial skills and wider social system supports necessary for sustainable enterprises, including favorable market conditions. The premise here is that incorporation into circuits of capital enables successful competition and hence prosperity; in other words, capitalism can fix the (poverty) problem that capitalism produces—hence this approach has been dubbed "poverty capitalism." These initiatives additionally presume that women can simply take on additional work responsibilities, will have the support of family and community members to do so and to prosper, and will be able to control how the money is invested and the profits used. The premise is that institutionalized gender and class inequalities can be overlooked or easily transformed. Although microcredit projects often emerge from laudable intentions, Anne Marie Goetz and Rina Sen Gupta summarize a number of feminist concerns:

> Improvements in women's productivity, mobility, access to markets, literacy, social status, and control of household decisions takes [*sic*] time, requires [*sic*] considerable commitment by development workers, a long-term investment in local-level processes of social changes, as well as a willingness to cope with the sometimes violent and disruptive consequences of challenging

class and gender privilege. This is even more true when it comes to changing social attitudes toward women's right of ownership over resources and to assigning value to women's contributions to household well-being. (1996: 61)

Critics raise other issues as well. A focus on microfinance avoids asking larger questions regarding the structural causes of poverty and its reproduction through neoliberal policies, the "quick fix" of microcredit projects shifts support from longer-term and more socially oriented programs addressing the complexity of effective social change, and the foregrounding of quantifiable success indicators (repayment rates) deflects attention from the quality of women's participation and whether and in what ways empowerment actually occurs. We see the power of gender operating in several ways: the framing of development strategies through a "paternalistic colonial lens" (Bergeron 2003:168), the reproduction of gender stereotypes and unchanged distributions of household labor, and simplistic expectations regarding domestic, gender, and class relations in community settings. In these senses, microcredit initiatives exemplify both the promise and flawed delivery of "women-oriented" policies that we reflect on throughout this text: they are a too-simplistic answer to complex problems. The popularization of microcredit, however, obscures this. Microcredit enthusiasts, who market it as an empowering solution for women's poverty in the South to consuming publics in the West through such images as a poor woman "photographed with both 'primitive' abacus and 'modern' calculator" that turn her into a "magical object," enable the financialization of development to carry on largely unquestioned "'in her name'" (Roy 2010: 71).

## Gendered Politics of Consumption

The financialization of development has in some sense democratized development, increasingly drawing ordinary consumers in the developed world into financially supporting campaigns for such things as microcredit, fair trade, and HIV/AIDS treatment initiatives sponsored by NGOs and corporations that frequently employ Western celebrities (Bono, Gwyneth Paltrow, Madonna, and so on) to encourage giving. This trend has been variously referred to as "celebrity-driven development," "philanthrocapitalism," or "brand aid" (Rowley 2011; Richey and Ponte 2011; King 2013) and often consists of campaigns that exhort consumers to buy products made available to them that supposedly "save" the lives of poor people, particularly women, in the global South who are to benefit from (some of) the proceeds from the products bought. Although more "ethical consumption" that foregrounds the needs of poor women and engages consumers in caring about them and doing something for them can be seen as a positive development, too often these campaigns obscure the poor working conditions of those who produce the items for sale, endear consumers to the very corporations involved in large-scale labor exploitation in the developing and developed worlds, play on stereotypical images of either victimized or beautified poor women generically from the global South (and especially the African continent) to open purse strings, and, in some cases, give little of the proceeds to combating the problems they claim they seek to solve. Just as problematically, these initiatives turn shopping into a moral act, feeding into the faulty assumption that this is all that is necessary to alleviate the pain of faraway vulnerable bodies of color, while increasing the profits of the corporations implicated in sustaining those vulnerabilities. Thus, this trend, which we call the new "gender equality by consumption" approach, constitutes only a new twist on the sordid relationship between global capitalism and consumerism that we detail below.

Market processes involve the production of goods and services, the circulation of cash or credit for purchasing them, and the creation of consumer desires that shape what we purchase. A great deal of attention and resources goes into producing a pervasive market *culture* that encourages consumption by inculcating consumer *subjectivities*—that is, orienting people to always desire and thus consume "more" and, more recently, to imagine that their endless consuming will "do good." The power of gender operates through marketing, advertising, and deepening the commodification of social life and relations. The politics of advertising—who decides what we "want"—is explicitly about using cultural codes to manipulate consciousness and create ever-changing tastes and fashions. Stereotypes of gender, ethnicity/race, sexuality, and age are used strategically and prominently in advertising to project selective images of bodies, cultures, sexualities, and lifestyles as the "most desired" and "most desirable" or the most "helpable," as in the case of marketing for ethical consumption. Celebrity-studded arts and entertainment are also big business on a global scale, where selling sex, sensationalism, stereotypes of "good" and "bad" cultures, and now "brand aid" is a lucrative strategy. At the same time, the more corporatized popular music and videos become, the more violent and sexually violent they become.

Women's bodies continue to be objectified, whether as hypersexual commodities available to consumers or as asexual victims in need of saving by consumers.

Although affluent consumption is the privilege of only a small elite, it shapes the desires, choices, and valorization of those without affluence. Pervasive advertising and global media encourage even the poorest to desire consumer goods as an expression of self-worth. Northern desires for cheap goods as well as luxury items—clothes, cars, electronics, flowers, furs, diamonds, gasoline—determine Southern patterns of production, including poorly paid workers, hazardous work conditions, and environmentally unsound practices. Even political activities shift to market-based expressions: identity-based groups become particular targets of marketing and use consumption as an identity "marker," and political action is increasingly consumer-based as people "vote" through what they do and do not buy, just as they are now expected to "save" feminized "others" by their mere purchases. But we might ask: Whose needs, desires, and interests are served by consumerism? Whose bodies and environments are devalorized—rendered disposable—in pursuit of consumerism and the neoliberal commitment to growth (rather than redistribution) that fuels it? These questions become focal points as we shift our attention to gendered divisions of resources.

## GENDERED RESOURCES

The devalorization of the environment upon which industrial capitalism and more recent neoliberal globalization rest has led to a wide array of resource shortages and maldistributions, ecological degradations, and "natural" disasters, the most serious of which in terms of global impact is the onset of global warming. Although there is finally a global scientific and even global political consensus that global warming is "man-made" by largely industrial pollutants, this has not yet caused a fundamental rethinking of commitments to neoliberal globalization that might curb this ecological meltdown.

Naomi Klein (2007) has recently traced the historical relationship between "free-market fundamentalism," initially championed by the Chicago School of neoclassical economists and imposed systematically from South to North and East to West since the Cold War period, and various economic, political, and "natural" disasters. Although she does not provide an epidemiology of the relationship between global warming and such disasters as Hurricane Katrina in 2005 and the Southeast Asian tsunami in 2004, she argues that these "natural" shocks were able to wreak such destruction and loss of human life because of the "policy trinity" of neoliberal globalization—"the elimination of the public sphere, total liberation for corporations, and skeletal social spending" (2007: 15). The range of social and technological safety nets that would have better protected people and their environments when disasters struck was structurally undermined by a free-market ideology that transferred resources from public services and works to private corporate hands. Moreover, she argues that such "natural disasters, rather than serving as wake-up calls to shift resources back into serving public needs, have actually accelerated private accumulation, deepened human immiseration, and worsened environmental vulnerability. She calls this purposive use of calamities, including environmental ones, to enrich corporations at the expense of human welfare and environmental stability "disaster capitalism," which relies on a neoliberal capitalist "shock doctrine" that works in the following way: "The coup, the terrorist attack, the market meltdown, the war, the tsunami, the hurricane—puts the entire population into a state of collective shock. The falling bombs, the bursts of terror, the pounding winds serve to soften up whole societies much as the blaring music and blows of the torture cells soften up prisoners. Like the terrorized prisoner who gives up the names of comrades and renounces his faith, shocked societies often give up things they would otherwise fiercely protect" (2007: 17).

We further argue that this softening up constitutes a feminizing of populations in relation to capital, and that racism, classism, and sexism operate to determine who and what is disposable, enabling further extractions of resources and violations of human and civil rights with relative impunity. Indeed, as Klein points out, in the wake of "natural disasters such as Hurricane Katrina, land developers, corporate contractors, and the politicians who allied with them saw an opportunity to "clean out" the majority poor African American population hardest hit and to start with a "clean slate." Their objective was not to "rebuild" what was lost for the people who had lost it, but rather to "reconstruct" selected spaces in ways that were most profitable for private industry and least affordable for those who were dislocated (Klein 2007: 8).

## GENDERED DIVISIONS OF RESOURCES

Although the racist and classist dimensions of the vulnerability to and the aftermath of Katrina have been heavily exposed, less well known are its impacts on women specifically. According to a US Institute for Women's Policy Research (IWPR) report (Jones-DeWeever 2008), poor women in New Orleans suffered particularly from further impoverishment and disease but also higher incidences of domestic violence and loss of child care as well as loss of jobs and health benefits. It is also estimated that three times more women than men died in the Southeast Asian tsunami in 2004, and a study of "natural" disasters between 1981 and 2002 (during which "natural" disasters began to climb exponentially) in 141 countries found that women died on the order of fourteen times more than men during disasters (True 2012: 161, 164). The major reasons for women's greater vulnerability in such disasters include the usual litany: they "are generally poorer than men, they do not own land, they are less likely to have an education or access to health care, they are often less mobile due to cultural constraints, and they have less of a political voice in environmental planning and decision making" (True 2012: 161). The loss of life and particularly women's disproportionate mortality in disasters are greatly lessened in developed country contexts where infrastructures are more solid and disaster relief is more available, but the majority of the world's women, most of whom inhabit the global South economically and racially, have particular stakes in confronting climate change and reversing the gender, race, and class environmental apartheid and triage that have contributed to it and that are being reimposed in its wake.

As such NGOs as the Women's Environment and Development Organization (WEDO) have pointed out, poor women are not just on the front lines of global warming but are also central to reversing it. In addition to the fact that women in aggregate have smaller carbon footprints than men in aggregate because they have fewer resources, less control over resources, and "own less than 2 percent of the world's private land" (Ghosh 2007: 444), poor women, as the producers of 60 to 80 percent of food consumed in households and the primary suppliers of water and fuel to households in the global South, have been most active in seeking to conserve and replenish natural resources vital to their families and communities (WEDO 2008). For example, the women's tree-planting Green Belt Movement in Kenya—for which its founder,

Wangari Maathai, received a Nobel Peace Prize—has been planting trees in mountain regions that by 2017 will absorb 375,000 tons of carbon dioxide, while also repairing soil erosion, enabling rainfall retention for farming and electricity, and providing income for poor women (WEDO 2007). The Green Belt Movement began as a grassroots women's movement, but this particular project, started in 2006, is being supported by the World Bank's Community Redevelopment Carbon Fund. This "partnership" is a result of linkages that were made between gender inequality and environmental crises by women's movements during the UN Decade for Women and at the UN Environmental Summit in Rio de Janeiro in 1992—linkages that IGOs have only begun to recognize very unevenly. As WEDO (2007) observes, although "every major global agreement on sustainable development acknowledges the importance of gender equality," the UN Framework Convention on Climate Change (UNFCCC) and the 1997 Kyoto Protocol that facilitates this treaty "are narrowly focused on emissions reductions, rather than social impacts" and social solutions. The largest contributor to greenhouse gases per capita, the United States, has thus far refused to ratify the Kyoto Protocol (yet China as the highest emitter has signed it), and by 2007 only two countries had used a gender perspective in their climate change initiatives reported to the United Nations Environment Program (UNEP) (WEDO 2007). Moreover, the MDG focused on environmental sustainability has no targets or indicators that address gender inequality as a source of or ending it as a solution to environmental breakdown, and few countries mention women in their National Adaptation Programmes of Action to deal with climate change (UN Women 2011: 116).

Contemporary official resistance to making the connection between gender inequality and global warming has its roots in the rise of Western colonization. This undermined communal land use and women's land rights. In addition, the rise of Western science transformed peoples' notions of nature and instituted a worldview that saw nature strictly as a resource for Eurocentric, "man-made" projects, thus discrediting belief systems associated with "primitive" cultures in which nature was revered as a manifestation of feminine divinity. Early Western science, coupled with Christian ideology, still thought of nature as feminine, but rather than powerful and goddesslike, nature in this view was a passive resource from which European men could take anything they needed or wanted without care for the effects of their interventions. This attitude paved the way for rapacious land-use patterns and technologies, which have led to numerous ecological crises since the advent of the industrial revolution (Merchant 1980). Western gender ideology continues to construe nature as a passive resource to be exploited, controlled, used, and abused. On the flip side, the concomitant racialization of nature as brute and savage during the colonial period has justified efforts to tame it for (white) "man's" purposes ever since. As these ideologies spread, environmental crises have followed, culminating in the contemporary problems of acid rain and global dumping, ozone depletion and global warming.

If we look through the lens of the *gendered divisions of resources,* we see that gender and race ideology contributes to the growth and perpetuation of these problems. The increasingly global aspects of the gendered divisions of resources rest upon dichotomies of culture-nature, active-passive, subject-object, users-resources, advanced-primitive, and exploitation-stewardship. These dichotomies are manifested in the contemporary situation in which women, especially in the global South, have a great deal of responsibility for caring for the environment but little say in how it will be used and for what purposes.

Neoliberal globalization has also ensured that environmental issues are subsumed to the interests of capital, constituting a colonization of nature itself while also naturalizing inequalities. As Nandita Ghosh puts it, "Promoting market values above all else also reduces complex human relationships with nature to ego-driven, need-based interactions. Nature is also perceived as universal and encompassing of all human society. Here too it is externalized and can be used to justify the 'natural' ethnic, sexual, and class oppressions that are always gendered. Both ideologies obfuscate the contributions of human labor to the process by which nature is externalized, produced, and consumed" (2007: 446).

This "marketization of nature" also pits "diverse cultures and ecosystems against the privatization and enclosure" of the global resource "commons" (Ghosh 2007: 446), but the neoliberal governmentality or "biopolitics" of Empire intervenes to "control and diffuse a diversity of crises" in the interest of capital (Ghosh 2007: 447) at the same time as whole populations (and, we could argue, the earth itself) are consigned to what Giorgio Agamben (1998) calls "bare life,"[23] a "state of exception" in which legal rights are suspended and bodies are excluded from moral calculus (Ghosh 2007: 448). This enables the continuation of the "shock doctrine" even as IGOs and their member states claim to be addressing environmental crises, but in ways that do not unduly disturb capital or the disposability of gendered, raced, classed, and sexualized bodies.

*Gendered Resource Depletion*

Although it was only recently that food safety, water access, and energy self-sufficiency became mantras of world politicians and took center stage in debates about global warming and global trade, it was poor, rural women in the global South who first alerted the world about what Sen and Grown (1987) back in the 1980s called the "food-fuel-water crises." Like the proverbial canaries in the mineshaft, women in subsistence economies bore the initial brunt and continue to be on the front lines of these crises, which are due to resource depletion. Women's displacement from the land by large-scale agricultural development for export has contributed to high levels of famine, particularly in Africa. But there are additional consequences of this displacement, contributing not only to continued hunger but also to deforestation and desertification. Women are the main food producers and processors in most of the rural areas of the global South, and they must have access to clean water and firewood for fuel. As their land is lost to corporate farms and as water sources are polluted by agricultural runoff from fertilizers and pesticides or suspended by large-scale dam projects or privatization efforts, rural women and children are forced to travel farther and farther in search of clean water, spending as much as 40 billion hours per year in this pursuit in Africa alone (UNIFEM 2008: 130).

Similarly, as forests are cut down for large-scale agricultural, industrial, tourist, or even residential enterprises, women must go farther afield to look for the firewood needed to cook and to boil water, making it safe to drink. This has exposed them even more to "firestick" rapes in such places as the DRC and the Darfur region of Sudan. When water and fuel sources are being depleted, not only does food become scarce, but also the basis for ecologically sound agricultural practices is eroded. First, female subsistence farmers are forced to cultivate small plots of land repeatedly rather than engage in crop rotation. Monoculture depletes vital soil nutrients and can eventually even lead to small-scale desertification. Large-scale desertification is the result of the overuse of crop lands by corporate farming practices, including not rotating crops, overwatering and salinating the soil, and/or growing crops using methods that destroy fragile topsoil.

Second, when the soil is too depleted to produce crops, rural populations are reduced to consuming the seeds for future crops, destroying their capability to produce their own food. Another alternative is to seek food, as well as fuel and water, farther away from their homes. This pushes rural peoples into marginal and therefore sensitive ecosystems, even conservation areas and parks. Different interests motivate poor rural peoples, who have few alternatives for survival in the short term, and ecologists, who take the longer view toward saving the environment but who do not work on remedies for the unequal distribution of land and resources that forces poor people to seek food, fuel, and water in protected areas.

This unequal distribution of land and resources arises not just from class status but also from gender divisions in a world in which women own only a tiny fraction of privately held land. The Western assumption that women are not farmers has led both to the loss of women's land rights and to the failure to provide technological assistance to women who work the land. As we have learned from the unforeseen consequences of high-technology experiments such as the green revolution, not all technology is good or appropriate for every socioeconomic and environmental context. Development mistakes—mistakes for the large number of people impoverished by them—might have been avoided if women farmers in the global South, who are central to subsistence food production and thus mindful of conserving the land, had been consulted about how best to use the land and what technologies are most appropriate (Rodda 1991).

Most women agricultural workers are not formally educated in modern, Western agricultural techniques. However, they work closely with and on the land and have developed significant informal knowledge about ecosystems and appropriate land-use patterns. As farmers, women often know which plants have the most nutritional value and what forms of cultivation lead to the least soil erosion and water consumption. As traditional healers, women often know which plants have medicinal value and what practices sustain the biodiversity of an ecosystem to ensure that such healing vegetation is preserved. As fuel gatherers, women know they are dependent on forests to provide renewable sources of firewood.[24] International and national development planners and agencies that ignore women's knowledge and introduce inappropriate technologies can do much more harm than good.

Globalization forces are constituting an even more serious threat to ecological sustainability and biodiversity as capitalist expansion spreads industries and enterprises into areas that were previously less affected by economic development. Trade liberalization policies, such as Trade-Related Intellectual Property Rights (TRIPs) that were codified in the 1995 General Agreement on Tariffs and Trade (also known as the GATT) agreement and are enshrined in the articles of the WTO, essentially allow the patenting of all slightly modified plants, animals, and building blocks of human life. As Vandana Shiva (2005) argues, this "biopiracy" constitutes multiple thefts, including the privatization of the environmental commons, the dispossession of the poor of public resources, and the disowning of the knowledge of ecological conservation that especially rural poor women have as a result of cultural assignments to be the custodians of seeds and plants over which companies like Monsanto are now gaining monopolistic rights. The privatization of even genetic materials undermines both public accountability for how the earth and living things on it are used (and abused) and women's capacity for developing more sustainable practices.

## Gendered Resource Destruction

Of course, women are not always kind to the environment, especially when they become members of consumer-oriented cultures, which are increasing in number as a result of globalization. Western gender ideology encourages women to adopt a consumer lifestyle through which they can beautify their bodies (according to Western standards), dress fashionably (as defined by male fashion designers), and stock their homes with modern "conveniences" (some of which actually create work). Beauty products are implicated in all manner of ecological harm, ranging from inhumane animal testing of makeup and shampoos to ozone depletion from aerosol spray use. Fur coats are products of the brutal destruction of animals for their pelts. Finally, "keeping up with the Joneses" keeps women (and men) enamored of the idea that they must have more cars, dishwashers, laundry machines, microwaves, refrigerators, computers, and other devices that require much energy to produce and operate, result in a great deal of air and water pollution, and create a significant amount of toxic garbage when they are thrown away to make way for new, improved models.

While middle- and upper-class consumers in "throwaway" societies are heavily implicated in resource waste and environmental pollution, poor and working-class women worldwide suffer the effects of environmental degradation and pollution. The poor and working class are concentrated in crowded and often highly polluted residential areas and largely unregulated, toxic workplaces. Moreover, given the rise in poor, female-headed households, a large number of women and children live in remote rural areas and urban slums, where toxic-waste dumps are common. This situation occurs frequently in countries of the global South that accept toxic refuse (for dumping and/or dismantlement) from the global North in order to earn foreign exchange.[25]

Women's reproductive organs are harmed by exposure to industrial toxins in workplaces and residential communities, resulting in ovarian cancer, infertility, miscarriages, and birth defects. Recognition of women's susceptibility to industrial toxins has led to some restrictions on where women are allowed to work. However, data on sterility, cancers, and genetic damage indicate that men's reproductive health is also put at risk by working in toxic environments. This suggests that the gendered solution of barring women from certain workplaces is simply an "industrial protection racket" that draws attention away from polluting industries as the real problem (Nelson 1990: 179). Similarly, women's reproductive failures have called attention to the hidden effects of nuclear testing and nuclear power plant emissions and accidents (Seager 1993). Yet it is rare that states and industries are held accountable for the extensive reproductive harm and genetic damage their nuclear programs have produced.

Militaries have been the worst polluters in the world, according to Seager, who has catalogued the many and extensive harms done to the environment by military installations by the end of the Cold War. This list includes such practices as the production and dumping of toxic wastes from chemical weapons programs, the appropriation of land equal to the size of Turkey in thirteen industrialized countries, the consumption of huge quantities of oil, the emission of large amounts of carbon dioxide and chlorofluorocarbons that cause global warming and ozone depletion, and the destruction of thousands of animals each year in weapons and other tests. The shroud of "national security" in combination with masculine privilege, however, ensured that in "virtually every country, military facilities are exempt from environmental regulations and monitoring requirements" (Seager 1993: 37). The US military has been subject to some environmental regulation since the Bill Clinton administration, but its penchant for secrecy and noninterference has meant that it monitors itself as opposed to being accountable to the civilian government or to citizens (Parr 2009: 83). The "war on drugs," too, which the US government uses to justify continual and widespread spraying of carcinogenic herbicides throughout the countrysides of Central and South America and Southeast Asia, has caused untold numbers of birth defects and reproductive disorders in rural women who live and work in these areas (Seager 1993: 30).

In recent years, "sustainability" has become a new global buzzword in IGO and NGO circles and has entered popular discourse. But it has also been taken up by the market, seeing more profits to be made by creating a niche market for "green" production and products. Like "brand aid," the "ecobranding" of products and corporations as "green" too often devolves into "green-washing," which both taps into and creates consumer desires for more ethical consumption but sells only somewhat modified versions of still polluting, wasteful, and labor-exploiting commodities (Parr 2009). And like brand aid, ecobranding and green-washing manufacture an essentially depoliticized response to the crisis of sustainability.

## Women as Disposable Resources

As Melissa Wright argues, one of the most economically and "socially useful lies" or "myths" is that of the "disposable third world woman" (2006: 2–3), who perhaps more than any other is rendered worthless and consigned to "bare life." This lie enables the superexploitation of the laboring bodies of these women while exposing them to a range of bodily harms without rights over their bodies. This accounts for the facts, as detailed in UNIFEM's 2008–2009 report on the world's women, that poor women in the global South have the highest rates of poverty, hunger, maternal mortality, poor maternal health, and HIV/AIDS, and their children are the most subject to high child mortality rates. Reductions in these rates constitute the bulk of the MDGs, but maternal health "is the most off-track of all MDGs" (UNIFEM 2008: 125; UN Women 2011: 112). In addition to the heteronormative reduction of women's health to "maternal" health, which assumes that all women are or will be mothers and the only aspect of their health worthy of protection is in relation to their reproductive labor, the broader notion of universal access to reproductive health, including family planning and contraception services, was added belatedly as a target to achieve the maternal health MDG. This was as a result of pressure from women's movements and the reality finally recognized that maternal deaths, which are nowhere near the 5.5 percent annual reduction targeted, could be reduced by one-quarter by access to contraceptives and safe terminations (UNIFEM 2008: 127; UN Women 2011: 112). However, in direct contradiction to this, the percentage of women denied access to contraceptives and family planning services they need increased from 55 percent in 1990 to 64 percent in 2005 (UNIFEM 2008: 127). The combination of further illegalizations of and legal, cultural, and geographical restrictions on contraceptive use and abortions, the rise of state-sponsored religious fundamentalisms, and the US "global gag rule" reimposed under the Bush administration (although lifted under Obama), which denied

US funding to any organization that even raises the option of abortion, have conspired to undermine meaningful progress on the very modest maternal health MDG.

A similar pattern of failing to address underlying causes because they would require women's rights over their bodies and their ability to exercise them can be found in the context of the MDG pertaining to HIV/AIDS. Far from being halted or reversed, women's contraction of HIV/AIDS continues to climb, particularly in sub-Saharan Africa and the Caribbean, where it is reportedly most prevalent and where women outpace men in its contraction or in the rates of contraction (UNIFEM 2008: 128). More women are living with HIV as a result of more dissemination of more affordable antiretroviral drugs, but many more need them to survive. The feminization of HIV/AIDS has been attributed to a combination of poverty, high rates of sexual assault in war and peace that lead to infections, a relative lack of information and treatment services provided to poor women, a greater stigma attached to having HIV/AIDs for women, and a relative lack of information and treatment services provided to poor women (UNIFEM 2008: 128; UN Women 2011: 114). Yet MDG targets and indicators are silent on such gender dimensions of the pandemic, with the exception of the use of condoms, which remains low.

The gendered divisions of power, violence, and labor and resources have conspired to construct official blinders, which ensure, especially, that young women of the global South will continue to be put at tremendous risk through prostitution, rape, poverty, and poor health care, as well as lack of contraceptive services and safe-sex education. These factors, along with a host of other health threats to women ranging from domestic violence to forced sterilizations and preferences for male children in many parts of the global South, have minimized women's power to control their own bodies, making them highly susceptible to contaminants and disease, which they end up passing on to their children, who, in turn, become damaged global resources.

In short, under the gendered division of resources, women in the aggregate but particularly in the global South not only have little access to resources that might make their lives longer and easier but also are treated as resources themselves, to be used, abused, and disposed of when it suits the purposes of powerful men, states, and industries. What most women need and want are rarely considered in the calculus of how resources are defined, divided, and used. Instead, under neoliberal governmentality, women are treated as abject beings without agency or rights; this occurs under a veneer of problem-solving that stigmatizes and colonizes so as to redirect attention away from the global capitalism, militarization, patriarchy, and racism that lie at the heart of global crises. As a result, women, the entire planet, and its other inhabitants suffer from this far-from-benign neglect. Such purposeful neglect is nevertheless still resisted by movements of poor and disenfranchised people around the world claiming "sovereignty" over their local resources (Patel 2009), as well as by "people's renewal movements," which "begin from the premise that there is no escape from the substantial messes we have created and that there has already been enough erasure—of history, of culture, of memory. These are movements that do not seek to start from scratch but rather from scrap, from the rubble that is all around . . . taking what's there and fixing it, reinforcing it, making it better and more equal. Most of all they are building resilience—for when the next shock comes" (Klein 2007: 466).

## TOWARD RESISTING NEOLIBERALISM

Feminists and other critics of neoliberalism raise a number of concerns. Some areas and sectors have indeed experienced significant growth, but instead of neoliberalism's promise to "lift all boats," the evidence shows that inequalities within and between countries have actually grown (Cornia 2004; Wade 2004; APSA 2008). The selective implementation of liberalization continues to favor the powerful nations of the North, whereas other nations have limited control over protecting domestic industries, goods produced, and jobs provided. Deregulation permitted the hypermobility of "footloose" capital and induced phenomenal growth in financial markets and high-risk transactions, which as critics predicted and the recent meltdown proves are unsustainable. Privatization entailed a decline of nationalized industries and a decrease in public-sector employment and the provision of social services worldwide. Women are disproportionately affected because they are more likely to depend on secure government jobs and on public resources in support of reproductive labor. At the same time and in spite of fewer available resources and more demands on their time, women are expected to fill the gap—thus "solving the problem"— when public provisioning declines. The poorest women and men—who in the global North tend to be ethnic/racial minorities—are especially hurt by reduced public spending because they have the fewest (private) resources and hence are most in need of public services and the support they provide.

The picture of GPE presented here reveals a polarization of income and status between masculinized elites and the global majority of feminized "others." This generalized analysis also exposed how the cultural code of feminization naturalizes the economic (material) devaluation of feminized work, whether that work is done by women or men who are culturally, racially, and/or economically marginalized. Hence, this chapter has illuminated not only how men and women are positioned and being repositioned globally by gendered divisions to maximize exploitation, but also how the power of gender continues to operate in ways that deflect attention away from such exploitation by naturalizing or depoliticizing it. At the same time, this chapter has exposed how neoliberal globalization has exacerbated the disposability of resources and bodies, particularly those that are most gendered, racialized, and classed, ultimately threatening the planet itself. In spite of the severity of human exploitation and environmental degradation, we note the continued resistance by national and international officialdom to reduce these harms significantly, as this would require fundamental shifts in human relationships and in human relationships with the environment, which are precluded by the maintenance of the power of gender.

Shiva (2005) calls for such a shift in her concept of "Earth Democracy." This is far from the contemporary top-down responses to global crises that are captured by Empire, or neoliberal governmentality coupled with imperialist security governmentality, and that stress corporate-led technological fixes and food-energy-water security only for those who can afford it and through violent means. Instead,

Earth Democracy allows us to overcome the artificial scarcity and manipulated and manufactured insecurities by seeing and experiencing connections. We begin to see the connections between corporations and corporate states, the connections between the economic wars and military wars, the connections between corporate profits and people's poverty, the connections between globalization and religious fundamentalism. We also start to discover the connections we have to the earth and one another. Exposing the connections of dominant powers enables us to evolve appropriate strategies to transform dead democracies into living democracies. Our ecological and social connectedness enables us to create living economies and living cultures, while building the solidarities which crack open the alliances of the powerful. (Shiva 2005: 185)

It is to such resistance and building of solidarity that we now turn to conclude this text. In the final chapter, we also explore what it might mean to degender world politics in order to enable more meaningful responses to the crises of representation, insecurity, and sustainability.

**Notes**

1. We prefer a reference to global political economy (GPE) rather than to international political economy insofar as GPE draws our attention to increasingly *transnational* processes and requires *transdisciplinary* perspectives. In contrast to many accounts, we also address discursive shifts, sociocultural changes, and shifting identities as these affect, and are affected by, globalization processes.

2. Overviews of feminist economics include Hewitson 1999; Ferber and Nelson 2003; and Barker and Feiner 2004.

3. Rai provides a very useful comparison and discussion of WID and GAD orientations (2002: 71–73).

4. For recent examples, see Marchand and Runyan 2000; Rai 2002; Mohanty 2003; Peterson 2003; Benería 2003; Parpart and Zalewski 2008; and Visvanathan et al. 2011.

5. For recent examples, see Agathangelou and Ling 2009; Lind 2010; and Marchand and Runyan 2011.

6. See Truong 1999; *World Development* 2000; Aslanbeigui and Summerfield 2000, 2001; Hooper 2001; Van Staveren 2002; Marchand and Runyan 2011; and True 2012.

7. On economics as the study of provisioning, see, for example, Nelson 1996; Ferber and Nelson 2003; and Power 2004. On feminist economics as offering not only a corrective but also an alternative and socially progressive understanding of economics, see Gibson-Graham 1996, 2006; and Barker and Feiner 2004. See also Bergeron 2001 for a critique of the continued masculinist, racist, and imperial underpinnings of even what some call the post–Washington Consensus.

8. See Federici 2004 for an extensive study of how capitalism and colonization brutally imposed gendered divisions of labor on colonizing and colonized societies.

9. The literature on women and the rise and consolidation of industrial capitalism and modernization is voluminous, but for germinal works see Rowbotham 1973; and Mies 1986.

10. There is a vast literature on this prompted early on by Fernandez-Kelly 1983; and Fuentes and Ehrenreich 1983.

11. For more visceral and lived accounts of the impact of SAPs on peoples in the global South, particularly in the Caribbean and Africa, see the films *Life + Debt* (2001) and *Bamako* (2006).

12. The literature is long-standing and extensive. See, for example, Sen and Grown 1987; Vickers 1991; *World Development* 1995, 2000; Bakker 1994; Einhorn and Yeo 1995; and Moghadam 1994, on transition economies of eastern and central Europe. For more recent literature on gender, structural adjustment, and global restructuring,

see Eisenstein 2009; and Marchand and Runyan 2011. See also Smiley and West (2012) on old and new impoverishment in the United States, particularly of women.

13. Although loss of economic resources is always problematic, Chant (2007) draws on extensive case studies to argue against automatically assuming that women are better off with, than without, men in their households.

14. Sexual minority (im)migrants are often rendered invisible by migration and refugee studies, both feminist and nonfeminist, and often face horrific treatment as they cross borders and in detention centers. See Luibhéid and Cantú 2005.

15. For more on gendered migration in the North American context, see Runyan et al. (2013).

16. Estimates vary, but in 1995 the world's "underground," or informal, economy was estimated to be worth US$9 trillion (*Economist* 1999: 59), the equivalent of one-fourth of the "gross global product" for that year, and the value of "housework" was estimated to be US$10–15 trillion (UNDP 1995: 6; Tetreault and Lipschutz 2005: 25). By the end of the 1990s, it was estimated that informal activities constituted more than one-half of all economic output and 75 percent of the GDP of some countries, that one-half to three-quarters of nonagricultural work in developing countries was informal, and that informal work in Africa accounted for more than 90 percent of new jobs during the 1990s (ILO 2002b: 5). By 2012, a joint study by the NGO Women in Informal Employment: Globalizing and Organizing and the ILO found that nonagricultural informal employment continues to outpace formal employment in most of the global South, where women also rely more on it than men as a source of income even though men are more employed generally and thus more employed in the nonagricultural informal sector as well. There is also evidence that large numbers of workers in the global North (in some places more than 20 percent) are in nonstandard and thus technically informal employment, working full-time or part-time with few or no benefits (see http://wiego.org/informal-economy/statistical-picture).

17. Virtually all researchers note the problematic nature of data on informality, but these generalizations are widely accepted. See UN 2000; ILO 2002a; ILO 2002b; Benería 2003; and Snyder 2005.

18. Dangler (2000) provides an in-depth history of homework as a structural feature of capitalism. Boris and Prügl provide the ILO definition of homework as "the production of goods or the provision of services for an employer or contractor under an arrangement whereby the work is carried out at the place of the worker's own choosing, often the worker's own home" (1996: 5).

19. Sex workers are not only women (and girls) but also men (and boys) and transgendered people, and their customers include not only heterosexual-identified men but also gay-identified men (and some women, straight and lesbian). As M. Jacqui Alexander argues, some male and female sex workers in the Caribbean (and the global South generally) are constituted as markets for the white gay (including lesbian) tourist industry and are thus subservient to "white gay capital" (2005: 11). This is yet another example of how otherwise progressive actors, in this case those who struggle for sexual minority rights at home, engage in colonizing and imperializing practices abroad.

20. Recent studies include Kempadoo and Doezema 1998; Hughes 2000; Hanochi 2001; Agathangelou 2004; Kempadoo 2005; Agustín 2007; Jeffreys 2009; and Dewey and Kelly 2011. Trafficking in women increasingly occurs in connection with transnational criminal networks operating in relation to militarized conflicts and trading in a variety of goods, including drugs, body parts, migrants, precious natural resources, arms, and nuclear materials.

21. Recent critical summaries with reference to hegemonic Western masculinity, especially for young men, include Kimmel 2008; and McCaughey 2008. See also True 2012 for examples of "globalizing masculinities."

22. On gendering global finance and its crises, see Aslanbeigui and Summerfield 2000, 2001; Truong 2000; Floro and Dymski 2000; Van Staveren 2002; Peterson 2003; De Goede 2005; and Marchand and Runyan 2011.

23. A related concept to this is "necropolitics" (Mbembe 2002), which is the ideological and systemic calculus of who can be killed or left to die and whose loss of life is ungrievable (Butler 2010), most typically racialized people of the global South deemed less than "human."

24. In Mali, for example, certain trees are designated as "women" trees. This means they are reserved for firewood, which is typically harvested from dead branches, and thus the trees are not to be cut down (Rodda 1991: 75).

25. It is estimated that up to 80 percent of North American electronic waste that is full of carcinogenic material is sent to Asia (Parr 2009: 100).

# 6

◄◦►

# Gendered Resistances

How have women resisted the gendered divisions of power, violence, labor, and resources? What new social movements have developed as a result of and in response to global restructuring? What are their problems and potentials in terms of disrupting power relations from the intimate to the global? How does feminist IR and transnational feminist scholarship center resistances to world-politics-as-usual by decentering the power of gender? Why is it necessary to go beyond "adding women" to challenge the crises of representation, insecurity, and sustainability?

As we have seen in our survey of gender and gendered processes in current world politics and the contemporary feminist IR inquiry that has brought these to light, the *power of gender* continues to foster dichotomizing, stratifying, "othering," and depoliticizing in thought and action. These moves produce and maintain *crises of representation, insecurity, and sustainability,* despite some *repositionings of some women and men* on the world stage. Repositionings, such as those moves that give some women greater access to the means of destruction and more men less access to the means of production, are more the result of the deepening and widening of militarization and economic globalization than of justice-inspired gender equality commitments and policies. Thus, *gendered divisions of power, violence, labor, and resources* are not seriously disturbed by some "resexing" of actors, especially when those actors are still expected to play dutiful or acquiescent roles in support of power-over, militarization, and economic and resource exploitations associated with imperial(ist) impulses. Thus, the question is not one of agency alone, but rather of whose agency for what.

This concluding chapter explores agency directed to resisting gendered divisions and the power of gender. Rather than offering inventories and

237

anatomies of social movements and their efficacies, we first examine the range of thinking about resistance practices and formations arising out of feminist IR and transnational feminist inquiry. We then provide our ruminations on *degendering* world politics to respond to global crises in ways that also promote gender—and more broadly social—justice.

## FEMINIST RESISTANCE POLITICS

### Women and Social Movements

Even as some women gain greater access to formal political power, it is more often the case that critical masses of female political actors who more radically challenge gender dichotomies are found outside of formal power structures. Because they typically organize outside of state apparatuses, these actors tend to be invisible through the state-centric lens on world politics that prevailed until recently. Now that market forces, in the form of private firms and IFIs, are challenging and complicating traditional state prerogatives in world politics, IR has begun to direct attention to what is frequently referred to as "civil society." Neoliberals and neoconservatives tend to conceptualize civil society in terms of the private sector, defined as corporate and individualist interests that are in tension with and seek to maintain autonomy from the state. Critical perspectives tend to view civil society in terms of social movements that resist both state domination and capitalist market exploitation (Macdonald 1994). This latter definition of civil society is making women more visible as actors in world politics. However, only feminist perspectives highlight the central roles that women play in social movement activism.

Women are found in large numbers in social movements for peace, human rights, economic justice, and environmental protection as members of both mixed organizations (which include men and women) and separate organizations (which are women-centered in terms of leadership, focus, and membership and thus are referred to as "women's movements"). Until recently, the activities of such social movements have been concentrated below the level of the state and confined within state boundaries. However, as economic, environmental, and social issues increasingly cut across state boundaries due to globalization forces, and as IGOs have become more significant sites for global policymaking and more open to NGO claimants and partnerships, women's movements, but particularly the NGOs that claim to represent such movements, are becoming more transnational in focus, organization, and impact. These processes are raising the profiles of women's movements in world politics. In this sense, they are part of what is being termed *global civil society,* which is seen as either a countervailing balance to or as an intervention against state and corporate power (Stienstra 1999: 262).

Women in their social movement roles as nonstate and transstate actors shift attention from "fitting women into" traditional IR frameworks and toward an understanding that accommodates and empowers women's struggles against the hierarchical consequences of practicing world-politics-as-usual. More often, women's activism not only resists oppressive state and market forces but also often seeks to transform civil society. Indeed, their emphasis on the transformation of civil society is what makes women's movements somewhat distinctive among social movements. Feminists tend to go beyond many critical formulations of civil society by arguing that civil society is not that autonomous from the state and the market, nor does it always resist the negative effects of these forces. All ideals and social movements have potential for variously regressive as well as progressive consequences. Just as there are progressive aspects to civil society, there are also regressive dimensions insofar as civil society reproduces oppressive structures (such as the heteronormative patriarchal family) and ideologies (such as sexism, racism, ableism, and homophobia) inculcated by a range of fundamentalisms. If these oppressive dimensions of civil society are not confronted and changed, it is unlikely that progressive, inclusive, and democratic social movements or global civil society more generally will flourish or that the negative effects of states and markets (reflecting problematic aspects of civil society) will be thoroughly challenged. Thus, even though there are liberating aspects of social movement struggles in which women significantly participate as members and leaders, such movements can perpetuate at the same time that they challenge gendered dichotomies. This caution is especially warranted when there is insufficient attention given to the transformation of civil society in the context of struggles to change states and markets.

*Transnational Feminist Movement Debates*

As indicated in Chapter 4—and exemplified in the problematics of the FMF campaign against gender apartheid in Afghanistan—there are major ongoing debates in feminist thought and movements, particularly those that are transnational in character, about how to resist regressive or imperial tendencies in order to build more equal and just solidarities to better confront crises of representation, insecurity, and sustainability. At core, anti-imperialist feminisms seek to enhance a "politics of recognition" in which the diverse voices and perspectives of subjugated women and men, or, more accurately, multiple sexes and genders, are represented equitably, and they seek to amplify a "politics of redistribution," which challenges the classist, sexist, racist, and heterosexist ways in which the material world is divided up (Fraser 1997). We see a politics of recognition as most central to ameliorating the crisis of representation but also key to challenging the crisis of insecurity, and a politics of redistribution as most central to countering the crisis of sustainability but also key to reducing the crisis of insecurity and enhancing a politics of recognition.

At various times, however, there have been tensions between a politics of recognition and a politics of redistribution because one has backgrounded the other. For example, early Marxist feminism was critiqued for focusing on only gendered class relations and material redistributions to solve these inequities without recognition of the need for a greater democratization of struggles to identify and resist not only gendered class exploitation but also other oppressions based on race, sexuality, and nation that intertwined with, variegated, and intensified class stratification. Later, various forms of cultural and ethnic feminisms were critiqued for a relative inattention to class analysis and a politics of material redistribution as they tended to pursue a kind of politics of recognition known as identity politics. Identity politics, while useful to foreground (and thus represent) the experiences and perspectives of a particular subjugated identity group (such as women, Asian women, Latinas, Chicanas, lesbians, and so on), also tended, on the one hand, to essentialize and homogenize such identity groups and, on the other hand, to so fragment identity into smaller and smaller groupings (young-disabled-lesbian-Chicanas) that no common cause could be seen among these groupings of infinite variety. The fragmentation of identity, however, served to draw attention to "hybrid" or "diasporic" identities that resist the forces of essentialism and homogenization and cut across identity groups (Anzaldúa 1999), and thus enable the development of coalition politics. Identity fragmentation (to the point of deconstructing all identities to expose them as always provisional and subject to change) also constitutes a poststructural feminist strategy (as well as a "queering" strategy) to denaturalize and thus destabilize identities, making them unavailable to be mobilized for the purposes of power and control or to be targets of power and control. Although, for a time, the developments of a politics of recognition overshadowed thinking about a politics of redistribution, today many contemporary feminist theorists and activists are emphasizing both to counter the rise of neoliberal globalization and governmentality and their security apparatuses. Developing and exercising both these politics entail anti-imperialist, antiracist, antiglobal-capitalist, antiheteronormative, and antihomonormative inquiry and political commitments.

Such inquiry and political commitments have been hampered by the ways that some feminist inquiry, both Western and non-Western, is conducted and informs social movements. Chandra Mohanty (2003) identifies practices that militate against anti-imperialist feminist thought and action. What she calls the "feminist-as-tourist" model arises from "brief forays into non-Euro-American cultures" in which "particular cultural sexist practices are addressed" through a Western "gaze" (2003: 239). This universalization of gender through a Eurocentric lens both subsumes more complex explanations for oppression under an overarching and ahistorical notion of gender and singles out for critique only certain forms of gender oppression associated with stigmatized local cultural "backwardness" as opposed to "modern" international political and economic forces. This yields social movements that can more easily become supporters and agents of imperial violence in the name of rescue missions. Social movement politics in this mode also tends to conceive of women as experiencing gender oppression in similar ways rather than as differently inflected by race, class, sexuality, and nationality. This cultivates "too-easy" assumptions that women share the same experiences and interests and thus constitute a global "sisterhood" (Grewal and Kaplan 2001: 19). Solidarity is then seen as flowing "naturally" from shared experiences and interests rather than as something that needs to be developed through political dialogue and action. As a result, more-privileged women end up speaking for less-privileged ones under the assumption that women's perspectives are interchangeable and even more insidiously, under the assumption that Western women, in particular, are more "liberated" than others and thus should lead—rather than listen—and forge "the" path for "other" sisters.

These perspectives and practices deny the realities on the ground. Consider, for example, that through a more significant embrace of quotas, women in the global South are gaining greater access to positions of formal power than are women in some of the most "developed" states. At the same time, even the most privileged Western women are subject to (economically motivated) cultural beauty standards, and to achieve these often involves bodily harm (whether through cosmetic surgeries, anorexia, or toxic cosmetics). And these women are just as subject to domestic violence as women elsewhere. Yet progress narratives in the West promote the continuation of colonial mind-sets, which find their way into feminist theorizing and social movements that are based on the feminist-as-tourist model. This contributes to crises of representation by failing to practice a politics of recognition.

Mohanty's "feminist-as-explorer" model refers to "area studies" approaches (2003: 240–241), which although more detailed, culturally sensitive, and historical in terms of examining women's lives in local, national, and/or regional contexts, still maintain a separation between the West and the non-West. In doing so, this model fails to see connections between global forces and national and local ones and the material conditions shared by the most subjugated women in both the South and North as a result of those global forces. Whether in cases of area studies performed by Western feminists or non-Western nationalist feminists, this model, in Mohanty's view, cultivates a kind of "cultural relativism" that erases any commonalities among women's struggles (2003: 240). This has the effect of confining social movements within state or regional borders and minimizing potential solidarities across those borders.

Catherine Eschle (2001) argues that these approaches set up a "universalist" versus "particularist" dichotomy from which polarizing debates ensue. The former is most implicated in imperialist impulses and actions; the latter, although also mired historically in Western anthropological practices that legitimated imperial conquest, is alternatively implicated in nationalist, statist, and thus ultimately conservative frameworks (Eschle 2001: 201). Not only does a particularistic approach feed into maintaining an oppositional and static view of "western feminism as unified and necessarily imperialist," but also a notion that those from outside a particular state or region are "inauthentic" knowers and actors who cannot understand or share in struggles outside of the locales from which they come (Eschle 2001: 201–202). Moreover, a vision of feminism organized on the basis of distinct ethnic and cultural identities frequently relies on a prepolitical notion of identity that delegitimizes contestation and dialogue within and across identities. It also marginalizes women who do not fit neatly into a predetermined category (Eschle 2001: 202). Such women who do not fit may be multiethnic, multinational, or sexual minorities; in this sense, just as a universalistic gender-based feminism undermines a politics of recognition, so, too, can a particularistic conception of ethnicity or culture-based feminism.

A related conundrum is the dichotomous construction of local versus global and the debates that ensue from this. Particularist advocates tend to privilege local or grassroots struggles as the most "authentic" and least contaminated by global power structures that co-opt and depoliticize social movements. Universalists tend to be most associated with global or international NGOs that lobby IGOs, garnering the majority of resources (although still relatively few compared with states, markets, and IGOs) for their larger-scale and more bureaucratic operations. International women's organizations are not new; they stretch back centuries in the form of women's peace movements, socialist women's *internationales,* and even missionary organizations that attended colonizing processes (Mackie 2001: 180–181). But the recent rise of feminist transnational NGOs has been met with a variety of concerns. First, there is the question of the relationship between the proliferation of contemporary NGOs and the rise of neoliberalism. As noted earlier, the "self-help" ideology of neoliberalism encourages private, voluntaristic, civil society operations to take up the slack—albeit with far fewer resources—for public welfare activities that states have been shedding. This reduces the accountability of states and markets, while also shifting services to unaccountable and relatively poorly resourced private bodies (as well as to underresourced households). Second, to the degree that NGOs are funded by states, IGOs, and, most often, private corporate foundations, they become more beholden to these interests and their priorities. Third, the "NGO-ization" of social movements, a concept Sonia Alvarez (1999) first coined in relation to Latin American regional women's NGOs she observed springing up during and after the UN Decade for Women, privileges middle-class actors with access to more resources and entrée into corridors of power. At the same time, this NGO-ization leaves behind poorer, more grassroots women who do not have the economic, social, and physical mobility (including foreign, high-theoretical, and bureaucratic language skills) to travel to and be heard at international conferences and sites of power, such as state and global capitals, where lobbying occurs. Moreover, grassroots movement demands get packaged by NGOs into policy bits that are digestible by states and IGOs and the femocrats within them, thereby taking off their radical edge.[1] In all these senses, it has been argued that the "revolution will not be funded" (INCITE! Women of Color Against Violence 2007).

This local-global split has also been manifested in distinctions sometimes made between transnational feminism(s) and global feminism. The former refers to a more postcolonial conception of transnational linkages among the many struggles of grassroots women of the global South, and the latter is tied to global (or cosmopolitan) feminist NGOs that are dominated by more resourced women from both the North and the South (Swarr and Nagar 2010). However, there have also been critiques of a fetishization of the local that is constructed as a more "innocent" space as if there were no power relations at the local level that silence some women over others and may result in parochial approaches that are unmindful of reproducing those power relations and their connections to larger and wider patterns and sources of abuse. Global feminism also can be charged with parochialism in representing only more privileged views or lenses. At the same time, there is worry that transnational feminism risks being reduced to "the romanticization of Third World activism in the global arena" and limits "transnational solidarity to Third World women workers across the First/Third World divide," thereby "becoming the 'other' to western white feminism" (Mendoza 2002: 309). In Breny Mendoza's view, this results from more attention given to cultural critique in much transnational feminist theorizing, which, although rightly directed to challenging ethnocentrism and confronting racism and heteronormativity as well as sexism, does not address sufficiently "political economic issues" that structure the lives of women in the South and North (2002: 310). This is the result of a politics of recognition overshadowing a politics of redistribution. The latter requires a more thoroughgoing solidarity of more-privileged women (and men) who choose to be against imperialism, racism, global capitalism, sexism, and heterosexism with less-privileged women (and men) who are critiquing and resisting these forces that ultimately threaten the planet and thus all on it.

Combining a politics of recognition with a politics of redistribution will also require coalitional solidarities among women's movements and mixed movements, as Catherine Eschle and Bice Maiguascha (2005) observe with respect to the antiglobalization movement. This movement is most associated with large-scale demonstrations outside various meetings of IFIs and economic elites held in various parts of the world, as well as the huge World Social Forums that have been held in South America, Asia, and Africa in the new millennium and most recently (2013) in Tunisia in honor of the Arab Spring. Variously referred to as the antiglobalization, global justice, new *internationale,* or world's peoples movement, it is constituted by congeries of local, national, and transnational social movements from around the world whose representatives gather periodically to dialogue with each other, bear witness to, and contest economic globalization and militarized violence. Conceived as a leaderless, memberless, nonorganizational model that stresses horizontal coalition-building, resists vertical control, and is open to all groups and individuals who wish to build a different world, the movement's main focus, as described in the World Forum Charter of Principles put forward at the first World Social Forum in Porte Alegre, Brazil, in 2001, is as follows: "The World Social Forum is opposed to all totalitarian and reductionist views of economy, development and history and to the use of violence as a means of social control by the State. It upholds respect for Human Rights, the practices of real democracy, participatory democracy, peaceful relations, in equality and solidarity, among people, ethnicities, genders, and peoples, and condemns all forms of domination and all subjection of one person by another" (Sen and Waterman 2009: 70).

These principles attest to the large presence of women and especially feminists in the movement, who made up, with youth, the majority of participants in the first World Social Forum (Eschle 2005: 23), as well as the considerable influence of feminist critiques of inequalities within civil society and global civil society.

Eschle points out, however, that the recognition of patriarchy and its relationship to globalization and militarism in movement documents and manifestos was hard won because of the more orthodox Marxism of predominantly male organizers of forums who could see the struggle only as a class-based one and thereby promoted that limited ideology through their behind-the-scenes leadership of what is supposed to be a leaderless movement (2005: 23–24). Moreover, as Johanna Brenner notes, just as some men in Marxist and labor movements attempted to marginalize feminist perspectives and issues such as reproductive rights in critiques of globalization generated at World Social Forums, women in some community-based movements—particularly those that are faith-based or receive funding from the Catholic church—have been silent on reproductive rights and the rights of sexual minorities even as they have advanced other feminist arguments at these forums, such as calling for attention to domestic violence as bound up in globalization (2009: 34–36). Thus, however much we can assume good intentions, there are no automatic solidarities, and intersectional ones are very hard to achieve in order to bring about both recognition and redistribution in the face of the *longue durée* of gendered divisions of power, violence, labor, and resources that structure global, national, and local spaces in North and South.

In order to build more intersectional coalitions, Mohanty (2003) recommends a "feminist solidarity" model for thought and action. This model sees the local and global as mutually constituted and, through comparative analysis, focuses "not just on the intersections of race, class, nation, and sexuality in different communities of women but on mutuality and co-implication, which suggests attentiveness to the interweaving of the histories of these communities" (Mohanty 2003: 242). This enables an alternative mapping of what connects and divides women (and men) based on redirecting attention to "global capitalism, and the uncovering of the naturalization of its masculinist and racist values," which compromise peoples and the planet (Mohanty 2003: 250). As we have argued, it is the power of gender that breeds the dichotomous thinking that operates to prevent or mitigate this remapping and the more fully developed solidarities that can arise from it. As Bernice Johnson Reagon (2000) has famously argued, coalitions are a matter of survival and can be built only through the praxis of acting together on particular projects at particular times (Gilmore 2008). They are not entered into because participants are like each other, like each other, or are safe from each other, but because "that's the only way you can figure you can stay alive" in the face of the widespread crises of representation, insecurity, and sustainability that affect all but the most privileged and that need to be resisted collectively in both small and large ways (Reagon 2000: 344).[2] And although, as Audre Lorde (2008) famously argued, it is problematic to "dismantle the Master's house" with the "Master's tools," even the tools that are implicated in neoliberal governmentality can be used for dismantling and rebuilding projects because many such tools arose, albeit in more de-radicalized and distanced form than was intended, from social movement analysis and agitation.

One such tool making headlines of late has been the Internet, especially in the form of social media, which has created a lively world of virtual politics that is having major material effects on offline worlds and is more accessible to more and more women. Although cyberpolitics, including "cyberfeminism," is not new, the use of Facebook, Twitter, YouTube, and blogs that circulate through smart phones and other handheld devices to mobilize ordinary people to take to the streets to successfully topple authoritarian governments, as during the Arab Spring in 2011, is an unprecedented phenomenon. Although already poor but even worsening economic conditions exacerbated by political repression motivated protesters to gather in great numbers and to "occupy" public places such as Tahrir Square in Cairo, horizontal social media messaging from a range of societal sectors, particularly young urban men and women, called upon people to assemble in ever-greater waves and coordinated on-the-ground protests. More privileged young Arab women living in and outside of the Arab world were particularly active, and remain so, in the blogosphere (sometimes writing in both Arabic and English), encouraging both men and women to be present at the protests during the Arab Spring and continuing to mobilize women to demand rights from post–Arab Spring political regimes.

As Judy Rebick (2012) argues, the global circulation of images and social media messaging from the Arab Spring also helped spawn the massive economic protests seen throughout western Europe, particularly in Spain and Greece, in 2011. Again, the imposition of austerity measures, which, among other harms, have been producing high youth unemployment rates (up to 43 percent in Spain alone), motivated resistance, but social media enabled the massification and coordination of street protests. Images and messaging from the May 15 Movement launched in Madrid by a coalition called the Indignados (the Indignant Ones), coupled with the Arab Spring, created a further contagion of protest, birthing "more than seven hundred occupations across Europe and Latin America" (Rebick 2012: 1–2), as well as the Occupy Wall Street movement that emerged in New York in September 2011.[3] Although the many Occupy "camps" typically set up in public parks and squares that spread throughout cities in the Americas, Europe, the Asia Pacific, and other parts of the world to demand economic justice for the "99 percent" were dismantled by local authorities and their security apparatuses, often very brutally and usually in the dead of night, occupy protests continue. And although social media attracted people to the camps and gave them global visibility, the process of deep coalition-building was conducted through face-to-face interactions within the camps that set up elaborate systems of shared communication and shared provisioning to ensure inclusion, democratized analysis of local and global economic crises, and democratized decision-making about how resistance was to proceed. Although not acknowledged, Occupy camps are, in fact, reminiscent of and replicate many organizing and democratizing practices developed in women's peace camps that were set up outside military installations in Europe and North America during the 1980s to protest nuclear weapons and the threats they pose to future generations and the planet.

Thus, it is important to refrain from imagining that social media are sufficient for building inclusive and sustainable social movements. Indeed, the digital divide between nations and genders is still wide and deep, and online media, like offline media, are still dominated by men as producers and subjects. According to Mary Hawkesworth, although the majority of males and females in the global North were Internet users and constituted the majority of Internet users in the world by 2006, relatively few people in the global South had access to the Internet, with, for example, only 15 percent of Brazilians, 8.6 percent of Chinese, 6.8 percent of Egyptians, and 3.6 percent of all Africans online and with women constituting only 20–24 percent of Internet users in Africa (2012: 307). Moreover, Hawkesworth points to a 2010 study of offline and online news media in 108 countries that found that women were the subjects of only 23 percent of offline news stories and only 11 percent of online news stories and rarely appeared in business and government news, were only 20 percent of experts quoted in all news stories, and were underrepresented as news reporters both offline (40 percent) and online (36 percent) (2012: 303). Even worse, she documents that in the wider world of the Internet, racist, sexist, and homophobic Web sites, social networking sites, and gaming sites proliferate, as do cyberharassment and cyberstalking, particularly of women (Hawkesworth 2012: 304–306). English, as the hegemonic language of global commerce and governance, dominates the Web, which is also the space most heavily surveilled by security states, most used for targeted marketing (both licit and illicit) to further ever-greater consumption of disposable goods and people, and least available to grassroots women's groups in the South (Hawkesworth 2012: 311). Thus, despite the Internet's promise of accessibility and inclusion, and the promise of the World Summits on the Information Society (WSIS) held since 2003 to empower women and other marginalized groups, it is more often a space of depoliticization than politicization, embodying and replicating gendered divisions of power, violence, labor, and resources and furthering the power of gender. Nevertheless, like all other "Master's" tools, it can be and has been used selectively, creatively, and subversively by feminist movements.

*Feminist Resistance Projects in Global Perspective*

There are easily millions of small and larger women's and feminist resistance projects directed in some way at challenging gendered divisions of power, violence, and resources as well as the crises of representation, insecurity, and sustainability they have spawned. Throughout this text, we have pointed to a few of them. Here we focus on a handful of those that have used global gender instruments instituted only recently to take them beyond the sorely circumscribed intent and use of them by IGOs and states. This is not to overshadow the many historical and contemporary equality, peace, labor, environmental, and Occupy movements within and across states that feminists continue to document as sources of resistance, some of which preceded world forums and others that do not make use of global gender policy instruments and may not be represented at World Social Forums. Nor is it to dismiss the very real power relations within, between, and among social movements and NGOs. Rather, we offer these examples as suggestive that the gendered dichotomies of universalist-particularist, local-global, online-offline, and transnational feminism–global feminism (see Table 6.1) are not always as operant on the ground. Instead, we see a mixing of strategies and actors engaged in ongoing coalitional struggles to build solidarity across internal and external borders through demanding much greater accountability from state, market, and civil society actors.

As Susanne Zwingel (2005) points out, there have been numerous efforts by local, national, and transnational women's movements to bring CEDAW "home"—that is, to have it implemented at the domestic level by state authorities. In the vast majority of states in which CEDAW has been ratified—with the most notable exception of the United States—feminists

TABLE 6.1
**Gendered Divisions of Resistance to and Produced by Governmentality, Militarization, and Neoliberalism**

| *Masculinized* | *Feminized* |
|---|---|
| Univeralist | Particularist |
| Global | Local |
| NGOs | Grassroots Organizations |
| Online | Offline |
| Global feminism | Transnational feminism |
| Theory | Practice |
| Experts | Activists |
| Individual | Collective |

have had to organize long and hard to get their states to adopt the legal provisions required by CEDAW even after lobbying long and hard for the ratification of it. Zwingel argues that the degree to which CEDAW can be brought home is dependent upon "first, the degree to which political institutions enable the representation of women's interests within public policy formations; second, the existence of transnational governmental or non-governmental activism that supports the appropriation and implementation of international norms; and third, the level of cultural affinity with the Convention" (2005: 408). In the case of Finland, which was alone among the Nordic states in not having a gender equality law when it ratified CEDAW, femocrats in the Council for Equality, a national women's policy agency, played upon the Finnish government's relative openness to women's interests and representation and its self-identity as space for socioeconomic equality to shame it into creating gender equality legislation by marshaling evidence from their femocrat contacts in other countries and at the global level that Finland was an outlier, particularly in the Nordic context (Zwingel 2005: 409). Chile first complied with CEDAW by creating a women's policy agency, SERNAM (Servicio Nacional de la Mujer). But in the relative absence of women in formal political positions at the national level and the presence of prevailing ideologies of "gender complementarity," which justify keeping women in their places rather than ensuring equality, SERNAM forged relationships with women's local NGOs and networks to bring some aspects of reproductive health onto the legislative agenda, including sex education and sterilization (Zwingel 2005: 410). As Zwingel notes, these local NGOs and networks advocated the more radical agenda of reproductive rights, including abortion, which SERNAM did not promote, but invocations of CEDAW by both SERNAM and networks of local movements pushed the right wing back to some degree, which included enabling the legalization of divorce (2005: 410–411). CEDAW has also spawned the development of transnational NGOs dedicated to disseminating information on CEDAW to women's groups at all levels and monitoring its implementation. Organizations such as the International Women's Rights Action Watch (IWRAW) in the United States and sister organizations like the IWRAW Asia Pacific located in Malaysia are part of a "transnational community of gender experts" (Zwingel 2005: 413). However, networks of local groups and NGOs that work with these organizations and are not part of national or international elites benefit from and use the intersectional interpretation of CEDAW that IWRAW offices provide by connecting gender, race, and class discrimination and, in turn, make such CEDAW interpretations relevant and responsive to "the particular shape of gender hierarchies in their own contexts" (Zwingel 2005: 412–413). Thus, the otherwise dead law of CEDAW is made live and is constantly reinterpreted to further radicalize its meanings and implementation from diverse women's perspectives at all levels of organizing.

A similar process has been observed in the case of UN Security Council Resolution 1325. For example, Carol Cohn (2008) reports that women's organizations in Kosovo and Afghanistan have translated the document into multiple languages used in their home countries, further translating UN-speak into understandable and useful language for grassroots women. Such practices are also occurring in the DRC, El Salvador, Iraq, Liberia, and Rwanda, in part because of connections made in transnational workshops focused on implementing 1325 (Cohn 2008: 190–191). Were it not for DRC women's lobbying of the UN peacekeeping mission there, there would not be even the one gender adviser finally put into place (Cohn 2008: 190). Jill Irvine refers to this process as a "double 'boomerang effect'" (2013: 21) in which local actors go beyond appealing to transnational intermediaries to bring their own recalcitrant states in line with international norms by generating grassroots and national campaigns to put pressure on transnational actors themselves, like the UN, to follow their own codified rules.

This effect was also observable in 2007 when more than 150 Iraqi women's organizations signed a letter, sent to the US Speaker of the House and the UN secretary-general, charging that the postinvasion constitutional process in Iraq was neither inclusive nor observant of CEDAW, 1325, or Security Council resolutions on Iraq specifically. Not only were secular women largely excluded from the drafting process of the Iraq constitution, but also personal status law was being subsumed under Islamic law with the help of Islamic women legislators who were the only beneficiaries of the recently introduced women's quota of 25 percent in the Iraqi parliament (Al-Ali and Pratt 2009: 135–137). This letter fell on deaf ears, but it exposed the hypocrisy of US unilateralism and its claims on behalf of democracy and gender equality and spoke to the widespread mobilizations of Iraqi women against the occupation and war. Moreover, continued dialogue and mobilization around 1325 are exposing its multiple problematics. These include the idea of protecting only women and only in war while leaving the prerogatives of war and the war system in place, making no connections between men and masculinities and war and thus doing nothing to address changing masculinities or men's participation in war, and leaving intact the idea that women are "more naturally" peaceful rather than widening responsibilities for all, elites and global civil society alike, to end war. As Cohn observes:

> While I do not think one can begin to understand war without gender; while I understand gender, war, nationalism, ethnicity, religion, capitalist forms of production, and consumption (how long should I make this list?) as mutually constitutive, I fear that "Women-as-peacemakers" places too much of war on gender. And in so doing, actually leaves the dominant political and epistemological frameworks untouched.
>
> I fear it is the easy way out. That it obscures all the parts of the war system, including, perhaps paradoxically, the working of gender regimes themselves. (2008: 202)

We return later to the challenges of breaking down the power of gender that undergirds war, but here our point is that policies such as 1325 are undergoing radical contestations and reformulations in the hands of the local, national, and transnational women's movements that use them. Even more recent analyses of organizing around and contestations of global governance instruments for gender equality (Caglar, Prügl, and Zwingel 2012) show further headway in terms of making these work better for more women, except when it comes to influencing financial institutions and their neoliberal policies. Still, there are multiple other strategies— grassroots, national, transnational, and translocal—for resisting neoliberal imperatives.

In terms of power differentials between grassroots and transnational women's organizations in the context of development, Millie Thayer's (2010) recent study reveals not only destructive, but also productive tensions between a Western feminist development organization and a rural women workers movement in Brazil. In their interactions, although structured by neocolonial and neoliberal relations, the women workers were able to openly assert their autonomy, demand a more radical aid agenda, and insist on projects that furthered their needs and politics in relation to their local conditions and struggles. As neoliberal pressures intensified on the development organization to increase "efficiencies" and employ quick fixes in its work, the grassroots organization allied with the development organization to push back on these donor demands, taking the most militant and uncompromising stands that enabled the development organization more negotiating space to resist new donor imperatives. Key to what

Amanda Lock Swarr and Richa Nagar (2010) call "critical transnational feminist praxis" is a refusal to enact the hierarchical dichotomies between experts and activists, theory and practice, and individual and collective knowledge and an ongoing commitment to be critical of one's own social and intellectual positions and accountable to others with whom one is collaborating through sustained dialogic encounters.

Latin America more generally has become a site of resistance to neoliberal governance. Leftist governments elected in such places as Ecuador, Bolivia, Brazil, and Venezuela have been experimenting with much greater involvement of civil society, including the poor, indigenous peoples, feminists, and LGBT activists, in governing and redistributing wealth and resources, particularly to the poor and indigenous. As feminist and other critical scholars (Macdonald and Ruckert 2009) note, there are reasons to be skeptical about how "post-neoliberal" and inclusive these states are as they are still embedded in the larger global economy, depend on resource exploitation, and are unevenly "democratic" and "progressive." Nevertheless, they do point to how national and regional contexts can begin to shift to other, nonmarket priorities.

As further evidenced by the World Social Forums and calls for "Earth Democracy" arising from them and the many social movements that make up the antiglobalization movement and Occupy movements,[4] resistance to the larger architectures and priorities of neoliberalism has not ended under neoliberal governmentality: its assumptions and rules continue to be contested both offline and online. Although digital divides continue between men and women, rich and poor, ethnic majorities and ethnic minorities, and North and South, the explosion of transnational, national, and even local organizing would not have been possible without ICTs. Cyberfeminism has enabled UN gender architectures, transnational and national feminist NGOs, and even grassroots women's organizations to monitor policies, exchange information, and build solidarity networks on an unprecedented scale. As Wendy Harcourt (1999) points out, the Web has opened up new political spaces for diverse women who can, at times, bypass discriminatory spatial structures and represent themselves and their struggles in less mediated ways, while also contesting exclusivist constructions of cultural and national identity. This is not to dismiss or underestimate the commercial control, violence promotion, and disembodiment in which the Web is deeply implicated, but it does tell a "tale" of another Internet that is being subversively appropriated to "confront political and social issues of the day" and to negotiate "intercultural and intracultural exchange" both online and offline (Franklin 2004: 2–3). However, as Gillian Youngs (2005) points out, "cybercitizenship" remains quite unequal, requiring a politics of redistribution in relation to ICTs as well.

Popular culture, despite the extreme commodification of it that promotes gratuitous violence, can also be a site and a stimulant of political resistance. Consider the case of Pussy Riot, the three-woman punk rock band in Russia that was sentenced to up to three years in prison for staging an iconoclastic performance against Russian authoritarian leader Valdimir Putin in a Russian Orthodox church in 2012. Scantily and provocatively dressed and rocking and railing against the state and the church for its complicity with the state, the band, which includes two mothers, courageously transgressed normative gender, political, and religious boundaries. Two members remained in jail as of 2013 and staged a hunger strike (a method most associated with feminist resistance to imprisonment stretching back to the Western suffragettes) after being denied parole, while the third released on appeal testified at a European Commission hearing about increasing human rights abuses in Putin's Russia.[5] Transgender and cultural studies theorist J. Jack Halberstam (2012) finds in pop star Lady Gaga's gender transgressive and bombastic performances (not her reformist politics) inspiration for what he calls "gaga feminism," which is about refusing the logic of domination in whatever form it takes and which continually seeks new forms of thinking, communicating, cooperating, provisioning, and organizing.[6] This feminism, he argues, infuses the translocally organized Occupy movement, whose transnational protests take multiple and evolving forms in and appropriate to each local context.

Feminist resistance directed at challenging the crises of representation, insecurity, and sustainability also takes other symbolic forms that do not require large-scale mobilizations, technological access, or pop culture fame. Women have used the few resources available to them to pioneer many forms of protest that have gained global recognition: These include donning the veil to protest Western imperialism, as women did in the Iranian Revolution; engaging in guerrilla theater, as the US feminist peace protest group CODEPINK does;[7] setting up women's peace camps outside nuclear weapons installations, as the women of Greenham Common in Britain pioneered; holding silent vigils to protest those "disappeared" by military dictatorships, for which the Argentinean Mothers of the Plaza de Mayo are famous; staging silent street protests against the Israeli occupation of Palestine, which was started by Women in Black (and which now has chapters in at least twenty-eight countries protesting war and violence); or hugging trees to save them, for which the local Chipko women's movement in India is internationally known. And as part of "peoples' renewal movements" and movements engaging in "postcapitalist" practices (Gibson-Graham 2006) such as barter and other reciprocal-provisioning activities, women, often in concert with many other "others," are working toward more feminist futures.

Feminist scholars, too, have been a part of the deconstruction and reconstruction of world politics, engaging in a range of theoretical, material, and discursive interventions. In our conclusion of this text, we consider some reconceptualizations of world politics offered by feminist, queer, and transgender theorizing. Such insights that rearrange how we think about world politics from feminist IR and related scholarship illuminate, without resolving, how the power of gender in world politics might be challenged. The stakes are high and the road is long, but the more ways to travel it, the better.

## TOWARD DEGENDERING WORLD POLITICS

After three decades of feminist IR analysis and intellectual activism, what have we learned? How do major changes in world politics in recent decades confirm, complicate, and contest feminist IR and related feminist lenses? The world faces old and new challenges, particularly in terms of global security and political economy. The post-9/11 climate of fear and uncertainty—exacerbated by the US-led "war on terror"—generates hypermasculine thinking and acting. The more recent breakdown of financial arrangements in the United States, with devastating effects worldwide, generates economic perplexity and a frantic search for fixes. In these contexts, realities and representations of uncertainty, chaotic conditions, and looming crises operate, not surprisingly, to amplify desires for clarity, predictability, and social order. As we have argued throughout this text, there are indeed multiple crises, and collective longing for easy answers and quick fixes is understandable. But the message of this text is cautionary, urging a fundamental transformation in ways of identifying, thinking, and acting that requires much more than any quick fix. We have argued that the power of gender as a meta-lens and hegemonic worldview itself is key to producing crises of global proportion. The problem then is that paths of least resistance—conventional ways of responding—are not only inadequate but also part of, indeed productive of, the problem. Hence, deconstructing the power of gender is a necessary component of addressing these crises and transforming world-politics-as-usual. This is obviously no simple or short-term project but one that is delayed or sidelined at great risk. It is urgent that we all get on with asking not only "How do we fix this problem?" but also "How do we transform the systems that produce and reproduce these problems?"

In concluding this text, we consider how its lessons might illuminate and potentially guide the development of alternative lenses and transformational politics. Recognizing that we are never "outside" of the system we critique means that no perspective can avoid complicity or claim innocence. The choice is not about whether we participate in the institutional practices constituting our life worlds but only how, in what ways, and with what effects. Do we take paths of least resistance that inexorably reproduce world-politics-as-usual, or do we attempt to be critically aware of structural violence and wary of too-easy analyses and quick fixes? What have we learned that might help us construct, however provisionally, forms of anti-imperialist feminism that avoid appropriations and impositions?

Brooke Ackerly and Jacqui True identify several ways in which feminist IR is distinguished from mainstream and other critical IR scholarship: it is "grounded in the human experience," "attentive to gender and other social constructions to identify emancipatory potential (and not practice forms of oppression in research)," "self-reflective," and "cognizant of the ongoing nature of the processes under study and the research process" (2006: 255–256). As such, feminist IR sees itself as collective inquiry that seeks to be supportive of and accountable to the struggles of subjugated people in world politics; this process entails not only privileging examinations of material oppressions and resistances, but also deconstructing oppressive discursive practices and reconstructing alternative conceptual frameworks for rethinking world politics. We engage some of these reconceptualization strategies in addressing the question of degendering world politics, by which we mean generating ideas and processes that decenter and destabilize gender difference, material gender divisions, and gender as a symbolic order or meta-lens, as well as decolonize and deneoliberalize feminism. As Maria Lugones puts it, a "decolonial feminist" sheds "her enchantment with 'woman,' the universal, and begins to learn about other resisters at the colonial difference" and in doing so affirms "life over profit, communalism over individualism, 'estar' [being] over enterprise, and beings in relation rather than dichotomously split over and over in hierarchically and violently ordered fragments" (2010: 753, 754). Adopting a decolonial feminist lens enables moving away from and decentering the preoccupations of mainstream IR with order, state sovereignty, national security, and capitalist development and toward democracy, human rights, human security, and human development. But such a lens also moves us even further on the path to degendering world politics in its insistence that we can imagine and practice more inclusive and equitable democratization, more widespread social provisioning for human and ecological well-being, and many more alternatives to the violence of securitization and neoliberalism. The following discussions offer further ideas for degendering our worldviews to release our thinking from the strictures of the power of gender. They are not prescriptive directions; rather, they are potential signposts on the road to such change.

## Degendering Power

When we recognize how much coercive power it takes to run this inequitable system, we begin to see why feminists argue that the deployment of coercive power is ultimately destructive of those who rule as well as those who are ruled. Disabling people—especially women—by depriving them of even the most basic needs so that the few can accumulate wealth and weaponry destroys genuinely popular support for states, international organizations, and their leaders. In the absence of popular support and consent as the sources of legitimacy for those in power, coercion is the only mechanism available to insecure rulers, who must rely on dividing, impoverishing, and degrading people and the planet to maintain their power. Therefore, "we" (referring here and throughout this conclusion to congeries of individuals, collectivities, and coalitions that make the political choice to challenge world-politics-as usual) must question not only the validity but also the efficacy of "power-over" as the mechanism for organizing world politics or solving world problems.

Effectively questioning power-over entails challenging the power of gender as a lens that privileges top-down masculinist, colonizing, and often coercive power that is associated with public (state, governmental) authority and institutions, at the expense of private (civil society and familial) sources of knowledge and potential authority. While doing so, we must also avoid romanticizing or interpreting as more "authentic" the experience or knowledge emanating from civil society or familial locations. Perhaps most crucial for avoiding the imperial impulse is recognizing that no single or universal answer to complex problems will be adequate and may even be disastrous. Hence, degendering also involves vigilance against the too-easy answers of "problem-solving" policy responses that are promulgated by elite decision-makers—whether in state governments, IGOs, NGOs, corporations, agencies, social movements, or communities—rather than addressing what keeps (re)producing systemic problems.

One alternative to coercive power is the more feminist concept of enabling power. In this model, conflicts of "difference"—as constituted through a self-other opposition and zero-sum lens—are addressed and ideally resolved not by force or its threat but by nonviolent interaction and mutual learning. Feminist postcolonial IR theorists Anna Agathangelou and L. H. M. Ling, for example, have coined the term "worldism" to describe a world politics that recognizes already existing multiple, history-making worlds that are inextricably embedded within each other, are capable of reframing each other's worldviews, and are mutually accountable to each other. Such recognition "brings with it duties and responsibilities, to be sure, but also possibilities" to "check and problematize hegemony" in order to open up critical "visions, strategies, and approaches" for a more "emancipatory" world politics (Agathangelou and Ling 2009: 86). In their view, shifting from the lens that the father, the metropole, and the general know best exposes how nonsensical it is to perpetuate the hegemonic self-other (non)relation in the face of the inescapable intertwinement and mutual constitution of worlds.

Feminist theorizing about the high degree of reciprocity, interconnectedness, and hybridity typifying most social relations and encounters recognizes that they take place in contexts of contingency and ambiguity. The concept of enabling power denies neither the need for autonomy nor the complexities of social interaction, but it does deny that a depiction of only hostile and competitive forces at work in the world is accurate or adequate. Christine Sylvester describes this model of enabling power as "relational autonomy" and contrasts it with the masculinist and imperialist ideal of "reactive autonomy" (valuing independence over interdependence and order over justice), which permeates the practice of international relations:

> In liberal political theory, the cast of masculine reactive autonomy appears in stories of abstract social contracts entered into, seemingly, by "orphans who have reared themselves, whose desires are situated within and reflect nothing but independently generated movement" [citation deleted]. Realist international relations theory follows this mold, even as it focuses on those anarchic spaces that elude social contract, for it depicts states as

primitive "individuals" separated from history and others by loner rights of sovereignty—backed up, for good measure, by military hardware—and involved in international conventions and institutions only on a voluntary basis. (1992: 157)

The reactive autonomy model in effect erases most social reality, especially the webbing that constructs meaning and order, as well as the practices of social reproduction that ensure everyday life and generational continuity. Reactive autonomy assumes that social order and cooperative relations are virtually impossible without some forms of hierarchy and coercion. This mind-set, or lens, encourages paths of least resistance that at best institutionalize a balance of forces and at worst rely on direct coercion. In contrast, relational autonomy assumes that cooperation typifies human relations when they are relatively equal and is destroyed in the presence of inequality, "othering," and coercion.

Moving toward a relational autonomy model for world politics would move us toward degendering world politics more deeply than we could simply by "adding women" (and other subjugated groups) to existing power structures. On the one hand, without deeper institutional changes, simply "adding women" can generate (still unrepresentative of all women) tokens whose presence may fuel complacency rather than sustained efforts at transforming representational politics. And simply "adding women" to public power without adding men to domestic labor and caretaking, and without holding elite men (and women) responsible for undermining webs of care, effectively exacerbates the crisis of social reproduction. On the other hand, "adding women" cannot take the form of a simple reversal that merely privileges feminine "care" over masculine "coercion." In such a reversal, not only gender dichotomies but also features of the feminine concept of care that oppress women would remain in place. Specifically, because caring has historically been a demand imposed upon subordinated groups and is, in this sense, inextricable from relations of inequality, a care model may offer insights on, but not solutions to, oppressive social relations. Caring that exclusively takes the form of sacrificing self or group interests is just another framing of inequality.

Emphasizing relational autonomy as a model of international relations would assist women in terms of a redistribution of resources to ease their lives, but we also need to facilitate women's autonomy (sometimes of the reactive sort) through the realization of a gender equality that entails a politics of recognition. Full equality, not only *between* men and women but also *among* women and *among* men, cannot be achieved unless all men have an equal responsibility for (social) reproductive or relational work (from the household through to the international arena) and diverse (in terms of race, class, sexuality, and nation) women have an equal say in how the world is organized.

Kathleen Jones (1993) posits a concept of "compassionate authority" (not to be confused with the Bush-ism of "compassionate conservativism") that foregrounds "humanizing authority." In the face of contemporary crises and the threats they pose, compassionate authority involves a shift away from the paternalism and the male protection racket as inefficient and heartless forms of social coordination no matter who practices them. Our understanding of authority changes if authoritative roles include female symbolism. Practices of leadership are altered toward a network model, and the relationship between leaders and followers shifts from a command-obedience structure based on fear of loss of protection toward a more consensual egalitarian model. Leadership and political action stimulate a move from efforts to destroy alternatives to those celebrating the birth of alternatives as new beginnings (Jones 1993: 240). Even though there is a strategic essentialism at work here, the process of redefining authority opens up the possibility for transforming who can lead, what the basis of leadership could be, how it could be more equal and consensual, and what shifts in direction it could take.

Degendering power then involves multiple moves, not least a turn away from power-over to enabling power. It involves recognizing that interdependence, differing perspectives, and uncertainty in outcomes are inescapable aspects of the human condition; we must acknowledge and address them rather than pursue the illusion of simple answers and the top-down, market-oriented fixes so endemic to neoliberal governmentality, which seeks to dispel politics understood as contestation of dominant scripts. We need to pursue a politics of recognition that acknowledges and empowers subjugated voices and marginalized alternatives, and a politics of redistribution that enables more democratic participation by the many and not just the elite few. Unless we degender power, we leave the crisis of representation in place, effectively disposing of identities, voices, and alternatives that lack requisite resources or do not comfortably fit.

*Degendering Violence*

The assumption that violence is largely the result of anarchic international relations—in contrast to supposedly "peaceful" domestic communities—obscures the question of the amount of and the way in which violence is deployed from the personal and local to the national and global levels. We know that domestic violence—a euphemism for the wide range of physical and emotional abuse suffered mostly by wives and children in families but also a reference to the everyday violence inflicted on a range of peoples subjugated by gender, race, sexuality, and national origin—is widespread throughout the world. Hence, it makes little sense to argue that the level and frequency of violent conflict are what separates international relations from domestic relations. A more productive starting point would be to see domestic and international violence as intimately connected and from that starting point investigate how and why this is the case and what the systemic implications are. Through this lens, international violence and the crisis of insecurity we identify in this text are bound up with historically institutionalized and deeply internalized constructions of gender and heteronormativity (which are always raced and classed). The power of gender establishes paths of least resistance in regard to gender performance that are so naturalized that they are difficult even to see and so internalized and normalized that they are even harder to defy. As we noted earlier, regardless of whether and to whatever extent we individually resist, none of us avoids gender socialization or lifelong pressures to conform to dominant gender norms and expectations.

The model of masculinity that is currently hegemonic encourages males to assume assertive, arrogant, aggressive, and power-over ways of thinking and acting that effectively produce conditions of conflict, "othering," competition, and structural violence. In addition, military security policies and practices can be seen, in part, as the pursuit of masculinist reactive autonomy, which can tolerate no interdependent relations. This model and its demands do less to empower men than subject them to crippling emotional (and physical) states and unrelenting pressure to prove their manhood, when, in reality, any claims to such status are fragile and precarious. Insofar as this model is valorized, women aspire to it as well—in part to enjoy the status and unreconstructed authority it affords and in part to realize its material benefits, such as higher pay.

But "adding women" to militaries where violence is constitutive raises different issues from adding them to positions of formal political authority. The aggressive and hypermasculinized climate of militaries is particularly hostile to feminized identities and bodies, which means that women and feminized men are not and arguably cannot be treated as equal, no matter how well intentioned individual agents and policies might be.

Merely increasing women's presence in militaries without also analyzing the power of gender will simply "resex" militaries to a certain degree without challenging the masculinism and imperialism of the war system and the ways of thinking and acting it engenders. Similarly, merely defining peace as the absence of the direct violence of war simply obscures the deep structural inequalities that both give rise to and are the result of violence. Sustaining sexism, racism, classism, heterosexism, and gendered nationalism has heretofore been vital to sustaining militarism and the "us" and "them" mentality that goes along with it. Thus, any serious attempt to end war must involve significant alterations in local, national, and global hierarchies.

With reference to the crisis of insecurity, the power of gender as a meta-lens naturalizes us-them as a necessarily hierarchical and oppositional dichotomy, which then fuels arrogance, distrust, fear, and often violence. Ultimately, it divides the human community into unequal and opposed beings who must resort to violence to settle disputes. This violent process may alter who the winners and losers are, but it rarely reduces systemic inequalities and keeps reproducing violence. By adopting the lens of reactive autonomy, IR practitioners—even without intending to—reproduce expectations of hostile and competitive behavior, which in turn generate uncooperative and defensive responses. This is how we find ourselves caught in self-perpetuating, vicious cycles, such as arms races and wars on terror, that produce more expressions of "terror" by hypermasculinist "othering" and outlawing all dissent. In contrast, the model of relational autonomy encourages mutual respect and cooperation. For this model to flourish in IR would require that we not only alter our lenses but also make profound changes in our individual and collective practices.

Simona Sharoni (2006) calls for an analytical approach and praxis of "compassionate resistance" to imperialist state violence. Arising out of her own scholarship on and resistance work in the context of the Palestinian-Israeli conflict, compassionate resistance refers to "analysis and targeting of oppressive systems and policies" but with "empathy," not only for those on the receiving end of violence, but also for those who are caught up in supporting and/or acting on behalf of oppressors because of uncritical acceptance of structural and ideological pressures (Sharoni 2006: 289). This "humanizes" conflicts while still maintaining clarity about the wrongs of them and who commits those wrongs. Rejecting the more liberal idea of "compassionate listening" between oppositional parties to reduce enmity because it assumes an "equal playing field, " Sharoni argues that compassion cannot be forged without oppressors taking respon-sibility for concrete acts that have led to unequal power relations on the ground and in a given encounter between those in conflict (2006: 289). This means that "one cannot speak of compassion between Palestinians and Israelis without specific reference to the Israeli occupation of the West Bank and the Gaza Strip and to such oppressive practices as the Apartheid Wall, checkpoints and home demolitions" (Sharoni 2006: 289). However, compassionate resistance can flow when people "become aware of their positions in and relationship to the conflict" (Sharoni 2006: 289–290), in-cluding deep complicity in it, and make conscious decisions about solidar-ity work against systems of power, privilege, and control as a result.

Another kind of analytical strategy, this one advocated by Cynthia Weber (1999), is "queering" the national security state. In her "queer" read-ing of US-Caribbean relations, she finds that the invasion and colonizing practices of the United States were fueled by a conception of itself as the male lover and of the Caribbean as the feminine object of "his" affections. Unable to maintain the affections of Cuba after "her" revolution against neocolonial rule, the United States, Weber argues, had "his" heterosexual prowess wounded, leading to a relative loss of "phallic" power that it has attempted to camouflage ever since. By seeing international relations as intersexual relations, Weber hopes to expose the very fragile (and, in fact, lost) hegemonic masculinity upon which the United States projects its power and, in the process, prompt a rethinking of US self-identity based on phallic power projection and its violent effects.

More recently, Laura Sjoberg (2012) finds in transgender, or trans, the-orizing concepts that can illuminate and reimagine difference in world politics. For example, the trans experience directs attention to "change"—not the instrumentalism of moving from one fixed gender to another, but rather the complexity of living in between genders and therefore worlds. This also requires "disidentification" with assigned sex and/or gender roles to enable the creation of hybrid sex and gender identities and relations that rest on reworking constructs of sex and gender in nonoppositional ways. This has implications not only for breaking down the psychosocial dynamics of oppositional gender identity formation from which we ar-gued the power of gender stems at its deepest level, but also for rethinking all oppositional relations and how "transitioning" away from them can re-duce violence.

Feminist inquiry into violence in its various forms has a long history and many diverse expressions. Cynthia Cockburn (1998, 2007) travels

widely to interview and work with women engaged in producing and negotiating solidarities in the context of often extremely violent conditions.
She wonders, along with other female antiwar activists she encounters,
why war continues and continues to be acceptable, despite its terrible
costs, and she determines that whatever other factors may be involved, the
cultivation of masculinities in and outside of militaries is key to the reproduction of violence as simply an acceptable way of being. In her words,
"War as institution is made up of, refreshed by and adaptively reproduced
by violence as banal practice. . . . Masculinity in its various forms is an
important content of that cycle: masculinity shapes war and war shapes
masculinity" (2007: 248). In concluding her 2007 book, Cockburn captures the power of gender—and its violence—in her own terms: "War is
the most violently coercive form taken by othering, the space in which
differentiation becomes lethal. Its means, the means of coercion, are fearful in the extreme. But it is the othering itself that is the problem. Assuring
the self by objectifying, excluding, diminishing, confining, oppressing and
exploiting an other" (2007: 258). In this sense, war, and its contemporary
form, Empire, is the absence of politics, for it shuts down dialogue and
contestation in favor of domination and the inculcation of thoroughgoing
complicities in it. The "security myth" ultimately holds all hostage to its
dictates and constant replay.

There is nothing simple or easy about identifying and institutionalizing alternatives to violence-as-usual. Generating alternatives presumes
as a starting point both a politics of recognition that cultivates respect
rather than "othering" and a politics of redistribution that minimizes
inequalities and the grievances that so often fuel conflicts. More specific anti-imperialist strategies entail an emphasis on dialogic, transver-
sal, discursive, and activist restructurings of valorized and devalorized
identities of states, nations, and people, coupled with analyses of class,
race, gender, nation, and sexuality stratifications and violences that produce and are produced by virulent us-them and self-other dichotomies.
Unless we degender violence, we leave structural violence in place, producing and reproducing not only others who are disposable but also violent practices of disposal.

## Degendering Labor and Resources

Whereas the desirability of "adding women" to institutions designed for
direct violence (and especially imperialist means and ends) is hotly de-
bated, "adding women" (and other less economically privileged people) to

the public realm of political power-wielders and the business world of economic income earners would seem a less contestable feminist goal. And, of course, feminists have worked long and hard to promote these projects. However, as we have seen, neoliberalism so marketizes and circumscribes political institutions and human relations and subjectivities that gaining such footholds does not necessarily translate into feminist gains more broadly defined as the development of social justice. It also has leavened gendered economic inequalities downward, with some women increasingly enjoying some of the benefits of access to higher political and economic positions, but many men "falling down" economically. This "race to the bottom" for many men and this "staying at the bottom" for many women are not the kind of equality that feminists envision. Far more people (women and subordinated men) should be "moving up," but this cannot occur without wider (not just women's) responsibilities for taking care of social reproduction upon which all else depends.

With reference to the crisis of sustainability, the power of gender operates to valorize productive over reproductive, formal over informal, and paid over unpaid labor. This has left women primarily responsible for serving others and ever willing to put family survival ahead of their own (despite small and problematic efforts to get men to shoulder more of this work), but it has also ensured that social reproduction more generally is devalorized and underresourced by those at the top. Even if increasing more diverse women's presence at the top of corporate and IFI hierarchies might translate into more humane and gender-sensitive labor and social reproduction policies, the fact remains that few women and few men can actually be at the top of pyramidal hierarchies. Increasing the number of women in higher-paying, male-dominated occupations may increase some women's wages and status. But that would not necessarily lead to challenging the global gendered dichotomy between productive and reproductive labor, which renders the latter "nonwork." Also, drawing poor rural women into circuits of capital through microcredit might enable some entrepreneurial women to prosper, and it might "feel good" to Western consumers to funnel a little of their shopping dollars to campaigns that assist such women to be entrepreneurs. But none of these moves disrupt the logic of capital accumulation or the growth imperative it establishes. They do not lead to questioning what is produced, why, and under what circumstance, or whose bodies are exploited in the process, whose backyards are surrendered to the waste produced, or how actual resources are distributed. Yet these are the underlying problems generating the crisis of sustainability, and to address them, we need transformative strategies.

In addition to others just cited, it is necessary to undermine the gendered dichotomy of "modern" and "traditional" that pervades the thinking and practices of development agencies. The power of gender creates an association between "women's work" and "primitive" economic and technological practices found in non-Western societies. This association tends to discredit the knowledge and agency of women in development processes and devalues the quite complex, self-sufficient, and ecologically sustainable economic activities and technologies in which many women (and some men) engage in traditional societies. Undermining this association and the devaluation of both women and traditional cultures that it entails requires questioning the kind of progress that masculinism and modernity have brought to us.

Moving beyond the power of gender involves questioning as well the premises of neoliberal capitalism: the imperative of growth, commodification of the life world, and pursuit of profits for some at the expense of well-being for all. By making visible the costs of current economic priorities, as well as who (most women and all marginalized peoples) and what (the environment) bear the brunt of these costs, states and corporations would find it harder to justify a great deal of what they claim is wealth-generating activity. Such costs include the realities that few are benefiting from the wealth that many workers are producing and that the formal sector of so-called productive work is dependent on the reproductive and informal sectors, rather than the reverse. Keeping the reproductive and informal sectors undervalued is "functional" only for those few at the top who reap greater profits as a result of this under- or devaluation.

Instead of having an equal say in what and how resources are to be used, women and people of the global South more generally are treated as resources themselves. Noting that "added resources" give added power to "states to do things that they could not have done previously," Christine Sylvester argues that "women are non-recognized resources for realist states, occupying positions ranking with oil, geography, industrial capacity, and military preparedness as contributions to power" (1992: 169). In fact, all states (and corporations) appropriate women's (and many men's) bodies and labor to extend their resource base and thus their power within and outside state borders. Yet this fact is concealed by the gendered division of resources. However, when a gender-sensitive lens is used to view world politics, the positions of women in a state's and a corporation's resource base are revealed, permitting women to specify strategies of resistance against this appropriation of their bodies and labor.

Individual women, too (particularly middle- and upper-class women in the global North), have a responsibility to change and curb their consumption patterns. These women benefit—in the form of cheap consumer goods—from the cheap labor of primarily poor and racialized women (and feminized men) of the global South. They do so, however, at the expense of creating international solidarity among women (and men) to struggle against the global gendered division of labor and the exploitative practices of neoliberal capitalism. Ultimately, degendering labor will involve increasing not only the presence of women in male-dominated occupations and institutions at all levels but also recognizing the power of gender to perpetuate differential valorization of skills, bodies, identities, jobs, and resources in ways that reproduce and cumulatively deepen inequalities.

Respect for nature as a partner in, not a slave to, the world community must be accompanied by respect for the needs of the vast majority of women and peoples of the global South to enjoy a much greater share of the world's resources. At the same time, it is incumbent on those who struggle for equity in parenting, work, consuming, soldiering, officeholding, decision-making, and property owning to concern themselves with transforming these activities in ways that are not ecologically harmful. We must engage a politics of redistribution to ensure more equitable access to and control over resources, and a politics of recognition to address shifting identities borne of global migrations and the citizenship claims they raise. Both entail rejecting the symbolic and material valorization of hegemonic masculinity at the expense of all that is feminized. Unless we degender labor and resources, we individually and collectively face an ever-deepening and widening crisis of sustainability. On the one hand, feminizing employment without enlarging responsibility for care undermines social reproduction, and exploitative production processes—especially the dangerous, debilitating, and demeaning work that is the survival option for too many—create disposable people and even countries. On the other hand, excessive and irresponsible growth disposes of natural resources, creates disposable waste that further degrades the environment, and depletes the resources upon which we all depend.

## Deconstructing the Power of Gender

In concluding this text, we observe that the early feminist insight asking, "Where are the women?" remains a productive starting point. This "add women" lens provides telling data on the differential positions and repositionings of women and men and, in the process, improves our knowledge of men and reveals problems and instabilities not foreseen when women are left out of the picture. Noting how repositionings are patterned provides us a more realistic picture of world politics and enables us to make better sense of what is going on. In effect, asking "the woman question" in a systematic fashion leads inevitably to asking "the man question." And as myriad feminist studies across the disciplines confirm, asking these questions leads to complicating sex itself as a constitutive binary and refiguring gender as not naturally "given" but as historically constructed and culturally varying.

Asking feminist questions about the hierarchical relationships between "men" and "women" further disrupts dichotomized thinking, as it leads to seeing there are no generic women or men but rather gendered identities crosscut by other dimensions of difference—especially ethnicity/race, nationality, and sexuality—so that hierarchies exist among genders as well as between them.

In these senses, "the woman question" remains an important and productive starting point because it leads us to more complex and contested terrain. In this text, it leads from "adding women" to recognizing intersectionality and adopting a postcolonial feminist lens, or "decolonial feminism." For us, a crucial key is exposing and deconstructing the power of gender as a meta-lens that naturalizes and reproduces essentializing, dichotomizing, stratifying, and depoliticizing thought and action. We have argued that the power of gender constitutes a resilient and adaptive lens, one that is taken for granted and naturalized because beliefs in, and identities based on, a simplistic binary of sex are deeply internalized and because there are powerful incentives for conforming to the paths of least resistance they constitute.

One objective in preceding chapters was to present a contemporary picture of global positionings and repositionings of women and men. The patterns that appear suggest in some ways an extraordinary shift in awareness of gender inequalities and a corollary commitment to improving hierarchical relationships between men and women through policy reorientations. We note here how these successes confirm the importance of visionary ideals, activist energies, and social movements—in this case women's and feminist movements—for altering social imaginaries and achieving large-scale change. At the same time, we observe that the power of gender as a meta-lens remains too often in place, making the strategy of "adding women" in order to degender world politics problematic in many ways. First, in spite of inclusive rhetoric, only some (typically elite) women get added, which exacerbates hierarchies among women and effectively pits subordinated groups against each other. Second, construing women as a generic group homogenizes their experiences and interests, rather than recognizing differences among women and the necessity of dealing with these through dialogue and in struggle. Third, "framing" women (particularly women of the global South) exclusively as victims or as people in need of help renders them a group to be "rescued," rather than listened to, learned from, and/or recognized as agents. Fourth, when essentializing stereotypes are deployed to promote raising the status of women (as incorruptible leaders, natural peacemakers), they often become tools for demonizing some men (as incorrigible tyrants, violence-prone rogues). Fifth, women as the object of policy recommendations become the solution to problems, rather than altering the institutional practices and underlying systems that continually generate problems. For example, feminizing employment enables women to serve more effectively as "buffers" ensuring family survival during economic crises, but only by increasing the workload for women and altering expectations only for poor men. Constituting women as the problem fixers not only increases their burdens and responsibilities, but also deflects attention away from what causes and reproduces systemic inequalities and who benefits from them. In this sense, the easy fix of "adding women" leaves governmentality, the war system, and global capitalism in place and fails to hold states, militaries, and corporations accountable for the crises of representation, insecurity, and sustainability they induce.

In short, and however well intended, simply "adding women" without transforming the power of gender is not only inadequate for addressing inequalities between women and men but also too often exacerbates inequalities among women (and among men and genders generally). We observe this in the new politics of gender equality at the international level, where gender equality is separated from other forms of equality, with the effect of increasing other forms of inequality that disadvantage women in other ways while also increasing subordinated men's resistance to gender equality. We also observe this in the new gender equality by consumption approach, which reduces social change to market forces in neoliberal fashion and replays neocolonial rescue missions, all the while dismissing the need for political analysis and activism.

Obviously, a great deal must change before world politics is degendered. Toward that end, we have identified some suggestive signposts, but these are only a beginning. They emerge from a wide-ranging but necessarily partial investigation of world-politics-as-usual, in which our attention has focused on the deeply problematic power of gender as a meta-lens and hegemonic worldview. The dichotomizing, stratifying, and depoliticizing effects of this meta-lens both produce and normalize global power structures and crises, hence precluding meaningful advances in social equality and justice. Degendering world politics requires then that we disrupt and transform these processes, which entails a serious rethinking of what it means to be human and how we might organize ourselves in more cooperative and mutually respectful ways. It requires no less than deconstructing the power of gender.

Overall, these changes are less a matter of identifying and promulgating policies than of individually and collectively remaking human society by reconstructing our identities, beliefs, expectations, and institutions. This is the most difficult and complex of human projects, but history shows that we are capable of such revolutionary transformations.

In one sense, we have no choice. Contemporary global processes force us to develop new understandings of who "we," as humans, are and how "we," as global citizens and planetary stewards, must act. In another sense, we willingly seek systemic transformations because we desire more than diffusely imposed discipline, globalized fear, and commodified life worlds. We demand lives of meaning and value and the actualization of justice. And whatever our commitments to justice, we cannot pursue them if we retain the power of gender as a meta-lens that produces and at the same time normalizes inequalities and hence injustice. There is no single or simple strategy to follow, but crucially important is a commitment to repoliticizing thought and action to *resist* what continually divides the world, yet binds it to deadening and destructive patterns.

### Notes

1. For a series of recent trenchant critiques of the co-optation and deradicalization of feminism by global capital, see Fraser 2009; McRobbie 2009; and Eisenstein 2009.

2. Staudt's (2008) extensive study of and participation in women's cross-border organizing against femicide at the US-Mexico border shows the extreme obstacles presented by "the border" to that organizing despite such proximity, but she argues that borderlands—as hybrid spaces where the intersection of local, national, and global is so visible—are particularly important sites for the development of coalition politics "on the ground."

3. See the film *Occupy Love* (2012) for a video diary featuring several feminist voices of Occupy movements, but especially Occupy Wall Street.

4. For numerous examples of explicitly and implicitly feminist struggles against globalization, see Naples and Desai 2002; Waller and Marcos 2005; Moghadam 2005; Hawkesworth 2006; and Marchand and Runyan 2011.

5. See http://www.commondreams.org/view/2013/06/03–9. Pussy Riot's imprisonment has spawned protests around the world. SlutWalks, which began in Canada in resistance to the assumption that women on the streets were soliciting sex and that sex workers did not deserve protection, are another example of recent feminist protest that has spread to other continents. See Borah 2012 for discussion of SlutWalk protests in India.

6. Zalewski (2013) urges a discontinuity project of breaking up the self-imposed boundaries of what constitutes feminism, particularly IR feminism, opening it up to new, unfamiliar, and even jarring formulations, such as, we would argue, "gaga feminism."

7. See Web and Video Resources at the end of this text for the online location of CODEPINK and other select feminist NGOs. The Boston Consortium on Gender, Security, and Human Rights is a particularly good source for learning about women engaged in peace-building projects in the global South, and other sites offer a wealth of information about contemporary struggles of women (at times, with men and other feminized others) for peace and economic, political, social, and environmental justice.

# Suggested Activities for Research and Discussion

Each of the chapters in this text begins with questions that not only organize the discussion, but also can serve as questions for discussion. Here we offer some suggested and adaptable individual and/or group activities to prompt further research and discussion and better engage readers with the text, including the list of Web and Video Resources provided.

## CHAPTER ONE

1 Go online (or consult your local newspaper for at least a week), and search for a sample of mainstream news stories about contemporary international relations between states. What gendered patterns (the absence or presence of women or men, the positions of power men versus women hold, the "masculine"/hard or "feminine"/soft nature of the issues discussed, and which states are featured as dominant or subordinate) do you notice in these stories? Consider in your gender analysis who wrote the stories, what the stories are about, which states they focus on, what state leaders are featured, how their leadership is characterized, and whether or not domestic populations are mentioned, who among them are featured, and how they are portrayed.

2 Read the text of CEDAW online (http://www.un.org/womenwatch/daw/cedaw/cedaw.htm), and consider why the United States has not ratified it. Do you think the United States needs gender (and even "diversity") electoral quotas? Why or why not?

3 Watch one or both parts of the two-part video entitled *Half the Sky* (available as streaming video on Netflix and on iTunes). Reflect on the following: (a) How well (or not) is poor women's agency (relative to the agency of NGO and Western actors) portrayed? (b) What solutions are being proposed? Market solutions? NGO solutions? Philanthropic solutions? Is there any discussion of political solutions such as local women organizing with the help of national women's movements and using international or national women's rights instruments or Western women demanding changes from their own governments to redistribute global power and wealth? (c) Why might it be problematic for US journalists and celebrities, with the help of a few local NGO "experts" and "informants" as opposed to more political women's movement representatives in these regions, to be the ones selecting and largely framing the stories of poor women in the global South in light of the history of colonial and neocolonial interventions? How do these stories tend to blame local cultures more than global economic and political structures? How would the stories change if these connections were made?

◄○►

## CHAPTER 2

1 Interview a few friends and/or family members, asking them how and when they were first conscious of being "male" or "female," if they felt comfortable with and accepting of their sex and gender assignments, and what they learned early on about the differences between how boys and girls should behave and what life directions/occupations they should pursue.

2 List the ways in which you are privileged or disadvantaged by your gender, race, class, sexuality, and nationality. Consider how the ways you are disadvantaged affect your life choices, such as aspiring to national or international office or becoming a corporate elite. Consider as well how your perspectives are different when you view the world from positions of disadvantage as opposed to privilege. How do you view "global" issues differently when you are a member of groups not visible or considered in relation to a particular global issue? What happens to how the issue is framed when you "add" such groups' interests and concerns?

**3** Choose a particular country, and research the percentage of women represented in national politics, the amount of direct violence present (e.g., armed conflict deaths and injuries, military spending, domestic violence and rape rates, incarceration rates), indicators of such structural violence as unemployment and poverty rates (by gender and race where possible), and pollution rates (by whatever measures you can find). Do you see any relationships among these?

◄◦►

## CHAPTER 3

**1** Find a list of recent and current (nonceremonial) female heads of state and government (such lists of women world leaders are available online), choose two such leaders, and research their paths to power and support (or not) of "women's issues" through their public pronouncements and the policies they have promoted.

**2** Visit the UN Women's Web site (http://www.unwomen.org/), enter the IKNOW Politics portal (under Resources tab), and join to participate interactively in international online discussions on increasing women's political participation. What would you recommend?

**3** When you visit the UN MDGs (http://www.un.org/millennium-goals/) Web site and go to the MyWorld survey to determine what people want beyond the year 2015, you can take the survey as to your priorities for a better world. Notice in the survey results so far, which you can also access, that male respondents list gender equality less frequently than female respondents do and place it almost at the bottom of their priorities, whereas female respondents list gender equality more frequently and in the middle of their priorities. How do you account for this? Where would you place this on your priorities? Why are racial, class, and national equalities not on the list? Notice as well that the survey does not ask what global governance structures need to change to get to the desired outcomes and therefore does not list such priorities as "more diversity in governing bodies," "more support for social movements," "more corporate responsibility/less corporate control," or "less militarization." Respondents can add their own priority. What would you add that is not on this list? How would the survey results look if the billions of people not able to access the Internet or the millions who cannot read, most of whom are women, could respond?

—◄o►—

## CHAPTER 4

1 When you are in department stores, at public events, playing video games, or even watching TV over a few days to a week, begin to pay attention (and make some notes) about how often you see manifestations of militarization or militarized security. Note as well gendered divisions in militarized goods (e.g., militarized toys and clothing marketed more to boys than girls), armed police and other security forces (e.g., more men than women), and visual representations of armed violence in the media (e.g., who are combatants and who are victims and how the latter are victimized if this is even visible). Note as well racial and national dimensions of this in visual representations (e.g., Are white Western men the heroes and racialized others the villains or in need of rescue by heroes?).

2 Watch the film *The Invisible War* (available as streaming video on Netflix), and then find stories (and images where available) about sexual abuse of local women around US military bases in foreign countries and about American servicewomen involved in the sexual abuse of male Iraqi prisoners in the Abu Ghraib prison. Do you think there is a relationship between sexual violence in the US military perpetrated by men against women and men and sexual violence perpetrated by US military members, male and female, against ally women and enemy men? Can this violence be stemmed in one context if not in others? Can "unsanctioned" violence be stopped in military institutions organized for violence? Do you think other world militaries (including peacekeeping forces) have high rates of sexual abuse within them and directed at others? This last question could lead you to further research.

3 Do some more research on women in peace-building by visiting the (Boston) Consortium on Gender, Security, and Women's Rights Web site (http://genderandsecurity.umb.edu/index.htm), which has links to PeaceWomen and the UN Women 1325 Portal and a number of other rich

resources. See also Cohn 2013 for a number of peace-building case studies. After you review some of this material, what do you see as the potentials of and problems with including women in peacemaking and peace-building projects? Does it matter which women are included and by whom? Do you think including more women in postconflict processes can help to prevent further armed conflict, or must other things also happen, and what might those be?

◄◉►

## CHAPTER 5

1 Go to YouTube (http://www.youtube.com/), and search using such terms as *women and globalization.* You will find such video resources as the multipart series "The Hidden Face of Globalization" and more recent commentaries on this topic. Based on a review of some of the material and noting who produced it, make a list of the many ways that these video resources argue that women, particularly poor, working-class, and racialized women in the global South and North, are affected negatively by globalization.

2 Visit the Human Rights Watch Web site (http://www.hrw.org/), go to Publications, and search under the Issues dropdown box for Women and then Domestic Workers. (You will see many other topics under Women, as well as LGBT rights, that you can also investigate on this site.) Choose "any country" for a full listing of publications on this topic produced by Human Rights Watch. What commonalities do you find in terms of the treatment of domestic workers across a range of host countries? How are these conditions related not only to a relative lack of informal labor and migrant labor protections but also to gendered assumptions about care work and the women (and girls) who do it. Do you think the new International Labour Organization convention for domestic worker protection will matter? Why or why not?

3 Visit the WEDO Web site (http://www.wedo.org/), and read the recent report "Sustainable Economy and Green Growth: Who Cares?" (you can download it). How has the financialization of environmental issues, which shifts attention from sustainable human and environmental

well-being and social equity to privatized green economy initiatives, marginalized women, care work, and environmental protection? At what costs when environmental crises are increasing? What would it mean to "reframe green from a care perspective" rather than a market one?

## CHAPTER 6

1 See the Uprising of Women in the Arab World Web site (http://uprisingofwomeninthearabworld.org/en/) and Facebook site for testimonial blogs and calls for mobilization (including in English) during and since the Arab Spring. Although few women in the Arab world are online or speak English, what kinds of concerns and organizing do you find on these sites? What do they tell us about the incompleteness of revolutions and the insufficiencies of democracies? Can you create your own "women's uprising" site(s)? What would you post/blog/tweet about with respect to gender (as it intersects with race, class, sexuality, nationality, and so on) issues of local-global import?

2 Look for images and videos and Twitter accounts of (and on) transnational phenomena, such as the World Social Forum and Occupy movements as well as CODEPINK, Pussy Riot, and SlutWalks, that focus in various ways on state and market violence against women and peoples. How visible are women in more mixed organizing versus more women-centered organizing? How could you analyze these movements as feminist (or not) in terms of their manifestos/philosophies, inclusiveness, and actions? For example, even if women (in all their diversity) may be less visible in mixed movements, are the goals and practices of these movements consistent with transnational feminist perspectives? Alternatively, there are some feminist controversies around the hypersexualized aspects of Pussy Riot and SlutWalk protests, including by women of color, who are most often constructed as hypersexualized. What do you think about these protests and the power of parody in relation to feminist resistance? Relatedly, there has been some controversy about the use of the term *occupy* as (neo)colonialized people have long been "occupied." What do you think about appropriations of such terms for transnational resistance movements?

3 Find (or create) an opportunity to participate (physically, not just on-line) in an organization or resistance action that is concerned with social inclusion, equity, and justice and is more feminist and political rather than charitable or market-based or market-promoting in orientation. Many transnational movements and organizations have or are, in fact, made up of local manifestations—such as actions by Occupy, (im)migrant rights, indigenous rights, SlutWalk, gay pride, and antiausterity (against defunding of education and health services) groups—and thus might be better thought of as translocal movements. There are also sometimes local and campus chapters of groups, such as Amnesty International, working on and with CEDAW, Security Council Resolution 1325, and other international women's human rights instruments. Regardless of your political orientation, what is the difference between engaging in a collective, face-to-face dialogic activity and just buying a T-shirt or making a donation or only being online? How might actions with (not over or under or distant from) others be more productive for crossing gendered divides and reversing the crises of representation, violence, and sustainability that ultimately hurt us all?

# Web and Video Resources

**Select Web Resources**

***Gender, Gender-Related, and Other Relevant IGO Policies/Documents***

*Beijing Platform for Action (BPA)—Fourth World Conference on Women (September 1995)*
http://www.un.org/womenwatch/daw/beijing/platform

*Convention on the Elimination of All Forms of Discrimination Against Women (CEDAW 1979)*
http://www.un.org/womenwatch/daw/cedaw

*International Convention on the Elimination of All Forms of Racial Discrimination (ICERD 1965)*
http://www2.ohchr.org/english/law/cerd.htm

*International Convention on the Protection of the Rights of All Migrant Workers and Members of Their Families (1990)*
http://www.humanrights.se/wp-content/uploads/2012/01/Convention-on
-the-Protection-of-all-Migrant-Workers.pdf

*International Labour Organization Convention on Domestic Workers (2011)*
http://www.ilo.org/migrant/areas/migrant-domestic-workers/
WCMS_168266
/lang—en/index.htm

*Rome Statute of the International Criminal Court (ICC) (1998)*
http://untreaty.un.org/cod/icc/index.html

*United Nations Convention on the Rights of the Child (1989)*
http://www.unhchr.ch/html/menu3/b/k2crc.htm

*United Nations Convention Relating to the Status of Refugees (1951)*
http://www.unhchr.ch/html/menu3/b/o_c_ref.htm

*United Nations Convention Relating to the Status of Stateless Persons (1954)*
http://www.unhchr.ch/html/menu3/b/o_c_sp.htm

*United Nations Development Programme Gender Inequality Index (2010)*
http://hdr.undp.org/en/statistics/gii/

*United Nations Economic and Social Council Resolution 1997/2 (Gender Mainstreaming 1997)*
http://www.un.org/womenwatch/daw/documents/ecosoc1997
/eresAgreedConclusions1997–2.pdf

*United Nations Framework Convention on Climate Change (UNFCCC)/Kyoto Protocol (1997)*
http://unfccc.int/kyoto_protocol/items/2830.php

*United Nations Millennium Development Goals (MDGs 2000)*
http://www.un.org/millenniumgoals

*United Nations Protocol to Prevent, Suppress, and Punish Trafficking in Persons (2000)*
http://www.uncjin.org/Documents/Conventions/dcatoc/final_
documents_2/convention_%20traff_eng.pdf

*United Nations Security Council Resolution 1325 (2000)*
http://www.un.org/events/res_1325e.pdf

*Universal Declaration of Human Rights (1948)*
http://un.org/Overview/rights.html

**Gender and Gender-Related IGOs**

*United Nations Development Fund for Women (UNIFEM)*
http://www.unifem.org

*United Nations Division for the Advancement of Women (UNDAW)*
http://www.un.org/womenwatch/daw

*United Nations Entity for the Gender Equality and the Empowerment of Women (UN Women)*
http://www.unwomen.org/

*United Nations Fund for Population Activities (UNFPA)*
http://www.unfpa.org/

*United Nations International Research and Training Institute for the Advancement of Women (UN-INSTRAW)*
http://www.un-instraw.org

*United Nations Office of the Special Adviser to the Secretary-General on Gender Issues and Advancement of Women (OSAGI)*
http://www.un.org/womenwatch/osagi

*Joint United Nations Program on HIV/AIDS (UNAIDS)*
http://www.unaids.org

### Other IGOs

*Food and Agriculture Organization of the United Nations (FAO)*
http://www.fao.org

*International Monetary Fund (IMF)*
http://www.imf.org

*International Organization for Migration (IOM)*
http://www.iom.int/jahia/jsp/index.jsp

*Inter-Parliamentary Union (IPU)*
http://www.ipu.org

*Office of the United Nations High Commissioner for Refugees (UNHCR)*
http://www.unhcr.org

*Organization for Economic Cooperation and Development (OECD)*
http://www.oecd.org

*United Nations (UN)*
http://www.un.org

*United Nations Development Programme (UNDP)*
http://www.undp.org

*United Nations Economic and Social Council (ECOSOC)*
http://www.un.org/ecosoc

*United Nations Educational, Scientific, and Cultural Organization (UNESCO)*
http://portal.unesco.org

*United Nations Environment Program (UNEP)*
http://www.unep.org

*World Bank*
http://www.worldbank.org

*World Health Organization (WHO)*
http://www.who.int

*World Trade Organization (WTO)*
http://www.wto.org

### Gender and Gender-Related NGOs and Information

*AI My Body, My Rights Campaign*
http://www.amnesty.org/campaigns/demand-dignity/my-body-my-rights

*Amnesty International (AI)*
http://www.amnesty.org

*Arab Women's Solidarity Association United (AWSA United)*
http://www.awsa.net

*Association for Women's Rights in Development (AWID)*
http://www.awid.org

*BLACKGIRL INTERNATIONAL*
http://www.blackgirl.org

*Boston Consortium on Gender, Security, and Human Rights*
http://www.genderandsecurity.org

*CEDAW Task Force, The Leadership Conference on Civil and Human Rights*
http://www.cedaw2011.org/index.php/about-us

*Center for Reproductive Rights*
http://reproductiverights.org

*Center for Women's Global Leadership*
http://www.cwgl.rutgers.edu

*CODEPINK*
http://www.codepink4peace.org

*Development Alternatives with Women for a New Era (DAWN)*
http://www.dawnnet.org

*Feminist Majority Foundation (FMF)*
http://feminist.org

*Feminist Theory and Gender Studies (FTGS) Section of the International Studies Association*
http://www.femisa.org, http://ftgss.blogspot.com

*Free Pussy Riot*
http://www.freepussyriot.org/

*Gender cc–Women for Climate Justice*
   http://www.gendercc.net/about-gendercc/activities.html

*Global Fund for Women*
   http://www.globalfundforwomen.org

*Green Belt Movement*
   http://www.greenbeltmovement.org

*Human Rights Watch*
   http://www.hrw.org

*Human Rights Watch—Women's Rights*
   http://www.hrw.org/en/category/topic/women%E2%80%99s-rights

*Institute for Women's Policy Research (IWPR)*
   http://www.iwpr.org

*Instituto Social y Político de la Mujer (ISPM)*
   http://www.ispm.org.ar

*International Center for Research on Women (ICRW)*
   http://www.icrw.org

*International Community of Women Living with HIV/AIDS (ICW)*
   http://www.icw.org

*International Feminist Journal of Politics (IFjP)*
   http://www.tandf.co.uk/journals/titles/14616742.asp

*International Gender and Trade Network*
   http://www.igtn.org

*International Lesbian and Gay Human Rights Commission (ILGHRC)*
   http://www.ilghrc.org

*International Lesbian, Gay, Bisexual, Trans, and Intersex Association (ILGA)*
   http://www.ilga.org

*International Women's Rights Action Watch (IWRAW)*
   http://www1.umn.edu/humanrts/iwraw

*International Women's Tribune Centre (IWTC)*
   http://www.iwtc.org

*Isis Women's International Cross Cultural Exchange (Isis-WICCE)*
   http://www.isis.or.ug

*MADRE*
http://www.madre.org

*National Council for Research on Women (NCRW)*
http://www.ncrw.org

*Navdanya—Research Foundation for Science, Technology, and Ecology (RFSTE)*
http://www.navdanya.org

*Occupy Wall Street*
http://occupywallst.org/

*Pan Pacific and Southeast Asia Women's Association (PPSEAWA)*
http://www.ppseawa.org

*PeaceWomen: A Project of the Women's International League for Peace and Freedom*
http://www.peacewomen.org

*Revolutionary Association of the Women of Afghanistan (RAWA)*
http://www.rawa.org

*SlutWalk*
https://www.facebook.com/SlutWalk

*Uprising of Women in the Arab World*
http://uprisingofwomeninthearabworld.org/en/
https://www.facebook.com/intifadat.almar2a

*WIDE Network*
http://www.wide-network.org

*Women Against Fundamentalism*
http://www.womenagainstfundamentalism.org.uk

*Women in Black*
http://www.womeninblack.org

*Women in International Security (WIIS)*
http://www.wiis-brussels.org

*Women Living Under Muslim Laws (WLUML)*
http://www.wluml.org

*Women Nobel Laureates*
http://nobelprize.org/nobel_prizes/lists/women.html

*Women's Environment and Development Organization (WEDO)*
http://www.wedo.org

*Women's International League for Peace and Freedom (WILPF)*
http://www.wilpf.int.ch

*Women's Research and Education Institute (WREI)*
http://www.wrei.org

*World Social Forum/Fórum Social Mundial*
http://www.forumsocialmundial.org.br

## Select Video Resources

*American Winter* (dir. Harry and Joe Gantz, 2013)

*Bamako* (dir. Abderrahmane Sissako, 2006)

*Beyond Gay: The Politics of Pride* (dir. Bob Christie, 2009)

*Can You Hear Me? Israeli and Palestinian Women Fight for Peace* (dir. Lily Rivlin and Margaret Murphy, 2006)

*Cowboys in Paradise* (dir. Amit Virmani, 2009)

*El Contrato* (dir. Min Sook Lee, 2003)

*G.I. Jane* (dir. Ridley Scott, 1997)

*Half the Sky: Turning Oppression into Opportunity for Women Worldwide* (dir. Maro Chermayeff, 2012) (Parts I and II)

*Life + Debt* (dir. Stephanie Black, 2001)

*Maquilapolis* (dir. Vicky Funari and Sergio de la Torre, 2006)

*Occupy Love* (dir. Velcrow Ripper, 2012)

*Rape Is . . .* (dir. Margaret Lazarus and Renner Wunderlich, 2002)

*Roger & Me* (dir. Michael Moore, 1989)

*Seek My Face, Hear My Voice: Foreign Domestic Workers in Hong Kong* (dir. Seyoung Lee, 2010)

*Seniorita Extraviada* (dir. Lourdes Portillo, 2001)

*The Invisible War* (dir. Kirby Dick, 2012)

*The Women Outside: Korean Women and the U.S. Military* (dir. J. T. Takagi and Hye Jung Park, 1995)

*Women on the Frontlines* (dir. Lisa Hepner and Patricia Smith Melton, 2003)

Women, Peace, and War (PBS TV) series (dir. Gini Reticker, 2011):
  *Peace Unveiled*
  *War Redefined*
  *The War We Are Living*
  *I Came to Testify*
  *Pray the Devil Back to Hell*

*Which Way Home* (dir. Rebecca Cammisa, 2009)

*Zero Dark Thirty* (dir. Kathryn Bigelow, 2012)


And countless YouTube and Vimeo resources on women, gender, and global issues, such as the following:

"Can We Shop to End Poverty?" with Ananya Roy (Global POV Production, 2013, http://www.youtube.com/watch?v=mpuf-N66CGI)

"The Hidden Face of Globalization" (four-part series produced by the National Labor Committee, 2008, http://www.youtube.com/watch?v=8Bhodyt4fmU)

"Side by Side—Women, Peace, and Security" (produced by UN Women, 2012, http://www.youtube.com/watch?v=a2Br8DCRxME)

"Who Sees Poverty?" with Ananya Roy (Global POV Production, 2012), http://www.youtube.com/watch?v=hrW8ier__4Q)

"Women and Climate Change" (produced by Gender cc–Women for Climate Justice, 2011, http://www.youtube.com/watch?v=j1JdAmCJF5o)

# References

Ackerly, Brooke A. 2008. *Universal Human Rights in a World of Difference.* Cambridge: Cambridge University Press.

Ackerly, Brooke A., Maria Stern, and Jacqui True, eds. 2006. *Feminist Methodologies for International Relations.* Cambridge: Cambridge University Press.

Ackerly, Brooke A., and Jacqui True. 2006. "Studying the Struggles and Wishes of the Age: Feminist Theoretical Methodology and Feminist Theoretical Methods." In Brooke A. Ackerly, Maria Stern, and Jacqui True, eds., *Feminist Methodologies for International Relations,* 241–260. Cambridge: Cambridge University Press.

Agamben, Giorgio. 1998. *Homo Sacer: Sovereign Power and Bare Life.* Trans. Daniel Heller-Roazen. Stanford, CA: Stanford University Press.

Agathangelou, Anna. 2004. *The Global Political Economy of Sex: Desire, Violence, and Insecurity in Mediterranean Nation-States.* New York: Palgrave Macmillan.

Agathangelou, Anna, and L. H. M. Ling. 2009. *Transforming World Politics: From Empire to Multiple Worlds.* London: Routledge.

Agustín, Laura Maria. 2007. *Sex at the Margins: Migration, Labour Markets, and the Rescue Industry.* London: Zed Books.

Al-Ali, Nadje, and Nicola Pratt. 2009. *What Kind of Liberation? Women and the Occupation of Iraq.* Berkeley: University of California Press.

Alexander, Karen, and Mary E. Hawkesworth, eds. 2008. *War and Terror: Feminist Perspectives.* Chicago: University of Chicago Press.

Alexander, M. Jacqui. 2005. *Pedagogies of Crossing: Meditations on Feminism, Sexual Politics, Memory, and the Sacred.* Durham, NC: Duke University Press.

Alvarez, Lizette, and Erik Eckholm. 2009. "Purple Heart Is Ruled Out for Traumatic Stress." *New York Times,* January 8. http://www.nytimes.com/2009/01/08/us/08purple.html (accessed February 9, 2009).

Alvarez, Sonia. 1999. "Advocating Feminism: The Latin American Feminist NGO 'Boom.'" *International Feminist Journal of Politics* 1(2): 181–209.

American Political Science Association (APSA). 2008. "The Persistent Problem: Inequality, Difference, and the Challenge of Development." Report of the Task Force on Difference, Inequality, and Developing Societies, July. http://www.apsanet.org/~globalinequality/imgtest/ThePersistentProblem.pdf (accessed February 6, 2009).

Andersen, Margaret L. 1983. *Thinking About Women: Sociological and Feminist Perspectives*. New York: Macmillan.

Anderson, Bridget. 2000. *Doing the Dirty Work? The Global Politics of Domestic Labour*. London: Zed Books.

Antrobus, Peggy. 2006. "Gender Equality in the New Millennium: Goal or Gimmick?" *Caribbean Quarterly* 52(2/3): 39–50.

Anzaldúa, Gloria. 1999. *Borderlands/La Frontera: The New Mestiza*. 2nd ed. San Francisco: Aunt Lute Books.

Araújo, Clara, and Ana Isabel García. 2006. "The Experience and the Impact of Quotas in Latin America." In Drude Dahlerup, ed., *Women, Quotas, and Politics*, 83–111. London: Routledge.

Ashley, Richard. 1989. "Living on Borderlines: Man, Poststructuralism, and War." In James Der Derian and Michael J. Shapiro, eds., *International/Intertextual Relations: Postmodern Readings of World Politics*, 259–322. Lexington, MA: Lexington Books.

Aslanbeigui, Nahid, and Gale Summerfield. 2000. "The Asian Crisis, Gender, and the International Financial Architecture." *Feminist Economics* 6(3): 81–104.

——. 2001. "Risk, Gender, and Development in the 21st Century." *International Journal of Politics, Culture, and Society* 15(1): 7–26.

Bach, Jonathan. 2011. "Remittances, Gender, and Development." In Marianne H. Marchand and Anne Sisson Runyan, eds., *Gender and Global Restructuring: Sightings, Sites, and Resistances*, 129–142. 2nd ed. London: Routledge.

Bakker, Isabella, ed. 1994. *The Strategic Silence: Gender and Economic Policy*. London: Zed Books.

——. 2007. "Social Reproduction and the Constitution of a Gendered Political Economy." *New Political Economy* 12(4): 541–556.

Bakker, Isabella, and Stephen Gill, eds. 2003. *Power, Production, and Social Reproduction: Human In/Security in the Global Political Economy*. Basingstoke, UK: Palgrave Macmillan.

Barber, Pauline Gardiner. 2011. "Women's Work *Unbound*: Philippine Development and Global Restructuring." In Marianne H. Marchand and Anne Sisson Runyan, eds., *Gender and Global Restructuring: Sightings, Sites, and Resistances*, 143–162. 2nd ed. London: Routledge.

Barker, Drucilla K., and Susan F. Feiner. 2004. *Liberating Economics: Feminist Perspectives on Families, Work, and Globalization*. Ann Arbor: University of Michigan Press.

Bedford, Kate. 2009. *Gender, Sexuality, and the Reformed World Bank*. Minneapolis: University of Minnesota Press.

Bedont, Barbara. 2005. "The Renewed Popularity of the Rule of Law: Implications for Women, Impunity, and Peacekeeping." In Dyan Mazurana, Angela Raven-Roberts, and Jane Parpart, eds., *Gender, Conflict, and Peacekeeping*, 83–108. Lanham, MD: Rowman and Littlefield.

Belkin, Aaron. 2012. *Bring Me Men: Military Masculinity and the Benign Façade of American Empire, 1898–2001*. New York: Columbia University Press.

Benería, Lourdes. 1995. "Toward a Greater Integration of Gender in Economics." *World Development* 23(11): 1839–1850.

———. 2003. *Gender, Development, and Globalization: Economics as if All People Mattered.* New York: Routledge.

Benhabib, Seyla, and Drucilla Cornell, eds. 1987. *Feminism as Critique: On the Politics of Gender in Late-Capitalist Societies.* Cambridge: Polity Press.

Bergeron, Suzanne L. 2001. "Political Economy Discourses of Globalization and Feminist Politics." *Signs: Journal of Women in Culture and Society* 26(4): 983–1006.

———. 2003. "Challenging the World Bank's Narrative of Inclusion." In Amitava Kumar, ed., *World Bank Literature,* 157–171. Minneapolis: University of Minnesota Press.

Borah, Rituparna. 2012. "Reclaiming the Feminist Politics of 'Slutwalk.'" *International Feminist Journal of Politics* 14(3): 415–421.

Boris, Eileen, and Elisabeth Prügl, eds. 1996. *Homeworkers in Global Perspective: Invisible No More.* New York: Routledge.

Boserup, Esther. 1970. *Woman's Role in Economic Development.* New York: St. Martin's Press.

Brah, Avtar. 2002. "Global Mobilities, Local Predicaments: Globalization and the Critical Imagination." *Feminist Review* 70: 30–45.

Brenner, Johanna. 2009. "Transnational Feminism and the Struggle for Global Justice." In Jai Sen and Peter Waterman, eds., *World Social Forum: Challenging Empires,* 26–37. 2nd ed. Montreal: Black Rose Books.

Brittan, Arthur. 1989. *Masculinity and Power.* Oxford: Basil Blackwell.

Brown, Katherine E. 2011. "Blinded by the Explosion? Security and Resistance in Muslim Women's Suicide Terrorism." In Laura Sjoberg and Caron E. Gentry, eds., *Women, Gender, and Terrorism,* 194–226. Athens: University of Georgia Press.

Brown, Sarah. 1988. "Feminism, International Theory, and International Relations of Gender Inequality." *Millennium Journal of International Studies* 17(3): 461–475.

Brown, Wendy. 1988. *Manhood and Politics: A Feminist Reading in Political Theory.* Totowa, NJ: Rowman and Littlefield.

Bunch, Charlotte, and Niamh Reilly. 1994. *Demanding Accountability: The Global Campaign and Vienna Tribunal for Women's Human Rights.* New York: United Nations Development Fund for Women (UNIFEM) and Center for Women's Global Leadership (CWGL).

Butler, Judith. 2010. *Frames of War: When Is Life Grievable?* London: Verso Books.

Caglar, Gülay, Elisabeth Prügl, and Susanne Zwingel, eds. 2012. *Feminist Strategies in International Governance.* London: Routledge.

Carver, Terrell. 1996. *Gender Is Not a Synonym for Women.* Boulder, CO: Lynne Rienner.

Chant, Sylvia. 2007. *Gender, Generation, and Poverty: Exploring the "Feminization of Poverty" in Africa, Asia, and Latin America.* Cheltenham, UK: Edward Elgar.

Chan-Tiberghien, Jennifer. 2004. "Gender Skepticism or Gender-Boom? Poststructural Feminisms, Transnational Feminisms, and the World Conference Against Racism." *International Feminist Journal of Politics* 6(3): 454–484.

Chappell, Louise, and Lisa Hill. 2006. *The Politics of Women's Interests: New Comparative Perspectives*. London: Routledge.

Chin, Christine B. N. 1998. *In Service and Servitude: Foreign Female Domestic Workers and the Malaysian "Modernity" Project*. New York: Columbia University Press.

Chowdhry, Geeta, and Sheila Nair, eds. 2002. *Power, Postcolonialism, and International Relations: Reading Race, Gender, and Class*. London: Routledge.

Chowdhury, Najma, and Barbara J. Nelson et al. 1994. "Redefining Politics: Patterns of Women's Political Engagement from a Global Perspective." In Barbara J. Nelson and Najma Chowdhury, eds., *Women and Politics Worldwide*, 3–24. New Haven, CT: Yale University Press.

Clancy-Smith, Julia, and Frances Gouda, eds. 1998. *Domesticating the Empire: Race, Gender, and Family Life in French and Dutch Colonialism*. Charlottesville: University Press of Virginia.

Clausewitz, Carl von. 2004. *On War*. Whitefish, MT: Kessinger.

Cockburn, Cynthia. 1998. *The Space Between Us: Negotiating Gender and National Identities in Conflict*. London: Zed Books.

———. 2007. *From Where We Stand: War, Women's Activism, and Feminist Analysis*. London: Zed Books.

Cohn, Carol. 2008. "Mainstreaming Gender in UN Security Policy: A Path to Political Transformation?" In Shirin Rai and Georgina Waylen, eds., *Global Governance: Feminist Perspectives*, 185–206. Basingstoke, UK: Palgrave Macmillan.

———, ed. 2013. *Women & Wars: Contested Histories, Uncertain Futures*. Cambridge: Polity Press.

Cohn, Carol, and Ruth Jacobson. 2013. "Women and Political Activism in the Face of War and Militarization." In Carol Cohn, ed., *Women & Wars: Contested Histories, Uncertain Futures*, 102–123. Cambridge: Polity Press.

Collins, Patricia Hill. 1991. *Black Feminist Thought: Knowledge, Consciousness, and the Politics of Empowerment*. New York: Routledge.

Connell, R. W. 1987. *Gender and Power*. Cambridge: Polity Press.

———. 1995. *Masculinities*. Berkeley: University of California Press.

Cook, Rebecca, ed. 1994. *Human Rights of Women: National and International Perspectives*. Philadelphia: University of Pennsylvania Press.

Cornia, Giovanni Andrea, ed. 2004. *Inequality, Growth, and Poverty in an Era of Liberalization and Globalization*. Oxford: Oxford University Press.

Crenshaw, Kimberlé. 1991. "Mapping the Margins: Intersectionality, Identity Politics, and Violence Against Women of Color." *Stanford Law Review* 43: 1241–1299.

Dahl, Robert A. 1961. *Who Governs? Democracy and Power in an American City*. New Haven, CT: Yale University Press.

Dahlerup, Drude. 2006a. "Conclusion." In Drude Dahlerup, ed., *Women, Quotas, and Politics*, 293–307. London: Routledge.

———. 2006b. "Introduction." In Drude Dahlerup, ed., *Women, Quotas, and Politics*, 3–31. London: Routledge.

D'Amico, Francine. 1997. "Policing the U.S. Military's Race and Gender Lines." In Laurie Weinstein and Christie C. White, eds., *Wives and Warriors: Women and the Military in the United States and Canada*, 199–234. Westport, CT: Bergin and Garvey.

Dangler, Jamie Faricellia. 2000. "The Periodic Resurgence of Non-Factory-Based Production." In Faruk Tabak and Michaeline A. Crichlow, eds., *Informalization: Process and Structure*, 47–68. Baltimore, MD: Johns Hopkins University Press.

De Goede, Marieke. 2005. *Virtue, Fortune, and Faith: A Genealogy of Finance*. Minneapolis: University of Minnesota Press.

DeLargy, Pamela. 2013. "Sexual Violence and Women's Health in War." In Carol Cohn, ed., *Women & Wars: Contested Histories, Uncertain Futures*, 54–79. Cambridge: Polity Press.

Devlin, Claire, and Robert Elgie. 2008. "The Effect of Increased Women's Representation in Parliament: The Case of Rwanda." *Parliamentary Affairs* 61(2): 237–254.

Dewey, Susan, and Patty Kelly, eds. 2011. *Policing Pleasure: Sex Work, Policy, and the State in Global Perspective*. New York: New York University Press.

*Economist, The*. 1999. August 28.

Ehrenreich, Barbara, and Arlie R. Hochschild, eds. 2002a. *Global Woman: Nannies, Maids, and Sex Workers in the New Economy*. New York: Metropolitan Books.

———. 2002b. "Introduction." In Barbara Ehrenreich and Arlie R. Hochschild, eds., *Global Woman: Nannies, Maids, and Sex Workers in the New Economy*, 1–14. New York: Metropolitan Books.

Einhorn, Barbara, and Eileen Janes Yeo, eds. 1995. *Women and Market Societies: Crisis and Opportunity*. Aldershot, UK: Edward Elgar.

Eisenstein, Hester. 2009. *Feminism Seduced: How Global Elites Use Women's Labor and Ideas to Exploit the World*. Boulder, CO: Paradigm Publishers.

Eisenstein, Zillah R. 2004. *Against Empire: Feminisms, Racisms, and the West*. London: Zed Books.

———. 2007. *Sexual Decoys: Gender, Race, and War in Imperial Democracy*. London: Zed Press.

Eisler, Riane. 2007. *The Real Wealth of Nations: Creating a Caring Economics*. San Francisco: Berrett-Koehler.

Eisler, Riane, David Loye, and Kari Norgaard. 1995. *Women, Men, and the Global Quality of Life*. Pacific Grove, CA: Center for Partnership Studies.

Elshtain, Jean Bethke. 1987. *Women and War*. New York: Basic Books.

———. 1992. "Sovereignty, Identity, Sacrifice." In V. Spike Peterson, ed., *Gendered States: Feminist (Re)Visions of International Relations Theory*, 141–154. Boulder, CO: Lynne Rienner.

Enloe, Cynthia. 1983. *Does Khaki Become You? The Militarization of Women's Lives*. Boston: South End Press.

———. 1989. *Bananas, Beaches, and Bases: Making Feminist Sense of International Politics.* Berkeley: University of California Press.

———. 1990. "Womenandchildren: Making Feminist Sense of the Persian Gulf Crisis." *Village Voice,* September 25: 29ff.

———. 1993. *The Morning After: Sexual Politics at the End of the Cold War.* Berkeley: University of California Press.

———. 2000. *Maneuvers: The International Politics of Militarizing Women's Lives.* Berkeley: University of California Press.

———. 2007. *Globalization and Militarism: Feminists Make the Link.* Lanham, MD: Rowman and Littlefield.

———. 2010. *Nimo's War, Emma's War: Making Feminist Sense of the Iraq War.* Berkeley: University of California Press.

Eschle, Catherine. 2001. *Global Democracy, Social Movements, and Feminism.* Boulder, CO: Westview Press.

———. 2005. "Constructing 'the Anti-Globalisation Movement.'" In Catherine Eschle and Bice Maiguascha, eds., *Critical Theories, International Relations, and the "Anti-Globalization Movement,"* 17–35. London: Routledge.

Eschle, Catherine, and Bice Maiguascha, eds. 2005. *Critical Theories, International Relations, and the "Anti-Globalization Movement."* London: Routledge.

Fall, Yassine. 2001. "Gender and Social Implications of Globalization: An African Perspective." In Rita Mae Kelly et al., eds., *Gender, Globalization, and Democratization,* 49–74. Lanham, MD: Rowman and Littlefield.

Faludi, Susan. 2007. *The Terror Dream: Fear and Fantasy in Post-9/11 America.* New York: Metropolitan Books/Henry Holt.

Farrell, Amy, and Patrice McDermott. 2005. "Claiming Afghan Women: The Challenge of Human Rights Discourse for Transnational Feminism." In Wendy S. Hesford and Wendy Kozol, eds., *Just Advocacy? Women's Human Rights, Transnational Feminisms, and the Politics of Representation,* 33–55. New Brunswick, NJ: Rutgers University Press.

Fausto-Sterling, Anne. 1992. *Myths of Gender: Biological Theories About Women and Men.* 2nd ed. New York: Basic Books.

———. 2000. "The Five Sexes, Revisited." *The Sciences* 40(4): 19–23.

Federici, Sylvia. 2004. *Caliban and the Witch: Women, the Body, and Primitive Accumulation.* New York: Autonomedia.

Ferber, Marianne A., and Julie A. Nelson, eds. 2003. *Feminist Economics Today: Beyond Economic Man.* Chicago: University of Chicago Press.

Ferguson, Ann. 1984. "On Conceiving Motherhood and Sexuality: A Feminist Materialist Approach." In Joyce Trebilcot, ed., *Mothering: Essays in Feminist Theory,* 153–182. Totowa, NJ: Rowman and Allanheld.

———. 1989. *Blood at the Root: Motherhood, Sexuality, and Male Dominance.* London: Pandora.

Fernandez-Kelly, Maria Patricia.1983. *For We Are Sold, I and My People: Women in Industry in Mexico's Frontier.* Albany: State University of New York Press.

Finlay, Barbara. 2006. *George W. Bush and the War on Women: Turning Back the Clock on Progress.* London: Zed Books.

Flanders, Laura, ed. 2004. *The W Effect: Bush's War on Women.* New York: Feminist Press at City University of New York.

Floro, Maria, and Gary Dymski. 2000. "Financial Crisis, Gender, and Power: An Analytical Framework." *World Development* 28(7): 1269–1283.

Foucault, Michel. 1991. "Governmentality." In Graham Burchell, Colin Gordon, and Peter Miller, eds., *The Foucault Effect: Studies in Governmentality,* 87–104. Chicago: University of Chicago Press.

Franklin, M. I. 2004. *Postcolonial Politics, the Internet, and Everyday Life: Pacific Traversals Online.* London: Routledge.

Fraser, Nancy. 1997. *Justice Interruptus: Critical Reflections on the "Postsocialist" Condition.* New York: Routledge.

———. 2009. "Feminism, Capitalism, and the Cunning of History." *New Left Review* 56: 97–117.

Friedenwall, Lenita, Drude Dahlerup, and Hege Skjeie. 2006. "The Nordic Countries: An Incremental Model." In Drude Dahlerup, ed., *Women, Quotas, and Politics,* 55–82. London: Routledge.

Fuentes, Annette, and Barbara Ehrenreich. 1983. *Women in the Global Factory.* Boston: South End Press.

Ghosh, Nandita. 2007. "Women and the Politics of Water: An Introduction." *International Feminist Journal of Politics* 9(4): 443–454.

Gibson-Graham, J. K. 1996. *The End of Capitalism (As We Knew It): A Feminist Critique of Political Economy.* Cambridge, MA: Blackwell.

———. 2006. *A Postcapitalist Politics.* Minneapolis: University of Minnesota Press.

Giddings, Paula. 1984. *When and Where I Enter: The Impact of Black Women on Race and Sex in America.* New York: Bantam Books.

Giles, Wenona, and Jennifer Hyndman. 2004. "Introduction: Gender and Conflict in a Global Context." In Wenona Giles and Jennifer Hyndman, eds., *Sites of Violence: Gender and Conflict Zones,* 3–23. Berkeley: University of California Press.

Gilmore, Stephanie, ed. 2008. *Feminist Coalitions: Historical Perspectives on Second-Wave Feminism in the United States.* Urbana: University of Illinois Press.

Goetz, Anne Marie, and Rina Sen Gupta. 1996. "Who Takes the Credit? Gender, Power, and Control over Loan Use in Rural Credit Programs in Bangladesh." *World Development* 24(1): 45–64.

Goldstein, Joshua S. 2001. *War and Gender: How Gender Shapes the War System and Vice Versa.* Cambridge: Cambridge University Press.

———. 2011. *Winning the War on War: The Decline of Armed Conflict Worldwide.* New York: Dutton.

Goodyear, Michael, and Ronald Weitzer. 2011. "International Trends in the Control of Sexual Services." In Susan Dewey and Patty Kelly, eds., *Policing Pleasure: Sex Work, Policy, and the State in Global Perspective,* 16–30. New York: New York University Press.

Grant, Rebecca. 1994. "The Cold War and the Feminine Mystique." In Peter R. Beckman and Francine D'Amico, eds., *Women, Gender, and World Politics: Perspectives, Policies, and Prospects,* 119–130. Westport, CT: Bergin and Garvey.

Grewal, Inderpal. 2005. *Transnational America: Feminisms, Diasporas, Neoliberalisms*. Durham, NC: Duke University Press.

Grewal, Inderpal, and Caren Kaplan, eds. 1994. *Scattered Hegemonies: Postmodernity and Transnational Feminist Practices*. Minneapolis: University of Minnesota Press.

———. 2001. "Global Identities: Theorizing Transnational Studies of Sexuality." *GLQ* 7(4): 663–679.

Guerrero, MA Jaimes. 1997. "Exemplars of Indigenism: Native North American Women for Decolonization and Liberation." In Cathy J. Cohen, Kathleen B. Jones, and Joan C. Tronto, eds., *Women Transforming Politics: An Alternative Reader*, 205–222. New York: New York University Press.

Hague, Euan. 1997. "Rape, Power, and Masculinity: The Construction of Gender and National Identities in the War in Bosnia-Herzegovina." In Ronit Lentin, ed., *Gender and Catastrophe*, 50–63. London: Zed Books.

Halberstam, J. Jack. 2012. *Gaga Feminism: Sex, Gender, and the End of Normal*. Boston: Beacon Press.

Hanochi, Seiko. 2001. "Japan and the Global Sex Industry." In Rita Mae Kelly et al., eds., *Gender, Globalization, and Democratization*, 137–148. Lanham, MD: Rowman and Littlefield.

Harcourt, Wendy, ed. 1999. *Women@Internet: Creating New Cultures in Cyberspace*. London: Zed Books.

Harding, Sandra. 1986. *The Science Question in Feminism*. Ithaca, NY: Cornell University Press.

———. 1991. *Whose Science? Whose Knowledge? Thinking from Women's Lives*. Ithaca, NY: Cornell University Press.

Hardt, Michael, and Antonio Negri. 2000. *Empire*. Cambridge, MA: Harvard University Press.

Hawkesworth, Mary E. 2006. *Globalization and Feminist Activism*. Lanham, MD: Rowman and Littlefield.

———. 2012. *Political Worlds of Women: Activism, Advocacy, and Governance in the Twenty-First Century*. Boulder, CO: Westview Press.

Hawthorne, Susan, and Bronwyn Winter, eds. 2002. *September 11, 2001: Feminist Perspectives*. North Melbourne, Australia: Spinifex.

Henderson, Sarah L., and Alana S. Jeydel. 2010. *Women and Politics in a Global World*, 2nd ed. Oxford: Oxford University Press.

Henry, Nicola. 2011. *War and Rape: Law, Memory, and Justice*. London: Routledge.

Hesford, Wendy S., and Wendy Kozol, eds. 2005. *Just Advocacy? Women's Human Rights, Transnational Feminisms, and the Politics of Representation*. New Brunswick, NJ: Rutgers University Press.

Hewitson, Gillian J. 1999. *Feminist Economics: Interrogating the Masculinity of Rational Economic Man*. Cheltenham, UK: Edward Elgar.

Hoogensen, Gunhild, and Bruce O. Solheim. 2006. *Women in Power: World Leaders Since 1960*. Westport, CT: Praeger.

Hooper, Charlotte. 1998. "Masculinist Practices and Gender Politics: The Operation of Multiple Masculinities in International Relations." In Marysia

Zalewski and Jane Parpart, eds., *The "Man" Question in International Relations*, 28–53. Boulder, CO: Westview Press.

———. 2001. *Manly States: Masculinities, International Relations, and Gender Politics*. New York: Columbia University Press.

Hua, Julietta. 2011. *Trafficking Women's Human Rights*. Minneapolis: University of Minnesota Press.

Hudson, Heidi. 2005. "Peacekeeping Trends and Their Gender Implications for Regional Peacekeeping Forces in Africa: Progress and Challenges." In Dyan Mazurana, Angela Raven-Roberts, and Jane Parpart, eds., *Gender, Conflict, and Peacekeeping*, 111–133. Lanham, MD: Rowman and Littlefield.

Hughes, Donna M. 2000. "The 'Natasha' Trade: The Transnational Shadow Market of Trafficking in Women." *Journal of International Affairs* 53(2): 625–652.

Hunt, Krista, and Kim Rygiel, eds. 2006. *(En)Gendering the War on Terror: War Stories and Camouflaged Politics*. Burlington, VT: Ashgate.

INCITE! Women of Color Against Violence. 2007. *The Revolution Will Not Be Funded: Beyond the Non-Profit Industrial Complex*. Cambridge, MA: South End Press.

International Labour Organization (ILO). 2002a. *Decent Work and the Informal Economy* (Report VI). Geneva: ILO. http://www.ilo.org/public/english/standards/relm/ilc/ilc90/pdf/rep-vi.pdf (accessed February 8, 2009).

———. 2002b. *Women and Men in the Informal Economy: A Statistical Picture*. Geneva: ILO. http://www.ilo.org/public/english/region/ampro/cinterfor/temas/informal/genero/doc.htm (accessed February 8, 2009).

International Lesbian and Gay Association (ILGA). 2012. *State-Sponsored Homophobia: A World Survey of Laws Criminalising Same-Sex Sexual Acts Between Consenting Adults*. Brussels: ILGA. http://www.iglhrc.org/content/ilga-state-sponsored-homophobia-report (accessed May 15, 2013).

Irvine, Jill A. 2013. "Leveraging Change: Women's Organizations and the Implementation of UNSCR 1325 in the Balkans." *International Feminist Journal of Politics* 15(1): 20–38.

Jagger, Alison M. 1983. *Feminist Politics and Human Nature*. Totowa, NJ: Rowman and Allenheld.

Jeffords, Susan. 1989. *The Remasculinization of America: Gender and the Vietnam War*. Bloomington: Indiana University Press.

Jeffreys, Sheila. 2009. *The Industrial Vagina: The Political Economy of the Global Sex Trade*. New York: Routledge.

Joachim, Jutta M. 2007. *Agenda Setting, the UN, and NGOs: Gender Violence and Reproductive Rights*. Washington, DC: Georgetown University Press.

Joekes, Susan, and Ann Weston. 1995. *Women and the New Trade Agenda*. New York: UNIFEM.

Johnson, Allan G. 2005. *The Gender Knot: Unraveling Our Patriarchal Legacy*. Philadelphia: Temple University Press.

———. 2006. *Power, Privilege, and Difference*. 2nd ed. Mountain View, CA: Mayfield.

Jones, David E. 1997. *Women Warriors: A History*. London: Brassey's.

Jones, Kathleen B. 1993. *Compassionate Authority: Democracy and the Representation of Women*. New York: Routledge.

Jones-DeWeever, Avis. 2008. "Executive Summary." In Avis Jones-DeWeever, Institute for Women's Policy Research (IWPR), *Women in the Wake of the Storm: Examining the Post-Katrina Realities of the Women of New Orleans and the Gulf Coast*. http://www.iwpr.org/pdf/GulfCoastExecutiveSummary.pdf (accessed March 17, 2009).

Joseph, Ammu, and Kalpan Sharma, eds. 2003. *Terror, Counter-Terror: Women Speak Out*. London: Zed Books.

Kampwirth, Karen. 2002. *Women and Guerilla Movements: Nicaragua, El Salvador, Chiapas, Cuba*. University Park: Penn State University Press.

Kamrani, Marjan E., and Federica Gentile. 2013. "Securing the State: The Relationship Between Anti–Sex Trafficking Legislation and Organizing and the Fortressing of North America." In Anne Sisson Runyan, Amy Lind, Patricia McDermott, and Marianne Marchand, eds., *Feminist (Im)Mobilities in Fortress(ing) North America: Rights, Citizenships, and Identities in Transnational Perspective*, 115–132. Surrey, UK: Ashgate.

Kaufman, Joyce P., and Kristen P. Williams. 2007. *Women, the State, and War: A Comparative Perspective on Citizenship and Nationalism*. Lanham, MD: Lexington Books.

Keck, Margaret, and Karen Sikkink. 1998. *Activists Beyond Borders: Transnational Advocacy Networks in International Politics*. Ithaca, NY: Cornell University Press.

Kempadoo, Kamala, ed. 2005. *Trafficking and Prostitution Reconsidered: New Perspectives on Migration, Sex Work, and Human Rights*. Boulder, CO: Paradigm Publishers.

Kempadoo, Kamala, and Jo Doezema, eds. 1998. *Global Sex Workers*. New York: Routledge.

Kimmel, Michael. 2008. *Guyland*. New York: HarperCollins.

King, Samantha. 2013. "Philanthrocapitalism and the Healthification of Everything." *International Political Sociology* 7(1): 96–98.

Klein, Naomi. 2007. *The Shock Doctrine: The Rise of Disaster Capitalism*. New York: Metropolitan Books/Henry Holt.

Knapp, Gudrun-Axeli. 2005. "Race, Class, Gender: Reclaiming Baggage in Fast Travelling Theories." *European Journal of Women's Studies* 12(3): 249–265.

Krisoff, Nicholas D., and Sheryl WuDunn. 2009. *Half the Sky: Turning Oppression into Opportunity for Women Worldwide*. New York: Vintage Books.

Laclau, Ernesto, and Chantal Mouffe. 1985. *Hegemony and the Socialist Strategy: Toward a Radical Democratic Politics*. London: Verso Books.

Leatherman, Janie L. 2011. *Sexual Violence and Armed Conflict*. Cambridge: Polity Press.

Levine, Philippa, ed. 2004. *Gender and Empire*. Oxford: Oxford University Press.

Lind, Amy, ed. 2010. *Development, Sexual Rights, and Global Governance*. New York: Routledge.

Lind, Amy, and Jill Williams. 2013. "Engendering Violence in De/Hyper-nationalized Spaces: Border Militarization, State Territorialization, and Embodied Politics at the US-Mexico Border." In Anne Sisson Runyan, Amy Lind, Patricia McDermott, and Marianne Marchand, eds., *Feminist (Im)Mobilities in Fortress(ing) North America: Rights, Citizenships, and Identities in Transnational Perspective*, 95–114. Surrey, UK: Ashgate.

Lips, Hilary. 1991. *Women, Men, and Power*. Mountain View, CA: Mayfield.

Lorde, Audre. 2008. "The Master's Tools Will Never Dismantle the Master's House." Reprinted in Alison Bailey and Chris Cuomo, eds., *The Feminist Philosophy Reader*, 49–50. New York: McGraw-Hill.

Lovenduski, Joni, ed. 2005. *State Feminism and Political Representation*. Cambridge: Cambridge University Press.

Lugones, Maria. 2010. "Toward a Decolonial Feminism." *Hypatia* 25(4): 742–759.

Luibhéid, Eithne, and Lionel Cantú Jr., eds. 2005. *Queer Migrations: Sexuality, U.S. Citizenship, and Border Crossings*. Minneapolis: University of Minnesota Press.

Macdonald, Cameron Lynne, and Carmen Sirianni, eds. 1996. *Working in the Service Society*. Philadelphia: Temple University Press.

Macdonald, Laura. 1994. "Globalizing Civil Society: Interpreting International NGOs in Central America." *Millennium* 23: 227–285.

Macdonald, Laura, and Arne Ruckert, eds. 2009. *Post-Neoliberalism in the Americas*. New York: Palgrave Macmillan.

Mackie, Vera. 2001. "The Language of Globalization, Transnationality, and Feminism." *International Feminist Journal of Politics* 3(2): 180–206.

Marchand, Marianne H., and Anne Sisson Runyan, eds. 2000. *Gender and Global Restructuring: Sightings, Sites, and Resistances*. London: Routledge.

———, eds. 2011. *Gender and Global Restructuring: Sightings, Sites, and Resistances*, 2nd ed. London: Routledge.

Masters, Cristina. 2008. "Bodies of Technology and the Politics of the Flesh." In Jane L. Parpart and Marysia Zalewski, eds., *Rethinking the Man Question: Sex, Gender, and Violence in International Relations*, 87–108. London: Zed Books.

Mathers, Jennifer G. 2013. "Women and State Military Forces." In Carol Cohn, ed., *Women & Wars: Contested Histories, Uncertain Futures*, 124–145. Cambridge: Polity Press.

Matland, Richard E. 2006. "Electoral Quotas: Frequency and Effectiveness." In Drude Dahlerup, ed., *Women, Quotas, and Politics*, 275–292. London: Routledge.

Mbembe, Achille. 2002. "Necropolitics." *Public Culture* 15(1): 11–40.

McCall, Leslie. 2001. *Complex Inequality: Gender, Class, and Race in the New Economy*. New York: Routledge.

McCaughey, Martha. 2008. *The Caveman Mystique: Pop-Darwinism and the Debates over Sex, Violence, and Science*. New York: Routledge.

McClintock, Anne. 1995. *Imperial Leather: Race, Gender, and Sexuality in the Colonial Contest*. New York: Routledge.

McIntosh, Peggy. 2007. "White Privilege and Male Privilege." In Vera Taylor, Nancy Whittier, and Leila J. Rupp, eds., *Feminist Frontiers*, 9–15. 7th ed. Boston: McGraw-Hill.

McRobbie, Angela. 2009. *The Aftermath of Feminism: Gender, Culture, and Social Change*. London: Sage.

Mendoza, Breny. 2002. "Transnational Feminisms in Question." *Feminist Theory* 3(3): 295–314.

Merchant, Carolyn. 1980. *The Death of Nature: Women, Ecology, and the Scientific Revolution*. San Francisco: Harper and Row.

Midgley, Claire, ed. 1998. *Gender and Imperialism*. Manchester, UK: Manchester University Press.

Mies, Maria. 1986. *Patriarchy and Accumulation on a World Scale: Women in the International Division of Labour*. London: Zed Books.

Mies, Maria, Veronika Bennholdt-Thomsen, and Claudia von Werlhof. 1988. *Women: The Last Colony*. London: Zed Books.

Moghadam, Valentine M. ed. 1994. *Democratic Reform and the Position of Women in Transitional Economies*. Oxford: Oxford University Press.

——. 2005. *Globalizing Women: Transnational Feminist Networks*. Baltimore, MD: Johns Hopkins University Press.

Mohanty, Chandra Talpade. 1991. "Under Western Eyes: Feminist Scholarship and Colonial Discourses." In Chandra Mohanty, Ann Russo, and Lourdes Torres, eds., *Third World Women and the Politics of Feminism*, 51–80. Bloomington: Indiana University Press.

——. 2003. *Feminism Without Borders: Decolonizing Theory, Practicing Solidarity*. Durham, NC: Duke University Press.

Montagu, Ashley. 1974. *The Natural Superiority of Women*. New York: Collier Books.

Moon, Katharine H. S. 1997. *Sex Among Allies: Military Prostitution in U.S.-Korea Relations*. New York: Columbia University Press.

Nanda, Serena. 1998. *Neither Man nor Woman: The Hijras of India*. New York: Wadsworth.

Naples, Nancy, and Manisha Desai, eds. 2002. *Women's Activism and Globalization: Linking Local Struggles and Transnational Politics*. New York: Routledge.

National Council for Research on Women (NCRW). 2006. *Gains and Gaps: A Look at the World's Women*. New York: NCRW.

Nayak, Meghana, and Eric Selbin. 2010. *Decentering International Relations*. London: Zed Books.

Nelson, Julie A. 1996. *Feminism, Objectivity, and Economics*. London: Routledge.

Nelson, Lin. 1990. "The Place of Women in Polluted Places." In Irene Diamond and Gloria Feman Orenstein, eds., *Reweaving the World: The Emergence of Ecofeminism*, 173–188. San Francisco: Sierra Club Books.

Nelson, Mariah Burton. 1994. *The Stronger Women Get, the More Men Love Football*. New York: Avon Books.

Nikolic-Ristanovic, Verna. 1996. "War and Violence Against Women." In Jennifer Turpin and Lois Ann Lorentzen, eds., *The Gendered New World Order: Militarism, Development, and the Environment*, 195–210. New York: Routledge.

Okin, Susan Moller. 1979. *Women in Western Political Thought.* Princeton, NJ: Princeton University Press.

Okojo, Kamene. 1994. "Women and the Evolution of a Ghanaian Political Synthesis." In Barbara J. Nelson and Najma Chowdhury, eds., *Women and Politics Worldwide*, 285–297. New Haven, CT: Yale University Press.

O'Leary, Anna Ochoa, and Gloria Ciria Valdéz-Garcia. 2013. "Neoliberalizing (Re) Production: Women, Migrants, and Family Planning in the Peripheries of the State." In Anne Sisson Runyan, Amy Lind, Patricia McDermott, and Marianne Marchand, eds., *Feminist (Im)Mobilities in Fortress(ing) North America: Rights, Citizenships, and Identities in Transnational Perspective*, 75–94. Surrey, UK: Ashgate.

Oliver, Kelly. 2007. *Women as Weapons of War: Iraq, Sex, and the Media.* New York: Columbia University Press.

Ong, Aihwa. 2006. *Neoliberalism as Exception: Mutations of Citizenship and Sovereignty.* Durham, NC: Duke University Press.

Oosterveld, Valerie. 2005. "Prosecution of Gender-Based Crimes in International Law." In Dyan Mazurana, Angela Raven-Roberts, and Jane Parpart, eds., *Gender, Conflict, and Peacekeeping*, 94–117. Lanham, MD: Rowman and Littlefield.

Parpart, Jane L., and Marysia Zalewski, eds. 2008. *Rethinking the Man Question: Sex, Gender, and Violence in International Relations.* London: Zed Books.

Parr, Adrian. 2009. *Hijacking Sustainability.* Cambridge, MA: MIT Press.

———. 2013. *The Wrath of Capital: Neoliberalism and Climate Change Politics.* New York: Columbia University Press.

Patel, Raj. 2009. *The Value of Nothing: How to Reshape Market Society and Redefine Democracy.* New York: Picador.

Pateman, Carole. 1988. *The Sexual Contract.* Cambridge: Polity Press.

Peters, Julia, and Andrea Wolper, eds. 1995. *Women's Rights, Human Rights: International Feminist Perspectives.* New York: Routledge.

Peterson, V. Spike. 2003. *A Critical Rewriting of Global Political Economy: Integrating Reproductive, Productive, and Virtual Economies.* London: Routledge.

———. 2007. "Thinking Through Intersectionality and War." Special Issue on "Race, Gender, Class, Sexuality, and War." *Race, Gender, and Class* 14(3/4): 10–27.

Peterson, V. Spike, and Laura Parisi. 1998. "Are Women Human? It's Not an Academic Question." In Tony Evans, ed., *Human Rights Fifty Years On: A Radical Reappraisal*, 132–160. Manchester, UK: University of Manchester Press.

Pettman, Jan Jindy. 1996. *Worlding Women: A Feminist International Politics.* London: Routledge.

———. 1997. "Body Politics: International Sex Tourism." *Third World Quarterly* 18(1): 93–108.

Phillips, Anne. 1991. *Engendering Democracy.* University Park: Penn State University Press.

Phoenix, Ann, and Pamela Pattynama, eds. 2006. Special Issue on "Intersectionality." *European Journal of Women's Studies* 13(3).

Pierson, Ruth Roach, ed. 1987. *Women and Peace: Theoretical, Historical, and Practical Perspectives.* London: Croom Helm.

Poster, Winifred, and Zakia Salime. 2002. "The Limits of Microcredit: Transnational Feminism and USAID Activities in the United States and Morocco." In Nancy A. Naples and Manisha Desai, eds., *Women's Activism and Globalization,* 189–219. New York: Routledge.

Power, Marilyn. 2004. "Social Provisioning as a Starting Point for Feminist Economics." *Feminist Economics* 10(3): 3–20.

Prügl, Elisabeth, and Markus Thiel, eds. 2009. *Diversity in the European Union.* New York: Palgrave Macmillan.

Puar, Jasbir. 2007. *Terrorist Assemblages: Homonationalism in Queer Times.* Durham, NC: Duke University Press.

Rai, Shirin M. 2002. *Gender and the Political Economy of Development.* Cambridge: Polity Press.

———. 2008. "Analyzing Global Governance." In Shirin Rai and Georgina Waylen, eds., *Global Governance: Feminist Perspectives,* 19–42. Basingstoke, UK: Palgrave Macmillan.

Randall, Vicky. 1987. *Women and Politics: An International Perspective.* 2nd ed. Chicago: University of Chicago Press.

Rayner, Richard. 1997. "The Warrior Besieged," New York Times Magazine, June 22, 24–29. http://query.nytimes.com/gst/fullpage.html?res=9C07E0D6113F931A15755C0A961958260&sec=&spon=&partner=permalink&exprod=permalink (accessed February 8, 2009).

Reagon, Bernice Johnson. 2000. "Coalition Politics: Turning the Century." In Barbara Smith, ed., *Home Girls: A Black Feminist Anthology,* 343–355. New Brunswick, NJ: Rutgers University Press.

Rebick, Judy. 2012. *Occupy This!* Toronto: Penguin Canada.

Richardson, Laurel W., and Verta A. Taylor, eds. 1983. *Feminist Frontiers: Rethinking Sex, Gender, and Society.* Reading, MA: Addison-Wesley.

Richey, Lisa Ann, and Stefano Ponte. 2011. *Brand Aid: Shopping Well to Save the World.* Minneapolis: Quadrant/University of Minnesota Press.

Rodda, Annabel. 1991. *Women and the Environment.* London: Zed Books.

Roscoe, Will. 2000. *Changing Ones: Third and Fourth Genders in Native North America.* London: Palgrave Macmillan.

Rowbotham, Sheila. 1973. *Hidden from History: Rediscovering Women in History from the 17th Century to the Present.* New York: Vintage Books.

Rowley, Michelle. 2011. "'Where the Streets Have No Name': Getting Development Out of the (RED)?" In Marianne H. Marchand and Anne Sisson Runyan, eds. *Gender and Global Restructuring: Sightings, Sites, and Resistances,* 78–98. 2nd ed. London: Routledge.

Roy, Ananya. 2010. *Poverty Capitalism.* New York: Routledge.

Roy, Arundhati. 2003. *War Talk.* Cambridge, MA: South End Press.

Ruddick, Sara. 1984. "Preservative Love and Military Destruction." In Joyce Trebilcot, ed., *Mothering: Essays in Feminist Theory*, 231–262. Totowa, NJ: Rowman and Allanheld.

Runyan, Anne Sisson, Amy Lind, Patricia McDermott, and Marianne H. Marchand, eds. 2013. *Feminist (Im)Mobilities in Fortress(ing) North America: Rights, Citizenships, and Identities in Transnational Perspective*. Surrey, UK: Ashgate.

Russo, Ann. 2006. "The Feminist Majority Foundation's Campaign to Stop Gender Apartheid: The Intersections of Feminism and Imperialism in the United States." *International Feminist Journal of Politics* 8(6): 557–580.

Said, Edward. 1979. *Orientalism*. New York: Vintage Books.

———. 1993. *Culture and Imperialism*. New York: Knopf.

Sang-Hun, Choe. 2009. "Ex-Prostitutes Say South Korea and the U.S. Enabled Sex Trade Near Bases." *New York Times*, January 8.

Seager, Joni. 1993. *Earth Follies: Coming to Feminist Terms with the Global Environmental Crisis*. New York: Routledge.

———. 1997. *The State of Women in the World Atlas*. 2nd ed. New York: Penguin Books.

———. 2009. *The Penguin Atlas of Women in the World*. 4th ed. New York: Penguin Books.

Sen, Gita, and Caren Grown for Development Alternatives with Women for a New Era (DAWN). 1987. *Development, Crises, and Alternative Visions: Third World Women's Perspectives*. New York: Monthly Review Press.

Sen, Jai, and Peter Waterman, eds. 2009. *World Social Forum: Challenging Empires*. Montreal: Black Rose Books.

Sharoni, Simona. 1995. *Gender and the Israeli-Palestinian Conflict: The Politics of Women's Resistance*. Syracuse, NY: Syracuse University Press.

———. 1998. "Gendering Conflict and Peace in Israel/Palestine and the North of Ireland." *Millennium: Journal of International Studies* 27: 1061–1089.

———. 2006. "Compassionate Resistance: A Personal/Political Journey to Israel/Palestine." *International Feminist Journal of Politics* 8(2): 288–299.

Shepherd, Laura J. 2008. *Gender, Violence, and Security*. London: Zed Books.

———. ed. 2010. *Gender Matters in Global Politics: A Feminist Introduction to International Relations*. London: Routledge.

Shiva, Vandana. 2005. *Earth Democracy*. Cambridge, MA: South End Press.

Sjoberg, Laura. 2012. "Toward Trans-Gendering International Relations." *International Political Sociology* 6(4): 337–354.

Sjoberg, Laura, Grace D. Cooke, and Stacy Reiter Neal. 2011. "Introduction: Women, Gender, and Terrorism." In Laura Sjoberg and Caron E. Gentry, eds., *Women, Gender, and Terrorism*, 1–25. Athens: University of Georgia Press.

Sjoberg, Laura, and Caron E. Gentry. 2007. *Mothers, Monsters, Whores: Women's Violence in Global Politics*. London: Zed Books.

———, eds. 2011. *Women, Gender, and Terrorism*. Athens: University of Georgia Press.

Smiley, Tavis, and Cornel West. 2012. *The Rich and the Rest of Us: A Poverty Manifesto*. New York: SmileyBooks.

Smith, Dan. 1997. *The State of War and Peace Atlas*. London: Penguin Books.

Smith, Hilda L., and Berenice A. Carroll. 2000. *Women's Political and Social Thought: An Anthology*. Bloomington: Indiana University Press.

Snyder, Karrie Ann. 2005. "Gender Segregation in the Hidden Labor Force: Looking at the Relationship Between the Formal and Informal Economies." *Gender Realities* 9: 1–27.

Spivak, Gayatri Chakravorty. 1987. *In Other Worlds: Essays in Cultural Politics*. London: Methuen.

———. 1988. "Can the Subaltern Speak?" In Cary Nelson and Lawrence Grossberg, eds., *Marxism and the Interpretation of Culture*, 271–313. Urbana: University of Illinois Press.

———. 1998. "Gender and International Studies." *Millennium: Journal of International Studies* 27(4): 809–831.

———. 1999. *A Critique of Postcolonial Reason: Toward a History of the Vanishing Present*. Cambridge, MA: Harvard University Press.

Squires, Judith. 2007. *The New Politics of Gender Equality*. Basingstoke, UK: Palgrave Macmillan.

Squires, Judith A., and Jutta Weldes. 2007. "Beyond Being Marginal: Gender and International Relations in Britain." *British Journal of Politics and International Relations* 9(2): 185–203.

Staudt, Kathleen. 2008. "Gender, Governance, and Globalization at Borders: Femicide at the US-Mexico Border." In Shirin Rai and Georgina Waylen, eds., *Global Governance: Feminist Perspectives*, 234–253. Basingstoke, UK: Palgrave Macmillan.

Steans, Jill. 2006. *Gender and International Relations*. 2nd ed. New Brunswick, NJ: Rutgers University Press.

Stiehm, Judith Hicks. 1989. *Arms and the Enlisted Woman*. Philadelphia: Temple University Press.

Stienstra, Deborah. 1999. "Of Roots, Leaves, and Trees: Gender, Social Movements, and Global Governance." In Mary K. Meyer and Elisabeth Prügl, eds., *Gender Politics in Global Governance*, 260–272. Lanham, MD: Rowman and Littlefield.

Sudbury, Julia, ed. 2005. *Global Lockdown: Race, Gender, and the Prison-Industrial Complex*. New York: Routledge.

Sutton, Barbara, Sandra Morgen, and Julie Novkov, eds. 2008. *Security Disarmed: Critical Perspectives on Gender, Race, and Militarization*. New Brunswick, NJ: Rutgers University Press.

Swarr, Amanda Lock, and Richa Nagar. 2010. *Critical Transnational Feminist Praxis*. Albany: State University of New York Press.

Sylvester, Christine. 1992. "Feminists and Realists View Autonomy and Obligation in International Relations." In V. Spike Peterson, ed., *Gendered States: Feminist (Re)Visions of International Relations Theory*, 155–178. Boulder, CO: Lynne Rienner.

———. 2002. *Feminist International Relations: An Unfinished Journey.* Cambridge: Cambridge University Press.

Tetreault, Mary Ann, and Ronnie D. Lipschutz. 2005. *Global Politics as if People Mattered.* Lanham, MD: Rowman and Littlefield.

Thames, Frank C., and Margaret S. Williams. 2013. *Contagious Representation: Women's Political Representation in Democracies Around the World.* New York: New York University Press.

Thayer, Millie. 2010. *Making Transnational Feminism: Rural Women, NGO Activists, and Northern Donors in Brazil.* New York: Routledge.

Tickner, J. Ann. 1993. *Gender in International Relations.* New York: Columbia University Press.

———. 2001. *Gendering World Politics: Issues and Approaches in the Post–Cold War Era.* New York: Columbia University Press.

———. 2006. "Feminism Meets International Relations: Some Methodological Issues." In Brooke Ackerly, Maria Stern, and Jacqui True, eds., *Feminist Methodologies for International Relations,* 19–41. Cambridge: Cambridge University Press.

True, Jacqui. 2012. *The Political Economy of Violence Against Women.* Oxford: Oxford University Press.

Truong, Thanh-Dam. 1999. "The Underbelly of the Tiger: Gender and the Demystification of the Asian Miracle." *Review of International Political Economy* 6(2): 133–165.

———. 2000. "A Feminist Perspective on the Asia Miracle and Crisis." *Journal of Human Development* 1(1): 159–164.

United Nations (UN). 1995. *The World's Women 1995: Trends and Statistics.* New York: United Nations.

———. 2000. *The World's Women 2000: Trends and Statistics.* New York: United Nations.

United Nations Development Fund for Women (UNIFEM). 2008. *Progress of the World's Women 2008/2009: Who Answers to Women?* New York: UNIFEM. http://www.unifem.org/progress/2008/media/POWW08_Report_Full_Text.pdf (accessed February 6, 2009).

United Nations Development Programme (UNDP). 1995. *Human Development Report 1995.* New York: Oxford University Press.

———. 1997. *Human Development Report 1997.* New York: Oxford University Press.

United Nations Entity for Gender Equality and the Empowerment of Women (UN Women). 2011. *Progress of the World's Women 2011–2012: In Pursuit of Justice.* New York: UN Women. http://progress.unwomen.org/pdfs/EN-Report-Progress.pdf (accessed May 1, 2013).

United Nations Secretariat Department of Social and Economic Affairs. 2010. *The World's Women 2010: Trends and Statistics.* New York: UN Secretariat Department of Social and Economic Affairs. http://unstats.un.org/unsd/demographic/products/Worldswomen/WW_full%20report_color.pdf (accessed May 1, 2013).

Van Staveren, Irene. 2002. "Global Finance and Gender." In Jan Aart Scholte and Albrecht Schnabel, eds., *Civil Society and Global Finance*, 228–246. London: Routledge.

Vickers, Jean. 1991. *Women and the World Economic Crisis*. London: Zed Books.

Vickers, Jill. 2006. "The Problem with Interests: Making Political Claims for Women." In Louise Chappell and Lisa Hill, eds., *The Politics of Women's Interests*, 5–38. London: Routledge.

Visvanathan, Nalini, Lynn Duggan, Nan Wiegersma, and Laurie Nisonoff, eds. 2011. *The Women, Gender, and Development Reader*, 2nd ed. London: Zed Books.

Wade, Robert H. 2004. "Is Globalization Reducing Poverty and Inequality?" *World Development* 32(4): 567–589.

Waller, Marguerite, and Sylvia Marcos, eds. 2005. *Dialogue and Difference: Feminisms Challenge Globalization*. New York: Palgrave Macmillan.

Weber, Cynthia. 1999. *Faking It: U.S. Hegemony in a "Post-Phallic" Era*. Minneapolis: University of Minnesota Press.

Whitworth, Sandra. 2004. *Men, Militarism, and UN Peacekeeping: A Gendered Analysis*. Boulder, CO: Lynne Rienner.

———. 2008. "Militarized Masculinity and Post-Traumatic Stress Disorder." In Jane L. Parpart and Marysia Zalewski, eds., *Rethinking the Man Question: Sex, Gender, and Violence in International Relations*, 109–126. London: Zed Books.

Woehl, Stephanie. 2008. "Global Governance as Neoliberal Governmentality: Gender Mainstreaming in the European Employment Strategy." In Shrin Rai and Georgina Waylen, eds., *Gender and Global Governance: Feminist Perspectives*, 64–83. Basingstoke, UK: Palgrave Macmillan.

Women's Environment and Development Organization (WEDO). 2007. "Changing the Climate: Why Women's Perspectives Matter" (Factsheet). http://www.awid.org/eng/Issues-and-Analysis/Library/Changing-the-Climate-Why-Women-s-Perspectives-Matter (accessed February 5, 2009).

———. 2008. "Women: Essential to Climate Change Solutions" (Factsheet). https://www.wedo.org/wp-content/uploads/wdaccmediafactsheet.pdf (accessed March 17, 2009).

World Council of Churches (WCC). 2005. *World Military Expenditures: A Compilation of Data and Facts Related to Military Spending, Education, and Health*. Geneva: WCC Coordination Office for the Decade to Overcome Violence. http://overcomingviolence.org/fileadmin/dov/files/wcc_resources/dov_documents/MilitarySpendingReport.pdf (accessed February 8, 2009).

*World Development*. 1995. Special Issue: Gender, Adjustment, and Macroeconomics. 23(11): 1825–2017.

———. 2000. Special Issue: Growth, Trade, Finance, and Gender Inequality. 28(7): 1145–1390.

Wright, Melissa. 2006. *Disposable Women and Other Myths of Global Capitalism*. New York: Routledge.

Young, Brigitte. 2001. "Globalization and Gender: A European Perspective." In Rita Mae Kelly et al., eds., *Gender, Globalization, and Democratization*, 27–47. Lanham, MD: Rowman and Littlefield.

Youngs, Gillian. 2005. "Ethics of Access: Globalization and the Information Society." *Journal of Global Ethics* 1(1): 69–83.

Yuval-Davis, Nira. 1997. *Gender and Nation*. London: Sage.

———. 2006. "Intersectionality and Feminist Politics." *European Journal of Women's Studies* 13(3): 193–209.

Zalewski, Marysia, and Jane Parpart, eds. 1998. *The "Man" Question in International Relations*. Boulder, CO: Westview Press.

Zine, Jasmin. 2006. "Between Orientalism and Fundamentalism: Muslim Women and Feminist Engagement." In Krista Hunt and Kim Rygiel, eds., *(En)Gendering the War on Terror: War Stories and Camouflaged Politics*, 27–49. Burlington, VT: Ashgate.

Zwingel, Susanne. 2005. "From Intergovernmental Negotiations to (Sub)National Change: A Transnational Perspective on the Impact of CEDAW." *International Feminist Journal of Politics* 7(3): 400–424.

# About the Authors

**Anne Sisson Runyan** is a professor in and a former head of the Department of Women's, Gender, and Sexuality Studies at the University of Cincinnati, where she holds affiliations with political science and the Taft Research Center, which she recently directed. Her books include *Gender and Global Restructuring* (2000, 2011) and *Feminist (Im)Mobilities in Fortress(ing) North America* (2013).

**V. Spike Peterson** is a professor in the Department of Political Science at the University of Arizona, where she holds courtesy affiliations in women's studies, the Institute for LGBT Studies, and international studies. Her books include *Gendered States* (1992) and *A Critical Rewriting of Global Political Economy* (2003). Index

# Index

Abortion, 230, 231, 250
Abu Ghraib prison, 155, 157
Ackerly, Brooke, 256
Afghanistan, 87, 153, 163, 169, 175
Africa, 226, 231
Agamben, Giorgio, 94, 225
Agathangelou, Anna, 258
Agustín, Laura Maria, 212
Alvarez, Sonia, 243
*American Winter* (documentary), 196
Amnesty International, 168
Andersen, Margaret, 47
Anderson, Bridget, 210
Androcentrism, 61–62, 82–83
Antiglobalization movement, 244–245
Antrobus, Peggy, 130
Arab Spring, 123, 246–247
Argentinian Mothers of the Plaza de
    Mayo, 254
Aristotle, 84
Arlie R. Hochschild, 210, 214
Arms, global dealers in, 168
Asia
    antiglobalization movement, 244
    food insecurity, 190–191
    gendered division of labor, 188
    global governance, 99, 105, 107,
        123, 153

herbicides, 229
Occupy movements, 247
sex industry, 165, 211, 213
toxic waste, 236n25
women in vulnerable employment,
    128–129

Bachelet, Michelle, 118
Bakker, Isabella, 91
Bedford, Kate, 192
Beijing Platform for Action (BPA), 22,
    23, 105, 121, 130
Belief systems, 50, 56, 69
Belkin, Aaron, 161
Binary sex differentiation, 35, 56–58,
    64, 70–71
Binary thinking, 44–46
Biological determinism, 48
Biopower, 38
Birth defects, 229
Boserup, Esther, 186
Bosnia-Herzegovina, 165, 168
Brazil, 245, 252
Brenner, Johanna, 245
Brittan, Arthur, 7
Burundi, 166
Bush, George W., 12, 28, 38, 87, 175,
    176, 230, 260

Capitalism
  climate, 185
  disaster, 184–185, 222
  global, 176, 198, 220–221, 246, 269
  industrial, 26, 48, 188, 189, 221
  neoliberal, 78, 88, 90, 193, 199, 266, 267
  poverty, 184, 218
Caribbean, 231
Catholic Church, 245
CEDAW (Convention on the Elimination of All Forms of Discrimination Against Women), 24, 121, 135, 136, 249–251
Chan-Tiberghien, Jennifer, 134–135
Children
  with ambiguous sexuality, 2
  child care, 60, 83–84, 89, 90, 149, 202, 208, 209, 223
  child soldiers, 23, 167, 168
  domestic violence and, 151, 158, 261
  labor by, 189, 208
  mortality rates of, 230
  poverty of, 10, 191, 228, 230
  as prostitutes, 164, 211, 213
  rape and, 167
  socialization of, 41–42, 58, 111–112, 201–202
  structural adjustment policies and, 195
Chile, 250
China, 196, 224
Chipko women's movement, 255
Civil society, 238–239
Civil wars, 12
Classism, 14, 30, 63, 85, 222, 262
Clausewitz, Carl von, 140
Climate capitalism, 185

Clinton, Bill, 229
Clinton, Hillary, 169
Coalition, politics of, 240
Cockburn, Cynthia, 263, 264
Cohn, Carol, 251, 252
Colonialism
  development and, 219
  effects of, 83, 84, 189, 210
  ethnic cleansing and, 12
  justification of, 84, 86
  peacekeeping as, 172–173
  racialization of nature, 225
Community Redevelopment Carbon Fund, 224
Compassionate authority, 260
Compassionate resistance, 262–263
Conceptual Hierarchical Dichotomies produced by the Power of Gender, 47 (table)
Conformity, 50–51
Constructivist lenses, 65–66
Consumption, politics of, 219–221
Contraceptives, 230, 231
Council for Equality, 250
Crisis of Insecurity, 13, 85–88, 139, 141 (table), 177, 262
Crisis of Representation, 12, 16, 84–85, 101, 102 (table), 134, 137
Crisis of Sustainability, 13, 91, 182, 183 (table), 265, 267
Cyberfeminism, 246, 253

Dahl, Robert, 100
Dahlerup, Drude, 21, 122
Deindustrialization, 205
Democracy
  Earth Democracy, 233–234, 253
  gender equality and, 122

global capitalism and, 176–177, 198
in military, 152, 155
undermining of, 84
Democratic Republic of Congo, 166, 251
Deregulation, 12, 26, 89, 193–194, 197, 215, 232
Desertification, 226
Development, 190–193, 219, 266
Dichotomies
gender, 5–6, 58–59, 71–72, 161, 174
heteronormative, 58–59
hierarchical, 47 (table)
as lenses, 44–45
local *vs.* global, 243–244
normalization of, 72
social relations and, 45–46
stereotypes, ideologies, and, 49–54
universalist *vs.* particularist, 242
Western thought and, 46–47
Dichotomized thinking, 70, 72–73, 95n1
Direct violence, 140–141, 144–145, 149, 162
Disaster capitalism, 184–185, 222
Disposability, 94–95, 225, 233
Domestic violence, 164, 245, 261
Domestic work, 208–210
Double boomerang effect, 251

Earth Democracy, 233, 253
Economy, global
effect of on women, 29
feminist approaches to, 185–188
financial crisis of 2008, 12
homework and, 207
private life and, 192

repositionings of women and men, 32, 181–183, 185
restructuring of, 200
specialization, promotion of, 194
study of, 91
women, role of in, 109
Education, of girls, 9
Ehrenreich, Barbara, 210, 214
Eisenstein, Zillah, 86, 147, 155, 158
El Salvador, 251
Elites, 35, 69, 89
Elshtain, Jean Bethke, 151
Empire, 37, 176–177, 225, 264
Employment. *See* Labor
Empowerment of Women (UN Women), 105
English, as hegemonic language, 248
Enloe, Cynthia, 148, 152, 159, 164
Epistemology, 67
Equity, crisis of, 84
Eschle, Catherine, 242, 244, 245
Essentialism, 16, 35, 78, 144, 178, 240, 260
Ethnicity. *See* Race
Eurocentrism, defined, 37
European Union, 195
Eurozone, 195

Fall, Yassine, 194
Faludi, Susan, 28, 146, 147, 151
Family planning services, 230
Femininity
assignment of to enemy groups, 87, 96–97n15
devalorization of, 6, 18 (table), 19, 62–64, 185–186
governance and, 117
idealized forms of, 30, 58, 86–87

Femininity (*continued*)
  labor patterns and stereotypes of,
    89–90
  masculinist violence and, 76–77
  militarized, 171–172
  romanticization of, 62, 73
  traditional manifestations of, 149
  variablility of, 3–5, 15
Feminism
  cultural and ethnic, 240
  cyberfeminism, 246, 253
  decolonial, 256–257, 268
  (de)militarizing, 173–177
  gaga, 240, 254, 271n6
  gender dichotomy and, 71
  gendered shifts in work and,
    215
  global political economy and,
    185–188
  imperial, 176
  international relations (IR) inquiry
    of, 9, 13–14, 17–21, 34–35,
    74–75, 78, 80–81, 142, 256, 258,
    263–264
  lenses of, 66, 73–81, 76 (table)
  liberal, 76
  Marxist, 240, 245
  microfinance and, 218–219
  movements, debates in, 239–248
  neoliberalism and, 232–234
  NGOs and, 243–246
  political theorizing, 103
  postcolonial, 78, 131, 134, 143, 268
  poststructural, 76, 78, 146
  radical, 76–77
  resistance projects of, 248–255, 249
    (table)
  security and, 142–146

  socialist, 76
  solidarity model of, 246
  structural adjustment programs,
    research on, 195
  transnational *vs.* global, 243–244
  women in military and, 155
Feminist-as-explorer model, 242
Feminist-as-tourist model, 241–242
Feminist Lenses for Intersectional and
    Transnational Theorizing: Both
    in Relation and in Tension, 76
    (figure)
Feminist Majority Foundation, 175
Feminization anxiety, 87, 96n13
Femocrats, 124, 125, 132, 243, 250
Financial crisis of 2008, global effects
    of, 12, 26, 91
Financialization, gendered, 215–221
Finland, 250
Flexibilization, 205–206
Food-fuel-water crisis, 226
Food insecurity, 128, 190–191,
    226
Food production, women's role in,
    188–191
Foucault, Michel, 131

GAD (gender and development)
    research, 187
Gays/lesbians
  development assistance for, 193
  discrimination, 136, 235n14
  femininity and, 4
  global gay tourism, 214, 235n19
  heads of government, 136
  homophobia, 79, 175, 176
  identity politics and, 240
  in militaries, 152, 155

violence and, 163
*See also* Sexual minorities
Gender
  appellations and metaphors, 7
  coding, 55
  defined, 2–3, 35
  dichotomies, 5–6, 58–59, 71–72, 174
  explanation of, 31–32
  gender-appropriate behaviors, 6, 57
  gender inquiry in international relations, 17–21
  gender-neutrality, 59–60
  global crises and, 11–17
  global issues and, 8–11
  hierarchy, 6, 27, 63, 71, 73, 76, 85, 120, 143
  identities, nonnormative, 136
  identity, 57, 60–61
  in international policymaking, 21–24
  intersectional study of, 2–5
  as lens on world politics, 5–8
  mainstreaming, 11, 22–23, 126
  as ordering power, 56–62
  polarization of, 58
  power of, 7–8, 29–30, 33–34, 39–40, 47 (table), 182, 267–270
  quotas, 11, 21–22, 106–107, 109, 111, 122–124, 127
  repositioning of in global policymaking, 21, 33
  socialization, 56–58
  stereotypes, 3, 13–14, 182, 185, 188, 206, 209, 219, 220
  third gender, 4
  universalization of, 241
  violence, 163–168

Gender Empowerment Measure, 126
Gender equality
  democratization and, 122
  global paradox of, 1, 13, 17, 39
  global warming and, 224–225
  IGOs and, 9, 11–12, 16, 33, 132, 135, 224
  indices of, 126–127
  institutionalizing, 121–131
  market-based economies and, 122
  as modern economic efficiency, 132
  NGOs and, 9
  relationship to quality of life, 20–21
  rethinking of, 74
  in United States, 127
  *See also* Financialization; Labor; Power; Resources; Security; Violence
Gender Inequality Index, 126
Gender quotas, 11, 21–22, 106–107, 109, 111, 122–124, 127
Gender-Related Development Index, 126
Gendered, defined, 35
Gendered division of labor, 182, 185, 188
Gendered division of power, 182
Gendered division of resources, 182
Gendered Divisions of Labor and Resources productive of the Crisis of Sustainability, 183 (table)
Gendered Divisions of Power productive of the Crisis of Representation, 102 (table)

Gendered Divisions of Resistance to and produced by Governmentality, Militarization, and Neoliberalism, 249 (table)

Gendered Divisions of Violence productive of the Crisis of Insecurity, 141 (table)

Gendered nationalism, 142, 262

General Agreement on Tariffs and Trade, 227

Genocide, 28, 109, 156, 158, 167, 169, 170

Gentry, Caron, 156, 157

Ghosh, Nandita, 225

Gill, Stephen, 91

Global, explanation of term, 30–31

Global crises. *See* Insecurity, crisis of; Representation, crisis of; Sustainability, crisis of

Global Gender Gap Index, 110

Global governance, defined, 99

Global North
care deficit in, 203
consumption patterns in, 267
defined, 37
exportation of toxic refuse to South by, 229, 236n25
masculinization of, 18 (table)
military spending in, 168
neoliberalism in, 26, 37–38, 88–89, 193
restructuring, effects of on, 197
undocumented workers in, 203

Global Political Economy (GPE), 39, 181, 184–188, 192–193, 201–203, 233–234

Global South
acceptance of toxic refuse by, 228
access to Internet in, 248
defined, 37
divisions of labor in, 89
economic shocks in, 129–130
effects of war in, 140
female activism in, 187
feminization of, 18 (table)
gender violence in, 168
global gay tourism in, 214
homophobia in, 175, 176
masculinism, 28–29
migration of women from, 202–203
military spending in, 167–168
neoliberalism and, 26, 37–38
news media and, 118
peacekeeping operations in, 173
poverty abatement in, 184
purchase of arms by, 168
restructuring, effects of on, 197
women in, 11, 78, 94, 105, 227, 230, 231–232, 266

Global warming, 26, 221, 224

Globalization
environmental effects of, 221–222, 225, 227–228, 233
informalization of work and, 204–207, 215
masculinization of, 28–29, 160–161
microfinance and, 217
neoliberal, 26, 88, 187, 193–200
social effects of, 78, 113–114, 130, 182, 185

Goetz, Anne Marie, 218

Goldstein, Joshua, 162, 167

Governmentality, neoliberal
defined, 37, 131
environmental crises and, 225
gender equality and, 132–133

global capitalism and, 26, 37–38, 131, 160, 176, 181
  NGOs and, 131–132
  resistance to, 132, 248–255, 249 (table), 253
  results of, 131–132
Greece, 247
Green Belt Movement, Kenya, 223–224
Green-washing, 230
Greenham Common, Britain, 254
Grown, Caren, 189, 226
Guantánamo Bay military prison, 38n1, 156
Gupta, Rina Sen, 218

Halberstam, J. Jack, 254
*Half the Sky: Turning Oppression into Opportunity for Women Worldwide* (Kristof and WuDunn), 9–11, 184, 212–213
Hanochi, Seiko, 213
Harcourt, Wendy, 253
Harding, Sandra, 69
Hawkesworth, Mary, 248
Health care, 94, 114, 196, 223, 231
Hegemonic masculinity, 3–4
Herbicides, 229
Heteronormative patriarchy, 36
Heteronormativity, 35, 58
Heteropatriarchy, 192–193, 211
Heterosexism, 35, 53 (box), 56, 58, 77, 120, 244, 262
Hierarchies, institutionalized, 54
HIV/AIDS, 135, 164–165, 168, 170, 219, 231
Hobbs, Thomas, 83

Homework (home-based production), 207–208, 235n18
Homonormativity, 36
Homophobia, 79, 175, 176
Hoogensen, Gunhild, 104, 106
Hooper, Charlotte, 28, 160
*Human Development Report,* United Nations Development Programme, 126
Human Rights Watch, 168
Hurricane Katrina, 222, 223

Identity, politics of, 240
Ideologies
  defined, 47
  dichotomies, stereotypes, and, 49–54
  Eurocentrism, 37
  fundamentalism, 27
  gender, 29
  heteronormative, 56
  in intersectional gender analysis, 31 (figure)
  masculinism, 6, 8, 73
  militarism, 27
  purpose of, 48
  *See also* Feminism; Neoliberalism
IGOs (intergovernmental organizations)
  financial matters and, 216
  gender equality and, 9, 11–12, 16–17, 33, 132
  gender inequality-environmental crisis linkage, 224
  gender inequality *vs.* race inequality, 135
  gender mainstreaming by, 125–126
  global governance and, 99

IGOs (*continued*)
    relationship with NGOs, 243
    women's issues and, 135
    women's representation in, 19,
      107–109
    women's security and, 178
Illuminating Invisible Privilege, 52–53
    (box)
ILO Domestic Workers Convention,
    210
(Im)migrant labor, 202–204, 235n14
Imperial(ist) impulse, 38
India, 255
Indignados, 247
Industrial capitalism, 26, 48, 188, 189,
    221
Industrialization, consequences of,
    189–190
Information and Communications
    Technologies (ICTs), 44, 205,
    211, 214, 253–254
Insecurity, crisis of, 13, 85–88, 139,
    141 (table), 177, 262
Inter-Parliamentary Union, 105
International Convention on the
    Elimination of All Forms of
    Racial Discrimination, 135
International Convention on the
    Protection of the Rights of all
    Migrant Workers and Members
    of Their Families, 204
International Court of Justice, 108
International Criminal Court,
    108–109
International Criminal Tribunal, 158
International Gay and Lesbian Human
    Rights Commission, 136
International Justice Mission, 212

International Labour Organization
    (ILO), 206
International Lesbian, Gay, Bisexual,
    Trans, and Intersex Association,
    136
International Monetary Fund (IMF),
    109, 194
International relations (IR)
    feminist definition of, 18–19
    feminist inquiry, 9, 13–14, 17–21,
      34–35, 74–75, 78, 80–81, 142,
      256, 258, 263–264
    traditional theory, 65–67, 70,
      91–92, 99–100, 140, 144–145,
      147, 238–239
International Trade Center, 109
International Women's Rights Action
    Watch, 250
Internet, 197, 211, 246–248, 253–254
Intersectional analysis, 14–16, 31
    (figure)
Iran, 175
Iraq, 87, 153, 159, 251
Ireland, 174
Irvine, Jill, 251
Israel, 152, 156
Israeli-Palestinian conflict, 174, 263
Issues, explanation of term, 32

Jeffords, Susan, 27
Johnson, Allan, 50, 51
Jones, David, 148
Jones, Kathleen, 260

Keck, Margaret, 110
Kenya, 223
Klein, Naomi, 221, 222
Kosovo, 251

Kristof, Nicholas D., 8
Kyoto Protocol, 224

Labor
    crisis of sustainability and, 182, 183
      (table)
    degendering, 264–267
    domestic, 208–210
    feminization of, 90, 191–192
    flexibilization of, 89
    gendered divisions of, 88–92,
      115–116, 182, 188–189
    (im)migrant, 202–204, 235n14
    informalization of, 204–207,
      235n16
    international sex work, 210–215,
      235n19, 271n5
    reproductive, 201–202
    sex/affective production and, 95n4
Lady Gaga, 254
LaGarde, Christine, 109
Land ownership, 22, 189–190,
    223–227
Latin America, 253
Leatherman, Janie, 166
Lenses
    acquisition of, 41–42
    dichotomies of, 44–47
    (Neo-)Marxist, 65
    (neo)liberal, 65
    positivist, 67–68
    postcolonial, 65, 70, 81
    postpositivist, 67–69, 70
    poststructural, 66, 70, 77–78,
      81
    purpose of, 40–41
    stereotypes as, 42–44
    types of, 65–66

Lesbians. *See* Gays/lesbians
LGBTQ, 36, 87, 136, 211
Liberalization, defined, 193
Liberia, 251
Ling, L. H. M., 258
Lipshutz, Ronnie, 137
Local *vs.* global dichotomy,
    243–244
Lorde, Audre, 246
Lugones, Maria, 256
Lynch, Jessica, 146
*Lysistrata* (play), 141

Maathai, Wangari, 224
Maiguascha, Bice, 244
Market fundamentalism, 37
Marketization of all life, 37
Marxism, 76, 245
Masculinism
    globalization and, 28–29, 160–161
    justification of male domination, 7,
      27–28
    media and academic studies and,
      96n8
    politics and, 82–85
Masculinity
    aggression and, 158
    idealized forms of, 30
    militarized, 159–163
    models of, 85–86, 261
    overvaluing of, 19
    privileging of, 6–7, 14, 51, 52–53
      (box), 62–63
    variability of, 3–5
    war and, 143, 264
    Western hegemonic, 160
Masculinization, 6, 27–28, 87,
    146–147

Masculinization as Valorization and Feminization as Devalorization, 18 (table)

Masters, Cristina, 162

McIntosh, Peggy, 51

Mendoza, Breny, 244

Meta-lenses, 19, 65

Microfinance, 217–219

Migration/immigration, 204, 235n14

Militaries
  adding women to, 261–262
  democratization of, 152, 155
  domestic violence in, 164
  functions of, 158–159
  gender dichotomies of, 161
  manhood and, 160–161
  as polluters, 229
  spending by, 25–26, 88, 130, 143, 167–168

Militarization, global, 88, 176

Militarized
  masculinity, 159–163
  prostitution, 164–165, 179n8, 211
  rape, 153, 164–165
  violence, 87, 145

Military sexual trauma (MST), 164

Millennium Development Goals, 127–129

Moghadam, Valentine, 110

Mohanty, Chandra, 241, 242, 246

Monsanto, 228

Montagu, Ashley, 85

Moon, Katherine, 165


Nagar, Richa, 253

National Adaptation Programmes of Action, 224

Nationalism, gendered, 142, 262

Nature, marketization of, 224–225

Necropolitics, 236n23

Nelson, Mariah, 85

(Neo-)Marxist lenses, 65

Neoclassical economic theory, 91

Neocolonialism, 37, 168, 172, 187, 189, 202, 212, 252, 263, 269

Neoconservativism, 26–27

Neoimperial rule, 37

(Neo)liberal lenses, 67

Neoliberalism
  business interests, domination by, 197–200
  capitalist, 78, 88, 90, 193, 266, 267
  defined, 26, 37
  as economic strategy, 91
  media giants and, 197
  as promoter of democracy, 91
  resistance to, 239–248, 254–255
  *See also* Globalization; Governmentality

(Neo)realist lenses, 65, 67

News media, 49, 55, 59, 85, 96n8, 106, 118, 119, 197–199, 221

NGO Forum, 135

NGOs (nongovernmental organizations)
  as advocate for women's rights, 24
  CEDAW and, 135
  celebrity-driven development and, 219–220
  crisis of representation and, 12, 134
  cyberfeminism and, 253
  evangelical, 212–213
  feminist, 243–246
  gender equality and, 9, 16–17
  gender mainstreaming and, 125–126

IGOs and, 243
NGO-ization, 243
as part of global civil society, 239
participation of women in, 110
peace and human rights and, 166
reproductive rights and, 250
sexual orientation discrimination
and, 136
universalism of, 243
women's security and, 168
Nyiramasuhuko, Pauline, 158

Obama, Barack, 38, 108, 136, 162
Occupy Wall Street movement, 247
Office of Global Women's Issues, US
State Department, 108
Ontology, 67
Organization for Economic
Cooperation and Development,
123
Orientalism (or Occidentalism), 37
"Othering," 62–64, 72, 78, 83, 86, 95,
101, 134, 147, 177, 237, 259, 261,
262, 264

Pakistan, 156
Palestinian-Israeli conflict, 174, 263
Paths of least resistance, 50, 54, 259,
261
Peacekeeping, 171–173
Pettman, Jan Jindy, 213
Philanthrocapitalism, 219
Platform for Action, UN Fourth
World Conference on Women
(1995), 22, 121, 168
Plavšić, Biljana, 158
Poland, 156
Policy agencies, women's, 124–125

Politics
coalition, 240
of consumption, 219–221
degendering, 255–270
feminist approaches to, 102–104,
134
feminist resistance, 238–255
identity, 240
imperial global gay, 176
masculinism and, 82–85
power and, 82–85
of recognition, 240
of redistribution, 240
stereotypes and, 71, 112, 114–120
valorization of feminine traits,
103–104
*See also* Repositionings of women
and men; Women, governance
and
Post-traumatic stress disorder (PTSD),
161–162, 163
Postcapitalist practices, 255
Postcolonialism
dichotomies and, 70
feminist, 77, 78, 131, 134, 143, 187,
243–244, 258, 268
lenses of, 65, 71, 81
Poverty
abatement of, 184, 190, 217–219
capitalism, 184, 218
crisis of insecurity and, 13
developmental agencies and,
191–193
females and, 168
feminization of, 208
gendered divisions of labor and, 89
in global South, 230
militarized violence and, 143

Poverty (*continued*)

    Millennium Development Goals and, 128

    patriarchal authority and, 10

    in Philippines, 164

    stereotypes of, 43

    time poverty, 113

    World Bank and, 130

Poverty capitalism, 184, 218

Power

    conventional definition of, 100

    degendering, 257–260

    enabling, 258

    feminist conception of, 111

    gendered divisions of, 84, 101, 102 (table)

    politics and, 82–85

    *See also* Power of Gender

Power of Gender, 7–8, 29–30, 33–34, 39–40, 47 (table), 182, 267–270

Power-over, 100, 103, 158, 257

Power-with/power-to, 103, 111

Prison-industrial complex, 159

Privatization, 194, 232

Privilege, 6–7, 14, 51, 52–53 (box), 54, 62–63

Progress of the World's Women report 2008/2009 and 2011/2012, 105

Prostitution, 164–165, 179n8, 210–215, 211, 235n19, 271n5

Protocol to Prevent, Suppress, and Punish the Trafficking of Persons, 212

PTSD. *See* Post-traumatic stress disorder

Pussy Riot, 254

Putin, Vladimir, 254

Queer/queering, 36, 66, 78–79, 240, 263

Quotas, gender, 11, 21–22, 106–107, 109, 111, 122–124, 127

Race

    CEDAW and, 135

    colonization and, 12, 189

    divisions of labor and, 116

    feminism and, 78, 240, 242

    fundamentalisms, 27–28

    gender and, 7

    identity and, 268

    inequalities and, 13, 245

    masculinism and, 62

    migrations and, 183, 203–204

    military service and, 116

    political participation and, 114–116, 122, 136

    power and, 100

    privilege and, 83, 182

    resources and, 94

    social Darwinism and, 48

    socialization and, 50, 65, 112, 201

    stereotypes, 43, 220

    structural adjustment programs and, 195

    violence and, 163, 166

Racial profiling, 148

Racialization, 15, 36–37

Racism

    discrimination, 120

    exploitation of women and, 78

    feminization of, 64, 222

    global crises and, 232

    intersectional gender analysis and, 30

militarism and, 262
privilege and, 14
stereotypes, 210
struggles against, 85
UN World Conference Against
Racism, 135
Racist hierarchy, 210, 213
Randall, Vicky, 119
Rape
firestick, 226
genocidal, 165–166
military, 24, 153, 164–167, 170
prosecution for, 170–171
Rayner, Richard, 165
Reactive autonomy, 258–259,
261–262
Reagan, Ronald, 27
Reagon, Bernice Johnson, 246
Rebick, Judy, 247
Recognition, politics of, 240
Redistribution, politics of, 240
Refugees/displaced people, 137
Relational autonomy, 258–259, 262
Religious belief systems, 114–115
Religious fundamentalisms, 27
Remasculinization, 25–30, 87,
146–147
Repositionings of women and men,
2, 17–24, 29–30, 32–33, 39, 100,
181–183, 185, 237, 268
Representation, crisis of, 12, 16,
84–85, 101, 102 (table), 134, 137
Reproductive labor, 201–202
Reproductive rights, 245
Resistance to neoliberal politics,
239–248, 254–255
Resources
degendering, 264–267

depletion of, 226–228
destruction of, 228–230
dichotomies of, 225
divisions of, 93, 182, 223–232
ecological, 94–95
gendered, 221–222
masculinist lenses and, 93–95
poor women and, 223–224
women as, 230–232, 266
*See also* Sustainability, crisis of
Revolutionary Association of Women
in Afghanistan, 175
*Roger and Me* (film), 196
Rome Statute of the International
Criminal Court, 170, 171
Roy, Arundhati, 177
Runaway norms, 166–167
Russo, Ann, 175
Rwanda, 105, 134, 158, 166, 168, 170,
251

Same-sex relations, illegality of, 136
Seager, Joni, 229
Security
defined, 83
disarming, 177–178
gendered, 144–148
myth, 178, 264
redefinitions of, 145
*See also* Insecurity, crisis of
Security-industrial complex, 159
Sen, Gita, 189, 226
Sequestration, 196
Serbia, 158
SERNAM (Servicio Nacional de la
Mujer), 250
Service Women's Action Network, 154
Sex, defined, 2

Sex workers, international, 210–215, 235n19, 271n5

Sexism, 30, 84, 120, 222, 239, 244, 262

Sexual harassment and assault, 153–154

Sexual minorities
defined, 35–36
discrimination against, 136, 235n14
invisibility of, 79
rights of, 245

Sexualization, 15, 36

Sharoni, Simona, 174, 262

Shiva, Vandana, 228, 233

Shock doctrine, 195, 225

Sierra Leone, 166, 171

Sigurdardottir, Johanna, 136

Sikkink, Karen, 110

Sjoberg, Laura, 156, 157, 263

Social Darwinism, 48

Social media, 246–248, 253–254

Social movements
coalitions, 244–246
debates about, 239–248
NGO-ization of, 243
Occupy Wall Street movement, 247
as rescue missions, 241
social media, use of by, 246–248, 253–254
women and, 238–239

Social relations, dichotomies and, 45–46

Social reproduction, crisis of, 91

Socialization
biological reproduction, 56
childhood, 41–42, 50, 58, 111–112, 201–202
gender, 56–58

Solheim, Bruce, 104, 106

South Africa, 152

South Korea, 165, 179n8

Spain, 247

Specialization, in economic activities, 194

Spivak, Gayatri, 86, 178, 218

Squires, Judith, 135

Stabilization policies, 194

Status of Forces Agreements (SOFAs), 164–165

Stereotypes
conformity to, 60–61
dichotomies, ideologies, and, 48–54
gender, 3, 13–14, 182, 185, 188, 206, 209, 219, 220
gender socialization and, 58
as lenses, 8, 42–44
of masculinity and femininity, 59, 74, 85
omnipresence of, 62
politics and, 71, 112, 114–120
racist, 210
sexual, 211, 213, 214
of women, 13–14, 88–90, 100–101, 113, 150, 158, 269

Stiehm, Judith Hicks, 173

Stockholm International Peace Research Institute, 25

Strauss-Kahn, Dominique, 109

Strong objectivity, 69–70

Structural adjustment programs (SAPs), 194–195

Structural violence, 26, 88, 167–168

Subic Bay Naval Base, Philippines, 164–165

Sudan, 169, 226

Sustainability, crisis of, 13, 91, 182, 183 (table), 265, 267

Swarr, Amanda Lock, 253
Sweatshops, 208
Sylvester, Christine, 258, 266

*The Terror Dream* (Faludi), 146
Terrorism, 9–10, 12, 38, 157
Terrorist attacks of 9/11, effects of, 21,
    25, 27, 48, 87, 145–146, 159, 160,
    164, 167–168, 174–175, 203, 255
Tetreault, Mary Ann, 137
Thames, Frank, 106
Thatcher, Margaret, 118
Thayer, Millie, 252
*The Invisible War* (documentary), 153
Tickner, Ann, 80, 145
Toxic waste, 228–229, 236n25
Trade-Related Intellectual Property
    Rights, 227–228
Trafficking, human, 212–214, 236n20
Transgender, 66, 78–79, 263
Transnational corporations,
    subordination of women and,
    11
Transnational feminist networks
    (TFNs), 110
Tree-planting, 223–224
"Trickle-down" economic theory,
    91–92
True, Jacqui, 204, 256

UNIFEM (UN Development Fund for
    Women), 105–106, 108, 133, 135,
    169, 230
United Nations
    CEDAW (Convention on the
    Elimination of All Forms of
    Discrimination Against Women),
    121, 135, 249–251

Decade for Women, 9, 110, 168,
    224
Economic and Social Council, 21
Entity for Gender Equality, 105
Environment Program, 224
Environmental Summit, 224
Fourth World Conference on
    Women (1995), 22, 121, 168
Framework Convention on Climate
    Change, 224
High Commission on Refugees,
    137
Human Rights Council, 136
International Labour Organization
    (ILO), 206
Millennium Development Goals,
    105
Protocol to Prevent, Suppress, and
    Punish the Trafficking of Persons,
    212
Security Council Resolution 1325,
    23, 169, 170, 171, 251–252
Security Council Resolutions 1820,
    1888, 1889, 1860, 1983, 170
System-Wide Action Plan (UN-
    SWAP), 108
UN Development Fund for Women
    (UNIFEM), 105–106, 108, 133,
    135, 169, 230
UN Development Programme, 126
UN Women, 25, 105, 108, 127
World Conference Against Racism,
    135
United Nations, women on
    professional staff of, 107–108
United States
    austerity policies of, 195
    biopower and, 38

United States (*continued*)
    enfranchisement of African
        American men, 15
    gender equality in, 127
    gender quotas, 123
    global capitalism and, 176
    herbicides, spraying of, 229
    Kyoto Protocol and, 224
    militarized rape, 164–165
    military as path to power in, 116
    military spending of, 25, 168
    ratification of CEDAW, 24, 121, 136
    remasculinization of, 27–28, 87,
        146–147
    Rome Statute of the International
        Criminal Court and, 171
    September 11, 2001 attacks on, 12
    support for nonnormative sexual
        and gender identities, 136
    "war on terror," 12, 25, 38, 87, 88,
        145, 175, 176
    women in government, 105
    women in military, 151–155
Universalism, 16, 35, 70, 77, 78, 81,
    134, 241, 242, 243
Universalist *vs.* particularist
    dichotomy, 242
US Institute for Women's Policy
    Research, 223

Venereal disease, 165
Verveer, Melanie, 169
Violence
    degendering, 260–264
    direct, 140–141, 144–145, 149,
        162
    domestic, 164, 245, 261
    gender, 163–168
    gendered divisions of, 140–141,
        149–151, 156, 171, 173
    international-domestic relationship
        of, 143, 261
    militarized, 87, 145
    political, 155–158, 174
    sexual, 170
    structural, 26, 88, 167–168
    women as perpetrators of,
        157–158
    *See also* Rape

Walmartization, 196
War
    changing nature of, 166
    civil wars, 12
    civilians in, 23
    justification for, 87, 140
    logic of, 147–148
    masculinity and, 143, 264
    as men's business, 149
    technologicalization of, 162
    traditional roles of women in,
        150–151
    "war on terror," 12, 25, 38, 87, 88,
        145, 175, 176
Weber, Cynthia, 263
Western-centrism, defined, 37
"Where are the women?," 19, 73, 75,
    77, 102, 267
White, defined, 36
White/Anglo privilege, 52 (box)
Whitworth, Sandra, 160, 172
WID (women in development)
    research, 186
Williams, Margaret, 106

Women
  addition of to existing paradigms, 77, 186–187, 259, 264–265, 268–270
  denigration of women's work, 91
  dual nature of, 156–157
  economic development and, 129, 171
  economy, effect of on, 29
  as engines of economic growth, 10
  environmental degradation and, 94
  as farmers, 188–190, 226, 227
  financial institutions, representation in, 216–217
  food production, role of in, 188–191, 226
  global business, representation in, 109
  global crises *vs.* empowerment, 10, 13
  increased demands on, 90–91, 94
  industrial toxins, susceptibility to, 229
  intergovernmental organizations (IGOs), participation in, 19, 107–109
  as justification for war, 86–87, 97n16
  land ownership and, 22, 189–190, 223–227
  microfinance and, 217–219
  nongovernmental organizations (NGOs), participation in, 110
  as peacemakers, 142, 178, 252
  as perpetrators of violence, 157–158
  physical strength of, 85
  political violence by, 155–158, 174
  presence in news media, 27, 248
  on professional staff of United Nations, 107–108
  repositioning of in work force, 89
  rights, recognition of, 24
  security of, 168, 178
  social movements and, 238–239
  terrorism and, 9–10, 157–158, 174
  traditional wartime roles of, 150–151
  universalist categorizations of, 134–135
  vulnerability of in disasters, 223
  war and militarization, effect of on, 168
  world affairs, role of in, 19–20
  *See also* Repositionings of women and men; Stereotypes, of women
Women, governance and
  gender conformity of in positions of power, 117–119
  gender socialization, 111–112
  as global market and NGO actors, 109–111
  institutional impediments to, 119–120
  legal barriers to, 116
  lobbying and policy groups, 108
  militaries, exclusion from, 116–117
  national cabinets, percentage in, 106–107
  national legislatures, proportion of in, 105
  peace negotiations, presence at, 23, 170–171
  policy agencies of, 124–125

Women, governance and
  gender conformity of in positions
    of power (*continued*)
  political action, interest in, 111
  political power, exclusion from, 83
  in politics, 133
  religious beliefs and, 114–115
  situational constraints of, 112–114
  as state and national leaders,
    104–107
  structural obstacles to, 114–119
  as United Nations and other IGO
    officials, 105, 107–109
  as world leaders, 21
Women, in military
  discrimination against, 152–153,
    155
  feminist view of, 155
  history of, 142
  as mark of modernity, 151
  sexual harassment and assault,
    153–154, 157
*Women, War & Peace* (documentary
  series), 169
Women in Black, 254
Women in Politics map (2012),
  106–107
Women trees, 236n24
*Women Warriors: A History* (Jones),
  148
Women worthies, 102–103
"Womenandchildren," 118, 140

Women's Environment and
  Development Organization, 223
Women's International League for
  Peace and Freedom, 25, 110
Women's Research and Education
  Institute, 155
Work. *See* Labor
Working Group on Women and
  International Peace and Security,
  169
World Bank, 109, 125, 129–130, 192,
  194, 224
World Conference on Human Rights
  (1993), 168
World Economic Forum, 109
World Forum Charter of Principles,
  245
World politics lenses, 66
World Social Forums, 244, 245
World Summits on the Information
  Society, 248
World Trade Organization, 109
Worldism, 258
Wright, Melissa, 230
WuDunn, Sheryl, 9

Youngs, Gillian, 254
Yugoslavia, 158, 170
Yuval-Davis, Nira, 63

*Zero Dark Thirty* (film), 156
Zwingel, Suzanne, 249, 250